'0

(١

(01

STEPS ALONG
HOPE STREET

Other books by David Sheppard

Bias to the Poor
Built as a City
The Other Britain (The Dimbleby Lecture)
Parson's Pitch

By David Sheppard and Derek Worlock

Better Together
With Christ in the Wilderness
With Hope in Our Hearts

Dedicated to

All those who have travelled with me on these Steps Along Hope Street. They have brought commitment, skill, hope and love in making it always a team journey.

STEPS ALONG HOPE STREET

My Life in Cricket, the Church and the Inner City

DAVID SHEPPARD

Hodder & Stoughton
LONDON SYDNEY AUCKLAND

British Library Cataloguing in Publication Data
A record for this book is available from the British Library

ISBN 0 340 86116 9

Typeset by Avon Dataset Ltd, Bidford-on-Avon, Warks

Printed and bound in Great Britain by
Clays Ltd, St Ives plc

Hodder & Stoughton Ltd
A Division of Hodder Headline Ltd
338 Euston Road
London NW1 3BH
www.madaboutbooks.com

Contents

Contents

Acknowledgments

I owe much to friends who have read and commented, some on parts, some on the whole of this book. As in all our journey together, my wife Grace has played the largest role, reading each chapter as it emerged and then the whole book. Our daughter Jenny Sinclair and my sister Mary Maxwell have given me creative reminders of parts of our family life.

Canon Eric James has persevered in reading aloud each chapter back to me. Charles Williams (Lord Williams of Elvel) opened my eyes with shrewd questions on the whole text. Bishop Michael Henshall, Professor Noel Boaden and Roger Morris have commented helpfully on the Liverpool chapters. Bishop Colin Buchanan read the South London chapters with keen eyes as the present Bishop of Woolwich. Jean Hewitt, a close colleague at the Mayflower Family Centre, gave me detailed and positive comments on our years there.

I owe much to Professor Martin Daunton, who took me on as a student of the history of my own time. The essays I wrote for him equipped me with the larger picture behind my own experiences. And I record my gratitude to Parthe Ward, a House of Lords' librarian, for her refusal to give up in finding books for the essays.

I am grateful to Sir Richard O'Brien for his careful reading of the chapter on *Faith in the City*; to David Skidmore and Ruth Badger for checking what I have written about my Board for Social Responsibility years; to the Revd Ernie Rea concerning broadcasting; to Patrick Coldstream on the Churches' Enquiry into Unemployment and the Future of Work; to Father Michael Gaine and John Wilkins for their view of what I have written about Archbishop Derek Worlock. A number of other friends have allowed me to check the accuracy of stories in which they were involved.

I am grateful to Stephen Shakeshaft and Tony Hall of the *Liverpool Post* and *Liverpool Echo* and to Tom Murphy of the *Catholic Pictorial* for their help in finding and accessing pictures.

Margaret Funnell did a huge job for me in Liverpool before I retired. I could not have written this book without her thorough sorting of my papers into yearly envelopes where I could retrieve them.

I am grateful to Judith Longman at Hodder for all her encouragement and advice.

Prologue

As a small boy, I was a devoted cricket follower, watching many days of first-class cricket. But all my imaginings never placed me out in the middle as a player. I was never quick to foresee where new beginnings might lead. It took a master at school when I was seventeen to lift that cricketing horizon. Micky Walford, a fine batsman himself, said, 'You ought to play first-class cricket.' At that age I had firm plans for a career. The changes of direction that were to lead to Hope Street were unpredictable from my background. Following in my solicitor father's footsteps, I planned to enter the law – as a barrister.

It was at Cambridge University, in a college founded for the study of the law, Trinity Hall, that the most far-reaching and unexpected change of direction took place. Evangelical conversion to Christ brought a new centre to life, including the belief that God would have a calling for me. Ideas about career now needed to be examined at a new depth. Surely God wanted Christian lawyers – and cricketers. Writing down the arguments seemed to point that way, but in my prayers that direction was gradually changed. It was like a divine hand pulling on the steering wheel. Now all the steps I most wanted to take meant asking for ordination to the ministry of the Church.

My steps along Hope Street have been a shared journey. I have always worked in a team with partners who have brought different gifts from mine. One partner in particular has shared the entire journey from two years after ordination. My mother had brought me up to assume that professional people did not marry until they were thirty. So it was another breaking in of the unexpected when I fell in love with Grace, and married at twenty-eight years of age. It would be a distortion of my story if I did not include an account of my closest partner.

Grace's many talents would have made her an outstanding teacher. But, like others of her generation of Christian women, she gave up her career in order to build a home and become a curate's wife. Early in our marriage, cancer and agoraphobia were life-threatening and limiting for her. But they were rich learning experiences too. Courage and determination, together with medical skills, have firmly put all that in the past. After our daughter Jenny had gone to university, Grace did not back away from the challenge to use her gifts. She wrote two books that have produced a wide and lasting response. Her writing, in turn, led to broadcasting and speaking engagements, bringing a new zest and fun into our lives. This was in addition to bringing a positive approach to the demanding and often unappreciated role of bishop's wife. I was always glad to come home.

She has stayed alongside me as we ventured into areas of life outside the boundaries we knew through our homes and schools. Often Grace saw the implications of new ventures and opportunities into which I was stumbling. Her candour has played a key part in my 'earthing' and growth as a human being. As her talents flourished, I had to learn not to compete with her. I am glad that I have a strong partner who has not let me get away with unconsidered assumptions.

As curate and wife, we had not stepped outside the expectations our upbringing might have raised. Two or three years in an inner-city parish like Islington might well have been followed by a chaplaincy in a public school. But the needs of those left behind both by the Church and by comfortable Britain now increasingly took centre stage. It was venturing into entirely fresh territory from my background to move at twenty-eight years of age to become warden of the Mayflower Family Centre in Canning Town.

The twelve years there were like a second conversion – conversion to Christ in the city. He was already there alongside those in the greatest need, beckoning to us to join him in working for his kingdom. Canning Town presented the steepest of learning curves. Respect for a different culture was replacing the assumption that someone with a public school education would do all the giving. In Canning Town there was a richness of community life from which there was much to receive. I learned, too, much about collaborative ministry. There was one partner in that part of the journey who had a lasting influence on my thinking and acting. George Burton had been born and bred in the Glasgow of the Depression years. Working alongside him meant that I would never write off the God-given intelligence that was present in the inner city. As had happened to George, that intelligence, trampled on in childhood, could be unlocked in later years by confidence-building.

Living in the East End of London, where many were excluded from good opportunities, helped to open my eyes to injustice. Now it stared me in the face in the world of cricket. Apartheid excluded black, Cape Coloured and Indian people from the South African team we were to play against. Making public my refusal to play meant stepping outside all the assumptions sportsmen had grown up with – 'No religion, no politics'. In turn, entering that controversy publicly in 1960 was a watershed that spilled over into wrestling with issues of justice in our own country. There was then the pain of conflict with cricketing friends during the 'D Oliveira affair' in 1968.

The Mayflower gave the opportunity to meet many who otherwise had nothing to do with the Church. Structures and theories of church life did not cross our path. It was an unexpected shock when I was invited to become Bishop of Woolwich. It took months of soul-searching before accepting. But I believed that God wanted there to be a visible Church for all people, and knew that the Church of England had always been weak in the inner city. The insights I had gained in Canning Town could be placed at the service of the Church. Finding my way through the thickets of church services, synods and committees meant learning new skills. This time the key partner was my senior, Mervyn Stockwood, the Bishop of Southwark. He trained me as a young bishop in the way a good vicar trains a new curate. In learning from Mervyn, I was receiving a tradition that stretched back to Archbishop William Temple. It made me love the Church, but also to look at the needs of society around us. Canning Town had been predominantly a white district at that time. Now we lived in Peckham and saw black people being doubly excluded – by race as well as social class. There were bitter voices, and it mattered to go on listening.

Becoming Bishop of Liverpool in 1975 seemed to stretch back in a straight line to the call to go to Canning Town. The post-war confidence that there was never again to be mass unemployment was collapsing, with closure of factory following closure. Here it was appropriate to use the word 'poor' in describing many white families in inner and outer urban priority areas. The Liverpool black community was excluded from mainstream life more completely than we had seen in London, as the Toxteth riots were to reveal in 1981. These were momentous years in Liverpool. They culminated in open confrontation between the Militant-led City Council and a Government in Westminster that was determined to break the power of local authorities. A student at the university chaplaincy challenged me during those years. He had heard me deliver a series of lectures on the theme of *Bias to the Poor*. He felt let down that the only Christian message he thought I had offered was that there were flickers of hope. He said someone who really believed in the power of God would have talked about great streams of light. I said that Easter and Christ's victory were part of my firm belief. But on Good Friday there would not have been great streams of light. Much of Liverpool was living through Good Friday, and flickers of hope were what sustained some of us.

Building bridges between divided groups seemed plain Christian duty. The most inflammatory division in Liverpool had been between Protestant and Catholic. A symbol of breaking down those barriers has been the Pentecost walk along Hope Street that links two parts of a service held in the two cathedrals. The partnership – and close friendship – that developed with Derek Worlock, the Roman Catholic Archbishop, also became highly visible. Central to our relationship were our meetings on Good Fridays. The first of these took place soon after his arrival in Liverpool. I rang him up, making it clear that this was not about business. Could we talk unhurriedly about Christ's death on the cross? Every year after that, we made a point of meeting on Good Friday, and sharing our meditations on our saviour. We were to face several issues where we did not agree, but always knew that we held the central truths of the cross and resurrection in common.

There were many more hopeful steps to be taken together by the churches at grass-roots level. Liverpool went through a series of painful events, such as the football crowd disaster at Hillsborough. At moments like these the community expected the churches to act together. Some Christians feared that the strong wine of evangelism might be diluted when we spoke together. On the contrary, many had written off Christianity because of the rivalry and bitterness they had seen. Now they saw that we were ready to learn from each other and to act together. And we saw at least some who had been sceptical open their minds to the possibility that the Church could be an ally. Some would even ask, 'And is it true?'

During these years, I served on Archbishop Runcie's Commission on Urban Priority Areas that in 1985 produced the report *Faith in the City*. Across the country this was followed by persistent attempts to get the priorities it called for into the bloodstream of the Church of England. Ten years later, I chaired an ecumenical enquiry into Unemployment and the Future of Work. Our report caught the wind of public opinion in 1997 with its insistence that good work for everyone was possible if the nation had the will. Both these reports made clear that the claims of justice for those who have been left behind are the proper concern of the Church.

In the Diocese of Liverpool there was another close partner for twenty years of our journey. Michael Henshall came as Bishop of Warrington with gifts that were quite different from mine. His understanding of the Lancashire parishes – so different from Liverpool – helped us offer leadership to the whole diocese. Out of 220, 80 parishes were designated Urban Priority Areas (UPAs). I saw flickers of hope there, as many parishes became more outward-looking. Christians in Merseyside are surrounded by obvious human needs. That has drawn us to look outwards rather than concentrate on inter-church rivalries or internal party divisions. Seeing Christians from other churches as partners has meant there are greater resources to deploy. Within our own ranks, programmes of 'second-chance learning' have unlocked gifts that had been ignored. The ordination of women has made for a more whole ministerial priesthood, more ready to welcome collaborative work in teams and with lay people. These were all 'Steps along Hope Street'.

The spread of secularisation has affected all the churches in the western world. That has placed intense pressure on the clergy and loyal lay people. The quality of those coming forward for ordination has encouraged me. A higher proportion have been in their thirties and forties, rather than those in their twenties who were able to give the Church the whole of their working life. The number of worshippers in the mainline western churches has continued to decline. Yet those who do come regularly to worship show greater commitment than those who came because it was expected by the culture in which they grew up. These smaller congregations bear larger burdens financially and in active service, both in church life and in voluntary work in the community. A significant step along Hope Street was to help establish a conversation between Christians and Jews, and then another between Christians, Jews and Muslims. We did not attempt to water down our beliefs. We learned together that full-blooded faith marches in step with respect for 'the others' and the steps they take towards God.

Observers confuse hope with optimism at times. They are not the same. At one of the most difficult moments, a journalist questioned me about church life in Liverpool. I encouraged him to go out to the large outer estate, Kirkby, to meet Terry Gibson, the team rector. The journalist reported back: 'I said to him, "So you're optimistic then?" Terry's reply was, "I didn't say that. I said I was full of hope." ' Through the darkest days in East London or Liverpool, I have found that hope in God has kept bubbling up. I am thankful at having been rescued from being a 'platform Christian', rushing from meeting to meeting. Burnout would have occurred long ago if work had been the sole preoccupation of my life.

Now in retirement, there is a rhythm to life that has picked up interests that were never wholly forgotten in the busiest days. There is time for watching cricket, singing, painting, gardening – as well as continuing a limited church ministry and interest in urban politics. There was the wholly unexpected privilege of a life peerage, which has taken me back to the House of Lords. Now the steps are along the beach most mornings in jumper and corduroys without a 'dog collar'. There is space to be still, and for creativity and the new delight of seeing two small grandsons. After forty-five years of marriage, it is a special gift to have time to enjoy each other's company without the demands of working as a bishop. The last lap on this earth tells me that every street is a Hope Street. Writing this book has meant reflecting on a journey that has been full of surprises and a good deal of fun.

1

Early Stepping Stones

Family

At the height of the Depression, the place where you were born made a decisive difference to the life chances of a child. I was born 'on the right side of the tracks' in 1929. My early years were lived in a comfortable part of Chelsea. My parents gave me the security of never doubting that I was loved. That was owed first and foremost to my mother Barbara. My father Stuart died at forty-two, when I was eight years old and my sister Mary, fourteen. My mother had to rebuild a life for us and for herself. We moved away from London, where my father had been a solicitor, to the village of Slinfold in Sussex. For my mother, children, and later grandchildren, became her life – together with her garden, and cricket.

In the small study of our retirement house, over the back of a chair, rests a tiny bib from my earliest years. It has a teddy bear batting – a symbol of my father's hope that I might be a cricketer! I also have a picture that shows the support that came from the other side of the family. My mother was a Shepherd who married a Sheppard. J. A. Shepherd, my grandfather, was an artist who drew regularly for *Punch* and other journals between 1890 and 1940. He gave me one of his drawings when I went to boarding school – of the Lions playing cricket against the Kangaroos. It had appeared in *Punch* in March 1895, when there was great interest in the Test series in Australia, with the matches standing at 2–2.

My mother always encouraged my cricket. My father had taken me to watch at Lord's and at Hove. Now my mother organised our holidays around cricket fixtures. My grandparents lived in Gloucestershire, so we went for an August holiday, coinciding with the Cheltenham cricket festival, where we would see three Gloucestershire matches. At Cheltenham and in matches at Lord's and The Oval, I saw the greatest English batsman of the day, Wally Hammond, score hundreds of runs. When the war started in 1939, first-class cricket came to an end. Aged ten, I had already watched most of the first-class counties play. Wartime holidays from boarding school in the country, with no petrol, meant entertaining myself. Various forms of cricket were invented; in good weather there was an endless game against the coalshed door – throwing a tennis ball against the door, and then batting against it as it bounced back. I would imitate the great players, playing the particular strokes for which each was famous, and wearing my cap at a suitably rakish angle. My mother listened patiently to my account of how each of these matches was progressing. In other forms of the game she would bowl underarm to me. My sister was not so cautious. She bowled overarm and rather fast, so the ball was liable to go in any direction.

Music, and particularly the ballet, were interests that I was drawn into with my mother. During the war, Mary became a junior programme engineer at Broadcasting House, and we lived in a London flat in Weymouth Street, where holidays from boarding school included concerts and the ballet, which was my mother's passion. We would go to the New Theatre to see the Sadler's Wells Ballet twice a week. Tickets were eight shillings and sixpence, and Margot Fonteyn danced every night. I thought I was in love with her when I was fifteen.

My mother was a gentle and elegant woman, rebuilding her life after my father's death. During the war she served in the Mechanised Transport Corps (MTC). We thought her very smart in her khaki uniform. She drove a car for the commandant of the Home Guard for Devon and Cornwall, and then lorries at an airfield near Gloucester. When we moved to London, she drove an ambulance at the docks. She fell in love with a Polish airman, Czeslaw. I learned all I could about his country's tragic history, sandwiched between the two giants, Germany and Russia. I regarded Czeslaw as a friend. On one walk with him he allowed me to fire his revolver. When he was posted abroad, we lost contact. Aged fourteen, I wrote to General Sikorski at The Hotel Anders, Buckingham Palace Road, where I knew that the exiled Polish Government had its headquarters. After a long delay, I received a reply that with much regret informed me that he was missing, believed killed. I did not know what to do with the letter, and put it in a drawer, where my mother found it some months later. That loss drew us close together in expressing our grief again. My sister, five years older than I, had the experience of her boyfriend being killed in North Africa, and of losing many friends of her generation – a loss our mother had also known in the first war.

My mother and I talked about the world around us. She was by nature a pessimist, as her own mother had been. She was also very insular, believing that God stopped at Dover. We were unswervingly patriotic; Mr Churchill could do no wrong. She showed implacable hostility to socialism, and, strangely, considering what we knew was going on in

Hitler's Germany, towards Jews. Did I know that Emmanuel Shinwell was a Polish Jew and that his real name was Shinward? I became aware of class prejudice early. She gladly reported to me that my housemaster had talked to her about people who 'Didn't speak our language', Recently I have been reading the letters I wrote during my first term at my public school, Sherborne. I wrote, 'Most of the boys here speak our language.' It was all right, my mother said, to 'level up', but socialism meant 'levelling down'. As well as Jews and socialists, Catholics were also on the list of her disapproval. As I grew up, I began to argue some of these points with her, often with the superior certainties of a teenager.

There were times when she took a dislike to someone that would prove hard to shift. She allowed a very small number of people to enter her inner circle. Mary's husband, Charles Maxwell, a distinguished BBC producer, was never given that chance, hard as he tried to find common ground. 'BBC types' as a group were disapproved of during the three years Mary worked there, and Charles was never given the chance to alter her views. Thankfully, when I brought Grace home, she was given the key to my mother's heart. When she did allow that access, she would give her time and love without stint. Then we experienced generosity, attentiveness, patience and support that included challenges when she thought we were wrong. She was a faithful cricket-watcher when I played – suffering all the agonies of supporting an opening batsman, when on occasions I was dismissed almost before she had found her seat. I have a picture in my mind of her, sun-bronzed, in old clothes, putting down her garden tools in order to give her whole attention to one of her grandchildren.

Mary saw part of her role as elder sister to introduce me to some of the realities of life. In Gloucestershire that might be in the world of hunt balls; in London, the milieu of broadcasting and theatre. Sometimes I had to learn to stand my ground in the face of her strong opinions. After her years at the BBC, she worked for TocH at Tower Hill, the base from which our cousin Tubby Clayton travelled the world, raising money for the rebuilding of All Hallows by the Tower – the church where I had been baptised, and where my father's ashes had been laid. This education in fundraising led to Mary working for three years for the NSPCC, travelling around England and Wales for its children's branch, the League of Pity. When she had her own children, she was a voluntary fundraiser for charities. For many years she ran a charity ball at Hurlingham in aid of the Chelsea Boys' Club, which our father had founded. When Charles retired and they moved to Rudgwick, a Sussex village where there is generous support for charities, Mary chaired Save the Children there for seventeen years and worked for the West Sussex Association for the Disabled.

I cannot recover any direct memory of my father Stuart, though I remember occasions when we were together. Perhaps the shock of his death, when I was eight years old, blanked out those memories. However, when our daughter Jenny was eight years old, my mother said to me, 'Your father gave a lot of time to playing with you, just as you are doing with Jenny.' It reminded me how important are the early years in building a secure personality, and made me understand how much I owed to him. He lived with a great deal of ill health, much of that dating from the First World War. My mother believed he smoked himself to death. The threat to health of smoking was unknown during the war. He believed cigarettes were vital for the morale of troops. This continued in civilian life, where his generation thought smoking was a necessary part of generous social life. I learned to fill up the silver cigarette box when there was a party.

He came out of the war as a founder member of TocH, a fellowship that had been established in Poperinghe by the Revd Tubby Clayton, his first cousin. My father's faith was important to him. Reading letters he had written to his father from the trenches in France, and later from the campaign based on Salonika – supporting 'our allies the Serbs' against the Bulgarians – I came across his account of a service of Holy Communion attended by just two others. In addition, there was an enthusiastic commentary on the parade service later the same day. When he died, my mother taught me his favourite verse from the Bible: 'Be thou strong and very courageous, for the Lord thy God is with thee whithersoever thou goest.'

The idea of service was firmly present in our home. My father was a member of the small Executive Committee of 'Children's Folk', founded in 1927, along with the secretary of the Charity Organisation Society and representatives of the National Association of Boys' Clubs and what was to be the National Association of Playing Fields. My sister recently discovered the brochure of Children's Folk. It began with an extract from a broadcast by Canon Dick (H. R. L.) Sheppard from St Martin in the Fields. At a charity cricket match my father introduced me to Dick Sheppard as a distant cousin. The broadcast quoted in the brochure took place on the evening of Armistice Day. Speaking of the ten million who gave their lives in the First World War, Dick Sheppard imagined what their message to those listening might be:

> Don't bother over much about singing our praises; don't set too much store on those granite memorials. They mean little to us. But claim for every child adequate education, physical, mental and spiritual; the decencies of home life; green places in which to play; and reasonable security against standing all the day idle in the market place, when schooldays are over, because no man hath hired us.

Those priorities moved my father to found the Chelsea Boys' Club with friends, and he gave much of his leisure time to that. My mother's love of the ballet stemmed from wanting to find an interest for herself when he was out so much.

I was taken in to see him in bed at home, when he was very ill. 'Look after Mummy,' he said. 'Yes, I will,' I assured him. What a promise for an 8-year-old to make! I think the sense of responsibility that stemmed from that has been strong. That night my mother said tearfully, 'God may want Daddy', and in the morning she said, 'God did want Daddy'. We wept a lot together, and, when I was sent to a boarding preparatory school a few months later, we set each other's tears off. Because my father had died, I was allowed to go as a weekly boarder to Northcliffe House School in Bognor Regis. That really made the homesickness worse, as we had to part every week. Until I was much older, I didn't get over the feeling of a blow in the pit of my stomach when I knew the holidays were coming to an end.

School

My mother disliked London, and when my father died we moved to Sussex. These changes – my father's death, moving house and being sent away to boarding school – meant that I learned to keep most of my feelings buried deep. In any case English people – especially boys – didn't display feelings. Going to Sherborne at thirteen, I was the third smallest in my house of seventy boys. I learned to keep out of trouble in the playground, and won some respect through doing well at cricket.

I wanted to please authority and keep out of trouble. I was only beaten once in a regime where beatings were quite frequent. In my circle there had been much talk about a prefect who was alleged to have drawn blood in beating boys. We held some indignant conversations about 'Bloody Erb'. In our dormitory of a dozen or more 15-year-olds, I remember summoning up my courage and saying just before lights were to go out, 'I see Bloody Erb has been at it again.' The prefect in the dormitory said ominously, 'Sheppard, I'll see you later.' Next day I was duly given five strokes of the cane, and very painful they were. It would be nice to portray myself as becoming a champion for fair dealing by protesting against injustice. The unfortunate truth is that as a prefect and head of the house later on, I never challenged that culture. I delivered a number of beatings, though I would like to have thought they were fair.

Some attitudes learned at home were being questioned. In 1945 the first post-war election took place. Frank Byers stood for North Dorset as a Liberal. I was impressed by what he had to say, and declared myself in our debates at Sherborne to be a Liberal. My first memory of political cut and thrust was a boy sitting on my head and saying, 'Now will you vote Conservative?'

There were negative effects from boarding school. But I am grateful to Sherborne for foundations that have served me well: loyalty to friends and the group I belonged to; the discipline of the classics; a good intellectual base; training in personal reliability; confidence and motivation; determination to achieve; some cricketing skills; a love of music. Music offered a gentler part of school life that I loved. My voice did not break until I was well over sixteen, and I was the leader of the trebles in the choir. That taught me a powerful sense of responsibility and concentration. The director of music, Mr Picton, planned for one of his boys to win a choral scholarship to King's College, Cambridge each year. I was lined up for that honour, but let him down and left a gap for that year. Exams and cricket were making heavy demands on my time; I had never broken through to playing the piano with real facility. Seeing me struggle in playing my piece, he would sometimes change course, and say, 'Now sing it!' When I told him I had decided to give up the piano, he raged at me, 'You won't have your cricket when you're old.' (As it happens, in retirement I have joined a choir, along with Grace, for the first time since I left school.)

We sang much of the great choral music, both in the school chapel and in Sherborne Abbey, with its magnificent vaulted roof. That music contained words from the Bible and Christian tradition that much later became part of the lifeblood of my faith. At the time, they rang round my mind as beautiful expressions of distant truths. Daily chapel services during those wartime years were connected with the Book of Remembrance that we passed as we entered, in which old boys who had been killed in the war were listed. I assumed that I was on God's side, and hoped – in an unexamined way – that was true.

My housemaster was the Mr Chips of Sherborne, Alick Trelawny Ross. He had been a boy in the school, and had taught there for thirty-two years when he retired. He believed in pushing boys into the fast track, telling me, aged fifteen, that he wanted me to be the head of the house at seventeen. That approach to school teaching raises questions about the boys of fifteen that he had decided would *not* be given any responsibility at seventeen. Having passed school certificate in this 'fast track' at fourteen, my option was to do history. Alick Ross said, 'No you're not. You're going to do classics.' He told my mother that the history master was a communist. The upshot was studying classics for the next four years, in a select group of six. I was by no means the brightest, having won a minor scholarship to Sherborne by much hard work and going on to win an exhibition to Trinity Hall at Cambridge. We knew where each of us was in the pecking order, and some of the others achieved major awards.

One way or another, I found myself programmed to achieve. Cricket added to those ambitions. At fourteen, I philosophised to myself that it seemed to be a very English thing to mess about at many sports, without excelling at any of them. Wouldn't it be better to play one game as well as possible? Cricket was the one game for me. I was never athletic, but had a natural ball game sense. At fifteen I was still small, and Alick Ross said that I could go into his dining room after lunch each day and drink a glass of his port! When he retired, his successor, Hughie Holmes, said he could not afford to give me port, but I could keep a crate of Guinness in my study and drink a bottle a day. Whatever the cause, I grew a foot taller within two years!

Cricket

I was no cricketing prodigy, unlike my contemporaries Peter May and Colin Cowdrey. By chance I went to Lord's and saw Colin playing at thirteen among 18-year-olds. In the Tonbridge team against Clifton, he took eight wickets with his leg breaks and googlies. He also scored 75 and 44. I was seventeen then, having won a place in the Sherborne first eleven that year. After a disastrous start, scoring a duck in both my first two innings, I started to make good scores. My mother had paid for me to have coaching at Lord's during the Easter holidays. A member of the Sussex committee, Roger Green, who lived with serious physical handicap, was a keen supporter of all cricket in the county. He saw me in the nets at Lord's, and told Sussex about this promising young batsman. That led to an invitation to play in the first junior county matches to be played after the war in 1946. Young Yorkshire came south and we played them in two matches, at Chichester and Hastings. I scored 50 in each game. The Sussex secretary, Billy Griffith, wrote me a letter afterwards, inviting me to come and practise with the county players the following Easter. I carried the letter around in my pocket throughout that winter!

I have written at length about my cricket career in *Parson's Pitch*,[1] and it is clearly not appropriate to repeat all of that here. But, because it was such a crucial part of my development, the influences that cricket may have had are worth some reflection. There is quite a long list: powers of concentration; determination to succeed; application and the need to review; coping with ordeal; handling the press; combining being a public person with private life; leadership in a team; playing hard and playing fair; seeking for justice.

A good colleague in my Bishop of Woolwich days, Canon Eric James, said that he could see the effect batting had left on me, in great powers of concentration. He observed that I did not notice interruptions! I have certainly found myself able to focus for long periods on a task, whether in writing or preparation by myself, or in a group that is working through a subject. Batting demands intense concentration and determination to succeed. One day at Lord's, I had been dismissed for a small score as opening bat for MCC against Yorkshire. So I was able to linger over lunch with Frank Lowson, who was twelfth man for Yorkshire. We were talking about our contemporary, Peter May. I said, 'Peter's hungry for runs.' Frank said, 'Yes, I think that's what I ought to be.' Frank was a fine player, who had played for England, but that conversation summed up the difference between a good player and a great one.

As a young player in first-class cricket, I was hungry for runs. There would be bad days, when receiving a good ball meant little or no score. But I reckoned that I should score not less than 100 runs from the two innings of each match; a good beginning should lead on to a big score. The discipline of building up a long innings was achieved more often when I played regularly and was perhaps fitter, than in those later years with only a holiday month in which to play. Taking *Wisden Cricketers' Almanack* from the shelves where it creates the colour scheme for my study, I see nine scores of more than 170 during the five full seasons, 1949–53. In the later seasons with only a month's cricket, there were some centuries, but rarely much more than 100.

Succeeding as a batsman also calls for application and constant review of technique. 'Jack Hobbs said' was a frequent refrain from Patsy Hendren, who was the Sussex coach, when I was playing in the second eleven. Jack Hobbs was the model for all that earlier generation of cricketers. An inveterate storyteller, Patsy passed on much of the lore of the game. 'Jack Hobbs said that it takes fifteen years to make a batsman.' That embedded itself in my mind, and application was one of the lessons cricket imbued in me. The technique of batsmanship needed to be under review all the time, with colleagues in a good team telling each other about mistakes that emerged. Test and county teams did not then have regular coaches as they do now.

I seized every chance to practise against different kinds of bowling. At Cambridge, we invited professional bowlers to come and coach us for a week at the start of the season. In the year I was captain, Jim Laker came, the greatest English spin bowler of my time. That year our university side included the South African Cuan McCarthy, then considered the fastest bowler in the world. I asked Cuan if he would come to the ground during the gap we had over the exam period, and 'slip himself at me' in a net. It was one of only two occasions when I thought the ball was going to knock the bat out of my hand! But he provided an important learning experience for me in sharpening up my reactions to the fastest bowlers.

As a boy, my technique was that of a typical public schoolboy batsman, 'sideways on', making classical drives through the covers, the bat going 'inside out'. Micky Walford talked to me about the times I missed easy runs from the ball bowled on my legs. 'You need to open your feet up,' he said, and showed me the movements I needed. Application was what was required. That winter I went into the gymnasium and moved my feet in the way he advised at least ten thousand times.

Sir Leonard Hutton was my idea of the master batsman. Playing with and against him, I noticed that when he played defensively the ball never went to the offside of the wicket. It always went straight back down the pitch, or came out on the onside, because he put head, eyes and hands behind the line of the ball. Soon I was doing the same. There followed a season when I hardly hit the ball through the offside, but developed strokes on the onside, because of the way I had positioned myself in line with the ball. In another year or so, the offside strokes came back as well. During that period I learned a sort of party piece of providing an imitation of Len Hutton batting. At the beginning of the war, as a PT instructor he sustained a fracture of his wrist in two places, with the result that his arm was shortened by two inches. Because of that he moved his top hand round the bat handle. This was a factor in the way his bat never went 'inside out'. I could put on a display of how he played.

Years later, during my last 'come-back' tour in 1962–63, in the Sydney Test, I was caught at second slip off Alan Davidson, the Australian fast bowler. Brian Johnston, the BBC commentator, asked me afterwards whether I realised that I had played the ball in the middle of the bat, yet it had gone as a catch to the slips. It dawned on me that I had unconsciously fallen back into the 'inside out' way of playing. I had not been reviewing my technique. In addition, most of my team mates had not known how I had batted in my regular years of playing – nine years before. I decided that it was too late to learn it all over again. There would be no more Test cricket, once the tour was over. Instead I decided to use the method with the Len Hutton grip, until we had seen off the opening bowlers and the new ball.

When it came to playing Test cricket, there was an element of ordeal to cope with. You are on your own when you go out to the wicket. Like many newcomers, I had known what it was to 'freeze' on the first big occasion, and to fail to produce any of the strokes that came naturally when relaxed. In 1953 I was given 'the full treatment' by Lindwall and Miller, in a match when we were leading Australia on the first innings. My mouth went dry. I resolved to chew gum to help still my nerves if ever I played big cricket again. Other techniques, like deep breathing, helped to calm me down when I found myself back in the Test match scene. There was another danger then, that I could become so calm that I might as well be asleep. So there needed to be a conscious sharpening up to move quickly when the ball was bowled.

There is another element to the ordeal that Test cricketers face: handling the criticism of the press. Most cricketers express varying degrees of hostility to the press and avoid talking to journalists if they can. That seemed foolish to me, as they were going to write about us anyway. Surely they were more likely to write something approximating to the truth if they were well informed. Cricket taught me to go to meet the press rather than avoid them. A free press is a very important estate in a democracy like ours. Years later, my staff had a standing order that we would always ring back if a journalist called. Even if it was clearly right not to make a statement, my chaplain or I offered briefing, so that the paper had some accurate information. It might still distort issues but, if the story pointed roughly in the right direction, I felt relief. Of course there have still been occasions, some of which I shall describe at a later point, when I have been angered and hurt by slanted and dishonest reporting.

In my time some teachers have expressed hostility to team games. It is true that there have been times when team games have been given too much prominence in the life of some schools; but playing as part of a team can teach lessons of lifelong value. Supporting and being supported through a bad patch can make all the difference to a player's morale. I dropped a straightforward catch from Neil Harvey in a Test at the Sydney cricket ground. I wanted the earth to open up. In the pandemonium of the crowd whooping at my failure, it lifted me from despair to see Brian Statham mouthing 'Bad luck!' and to feel his support at such a moment. A cricket team spends many days together on and off the field. Learning to live together can be demanding, and can make all the difference between a team that achieves its potential and one that is at sixes and sevens. I caught myself treating a team member as a joke machine. We were tempted to put in the right feedline to draw out the funny remarks in which he excelled. But it dawned on me that we were indulging ourselves, rather than treating him as a person who had sensitive feelings and a serious side.

Cricket gave me varied experience of leadership roles. During my national service in the army, I arrived as a brand new second lieutenant at Shorncliffe Barracks. I was told to report to C Company office. I walked in the door and saluted. The Company commander did not look up. His first words were, 'Can you play cricket?' I quickly found myself in command of the unit's cricket team. It was, however, a surprise to be elected captain of the Cambridge University team. I had not captained my school team. Peter May had been the outstanding school cricketer of my year, and had captained the Charterhouse School team. I had assumed that he would be made captain. The team elected the next year's captain and secretary at the end of the University Match with Oxford. It took my breath away when I was elected secretary after my first year; that usually meant that the secretary was elected captain the following year, as I duly was. I was made captain of Sussex the year after finishing at university, in spite of making it clear to them that I was likely to offer for ordination later that year. The following year there was an even greater surprise when I was made captain of England.

Taking care about how other members of a team are treated is a key part of captaining a side. Mike Brearley has been an outstanding example of a captain sensitive to the different personalities of his team. Drawing out the best often calls for patience and encouragement. Sometimes a player responds to needling at the right moment, but that can go badly adrift with the wrong person. Once I chided a bowler at an inappropriate time, and the result was the puncturing of his confidence in a damaging way. And the moment when someone had scored 0 and was clearly judging himself harshly was not the right time to criticise. It was wise to build someone up with the praise that he deserved, before tackling what was wrong.

Friends who comment on present-day cricket are inclined to say to my generation, 'Of course it was more of a game when you played. Now it's all about money.' There is truth in that, but there has always been playing to win, and some sharp practice in pursuing that goal. One of the features of today's game that I regret is the 'sledging' – verbal abuse that is aimed at intimidating a batsman. So is the constant appealing for catches that puts enormous additional pressure on the umpires, when an honest question and answer between batsman and catcher used often to sort out the truth. We certainly played hard and played to win. I hope that we played fair too.

When I first played for Sussex, our opponents were inclined to say, 'We like playing against Sussex.' That wasn't very difficult, because that year, 1947, we were bottom of the championship. We played in a friendly way. If everything went right, we won a match every now and then. In 1950 I was picked for England and at the end of the summer went on tour to Australia. Len Hutton, who had been the chief target of the roughest treatment from the Australian fast bowlers, said to me, 'Do you think you can learn to hate these Australians for the next six months?'

The passion to win at all costs was reflected in a conversation at the end of the 1952 season. I was playing at Swindon in the National Playing Fields charity match, in which the Duke of Edinburgh played each year. Some of us were staying in the same house before the match, including Freddie Brown and E. R. T. Holmes. Errol Holmes said, 'I played with Wilfred Rhodes. I played with Hedley Verity. However, this Tony Lock is the greatest left-hand bowler I have ever seen. But I think he throws, and we in Surrey ought to stop him.' Freddie Brown said, 'You've no right to stop him. I don't care what we do to beat Australia.' I joined in, 'Come on Freddie, you went to Australia with Douglas Jardine. Would you have bowled bodyline in order to beat Australia?' He muttered, 'I wouldn't have had the same field placing.' I remembered that conversation, when in 1958–59 the England team, with Freddie Brown as its manager, was defeated 4–0 by an Australian side in which bowlers who were widely held to be throwers, Meckiff and Rorke, played a key part. English complaints were met with a lack of sympathy, with reminders of how many wickets Tony Lock had taken.

Test cricket has always been played hard. My first matches against Australia still had the shadow of Sir Donald Bradman falling across them. He had been the target of bodyline, which was the most brutal exploiting of the pace of Larwood and Voce, our great fast bowlers. When he had Lindwall and Miller at his command, Bradman unleashed them without any holding back, especially at Len Hutton. Lindsay Hassett succeeded him as captain. Hassett had been something of a joker, and, I think, calculated that he must not be seen to be any less tough than Bradman. So nobody on the field looked at you when you were batting, much less spoke to you – with the notable exception of Keith Miller, who played as hard as anyone ever did, but always believed this could be done alongside warm personal relationships. The captain of the stronger team sets the pace for much of what takes place on the field. When I was brought back into the Test team in 1956, the blocks that forbade players from talking to each other had been removed. The credit for that should go to Peter May, as the captain of the stronger side in that series. We still played as hard as ever – and to win.

Some of Test cricket's examples of toughness rubbed off on me more than I like to admit. In 1953 England saved a key Test when Trevor Bailey bowled down the leg side, making it almost impossible for the Australian batsmen to play their normal strokes. Like all cricketers, we discussed the rights and wrongs of this. The following month at Cheltenham, after a keenly fought game, Gloucestershire had quite a small number of runs to win but with a short time left. As captain, I instructed our bowlers to bowl down the leg side, with most of the fielders placed there. There was what *Wisden Cricketers' Almanack* described as 'a thrilling finish', but I was ashamed at the tactics I had employed. We played Gloucestershire again a few weeks later, and I went into their dressing room before the match and apologised to Jack Crapp their captain.

There was another occasion when I felt the need to apologise to the other team. Jim Laker had bowled Australia out for 84 on the Saturday of his famous 1956 Old Trafford Test. On the Sunday, I kept a long-promised preaching engagement. After church there was an informal meeting with some club cricketers, who asked me about the astonishing collapse on the previous day. Unguardedly I said that I thought an English county team might have battled it out and scored 200. I was devastated to see my comment splashed all over a tabloid newspaper on the Monday morning. I believe that going into the Australian dressing room to apologise prevented the possibility of a feud becoming established.

The senior Sussex professionals set a high standard of fair play. George Cox was a great encourager to me from the beginning. Cricket to him was to be played as a game, and for fun, as well as being a test of skills and courage. He was angry with me that day at Cheltenham, and tried to warn me against using such questionable tactics. I ignored one of the lessons about leadership that cricket was teaching me – to listen carefully to advice from within the team. John Langridge, my opening partner, who had started playing for Sussex before I was born, never failed to walk out if he knew that he had touched the ball for a catch behind the wicket. Watching him from the other end made me change the practice I had learned from school and club cricket. They had said that sometimes you were given out when you were not out, and therefore it was fair that, on occasions, you 'got away with it'. 'Walking' when you know you are out has divided different generations of cricketers. On my last tour, I was batting at Melbourne against the fast bowler Alan Connolly. There was the lightest of touches to a ball on the leg side that was caught by the wicketkeeper. He did not appeal. Only the bowler did, in a rather half-hearted way. I walked out, knowing there had been an edge. Jack Fingleton, an Australian cricketer from an earlier generation, said, 'You made the umpire look silly. He was shaking his head as you walked out.' I said that surely, if the umpire had any sense, he would have watched my reaction before giving his decision.

Another issue in the cricket world started to impinge on my consciousness. Several cricketers, like George Cox and Billy Griffith, went to South Africa to coach or to play. They came back with disturbing accounts of the way black people were treated. Cricket, justice and apartheid in South Africa were to become a significant part of my story that will be picked up in a later chapter.

2

New Directions

Cambridge University brought a watershed in more ways than one. At the end of my time in university, I had turned in new directions of career and belief. Two years of national service in the army made me more conscious of what university offered. I went to Trinity Hall, a college founded for the study of law. The ambition was to become a barrister. I did not want to embark on law straight away, nor to go back to classics after two years' gap; so I opted for the subject I had always wanted to study – history – for part 1 of the 'Cambridge tripos', with the intention of moving on to law for part 2. The first supervision produced a shock. At school, studying Latin and Greek, my work was 'right' or 'wrong'. Now, after reading my first history essay, I nervously waited for judgment. My tutor simply said, 'Yes', and moved on to discuss some of the ideas raised in the essay! History is the hardest subject to obtain first-class honours, and the easiest simply to pass – for the same reason, that you cannot be absolutely right or wrong with history. The skill lies in marshalling the evidence and arguing the case. The fact that I had not studied history at school meant that university lectures, that naturally assumed we had basic knowledge, were hardly geared for my needs. After a while I preferred to take whole days in the university library, where I could find all the books I required and move at my own speed.

A further problem was soon to arise. Cricket called. After my first summer, I was chosen for the England tour of Australia. The college authorities agreed that they would not send me down if I failed, but that I must take my part 1 exams. I returned from the cricket tour with six weeks left before those examinations. That meant shrewd advice from tutors about likely questions, and cramming from chosen books. I achieved a 2:2. The following year for part 2 of the tripos I studied much more thoroughly, but still only achieved a 2:2.

Cambridge conversion

All new students receive visits and invitations from a plethora of societies, sporting, political or religious, and I was no exception. All of the invitations went in to the waste-paper basket. I was determined to make up my own mind what to pursue, after taking the measure of life at Cambridge. I went at times to College chapel, going on to sherry in the dean's rooms after evening service. The dean was Owen Chadwick,[1] whose influence was quiet and gentle. My mind was open to a good argument, and there were plenty of those between students until late at night.

My winter game was squash. I had a keen match with John Collins[2] who, I discovered, was studying for ordination. He invited me back to tea. As I left, he asked me if I would like to come with him to a sermon at the start of the University Mission that was about to begin. My answer – a mixture of the encouraging and the cautious – was, 'Yes, I'd like to come, but I won't be able to come to them all.'

The large University Church, Great St Mary's, was full. The pulpit had been wheeled along rails into the middle. The preacher was an American Presbyterian, Dr Donald Gray Barnhouse. He was aggressive, his target formal religion. Simply keeping religious duties would never make us acceptable to God. Preachers I had heard before had assumed that we were on the road, and needed to make progress along it, by learning to pray better, or live better. Barnhouse made no such assumption. Only a conscious response to the undeserved love of God in Christ could make us at one with God. If we had not responded directly to that love, we were not on the road at all. I did not agree with several parts of what he said, but the central thrust penetrated all my 'good-as-most and better-than-some-I-can-think-of' defences.

John Collins and I walked back to his rooms. A central memory of what he said to me was his explanation of Jesus bearing our sin. He read the words from Isaiah about the suffering servant that I had sung in Handel's *Messiah*: 'The Lord has laid on him the iniquity of us all.' He took a Bible and placed it on one hand. This represented my sin, coming between me and God, like a cloud. When he quoted the words about the suffering servant, he placed the Bible on the other hand. Jesus on the cross, the suffering servant, took our sin on himself. He cried the sinner's cry: 'My God, my God, why have you forsaken me?'

Certainly the penny dropped for me at that moment. I believed that Jesus died for me. In the sermon, Dr Barnhouse had explained Christ's death on the cross by using a deliberately crude illustration to shock us into thinking, 'God sheathed his sword of wrath in the head of an innocent Christ.' Looking back, I find Barnhouse's words unworthy of

God, our loving Father. There remains mystery surrounding this deepest moment in God's reaching out to us. Human illustrations can undoubtedly point us in some right directions, but should not be required to produce neat answers as though there is no further mystery. Whatever the human means, that day I grasped the truth that Christian faith rests on the undeserved love of God. Of course, he uses imperfect people to do his work – and imperfect ideas. The fact that we owe great spiritual blessings to someone does not mean that we must remain their unquestioning disciples. That grasp of the undeserved love of God has been refreshed and strengthened from many and varied sources over the years. The life of faith calls us to go on travelling and learning, without believing that we shall set aside all the mystery in this life.

It was a clear and starry night as I walked home across the small bridge that leads to Trinity Hall. The greatness of God felt overwhelming. John Collins had introduced me to one of the texts that has touched the lives of countless English Christians who have seen Holman Hunt's painting, *The Light of the World*: 'Behold I stand at the door and knock. If any one hears my voice and opens the door, I will come in to sup with him and he with me.' Now, in my rooms, I knelt and prayed, using my own words to 'open the door' and ask Christ to enter my life, imagining him knocking at the door. Then a fresh fear appeared, that I wouldn't 'keep it up'. This was what I wanted today – with all my heart; but what if my heart changed tomorrow? So I prayed 'Lord, I don't know where this is going to take me, but I'm willing to go with you. Please make me willing.' That was my conversion to Christ. In some ways it was all utterly new and different; it was also the pulling together of many loose threads that had been woven in my life through my background and growing up.

That first term at Cambridge was coming to an end. John Collins asked me whether I meant to take my new faith seriously. If so, would I come to a 'camp' during the vacation? I agreed, and this began a regular involvement with Iwerne (pronounced Euan) Minster Varsity and Public Schools (VPS) Camp. In fact the 'camp' was a house party, using Cla(y)esmore School in the holidays. I went every vacation until my ordination five years later. I went first as a helper, and then as an 'officer'. I owe much to Iwerne. Disciplined personal devotion and a pastoral care for each boy gave me a firm base for Christian service. There was an unswerving pattern in the series of talks at 'camp', calling boys to personal faith in Jesus who could be their friend and saviour. The key to Christian growth was seen as the 'quiet time' every day, with Bible reading and prayer. If I asked a boy how his Christian life was progressing, he was likely to reply that he was keeping up his quiet time – or not. What I now think left a major gap was to leave out what Jesus taught in the Gospels about 'the kingdom of God'. The kingdom, presented by a parable or a saying following a miracle, spoke of God's rule in the whole world – the kingdom of right relationships, the kingdom of God and his justice. It was not all about my Lord and me. It was also about belonging to the company of Christians and together serving 'the others'.

Many years later I preached for John Collins at Holy Trinity, Brompton, and stayed in the vicarage the night before. In the bedroom was a copy of a memoir of 'Bash'.[3] 'Bash', a most unlikely name for this outwardly timid and eccentric man, was the Revd E. J. H. Nash, who led the team at Iwerne Minster. The book was a compulsive read. It evoked vivid memories of Bash. He was single-minded, unashamedly elitist. The role of women was merely to be supportive. He had no hesitations about concentrating on boys from the 'top thirty schools'. I recall one day when he and I were together. He prayed, 'Lord, we know that thou dost love one talent and two talent men, but we pray that thou wouldst give us a five talent man.' He was single-minded to the point of ruthlessness about the work of Iwerne. He was often courageous in challenging people about their actions or priorities. Many years later, as a bishop, a letter from Bash arrived; did I not think that I could use my influence to preach the gospel to the nation, rather than involve myself in the 'social Gospel'? That courage in challenging people sometimes became over-direction. There were several who felt they had to make a total break in order to be free from his influence.

To be fair, in assessing the influence of Iwerne in my life, the memories of Bash make him a more dominant figure than he was. It leaves out the lively debates that went on in the Officers' Room, in which we laughed at ourselves and criticised our ways vigorously. This was carried on within clearly accepted boundaries. I came to understand that we accepted the whole Bible at face value. At Iwerne, I worked closely with Bash, with the senior dormitory, made up of boys who had all been to camp before and professed to be committed Christians. This was because we agreed that my cricketing status ought not to be used to influence boys towards commitment. I always kept some distance between Bash and myself, so there was never the feeling that he was directing me, rather than offering honest advice that I could accept or reject.

Reading that book about him, nearly thirty years after I had last been to Iwerne, for a few moments I felt the enormous attraction of belonging to that tight-knit team. We had been so sure of what we were called to be and to do. That 'back-to-the-womb' attraction only lasted for a few moments. Then I shook myself, knowing that I did not want to go back. I remain enormously grateful for so much that God gave me through Iwerne, one of the many limbs of Christ's body. At the same time there is a firm conviction that the life of faith called me to move on to further parts of the journey.

Back in Cambridge, new understandings about the Church dawned. There were different theological parties – high and low, catholic and evangelical, liberal and conservative – which were sometimes in rivalry. I grasped that 'we' were 'conservative evangelicals'. So I asked my evangelical friends, 'Which church do we go to?' I duly started to go to St Paul's, Cambridge, on Sundays. I had never been to a church where there seemed to be so many activities going on throughout the week. In the student world, I would go regularly to the CICCU (Cambridge Inter-Collegiate Christian Union) sermon on Sunday nights in Holy Trinity. In addition there was a Saturday evening Bible reading, held in the Union Society building, and small group Bible readings in the college.

In the CICCU we talked about being 'a real Christian'. Because many of us had memories of having grown up as formal churchgoers, it seemed natural to say that we were now real Christians, without realising the insult that implied to other practising Christians, both in our own churches and, for example, in the Roman Catholic Church. We would not have thought of RCs as 'real Christians'! Christian unity was seen as a spiritual unity between believers, who recognised the same experience of the living Christ in each other. The CICCU dealt with the problems of divisions by avoiding any teaching about the sacraments, with the conflicting teachings different churches held about baptism and the Holy Communion. We also fought shy of any question of politics.

Evangelicals laid great emphasis on the Word. It became a priority to set aside time each morning for Bible reading and prayer. I started keeping notes, and wrote, after reading St Paul's Letter to the Romans, chapter 8 for the first time, 'Read it again. It's terrific!' The excitement that we had good news to share made me an enthusiastic evangelist. I would invite friends to the CICCU sermon on Sunday nights and talk about the faith, as John Collins had with me. There were times when perhaps I pressed the good news too eagerly on people who were not ready for it. I needed to learn more about respect – the need to listen and understand where others were standing. But undoubtedly the strength of the CICCU lay in the readiness of its rank and file members to pray for friends, invite them to the evangelistic services and to speak of their own faith.

For two years I was the Iwerne 'representative' at Cambridge. The responsibility that went with that was to ensure that every former 'camper' who came up to the University was given the chance of meeting regularly with an older Christian. I would consult with Mark Ruston, who was then vicar of The Round Church in Cambridge, about the most appropriate person to ask to take on such links. We would not have used the word, but we were making sure that there would be a 'soul friend', if wanted. I spent many hours thinking faith matters through with people who were my responsibility to 'cover'. One of them was David Watson, who wrote, 'It is impossible to stress how important those sessions were for me. Without them, humanly speaking, I should never have survived as a Christian.'[4]

I had myself welcomed a resource like that when I came back from my first camp at Iwerne. John Collins had passed me on to someone he thought would be more appropriate; I've sometimes wondered whether that was because he did not know anything about cricket, and believed that would limit what he could give me! Teddy Saunders, also an ordinand at Ridley Hall, took me on. That next term, a new chaplain came to Trinity Hall, Tony Tremlett.[5] It seemed natural to sign up for instruction every week with him too. To my infant Christian mind it seemed that my two guides were rivals, presenting contradictory teachings. In the long run, few experiences have been so good for me in my pilgrimage, painful as this was. It made me resolve that I would think for myself rather than depend on either of them as my authority figure.

Within a year of my conversion, I was travelling to Australia and New Zealand with the England cricket team. John Dewes, another member of the team, and I were known to be evangelical Christians. We were invited to speak at a number of meetings for young people in Australia and New Zealand during the six months' tour, and were also invited into the homes of Christians from various denominations. Times of prayer, hymns round the piano, the warm welcome from families, meant that the spiritual unity that evangelicals know became a reality to me. Speaking at so many meetings brought the danger of becoming a 'platform Christian'. Sporting heroes are in danger of being lionised, and Christian sporting heroes, invited to repeat their 'testimony', face the additional danger of their faith becoming stuck. That danger was real enough for me, of repeating the story too often, and giving out more than I took in. I kept a log of all my speaking engagements before ordination. There were 402 in that period of five years. The demands of local ministry at the Mayflower Family Centre were to rescue me from too many platform meetings.

Calling to ordination

There were walks with God, seeking to test my thoughts about what his calling to me might be. One of them took me alongside the playing fields of Harrow School. I was early for a meeting at another school nearby. With my involvement with Iwerne it was natural that I thought about the possibility of becoming a chaplain at a public school, and just that was in my mind as I walked. I ran into a housemaster at Harrow School whom I knew. 'Are you thinking of coming here?' he asked. 'That would be a great idea.' As it happened, I was asked to consider a post as chaplain at Harrow years later. However, other influences were at work too! Quite recently I discovered that a friend in the CICCU was praying that I should not go to a public school, but work with less privileged people.

Another walk was when Sussex was playing Lancashire at Blackpool. On the Sunday, I walked along the front, which was crowded. It was Bolton 'Wakes Week', when all the factories in Bolton closed, and the entire town seemed to be there. Walking along the front, I talked to God about so many people in Britain who did not have any connection with the Church. Perhaps my calling was to reach out to them. At the time I thought such reaching out might be through preaching to large gatherings. I was to learn that those right outside the Church's life were not likely to be reached without the patient building of bridges of human caring and contact.

The need to clarify God's calling grew more urgent during the cricket season of 1953. So far, student years had made it possible to play cricket. Now, what career beckoned? I wrote an 'Appreciation of the Situation', as the army had taught me, setting out object–courses–factors–plan. That paper exercise proved to my own satisfaction that the best way to serve God would be to stay in cricket for some years and use the many opportunities to spread the faith that were coming my way. Alongside the paper exercise, however, in my prayers I was asking God to confirm what seemed to be best, or to pull me back, if that was not his will. Soon every task that attracted me seemed to involve ordination. Towards the end of the 1953 season, I went to a selection conference, knowing that being ordained was what I most wanted in the world. A recommendation followed, and an interview with my bishop – George Bell, Bishop of Chichester. The main memory I have of my meeting with him was that he made it clear to me that he expected me to serve in another diocese, rather than in comfortable Chichester.

Theological college training at Ridley Hall took me back to Cambridge. Enrolling in the life of a company of sixty felt all too like school again. So the introductory talk from Cyril Bowles our principal[6] on the first evening was reassuring. He told us that the front gate was always locked at 10 p.m. The college only had one porter, and under no circumstances was he to be disturbed at night. If we came in after 10 p.m, the way in was over the wall. Since Ridley was next door to Newnham, a women's college, there were moments when policemen took a keen interest in young men climbing over that wall!

When faced with academic theology, we members of the CICCU saw ourselves as on the defensive. Our elders warned us that it was in the grip of liberal scholarship, which did not respect belief in the inspired

Word of God in the Bible. We were inclined to regard with suspicion much of what we were taught. However, sitting at the feet of Christians of other traditions I learned to respect their faith and their searching. My last two terms at Trinity Hall – making up for the winter spent cricketing in Australia – had required me to receive a 'certificate of diligent study'. That was obtained by writing some major essays for Owen Chadwick, the dean of the college and foremost church historian. In supervisions with Owen I learned from his clear mind to appraise with a cooler detachment those figures of history I had regarded as heroes or villains. Maurice Wiles,[7] a member of the Ridley Hall staff, encouraged us to think freshly about great issues in the world. It was Maurice who led me into reading the main message of Old Testament prophets like Amos, Isaiah, Hosea and Jeremiah. This was about justice and the knowledge of God, and not simply their foretelling the coming of the Christ. Cyril Bowles was fair-minded, clearly a man of prayer and of deep faith, who understood those who came from a position like mine and listened carefully to us. His method of interview was effective for someone like me. He spent most of the time in silence, waiting for what I might want to raise with him. I duly filled in the spaces!

I had not thought too deeply about what it meant to be an Anglican, and Ridley Hall began to open my mind not only to what it meant to serve in the Church of England, but also in partnership with other churches. Dr Donald Soper,[8] the great Methodist minister, was one of our visiting speakers; he loved to remind me many years later that I had driven him to the station after his talks. Overnight he had focused on human needs and the social responsibility of the Church. Question time had produced fierce insistence from students on the primacy of 'preaching the Gospel'. In his talk in the morning, Donald Soper began: 'I want you to know that I believe with all my heart that people need to hear of the personal salvation that Christ offers. But I didn't think it would do you any harm to wait overnight to know that!'

Marriage to Grace

It was at Ridley Hall that I met my future wife, Grace. A cousin of mine was in Cambridge and I wanted her to meet some Christian company. I asked the president of the CICCU to tell me who was the best girl he could recommend for this. The following day I found a note in my room which said, 'Grace Isaac's the name', with her address at Homerton College. So I invited her to tea with my cousin. Grace came along, but regarded it as necessary to bring a chaperone too, another friend from college. It reflected the culture of that part of the Christian world at that time – both that I needed to ask for such an introduction and that Grace felt that she needed a chaperone. Men and women lived within our segregated institutions and activities. If a boy and girl went out together, we were inclined to assume that they were about to announce their engagement. Both Grace and I believed that God would have a partner for us, if that were his will, and that therefore we did not need to do too much about finding one. Besides, my mother had brought me up to think that 'people like us' – presumably those with professional careers – did not get married until we were thirty. I did not quite make it, being twenty-eight when we married.

Regardless of 'what Mother said', that first meeting led to a sleepless night, thinking of this tall, fair and natural young woman. There was a whole new level of excitement every time there was a possibility of seeing Grace. Another part of me told me to back away from the longed-for further contact, because that might have been imposing my will rather than God's. When we compared notes later we found that we had both felt strong attraction from the beginning, and both tried to discipline ourselves not to seek out the other. Perhaps our insistence that we leave it all to God may have been a way of avoiding the responsibility for making important decisions ourselves. Anyway, at the time winning her seemed out of my reach. There she was, talking easily with other men after church services, leading me to believe I stood no chance. She was thinking similar thoughts about my presumed inaccessibility. Some brief, unsought encounters increased my attraction for Grace. At last I realised the danger of falling in love with an idea rather than with a real person. We still needed to get to know each other. Then I summoned up the courage and asked her out to dinner. I found myself at ease in her company from the beginning. She enjoyed sport, loved music and spoke naturally about her faith.

She reminds me that I spent part of the evening cross-examining her about the Ruanda Mission, part of the Church Missionary Society (CMS). Her clergyman father, Bryan Isaac, was the Home Secretary of the Mission. 'Ruanda' and the East African Revival, were understood to go in for public confession – 'living in the light' – and I wanted to know if she would expect us to live like that. Some years later on, we had reason to be thankful for this Revival teaching. A Rwandan Christian, William Nagenda, asked us at an important moment early in our married life if we lived in the light with each other. His question came at a moment when we needed to be more open in our communicating – a lesson we have gone on learning. For the moment, nervously wondering whether we should commit ourselves to marriage, I was happy that we could share our understanding of the faith. Grace came through my rather earnest 'vetting' with flying colours. When I told Bash that we were engaged, he said, 'Good evangelical stock!'

Ordination and curacy

My ordination was on Michaelmas Day 1955, in St Paul's Cathedral, Bishop J. W. C. Wand's last ordination. Church party divisions had been apparent in Cambridge. Now I saw them enshrined in the Diocese of London – as they have continued to be. Thirty of us were ordained. Half genuflected and crossed themselves at all possible points in the service. Half of us stood ramrod straight, to demonstrate that we disowned such ritual. It was hard to detach ourselves from these sad divisions. At the end of the service, outside the public service, each of us had to receive the document containing his orders from Bishop Wand. He sat in a bishop's chair, and gave our orders to each of us with his episcopal ring turned towards the recipient. The High-Church ordinands knelt and kissed his ring. The Low-Church ones didn't. I decided that I would give him a deep bow, as a sign of my respect for him. When I went to take my orders from him, I froze, because he did not let go of the document. The only thought in my mind was, 'I haven't done enough.' What the bishop knew, and I didn't, was that he had agreed for a photographer to take a photo of this cricketer receiving his orders!

Living in inner-city London brought the challenge to listen and enter into a life and culture that was quite new to me. Maurice Wood, Vicar of St Mary's, Islington, had invited me to join him as one of two curates. Islington was then still largely a working-class area, and St Mary's was typical of many evangelical parishes in inner-city areas. Its strengths included: a strong belief in the power of Christ in the life of the individual; loyalty to the Bible; a warm welcome into the fellowship for those who came to us; a determined fight for standards of behaviour; courageous personal discipleship; faithful visiting of homes by staff and by some of the congregation; compassion for individuals; individual care for immigrants who were newly arriving; concern for children and for the elderly. St Mary's Church had been bombed during the 1939–45 war and was rebuilt on its former grand scale while I was working there. A loyal group, perhaps thirty to forty in number, had bravely kept the flag flying during those difficult years. Some of these had moved away to the suburbs but continued to come back to support the church where they had grown up.

Maurice Wood[9] was energetic, keen to spread the Gospel in every possible situation. He published a series of booklets in accessible English which we carried everywhere with us. Maurice was a shrewd pastor who had practical advice. For example, I had allowed myself to become trapped in trying to sort out the problems of a disturbed person who really needed professional help. The penny dropped for me when Maurice asked me how many other people I would be able to help if there were a second person with needs like that for me to take on. He expected the two curates to carry a black-bound copy of the Bible and to wear a black Homburg hat as we went round the parish. Yet life was fun around Maurice. Stories abounded, for example, of his wartime experiences as a chaplain with the Marine Commandos. He had time-consuming outside commitments, in the Church Assembly and as chairman of the national Islington Clerical Conference. For some years he took the conference on tour round the country in addition to its January meeting in Church House, Westminster. I was included to take part in the public rallies that were also part of what we referred to as the 'Islington circus'.

When I added to the full programme of a parish like that the invitations that came to me on the Christian sportsman ticket, it was all a bit hectic. I can't have been the easiest curate to handle, with these outside commitments. Maurice was generous and encouraging. He understood about many demands. He had married a second time, following the death of Marjorie his first wife, to Margaret, who made the vicarage a welcoming home, while she bore two children to add to the three from the first marriage. Maurice went through a period of nervous exhaustion while I was there, and was unable to take a service for some months. Perhaps the exhaustion was a delayed working out of bereavement. It was an education to me to be close to him, as he slowly found his way back to full health and activity. He asked me to be there, and ready to take over, when for the first time after going through this trough he presided again at the communion service. It was during that period of personal rehabilitation that he agreed to marry Grace and me. Our first married home was on the two top floors of a terraced house. We shared with our landlords the bathroom, complete with gas geyser, opposite the front door. The loo was down another floor again, in the basement where they lived.

Maurice strongly encouraged lay leadership in parish life. Yet there was an issue about where we believed such lay leadership might appear. He encouraged students and nurses to come to St Mary's, believing that they would provide the leaders to establish youth and children's organisations and a visiting programme. There was a 'Guest Service' one evening each month, at the end of which there was an opportunity to come forward for any who wanted to show their fresh commitment to Christ. Maurice said that there had never been a Guest Service without at least one person making a Christian commitment. But he agreed that more often than not they were students or nurses. Their presence played an influential part in determining the character of the Young People's Fellowship. I remember, with shame, saying to a friend, 'I don't believe leader types live around here. We can't avoid importing leaders.' That remark needed to be disowned before I moved on to the Mayflower.

The tidy, bookish programme St Mary's offered meant that the youngsters who represented the majority in the area either never came, or, because they didn't like the type of programme, drifted away. I learned that there had been a Crypt Club in the pre-war years, run by a London City Missionary, Daddy Daniels. Visiting around the parish his name was heard more frequently than that of any vicar. There had been a church football team for a while, but the boys from the Crypt Club had refused to pass the ball to the boys from the choir in the 'upstairs church'.

I became involved with the Islington Boys' Club, helping them by recruiting a young leader, Mike Miller, while our regular leader was recovering from an accident. We needed some money for improvements to an old building, and I wrote a letter to the *Daily Telegraph* drawing attention to the needs. As a result, £1,100 came in – quite good money then. That involvement drew me into the circle of Boys' Clubs, and I started to grasp how many potential allies there could be in parishes like Islington. Talking to boys in the club made it clear how limited were the jobs they were able to obtain. Giving the prizes away at a local primary school opened my eyes wider; reporting on the school's achievements, a duplicated piece of paper told us that of thirty-nine leavers one had passed the eleven-plus exam. The report went on: 'With the material available, this was a very creditable result.' Even then, new to the inner city, I suspected that with teachers having such low expectations, children were most unlikely to fulfil their potential.

In the street where we lived I visited a lifelong Islington man, who became deeply interested in our talks about God. Like many he could not get past the question of God allowing suffering. I read him a poem, 'The Sufferings of God',[10] by 'Woodbine Willie' (G. A. Studdert-Kennedy), from his poems of the First World War. At the end he said, 'That's the best poem I ever heard.' My problem in trying to help him further towards a living faith was my own strong sense that he would be out of place if he were to come to church. We needed bridges, stepping stones that would enable honest searchers to meet up with local Christians, before they would feel able to approach the institutional church.

Two streets away a small group was coming into being, in a flat. It proved a significant bridge for some neighbours. Ethel Noble had been nervously ill for a long time; unfortunately the doctor was alleged to have told someone else in the parish that there was nothing wrong with her. The result of that was that the close-knit, small congregation that had survived the bombing of the church and the migration of many of its members decided that she must be malingering, and dropped visiting her. She had sad days, but also times of great perception. She agreed that we might invite some others to meet in her room for a discussion. Tom and Barbara Quantrill, her next-door neighbours, were among those who came. For them this was the first step towards a lasting faith. It was a step forward for me too, in learning that those who have great personal *needs* may also have *gifts* from which those who appear stronger may receive. I learned too that someone's home could itself provide the bridge on which neighbours would meet with Christians.

The majority of our white neighbours in Islington had no church background that had survived beyond childhood. One family said, 'Johnny's the religious one in this family. He goes to your church.' But I had never seen Johnny before. He blushed scarlet, and it became plain that, though he might have been *sent* to Sunday school, not surprisingly he had never arrived. Those who did come usually regarded approaching adulthood as time to leave church behind. The arrival of West Indians and Nigerians provided a striking contrast, for we could expect many of them to know the Christian story in a way that the majority in the host community did not. Sadly in the 1950s we did not see what an opportunity there was for us if we had given priority to showing these black newcomers to London that there was a place for them in the Church.

Mildred came to church one Sunday, grasping tightly in her hand a letter from her vicar in the West Indies. She had been in Britain about a month. She had been scared by the stories other West Indian friends told her. They said that white people would get up and move from their seat if a black person tried to sit in the same pew. The letter she grasped was addressed 'To any priest in the Church of England', commending her as a loyal church member. When she came to St Mary's the first person she met said, 'You're new aren't you? Come and sit with me.' Mildred's fears faded away and soon she had settled into the fellowship in the parish.

The media posed some fresh challenges; as a cricketer, I had learned to be cautious in my dealings with them. In my brief introductory word on my first evening in the parish, I said that my ambition was like St Paul's in the text, 'I determined not to know anything but Jesus Christ and him crucified.' Maurice Wood had pressed me not to say anything that was not explicitly Christian, so that gospel words might find their way into the local newspaper. The only exception I made was to mention my enthusiasm for the National Playing Fields Association and what it could do in areas like Islington. The account in the paper confined itself to saying that I was 'very interested in the National Playing Fields Association'.

In 1956 I was invited to write a weekly column for six months in the *Daily Mail*. Maurice Wood encouraged me to see this as a great opportunity to preach the Gospel. Hopefully, it touched some chords. At the same time there were several moments of embarrassment and pain. I wrote an introductory piece for *Daily Mail* readers, expressing the hope that I might offer helpful advice. Without mentioning it to me, *Daily*

Mail Promotions copied my piece, put a purple border round it, and sent a copy to every clergyman in the Church of England! One clergyman sent a copy to the Archbishop of Canterbury, complaining about the arrogance of this novice priest. Geoffrey Fisher, the Archbishop, wrote, asking me what had happened and acknowledging the difficulties that press treatment could cause. Having received an explanation of what had happened, he wrote again supportively and encouragingly.

Geoffrey Fisher's reputation has been that of a schoolmaster, bringing discipline to the Church of England by the revision of Canon Law. His letters to me on this occasion showed another side to him. He had also written to me two years earlier. Ronnie Aird, the secretary of the MCC, had sounded me out about the possibility of captaining the England team in Australia in 1954–55. Cyril Bowles, my theological college principal, had consulted the Archbishop about the wisdom of releasing me for a year if that invitation came. I have included Geoffrey Fisher's reply in this book, because it reveals a concern for much more than a 'churchy' view of the Kingdom of God. He wrote, 'Here is a piece of what I should regard as direct service to the wider interests of the Kingdom of God.' Perhaps the headmaster in him reappeared when his letter went on, 'there really is a crying need for someone to bring back into the higher ranks of English cricket a sort of moral decisiveness and discipline which has been slipping'.

There were some difficult times with my sub-editor at the *Daily Mail*. Sometimes he cut whole paragraphs without consulting me. Often headlines appeared at the top, altering the thrust of the article below. But one challenge he made hit the nail on the head in a way that taught me some important lessons. He said, 'If I am prepared to come all the way to the commitment to God you write about, your piece might touch me. But, suppose for the moment I am only prepared to take some small steps in my daily life, I feel you have nothing to say to me.' It dawned that, while expecting readers to follow me on to Christian territory, I was not prepared to make the effort to meet them on their ground. I remembered that, when my six months finished, and an invitation came to write a weekly column for *Woman's Own*. That went on for seventeen years. There was rich material to write about from conversations in the homes of people who were not committed Christians, but who were prepared to think about the challenges that met them every day. Writing 520 words each week in my own hand was a discipline that stood me in good stead, trying to make one point that had something to say about the everyday God in an accessible way.

It had become quite usual to write engagements in the diary and then forget about them until the day arrived. One day in 1956 the diary showed an agreement to go to the *Daily Telegraph* cricket correspondent

Lambeth Palace, S.E.1

28th June, 1954.

Dear Mr. Sheppard,

      I do not think I have ever had the pleasure of meeting you, but perhaps I may be allowed to send this little note. Your Principal has written to me and explained what was in your mind when you made your decision to accept the invitation to captain the Test and to give your time for the rest of this season largely to cricket, with the strong probability that it will mean your going to Australia, captaining our side there. One can quite understand that it was a difficult decision for you to make. Whatever else is said it delays your Ordination by some time. I would like merely to tell you that, so far as I can judge, I entirely approve of your decision. The Kingdom of God has many different aspects. Here is a piece of what I should regard as direct service to the wider interests of the Kingdom of God which you can render; and, as I understand, there really is a crying need for someone to bring back into the higher ranks of English cricket a sort of moral decisiveness and discipline which has been slipping. And I agree with you that you are right to regard this as a direct call, which delays your final vocation, but by no means interferes with but rather assists your service now to the Kingdom of God.

      There is always the danger that people who get involved in secular occupations of one kind and another may lose their sense of vocation. I do not believe for a moment that you are in any danger of that kind. On the contrary, by the Grace of God I am sure that this experience will deepen your sense of vocation and greatly increase your powers under God to serve Him in the Church in the years to come. May all blessing be with you in this decision, in what follows from it and, in due course, in your Ordination to the whole-time service of the Church.

      Yours sincerely,

      Geoffrey Cantuar:

D.S. Sheppard, Esq.

Jim Swanton's box at Lord's during the Oxford–Cambridge match. I went, hardly switched on to cricket. Jim said, 'Oh, Gubby wants to talk to you.' Gubby Allen was the chairman of the England selectors. He said, 'They are telling me I ought to press you to come and play. But when someone has decided to follow another career, I don't think we should press him to come back.' I said, 'Well, I am going to play a month's cricket for Sussex.' 'Now you're talking,' he said. 'When are you going to start?' The first date would only have allowed one match before the selectors met to pick the side for the fourth Test match. I said, 'You've had a bad match at Lord's. It'll come right in the next Test, and you won't need me.' We agreed to meet at Headingley, where I would be watching the first day's play. We could decide then whether an extra match for Sussex could be squeezed in. That would mean driving to Worcester overnight after a youth service in Portsmouth. At Headingley, England lost their first three wickets for 17 on a beautiful batting wicket. When we met at lunchtime, Gubby said, 'I think you had better go and play your match at Worcester!'

So the selectors took the risk of picking me for the fourth Test after no more than two county matches. It became famous as Laker's match, when Jim Laker broke every bowling record, taking 19 wickets in the match. Some newspapers had enjoyed a field day, joking at the curate being taken from teaching the Sunday school to batting against Lindwall and Miller. Lindwall was bowling when I went in to bat. He bowled a bumper first ball that whistled over my head as I ducked. It was the best thing he could have done for me, as I said to myself, 'This is a serious game!' and adjusted to the reality of what was going on. I was as amazed as everyone else that I scored 113.

Special media interest in the Islington curate followed. Maurice Wood was keen on making the most of this interest. That summer we had a public meeting in Islington Town Hall. Don Bradman, no less, came to read a lesson. I preached. The following year, having been recalled again for the last two Tests against the West Indies, I preached in St George's, Leeds, during the Headingley Test. Colin Cowdrey and the great young West Indies batsman Collie Smith read the lessons. There were other large-scale preaching moments. Reflecting on them, the evidence seemed to show that people like those I met out visiting in Islington were not present at these meetings any more than at 'ordinary' church services. These special occasions were inclined to attract those who were already on the fringe of church membership. In 1954, Billy Graham had led a three months' Greater London Crusade at Harringay Arena, four miles up the road from Islington. A curate arriving there in 1955 might have expected to meet converts from the crusade. There were indeed a number of people for whom that had been a decisive turning point. But they usually had a church background, as I had myself before the mission in Cambridge. I don't remember meeting any local Islington people not previously church members who had professed conversion through the Billy Graham crusade.

All that added up to an increasing belief that there needed to be many 'bridges' before those outside the churches would want to hear our preaching. After our twelve years at the Mayflower Family Centre, I agreed to a debriefing. This appeared in a 'Correspondence' I had helped to launch, *Christians in Industrial Areas*, now called *City Cries*. What lay behind going to Canning Town? I replied, 'It was Islington that changed me. Living in Inner London, becoming concerned for people there and feeling how much the Church was struggling in such areas. By the time I finished at Islington there was only one thing I wanted to do – to serve in an inner-city area.'

3

East Enders

Canning Town

One spring night in 1957 I parked the car by derelict land in Canning Town. I walked all round the district, trying to put my thoughts into words to God and to listen for what he might be saying. That walk with God was to test the hints and the hunch that might be leading to a new calling. A few weeks before, I had visited the Dockland No 1 Settlement in Canning Town, near the Royal Docks in the East End of London, to address a small Bible class. The staff there had told me that they did not know if there would be any jobs for them by the following week. The Settlement was about to be closed. I had been wondering whether there might be an inner-city task for me after my curacy finished in Islington.

Much of Canning Town was still derelict from the wartime bombing. Half of all the dwellings in that southern part of the Borough of West Ham had been demolished. In the middle of this dereliction, the mock-Tudor buildings of the Settlement, more sturdily built, had survived. They were built, Oxbridge college in style, around a courtyard, with a large block of club buildings that had been constructed in the 1890s and the 1930s. Across the road stood old terraced streets, a scrap yard and some maisonettes and houses, brick-built in the last few years. The wide open spaces left by Hitler's bombs were referred to as 'the debris'. They provided a playground for the children, until they were tidied up in later housing schemes. Often on winter evenings a small group would be huddled round a bonfire.

I have often held conversations with God on walks. Thoughts of what inner-city life had been teaching me led to a prayer that night: 'People like me say, "Lord, You are God the Father Almighty. We believe we can bring children up to Your glory, provided we have some nice gardens and trees in the street. But we don't think it is possible in places like this." ' That walk and reflection was far-reaching – more than was clear at the time. I had not grasped many of the implications yet. However, it began to dawn that a concern for the glory of God should produce indignation at living conditions where people could see no presence of God, and no place to bring up children.

At the top of my motives was a longing for the Christian gospel to be credible to inner-city people. Two years in Islington had taught me that the preaching that had 'worked' in Cambridge University for me, and in the suburbs for large numbers of people, had not been effective in the inner city. Much of the church growth that I saw at St Mary's, Islington, was among nurses and students. By contrast, most long-established Islingtonians, whom I met while visiting, and the youngsters that I came to know through my involvement with the Islington Boys' Club, assumed that the church was not for them.

A bishop has responsibility for helping to guide young clergy about their next move, and the Bishop of Stepney, Joost de Blank, quite soon to become Archbishop of Cape Town, asked to see me. He had a suggestion: 'We could cash in on your cricket, and young people's interest. Perhaps we could make you an extra diocesan youth chaplain.' Others also were keen to advise me. Through my involvement with the Islington Boys' Club I was drawn into some activities of the National Association of Boys' Clubs.[1] One of their staff, Neville Goodridge, said, 'Don't go round telling other people what to do. Go and do a piece of work and let others come and see what you're doing.' It was seminal advice. I recognised my need to tackle a long-term piece of work.

My first visit to speak to the Bible class at the Dockland Settlement had set the mind racing. Club buildings and a hostel surrounded the courtyard. Was this a place where I might work and to which others might come and share the vision of such work? That same Sunday evening I took my courage in both hands and wrote to the Bishop of Barking, Hugh Gough. He was a member of the Dockland Settlements Committee. Could I come and see him? He rang me back on the following day, and on the Tuesday afternoon I climbed on a Number 38 bus that went all the way from Islington to his house in Loughton. We talked so long that he said I'd better stay the night. In backing my enthusiasm, he took on a weighty responsibility. He agreed to become the chairman of a new committee, and a week or two later the Dockland Settlements Committee handed over the Settlement to 'the Bishop of Barking's Committee'. That new committee invited me to become the warden. We decided to take a new name – the Mayflower Family Centre. It all happened at breakneck speed.

Deep waters

If Hugh Gough took on heavy responsibility, I myself was plunging into deep waters. I was twenty-eight years old, getting married in June, two months away. Of course, Grace and I discussed the possibility of this new adventure in East London, and she said that she was ready to come with me. The programme was congested. I was still a curate in Islington. There was the recruiting of a new council who would accept responsibility for the large set of buildings and the staff that would be needed to run them. The remaining staff members needed reassurance about their jobs. New colleagues had to be found to join the venture.

In 1957 everything was still in the diary, including cricket. The previous year, as a bachelor, I had played my holiday month for my county, Sussex. Against all the odds, that had led to a recall to the England team against Australia for the last two Test matches. So in that breathless April, I crossed London to the Oval to put in some serious practice with the Surrey team. After our honeymoon I planned to play for another month.

Alas, the honeymoon was a disaster. We went to Italy in June. In the intense heat Grace fell ill. Eventually it was diagnosed as chicken pox; my non-existent Italian, mixed with broken French, broke down in trying to tell the doctor what was the matter. After references to *poulets*, I said desperately, 'Elle est plein de ah ah ah', with graphic gestures of scratching. 'Ah', he said, 'Varicella.' She was very ill and was placed in the isolation ward of a hospital. Grace persuaded me that she would be all right, and that I should go home and not miss the Sussex cricket match that might make it possible for the selectors to pick me for England against the West Indies that summer.

She kept going through the weeks that followed her return, without convalescing. She was conscious of living up to the expectations that Test matches brought for the new wife of a cricketer, and that the parish had for a curate's wife. In September she collapsed in the London Underground. After various attempts at diagnosis, she was taken into the London Hospital. The hospital was in some chaos, as there was an epidemic of Asian flu, and half the nurses were ill. The physician came and stood at the foot of her bed, and said that nothing was organically wrong. That phrase often sounds as though *nothing* is wrong.

We were both beginning to open our minds to the reality of nervous and mental illness – we had shrunk from that. Grace was later to write *An Aspect of Fear* about her experience that started then. It has helped many people to learn, as we slowly did, that there is nothing wrong with being afraid, but that you do not have to be controlled by fear. She wrote:

In the past I had had a strong faith which had stood me in good stead. But now somehow I was losing my grip. The awful prospect dawned on me that God might leave me. I dreamed one night that He was holding on to my fingertips; I felt that my hand would slip out of His at any moment. I was very distressed and frightened, and confided this dream to David. He did not appear to be shocked, neither did he offer any magic solutions. Quite calmly he accepted my word and suggested that for the time being I trusted in something that I could see and touch. I could trust him. His faith would have to do for both of us. This carried me through that crisis, and I did not feel so alone and afraid.[2]

It was clear that Grace was trusting in God as deeply as anyone I knew. That conversation in the hospital was a growing moment for me, as well as for her. Both of us had been brought up to think that as good Christians we should be able to stand on our own two feet. Now our growing realisation was that God never promised to protect trusting Christians from the sicknesses and fears that other human beings face. Often the Christian answers are not individualistic. These painful experiences opened our eyes to the corporate answers that the New Testament gives – like, 'Bear one another's burdens, and so fulfil the law of Christ.'

There has been much for me to learn from weakness, illness and failure that would never have been learned any other way. When the time came to move into our flat at the Mayflower, Grace had become a voluntary patient at the York Clinic at Guy's Hospital, and it was on my own that I moved into the Mayflower and our flat there. Touching rock bottom in this way was the beginning for both of us of climbing up to a shared life that was more honest and open. Being part of the venture at the Mayflower, Grace started to feel some excitement – and apprehension. An electrician came to do some work under the floorboards in the flat. He asked her, 'Do you think you're going to like it round here?' She thought for a moment, then said, 'Yes, the people have been so friendly and helpful, I expect I shall get used to it.' He said, 'You hesitated then.' She said he had spotted all too quickly her underlying fear that she wasn't going to cope.

After the period in the London Hospital, Grace had started seeing a psychiatrist. I always joined them for the last quarter of an hour. He said to me, 'You are to take six weeks holiday a year. It's not temporary. You will need more when you're older.' That was life-giving advice. So was the remark of an elderly clergyman that year, who asked me if I took my day off. 'Yes, always,' I said. 'Good,' he replied. 'It's not fair on your people not to.' Years later, as a bishop, I pressed clergy to build in proper holidays and time off. Ours is perhaps the easiest profession in which to be lazy. It also has the greatest temptations of trying to be God, always available, thinking you can meet everyone's cry for help.

The Mayflower

The last crowded months of 1957 saw us still living in Islington, with me as the parish curate, but going over to Canning Town two days a week. At the beginning of January 1958, I was licensed as warden and chaplain of the Mayflower. The large chapel in the Centre was crowded. A good number of well-wishers had come from Islington and from other churches. As the evening drew to a close, they drifted away and I began to wonder if anyone was going to be there on a regular basis. It turned out that there were six regular communicants, and twenty for a special service.

We created a pleasant flat out of a corridor in the hostel, the first married couple to live there. The kitchen had wire guards across the windows to stop tin cans – and worse – from being thrown in. It overlooked a busy scrapyard which was guarded by an Alsatian. From outside, the Centre had a fortress look. Friendly visitors often found it hard to spot just where you were meant to enter. Unfriendly ones never seemed to have much trouble! Inside the courtyard we looked out on a pleasant garden. The buildings of the Centre included nineteen club rooms of varying sizes, a nursery school, a swimming pool and the hostel that accommodated up to twenty 'residents' that we invited to join us – to serve in the district or to help in the Centre. These were in addition to the full-time staff. Some of the 'residents' were teachers in the district. Others were young men and women, who might have finished at university, spending a year or more offering supporting roles in the Centre. We would tell them to go out and find a job, in a way that would not have been possible twenty years later when jobs had become scarcer. The national background to our arrival in Canning Town in 1957 was optimistic. Harold Macmillan was Prime Minister, claiming 'You've never had it so good'. It was a time of near full employment. 'Never again' was the watchword that held together a consensus for those post-war years. The mass unemployment of the 1930s must never come back. When we moved to Canning Town everyone was in work, though most of it would have been unskilled or semi-skilled.

Grace brought sensitive gifts to the community. It was important to me that she – and, later, other spouses – was a full member of the staff team. At the same time she was grappling with fears that would leave her for several years with agoraphobia – the fear of public places. Relaxed and comfortable in our small flat, she found going outside our front door a formidable enterprise at times. A major factor in her healing was that she found herself regarded as a gifted person and not as an invalid in those difficult years. She found the Mayflower community unjudging. They accepted her as she was, and did not load heavy expectations on her of what a 'vicar's wife' was supposed to do. There were bad days and there were more hopeful ones, when her confidence was stronger. She learned not to try to conquer the great mountains all at once, but to make hay when the sun shone, and to climb more modest foothills. She was a good cook and was happy to entertain in our flat.

I had to learn that my first responsibility was to recruit and support a team, rather than be the one who was always in the front line. The full-time members of staff lived in the Centre or nearby. They included the warden, chaplain, parish worker, youth leaders, nursery school head-teacher, and housekeeper. Together with spouses, we met each week for an unhurried meeting. This was an important time of communication and mutual understanding. It wasn't just about making arrangements and dates, but wrestling with long-term policies and arguing about immediate priorities. Serving and living in a community that had more than its share of hurts could create pressures that crushed vision and enthusiasm. In addition to the day off and proper holidays, we established a pattern that each member of staff was expected to take a long leave of three or four months every three or four years. That was a significant factor in maintaining stability over the years. During the first fifteen years after the Mayflower was established, eleven staff members stayed for seven years or more. When I was appointed, I made a public promise that I would stay for at least ten years, and in the event stayed for twelve.

George Burton

No account of the Mayflower and its leadership could omit the place George Burton filled for eight years, until his death in 1966. Working closely with George left an indelible imprint on my approach to inner-city mission. Without him, we might have developed a warm and harmonious team that ran smoothly, but cut little ice locally. George was a disturbing – and at times disturbed – person, whose influence on many people of different ages and classes was deep and lasting. Born and bred in Glasgow, in the Depression of the 1930s, he had a brilliant mind that had been denied educational opportunities. He said to me, 'I've been fighting you educated people all my life.' When his trust had been hard-won by a very few of us, he revealed how deep were the hurts that tormented him. He had been large for his age. At fifteen he had lied about his age and joined the army. He was posted to India. From there he wrote stumbling love letters to a girl at home who was better educated than he was. She returned his letters, rejecting his love and crossing out all the wrong uses of words and mis-spellings. As a result he became unable to write at all for many years, which in turn caused a long rift in the family. His inability to write letters cut him off from his mother whom he adored. The family assumed that he no longer cared about her.

George understood Canning Town youngsters and adults at a deep level because he had grown up in situations akin to theirs. He had a powerful sense of God's leading and a passion to share his faith. He spoke openly of Christ in a way that made some think he was simply a 'Bible-basher'. But with local people he was ready to be patient until they wanted to hear. George, when relaxed, was a sensitive listener, quick to respond to practical human needs in a youngster's life or in his or her family. Jean Lodge Patch – later Jean Hewitt –had already left her career as a hospital almoner to join us as a youth leader. When George first arrived, the teenage youth club was at a low level. One evening, just fifteen young people came. Jean described George's response:

> The annual fair at Beckton Park, which had opened that night, was a strong counter attraction. 'Let's go and see the kids at the fairground', George urged. Leaving the handful of youngsters in the club room with the other helpers, we drove off to spend the evening strolling round the stalls and sideshows, observing the teenagers and stopping to chat with the few we already recognised.[3]

Soon he had established a lively, often disorderly club, to which a good number came. Before meeting George, I had said that what was wanted in the club was a bit of a riot going on, and the leader leading the riot. That's what we got with George Burton. He had a great gift for creating fun. There was much noise, with few rules, but he could crack the whip when he needed to. If there was trouble, he did not hesitate to turn the whole club out. He would then go out on to the street and talk with them, making it clear that they must help him build the spirit of the club. One evening in the week there was a short talk and a prayer in the clubroom. On one occasion a billiard ball was thrown while the prayer was going on. Immediately afterwards, George apprehended the culprit. 'How did you know I threw it? You were praying.' 'Yes I know,' said George, 'but I was looking through my fingers!' We had to keep good relations with our immediate neighbours. That wasn't always easy – especially when the neighbours brought round a billiard ball that had come through their window, saying, 'I believe this belongs to you!'

If his members were in trouble with the law, he would speak up for them in court, and follow them up if they were 'sent away'. I recall George coming home from one court visit. He was trembling all over. I understood then the degree to which he identified with club members. He would stop and chat with young people as he drove around the district, always with a helper, for he hated being alone. He became an accepted visitor in the homes of a number of members. His work was not confined to young people. He made friends with other local couples, and led several to a lasting faith in Christ. He was a remarkable example of a Spirit-filled person. There were moments when he responded to promptings that led him to walk into situations of personal need, which he would love to say 'were too much of a coincidence'. For example, one prompting told him that he must call on the mother of a member. As she opened the door to him, she said, 'Thank God you've come'. She had just discovered a serious crisis in the family.

I learned with George that working-class people are used to moving in groups and thinking in groups. The individualistic approach of much church life made it impossible for many East Enders to believe that 'This Christ could be for me'. As well as the Open Youth club, George brought together a 'Sunday Group', in which young people took a corporate step towards God by joining a group that included going to church and discussing Christian faith. That seemed to set them free to think as individuals about the claims of Christ. I used to speak of the *vision* that God could raise up local leaders in any community. It became an article of faith to George. He gave special time to members of the Sunday Group, believing that they were the leaders God was giving us. More than thirty years after his death several of them have proved themselves as gifted Christian leaders locally and on a wider canvas.

George insisted to us that, if we ever wrote about him, we should paint the picture 'warts and all'. When relaxed, he was as skilful and shrewd a colleague as I have ever known. George, when on edge, was raw, and could be brutal and crude in attacking those he saw as his enemies. It worried me that some of those who received the sharp edge of his tongue would not have understood what was happening. However, in 'picking up the pieces' after such rows, I found more than once that they *had* met such anger before – on occasions from their own father – and the hurt was not because of ignorance, but because it was uncovering old and painful sores. The 'warts and all' description makes much of our life sound as if free communications with George and with each other must have been suffocated. The reality was far different. There were indeed times when we 'walked on egg shells', but his challenges blew open barriers that middle-class politeness would have kept bolted and barred. Deep feelings came to be shared; we put away inhibitions that stopped sensitive questions being asked; there were many times of uproarious fun – provoked by George. When he died, I said that the rest of us were more polite than he was, so we were in danger now of allowing the gates that he had blown open to shut between us, blocking honest communication of our feelings.

George Burton's inability to write, dating from that rejection by his girlfriend in Glasgow who had made him believe he was an ignorant slum kid, became a near suicidal secret. Those of us to whom he disclosed it were then suspected of betraying his confidence. This sometimes led to angry and suspicious attacks on those closest to him. It was as though he was pressing us to kick him out, testing us whether we really meant it when we said that we valued him and wanted him there. Jean Hewitt, more than any of us, bore his resentment at her university degree. Once, he spat in my face from six inches away. Christmas was the time he dreaded most – when happy families gloried in their warmth. One year he pressed me to stay with him in his room, while he grew more and more morose. He brought out his trunk in which he kept some of the secrets he feared most. At the lowest point he took out the letters he had written in his forties to a girlfriend who had understood his fears. She had given them back in order to help him know that he could write again. Now he ripped them to pieces.

George forbade Grace and me to discuss him. There were late-night sessions when he manipulated the conversation in order to delay me. I had to prove willingness to stay with him till a very late hour rather than go downstairs to our flat and my wife. Staff meetings had their stormy moments. At one, George started to analyse Grace in front of the others. At last she exploded, 'I can't stand people who set themselves up as amateur psychiatrists.' George walked out of the room, and it was some weeks before communications were restored. Through the pain of moments like this, Grace and George built a bond of understanding. He often prayed, 'Lord, give Grace a baby', and he was overjoyed when Jenny was born. He loved to sprawl on the floor and enter into a tea party with Jenny and her dolls. The bond between Grace and George grew stronger still when she underwent major surgery for ovarian cancer, and the next year, 1996, he had his lung removed, also for cancer.

He had a fantasy of the ideal post for him. This was to run his own mission hall, where he would not have to work with a team like ours! His insecurity meant that he must always be able to leave, in case the strains became unbearable. There were three occasions when he actually had his bags packed and loaded in his small Ford car, ready to take off. I often thought that my first task was to keep George at the Mayflower. Not for the last time in my life, I was accused of letting someone else run the show. When he was in a raw mood, George would say that he did not care what I thought; he had come to serve the Lord Jesus Christ, no one else. But I knew that he was glad that I was the warden, and never doubted that he gave me his loyalty, whatever might be said in the heat of the moment. He would press me to come into the club, and to join weekends for the Sunday Group, and would build me up in front of the young people.

My unhappiest day at the Mayflower was when George had been on the staff for a year or two. I had an increasing feeling that I must ask him to leave. The rows between staff members seemed so incompatible with a Christian community. It was Jean Hewitt, seeing him with the young people every day, who persuaded me that he was God's right man for the job. Another factor in persuading me that he should stay, and that we should support him in his approach to the work, was that I was reading Alan Bullock's newly published *The Life and Times of Ernest Bevin*. He said that Bevin found it easier to hit on a way of solving a problem by talking than by putting his ideas down on paper with his clumsy handwriting. Bevin read comparatively little and never widely. He picked up ideas far more from conversation than from reading, using the people he met 'as other men use books'.[4] 'He was highly sensitive to criticism, quick to resent opposition and to take it as a personal attack. Once he suspected that someone was trying to get at him, or down him, he could be brutal in the vehemence with which he hit back.' I asked myself if the Church would have made space, had he been available, for Ernest Bevin – probably the greatest working-class Englishman of the century; and I knew that the answer was that we would not. The conviction grew that it was right now to shape our staff team in a way that would support George Burton.

When he died from lung cancer at the age of fifty-one, all the members of the Sunday Group came to the funeral service and then to the burial in East London Cemetery. It was a sunny day, and we sang their favourite hymn, 'Jesus Christ is risen today' as we stood round the grave. Most of them owed their faith to this man, both gifted and flawed as he was. When I think of George, the text comes to mind, 'We have this treasure in earthenware pots.' George was very earthy. But, as soon as I catch myself thinking that, another question crowds in, 'Who is calling the pot earthy? Aren't you earthy too?'

With all that background, it was a remarkable evidence of healing that George wrote a book in his own hand – *People Matter More than Things*.[5] It was one of those books that circulate widely through informal recommendation. Its challenge to tidy-minded Christians was that many young people, who are today outside any church circles, can be reached if we are prepared to stay with awkward behaviour and aggressive rejections.

Those years when I worked beside George Burton taught me several lessons that I hope I have never forgotten: God can and does use disturbing, even disturbed people to bring his love into the world; there are God-given gifts that home and school may have trampled on, which can be released and greatly used; it is practical to introduce such people to leadership provided you stand by them; space should be made in youth leadership and in other professions for some of those who have learned in the school of life and received hard knocks; strength can come from encouraging small groups to think about the faith together; anger should be listened to, and can be creative; the Holy Spirit moves us, if we open ourselves to him and are ready to test with others whether the promptings we feel are in tune with what we know of Christ; raw wounds in a personality can be healed, but will need costly loving from others.

This relationship with George Burton was a cameo of our experience in the East End. We were right to be indignant at the way in which so many human gifts were being blocked and wasted. Most of our neighbours had no access to places where decisions were taken. Often that led to frustrations and anger that was expressed without polite reserve. But, concentrating only on these features of life ignores the openness, the generosity, the humour and the loyalties that brought me the biggest education of my life.

Stepping stones

It was a blessing in disguise that the large chapel at the Mayflower had become unheatable. The small congregation decorated one of the club rooms, which for five years provided a more intimate setting for worship. The first year saw small additions to our number of worshippers. We had established 'Fellowship Hour', which followed the Sunday evening service, when the larger numbers came. This offered the chance for discussion that questioned the sermon and raised issues that were bothering members. Reviewing progress in staff meeting after two or three years, we arrived at a painful, if honest, assessment; hardly anyone was coming regularly to 'Fellowship Hour' who did not bring large personal problems. In contrast, most of our neighbours did not see themselves as unhappy or in special need. We coined the phrase 'happy pagans' to describe the majority of our neighbours. We believed that the Gospel, with its call to join as responsible servants of God's kingdom, challenged people like them to use the God-given talents they possessed. East Londoners were not anti-clerical; many were grateful to us for offering facilities for their children and for the neediest in the community. But they did not see the Christ we preached as being for them.

There were some difficult personal decisions to make about how much time to give to preparing for preaching and worship. What we did in our worship was important, but most battles were being lost and won long before our neighbours entered the church building. So, in order to protect space for meeting people outside church services, I decided only to prepare one address thoroughly each week. For the other Sunday service, I would give just an hour to preparation and think aloud about the reading for the day. One annoying result of this was that several members told me they liked these talks better than those that had been prepared as carefully as possible! However, my carefully prepared sermons often included visual aids that seemed to fit in with the small temporary chapel. These included paintings that Grace did. They made my addresses more accessible. One painting of a country scene side by side with a heavily urban setting has been remembered long after the rest of the sermon. Showing the two pictures, I asked, 'Where is God?' It helped people to reject the assumption that he would only be present in the country scene. He is equally present – sometimes hurt – in the roughest parts of a city.

It is not easy to 'change gear'. Priorities should be reviewed at intervals. It was a significant failure later on, when a congregation had grown, not to have given more substantial time to thinking imaginatively about our worship. I still believe it was right in those first years to keep good time to meet and listen to people who had little contact with the organised church. That brought an understanding of the area that could never have been learned from books. How would I have managed if there had been a congregation of seventy or so? It would have been hard to resist spending the lion's share of my time being a pastor to them.

The many contacts made through the activities at the Mayflower made for the easiest visiting. We particularly wanted to reach the 20–50 age group, which was conspicuous by its absence from worship. There were natural contacts with parents and grandparents of nursery school children, and of those who came to the children's clubs and youth clubs, as well as those who themselves came to the 'Mums' or 'Grandads' clubs. When I was able to appoint a chaplain to the staff, the job description I gave to Brian Seaman was to focus his time on this adult age group. Brian, wholeheartedly supported by his wife Marion, persevered faithfully with this personal ministry, based on visiting and group work, for ten years at the Mayflower. Then they moved on to more than twenty years of similar ministry in inner-city Newcastle.[6]

Our problem at the Mayflower was never how to establish first contacts. We saw the importance of establishing 'stepping stones', where members might meet Christians on common ground. In our situation we came to feel that the home was the most natural meeting place, and that it was good to try to meet as couples. With our tiny congregation at the time, Grace and I realised that we did have one home in the district that could be a base for a group – our own. We enlisted a young engaged couple as our partners. When they married, they stayed in the area. Since then Colin and Mary Watts have consistently made their home a hospitable place, a base for a Christian group and for many neighbours.

We kept one evening in the week free to meet couples who didn't come to church. The log that I kept of those evenings shows that they involved just seventeen couples over two and a half years. We made friends. Often the point of contact was with their children coming to the Centre. Sometimes they would tell us that their own children's faith was a challenge to them. One week we would visit them. The next week we tried to bring together a small group in our flat. We would have a friendly, light-hearted evening together, starting with a noisy game – 'Pit' – that had most of us shouting for our corner. Towards the end of the evening there was a discussion. Usually this would start with a problem that touched each of our lives – a row at work, or in our street, the rights and wrongs of a strike, the difficulty of forgiving and forgetting, why God allowed suffering. Nearly everyone joined in, though there was one evening when no one came at all. If we started on a 'religious' topic, newcomers would sit politely and listen to us. But when we had talked about more familiar subjects a few times, *they* often raised 'religious' questions. This small group was only one of several planned, or spontaneous, 'talking groups' in which people found the self-confidence to come out with their own ideas and questions. For a number these groups were stepping stones to 'The Searching Group' that we formed each year – and perhaps to churchgoing and to personal faith in Christ.

Books, culture and tactics

In the early years of the Mayflower we made three decisions about policy, which called in question some of the approaches we had experienced in evangelical parishes. First, we questioned the place of *books* in a district where few people were in the habit of reading. Second, we questioned the passing of moral judgments about a *culture* very different from middle-class areas where the churches were strong in numbers. Third, we questioned the *tactics* of presenting a 'white-hot' challenge in preaching and worship.

First, the place of books. In the evangelical culture from which we were coming, any well-run church was expected to have a bookstall. At a deeper level, it was assumed that every keen Christian would read the Bible every day. The bookstall disappeared first. It had been the first feature on entering the chapel to confront a newcomer for whom books were part of another world. Several men told me, 'I've been reading your piece in my wife's book.' They meant *Woman's Own* magazine. There was no other book in their home. The bookstall shouted at them that

Christians were expected to read books. So we moved the bookstall out of the church and into the room where Fellowship Hour took place. It was tucked round the corner, available for those who were confident about learning in that way.

The boys that I had known at Iwerne Minster in earlier years took the temperature of their discipleship by whether they were keeping up their quiet time of prayer and Bible reading. They were typical of Christians trained in the evangelical way. That was within reach for people who were used to books and individual disciplines. For those who struggled to read solid blocks of print, it must have felt like plunging into unknown, deep water. In Canning Town, with those who had not had a good experience at school, emphasis on books could all too easily associate church with school and failure.

I worked out a form of words about reading the Bible, designed to encourage rather than make people feel 'put down'. There were perhaps three ways in which Christians could feed on the Bible. First, when at worship scriptures were read and someone explained them in a sermon. Second, when a group discussed what a part of the Bible meant for them. Third, when someone attempted to read it on their own. This was an attempt to 'cool it'. I had seen good Christians despair at their failure to sustain the demanding discipline of individual Bible reading. If we told them that all good Christians read the Bible every day, they would try, but many would fail. Those with sensitive consciences would tell themselves, 'I can't read the Bible' (not true). Others might well go on to say, 'I'm not like these people, so I can't be a Christian.'

I wrote about this in the circular we sent to our supporters, *The Log of the Mayflower*. One university graduate wrote to say how much it had helped her, because she had felt so guilty that she had not kept up her daily reading. Another told me of standing up as a teenager at a meeting to make a promise to God that she would read the Bible every day before reading anything else. She had failed to keep this impossible promise that she had been encouraged to make. That failure had left her with deep feelings of guilt. Reflection on this suggested that a rule of life may be a fine thing to bind on yourself, but only when convinced that it fits you and your situation. It followed that preachers should not hold up impractical standards as the normal Christian life. A visiting overseas missionary told a story about an illiterate Rwandan who had been converted to Christ. He had taught himself to read and soaked himself in the Scriptures. He was a good enough friend for me to ask him whether that story was an exceptional one. He acknowledged that it would not be true of the majority of Christians there.

The second decision about policy had to do with passing moral judgments about the culture of the district. At this time I read Ted

Wickham's recently published book *Church and People in an Industrial City*.[7] In it he described evangelicals as 'moralisers'. I objected to that description of 'us'. Surely we wanted to bring the Gospel of God's undeserved love to people. However, on weighing up that description as moralisers, the result seemed plain. If we marched in with all guns blazing on 'worldliness', we would never get as far as revealing the grace of God in our lives. We would have kept ourselves separate from the local life.

The point is illustrated by our attitude to local weddings. At Islington, Maurice Wood had suggested that it was wise to have a firm commitment elsewhere, so as to be able to refuse any invitation to a wedding reception. The assumption that lay behind this was that an atmosphere of dancing and too much drink would make Christian witness difficult. In Canning Town we decided differently. I recall the first time that Grace and I went to a local wedding reception. We were dancing together, along with the families and their friends. We both felt that we were in the right place, and that the party at which Jesus turned the water into wine was probably rather similar in its atmosphere. Conversations took place with freedom, because we had shown our gladness to be part of their celebration and their world.

Ted Wickham argued that the moral judgments Christians made were often limited to *private* morality – swearing, drunkenness, dishonesty, sexual immorality, and hooliganism. But equally damaging to God's good world was the tolerating of poor housing, lack of training for decent jobs, prejudice against newcomers. I came to look more carefully at the use we made of the Old Testament prophets. For example, gospel sermons had used the text in the first chapter of Isaiah: 'Come, let us reason together. Though your sins are as scarlet, they shall be white as snow.' The 'scarlet sins' were then listed. They do not include one from that private morality list. Isaiah spoke of pursuing justice, championing the oppressed, giving the orphan his rights, pleading the widow's cause.[8] In Canning Town we found that local people were ready to enter into serious discussion about some issues like that.

The third decision was to question the tactics of 'white-hot' presentations of the gospel. One young man, new in his faith, was posted to Cardiff for his work. There he went to a Pentecostal church, and came home full of enthusiasm for the exciting singing and worship there. I said that we could make our worship 'hotter', but my experience was that, if we did, only a few would want to come with us. I believed we were called to reach the main body of our neighbours. Immediate 'preaching for a decision' would ask them to make a life-changing decision before they knew what was at stake. I hoped we could help people come to lasting commitment to Christ, when they had thought about what that might involve in their own community. An illustration of those hopes being fulfilled emerged some years later. Bill described how he had come to faith in Christ. He had joined the Sunday Group, and found himself exposed for the first time to Christian teaching. He said: 'At first, I thought it was all a fairy tale, but, after a bit, I started to argue and think and tried to reason it out. Quite a bit later, I prayed and asked Christ to come into my life.' Belonging to the group gradually led him to the place where he could contemplate believing for himself.

The presence in our evening service of young people from the Sunday Group had an important influence in keeping our church life earthed in the culture of the district. They were never perfectly still or silent, usually arriving after worship had begun, eating sweets in the back row. They frequently talked through the sermon. Grace, who often sat near them, defended them against some critics of their behaviour. Though noisy at times, they had been listening, as their chattering was a commentary on the sermon. When members of the Sunday Group began to pray out loud together, Joe prayed one day, 'And thank you, Lord, that Mrs Olley don't shush us like she used to!'

From the beginning, I felt that we must listen to the local culture with respect. Supposing my calling had been to go to India, it would have been wrong to think that I was leaving a continent of superior beings – Europe – to preach to an ignorant people. It would have been right to learn that the transition from one culture to another was an opportunity to learn the distinctive richness of the other. The Church and the Settlements had often made the mistake of assuming that educated, middle-class people, when they went to working-class communities, should expect to give, but not to receive anything. As a young man, Tubby Clayton had lived at the Oxford and Bermondsey clubs, led by 'The Doctor', John Stansfeld. 'The Doctor' took a local young man from Bermondsey with him to the Annual Meeting in Oxford. Tubby said that the room was filled with Fellows of All Souls. The young Bermondsey man, desperately nervous as he looked round this august company, said, 'Of course you lot are all so ignorant.'

George Burton certainly believed 'we educated people' were ignorant. So did I. In the Gospel we had something precious to bring, but we had also much to learn and receive from Canning Town and its different culture. We needed to listen for a long time before we could challenge the local ways of doing things. Looking back, I see myself defending 'Canning Town, right or wrong' during the first six years. That is not something to be ashamed of. Perhaps accepting uncritically is a necessary phase to move through before we can offer a proper critique of local attitudes, as hopefully I was able to do on occasions during the second six years.

During that second period, Roy Trevivian came to the Mayflower to produce four *People's Services* for BBC Radio 2.[9] He told me he had not wanted to come. He was cynical about this public schoolboy, ex-cricketer, playing around in the East End of London. He said that an incident during this visit changed his attitude to me. Ronan Point, a 21-storey block of flats half a mile from the Mayflower, had collapsed that week, with loss of life. After the broadcast *People's Service* that Sunday morning, there was a cup of tea in the garden. One of our local men was holding forth to all who would listen about the unreasonable behaviour of his employer. He had disciplined him for missing work when he had gone round to Ronan Point to see what help he could offer. Roy Trevivian was impressed that I did not join in the general seal of approval that our man was receiving. He was all too ready to skive off work if there was half an excuse. Believing that I knew him well enough to have earned the right to do so, I challenged him about his attitude.

I felt more solidarity with dockers who were increasingly fearful about the survival of their jobs. Jack Dash carried many of our neighbours with him in the 1960s, leading unofficial strikes. There was distrust of national organisers. At one of the Thursday evenings for a small group in our flat, a piece of old folklore came to the surface. A woman said, 'Bevin sold out to the bosses. All our fathers believed that.' In the Royal Docks, membership was inclined to be of the 'Blue' Union, not of the 'White' Transport and General Workers Union, that Ernest Bevin had built up after the First World War. He received a bloody nose both in East London and in Liverpool, and the distrust of national trade union structures still continued. By the 1960s the introduction of new technology had become a prime reason for fear of unemployment. 'New technology always produces new jobs' was the slogan regularly repeated. We heard it again when we moved to Liverpool in 1975. No one gave an account of what those new jobs would be for the dockers and their sons. The following year I was present at a rally at the Pier Head in Liverpool, held to protest against the closure of Dunlop's. One of the speakers asked, 'What will you tell your son, when he asks you what you were doing when they closed Dunlop's?' In Canning Town, as in Liverpool, the culture of the district was built round the father and son industry of the Docks. Militancy, which seemed irrational to those who already had secure jobs, found a fertile seed bed when unemployment appeared inevitable for a whole locality. It was difficult then for the wider community to bring pressure to bear.

When we spent days off with some of our friends who had very different perspectives at the other end of London, Grace and I had some confrontations. As we pulled up outside Jane's house in the West End, the problem seemed to be whether I should write my letter of apology then, or wait till afterwards. I would try my best to behave calmly through the evening, when smart young men made scathing comments about 'these dockers'. It always seemed to be at the end of the evening, when some guests finally put me on the spot or even goaded me. I would boil over at what seemed to me ignorant and insulting to people who were my neighbours and friends. There would be a sharp exchange. Jane nevertheless seemed to want us to come again.

The Mayflower was not a parish church, so there was no requirement for a Parochial Church Council. Once a modest congregation had emerged, it was clearly right that a local committee should be brought into being which would take on the responsibilities for the life of the church at the Mayflower. The arrival of this local committee raised some fresh dynamics. Dave, for instance, refused to stand for election to it. He then found it a great threat, and harked back to what he saw as a beautiful time when he could come straight to me to argue a point about the way church life was moving. He couldn't bear the thought of being under the authority of his own peer group. So he stopped coming to church. I have a vivid memory of sitting in his flat at the top of a tower block late one night. Dave was in a depressed mood, full of the injustices of life. He had never had any decent education. My comment that the eleven-plus examination unfairly favoured those who felt at ease in the world of teachers and books did not get us further forward. 'I don't remember any eleven-plus,' he said. 'Don't be silly,' his wife chipped in, 'you played hooky most of the time you were meant to be at school.' Dave relentlessly continued with his tirade. Eventually, I burst out angrily: 'I know that I was born on the "right side of the tracks". There are divisions of class and opportunity between us. But surely Christian love can bridge those divisions.' Perhaps my explosion helped us both to reach across to each other. In the end Dave found ways of relating to the organised church, at least for some years.

It was part of my role to enable people like Dave to stay in the ring. They often had gifts and insight to bear effective witness in their community. We needed some of the steadier members to come regularly to ensure that there was stability in church life. But space needed to be kept also for gifted people who came more erratically. One of our members, Tom Ham, held high office in his trade union. I encouraged him to see that this was his prime calling as a Christian. He came to me once, telling me that he was under enormous pressure from militants in his union, and asking for my prayers for the Branch meeting that week. I asked him to come that Sunday evening and tell the congregation, so that we could all pray intelligently. I made it clear that, with his union commitments, he was not expected to attend all our meetings and services. He usually came to church every other week, but we regarded him as a regular member, as much as those who served on the committee and never missed a service.

Many of the more confident members were inclined to move out of the district, seeking better opportunities for their children. 'Getting education, whether that came through school, a good club or church, was often the route to 'going up in the world'. When members moved away we commended them to their local church where they were moving. Some were hurt that we discouraged them from still regarding the Mayflower as their church once they had moved. We had seen many churches where those who had once lived in the district, and had moved away, travelled back to hold key positions. That prevented local leadership from emerging. This 'upward and outward' movement threatened to produce a 'community of the left-behind'.

I risked raising this sensitive subject: what did it do to the neighbourhood and to the children growing up in it if those who had experienced the best of education and church life all went away each generation? The grapevine played back to me that 'Mr Sheppard don't hold with going up in the world'. That made me think furiously about what I did hold with. In his summary of the Old Testament Law, Jesus said, 'You shall love your neighbour as yourself.' Loving yourself means that you should indeed want the best opportunities for yourself and for your children. But loving your neighbour as yourself – wanting the best for him or her – might cause you to ask what you are doing to them if you remove the contribution you can make to your community. Perhaps when you make decisions about where you want to live, your neighbours' needs should go into the scales as well as your family's needs. Speaking in suburban churches, where what was later called 'Essex man' was to be found, I found there was a tense silence when I described the effect on communities like Canning Town when all those who had done well in school moved away each generation.

Segregated housing – huge zones of council housing, kept well apart from equally large belts of private housing – produced one-class quarters. And the bigger the city, the greater was the segregation. In London it meant that when a young couple moved out of the area, they had to move several miles away. The lack of any privately owned housing in Canning Town meant that it was impossible for young couples who wanted to buy a house or flat in their own area to do so. This was a moment before the major growth of housing associations. I heard about the long-established St Pancras Housing Association, and went to knock on their door. That led on to contacts that made it possible for us to form a small 'Mayflower Housing Association' that would help provide modest-cost housing for those who wanted to stay.

It was encouraging that some new Christians thought this issue out and determined to stay in the area. Like Colin and Mary Watts, they are still there, giving firm local foundations to church life and to care in the community. Towards the end of my time there, Bert Girard came to me. He said, 'You know that I've always wanted a little garden. Well, Tate and Lyle's are offering to relocate staff, which would mean that I could buy a house in the country with a garden. I've put my name down for a place.' As it happened, Bert was the fifth member of our congregation who had come to me during that one week to say that they were intending to move away. I tried to avoid showing my disappointment. He had a perfect right to make that decision. A week or two later, he came to me again. 'You know I told you I'd put my name down for a place in the country,' he said. 'Well, I've been thinking about the old people that I've been visiting, and wondering who is going to take that on, if we all move away. So I've been back and crossed my name off the list.'

The hostel at the Mayflower provided rooms for twenty residents, in addition to the regular staff. Some of these residents came as teachers in the district; one worked in the laboratory of a local hospital. Several each year would come after university, often thinking about ordination. In an interview with each would-be resident, I made the point that if outsiders took on the leadership, they could block the way to achieving a locally rooted work. We would ask them to help, sometimes in menial ways, sometimes taking responsibility for a project, but ready to step back if a local person emerged who would take it on. One of the most rewarding results of those years at the Mayflower has been to know of former residents now in different parts of the world serving church and community in similar areas. Spending a year or more in Canning Town opened their eyes to needs and possibilities.

The Dockland Settlement in Canning Town demonstrated a number of features of the Settlement Movement that we had to reconsider. At one time it had employed forty paid workers – many paid not much more than pocket money. Down the road, the Parish Church of St Luke's, Victoria Docks, had, in the 1930s, fifteen clergy and twenty paid lay workers. When considering these large staffs in East London, it should be remembered that they attempted in amateur fashion much of what professional social and community workers tackle today. Even so, numbers like that carried with them the strong expectation that leadership could not be expected from local volunteers. I found that there was suspicion of Settlements and churches among Labour Party councillors in West Ham. We felt the mistrust. One councillor asked me, 'Doesn't the Church with its millions fund the Mayflower Centre?' I explained that the only contribution from that source was that the Diocese of Chelmsford paid me on the minimum stipend for a vicar in the diocese – then £1,100 a year. In fact, we depended on generous giving from the list of supporters across the country that gradually built up. So it was quite a remarkable turn-around of attitudes when Roger Sainsbury, who was warden of the Mayflower from 1974 to 1981, was made an Alderman of the Borough of Newham.[10]

Settlements and Missions had been founded in inner cities in the nineteenth century, often with a religious basis. Many moved away from the practising faith of their founders to play an important part in secular social work. Sometimes the movement went in the opposite direction, with Christian motivation being established or renewed where it had been nominal. We tried to learn from mistakes made by both Missions and Settlements. We set out to offer the resources of the Centre to serve the area, respecting its distinctive culture, and to help bring to birth a church with strong roots in the local community. We believed that there were God-given talents among local people that could be unlocked if these people could be helped over a lack of self-confidence. That belief made us ask questions especially about approaches to young people.

4

Young People – Problems or Possibilities?

A group of us were sitting on a groundsheet outside a tent. In the first years at the Mayflower we ran a 'families camp' at Bracklesham Bay in Sussex. A thoughtful discussion developed, one boy in particular asking searching questions. The next day I asked him if he would like to come for a walk and talk some more with me. He looked scared, then said, 'Can I bring my mate with me?' It provided a far-reaching lesson for me. Public school boys, in the house parties at Iwerne Minster for instance, would have welcomed a private talk rather than speaking in front of anyone else. Youngsters in Canning Town wanted the solidarity of the group.

Open youth work

The youth work that emerged under George Burton's leadership was at two levels. There was the Open Youth Club and the Sunday Group. The Open Youth Club deliberately made no demands at the door. We were glad when the 1960 Albemarle Report on the Youth Service said that the first reason for youth work was 'association'.[1] It went on to say that association could be no more than neutral, or it could be highly creative.

The majority of youngsters in the Open Youth Club at the Mayflower were not ready to face challenges to them as individuals. They wanted to remain in the security of a group of friends. Homework, books and evening classes were not part of their life. That generation still left school at fifteen, coming home tired from work, which was often heavy and monotonous. Boys and girls wanted to be able to mix, though they spent most of a club evening in their separate groups. Life to them *was* personal relationships, with fierce loyalties and fierce rows. They liked noise and freedom. Young people like these were often called 'unclub-bable', because of the tidy behaviour many clubs demanded. Seeing

George Burton's lively club in action, it seemed that these were the very kind of youngsters whom the club method, rightly handled, could suit best.

Working-class parents would distinguish between 'respectable' and 'rough' groups with whom they went around. We felt it right to cater in our Open Youth Club for the 'rougher' group, so often excluded. In the 1960s more money came into the pockets of young people and provided a growing market for goods such as clothes and records. Adolescent wages doubled, opening the way for some to take up music with its expensive instruments and recordings. That left poorer youngsters behind yet again.

In the Open Youth Club, activities were our servants, not our masters. The different rooms in the club block at the Mayflower made it possible to offer activities like judo, five-a-side football, swimming, a girls' room where there was a mirror, some easy chairs and magazines, wash basin and hair dryer. In the main club room there was a canteen, snooker, table tennis and a record player. My picture of George Burton in the club has him always on the move, hitching up his trousers, with an old jumper covering an ample figure. He might be joking with the girls about their hair styles; sparring good naturedly with the rebels in the club, who had run a stick along the window guards when the club service was on, shouting 'Fatty Burton'; or taking time for a serious talk with a boy who was waiting for sentence, knowing he was going to be sent away. He was quick to notice his helpers. Some needed a lot of affirming – like Grace Spencer, a member of the local church who ran the club canteen one evening a week. More than anyone, she was the motherly person to whom youngsters opened their hearts. Or a young man who would never have seen himself as a leader; George took him into the indoor swimming pool and asked him to take charge. He did not leave him alone there for more than ten minutes. Then he praised him and told the helpers' debriefing at the end of the evening how he had taken charge in the swimming pool.

He gave much personal support to those he believed were to be the leaders of the next generation. In a Sunday Group discussion, Jim Gosling described some of the stresses that he had to overcome in developing confidence as a leader:[2]

> Mr Burton, who's usually around, says, 'I'll leave it to you'. First thing that happens is that someone runs away with the keys and locks them out in the playground. They're all trying to break down the door, jumping over the roof. A year ago – I've been a Christian two years – probably I'd have got flustered over it and just left it and walked out. Yet I simply stood there and said a prayer, and after that things turned up.

A key was produced. Mind you, it may work out all different. Often we fall short of his ways. Only a few months ago something turned up and I went and punched someone. It's not a very good witness. But I believe that once a person realizes what they've done afterwards, and prays more about it, probably the next punch won't be for four or five years, or probably not at all.

When I spent an evening in the club, there was the need to learn how to talk and listen while the record player was going full blast. Again I discovered that young people were prepared to discuss deep matters when they were in a safe context, wrapped around with noise and in a crowd. Two summers saw me leading a short cricket tour in Sussex that included some of the club rebels. It was difficult for the village teams we played to assess the strength of our team. Some wore winkle-picker shoes and drainpipe trousers – a few of us white flannels. But there were some surprising talents, and we were a reasonable match for village sides.

We recruited a good number of helpers, some from among the 'residents', some who came from other parts of London after work, and an increasing number of local people, as the Mayflower church and the Sunday Group grew. That team of helpers meant that trusting relationships could be established, even when the attendance of members was erratic. Two teenage girls came into the club one Monday evening after a gap of months. 'Where's Pam?' they demanded. Pam was a helper who travelled across London to be there every Monday. Thankfully she was present. For those two girls, one of the attractions of the club was that there was an adult whose company they enjoyed. Another bridge between helpers and members resulted from the somewhat ramshackle nature of the club buildings – nineteen different rooms – which often called for repairs and alterations. Club members enjoyed working alongside helpers.

'Troublemakers'

When the leader went to court to appear for someone in trouble, it often created a particularly trusting association. Over subsequent years there have been a number of letters from former members who had been in trouble and wanted to tell me how much they valued George Burton's help in starting to build a more responsible life. One boy I visited in borstal started to make promises about coming to church when he came home. I said, 'Don't make any promises now. Come and see me when you get home.' In the event, he was back in the scrapyard with his former companions as soon as he came home. None of the intentions he expressed when he was away were fulfilled. It made me question how much can be achieved when youngsters are sent away. New intentions have to be worked out in the old context. Often attendance centres seem to be more effective than custodial sentences.

Outings with a smaller group for the day or the weekend strengthened relationships between leaders and members. An old coach produced its own adventures on trips 'up the other end' in central London, or to the seaside at Southend. One weekend they went to Maldon on the Essex coast. A fight developed between some of our girls and local girls. The chief fury of the girls was that their boys refused to join in, but stayed chatting in an amicable manner! That was at a time when 'Mods' and 'Rockers' were written about as though they were dangerous hooligans who wrecked seaside resorts like Margate or Brighton. Dressing that way did not imply that these young people were likely to use violent behaviour. The way the media portrayed groups of young people led many adults to classify them as 'folk devils'. I had seen some of that stereotyping at work, as a new curate in Islington. A reporter from the *Daily Sketch* interviewed me. She wrote that she asked me if any cricket was played around there. In a piece of highly imaginative writing, her account of my response was, 'He rolled his green eyes and said, "They're more interested in flick knives than cricket bats round here." ' I don't even have green eyes! Nor did I say anything like her report.

Canning Town, still a predominantly white area, did sometimes see real violence. One of a group who came to train for boxing at the Mayflower had his eye shot out in the middle of the day 200 yards from the Centre. The police could not obtain a single witness. He had been going with an axe to hack down the door of a rival gang leader. I visited another member of that group in Durham high security prison. He told me that when he was in borstal his housemaster had described him in his report as 'indifferent'. 'Indifference' had a particular meaning; it meant that he never showed any feelings. After a long talk he told me why. As a boy he had got into trouble. When his father heard, he went upstairs 'to put his kicking boots on'. He then gave him a kicking, and followed that by weeping all over him because he had hurt him badly. The boy resolved that he would never let anyone see his feelings again.

One of our members, working as a waitress in a local café, saw a vicious attack on a foreign seaman. They were often seen as 'fair game', because going to the police would risk missing the sailing of their ship. Friends at the Mayflower promised her that they would stand by her if she gave evidence – but I saw the fear of reprisals and the breaking with the culture in which she had grown up. As a boy, I had been brought up to believe that a policeman would always help me. So he should always receive help. The culture of East London was very different. Many people distrusted the forces of law, and would have been reluctant to come forward as witnesses. The result of being unable to find witnesses sometimes tempted police officers to 'plant' evidence. The hostility they met in local groups perhaps led them to 'show them who is boss' by belligerent approaches.

I saw that for myself late one evening. Walking back from the station in Stratford Broadway, I stopped to talk with a group of our youth club members. Suddenly a police officer tried to move us on very aggressively. It was bad luck for him that he did not see my clerical collar before he had committed himself to assuming that we were up to no good. On another occasion, when George Burton had died and I had taken over as youth leader, there was some trouble outside the entrance to the club. Our local police at Plaistow were very co-operative when we needed them to show their face, without becoming too heavy. Unfortunately on this occasion it was a mobile police group who did not know us. They snatched one boy – who had some learning difficulties – and charged him. I went with him to the magistrates' court, where he was put on probation and where the magistrate lectured us about the need for the Mayflower club to keep order more effectively. Seething inside, I was tempted to answer back, since the trouble had taken place outside on the street. I managed to restrain myself, wondering at the same time how George would have managed had he still been there! That experience helped me to understand feelings of those who were unjustly treated by the law. It also led me to pray for police officers who have to face some very frightening situations.

Going out together as a group of young people sometimes provided association that was what the Albemarle Report would call 'highly creative'. Attitudes could be challenged when the group saw their leader's reactions. Pip Wilson, who was youth leader at the Mayflower some years after our time, told me of one evening when he drove a group up to the West End in a minibus. While they were stopped at a set of traffic lights, one of the club members leaned out of the window and unleashed a volley of racist abuse at a black man standing there. The man came round the front of the stationary vehicle and punched Pip hard in the face. The drive home took place in absolute silence, shaken by seeing their leader bearing the blame for them.

Detached youth work

During our years at the Mayflower, I joined the Executive Committee of the National Association of Youth Clubs (NAYC)[3] and a working party. This oversaw a project that tested the idea of 'detached youth workers'. We appointed five workers to live and operate in differing parts of the country. As members of the working party we received monthly reports from each of the workers. Their freedom to meet young people on their own ground seemed to offer important opportunities for creative meeting. The report was published in the form of a Penguin book, *The Unattached*, by Mary Morse.[4]

When I moved to Liverpool, I found that there was a detached youth work project that had initially been chaired by Edward Patey, the Dean of Liverpool. The first project worker, Jude Wild, and her colleague Bill Cox, continued over the years to have a strong influence in Youth Work in Liverpool. Jude Wild said there were fewer obstacles to get over in talking to young people than there were in a youth centre. Locking and unlocking of doors, the telephone ringing or equipment needing to be handed out prevented a leader from spending uninterrupted time with individuals or groups of young people.[5] She described the way in which some young people, who had felt they did not belong in any form of institutional life, came to trust her with questions they would have been embarrassed to raise in other contexts.

In our last year in Liverpool, Grace and I spent half a day with a new detached youth work project in inner-city Breckfield. This had been set in motion by a Church Urban Fund grant, an example of a church initiative in which there was no attempt to retain church control. The management committee was made up of local people, with the diocesan youth officer offering professional advice. We were deeply impressed by the way the team of leaders accompanied young people. A number of these had been suspended from school, and others had dropped out from employment training projects. Here too association could be simply *neutral*, but it could also be highly *creative*, as adults and young people faced different issues together. Coping with violent behaviour was made easier, they said. In a club, a leader was bound to stay on the spot if trouble flared. In detached youth work, he or she could move on, then come back the next day and pick up with the group again. That does not lead to dropping club-based work. Rather there is room for both.

Over subsequent years, savage cuts were made to the youth service, as local authorities came under pressure to square their budgets. In London there were at one time some fifty detached youth work projects. Most have been abandoned by the individual boroughs, since the Inner London Education Authority (ILEA), with its more generous funding, was abolished. Detached youth work was not held to produce the 'outcomes' that justified public money being spent. That wish for measurable outcomes is understandable. At the Mayflower, we inherited a youth leader of the old school, Douglas Minton, who completed forty years in the Centre with us. 'Minnie' used to say that he wanted his boys (from the younger clubs) 'to be a credit to the Mayflower'. Of course, I wanted that too. But that could lead to our only recruiting 'nicer' young people. 'Successful' youth ventures frequently failed to provide the settings where 'rough' youngsters would feel at home. The attempt to measure 'outcomes' – like the publishing of raw school league tables – did not take into account the different starting places that young people were coming from.

In a Merseyside outer estate, Kirkby, three different detached workers have been employed for some years around Centre 63. Anthony Hawley, the current team rector, described to me the flexibility of the roles the three workers played according to the needs most felt at a given time. One might be a women's health worker; one have particular contact with schools and those who were suspended; one have special interest in finding employment; one have a general contact, going with groups to different activities that the district offers. Detached workers have shown that we need not wash our hands of young people who do not fit into our tidy plans for them.

Christians thinking about youth work are tempted, like local authorities, to look at the likely 'outcomes' – in this case measured by how many start coming to church. My years at the Mayflower, alongside George Burton, made me say that the Jesus of the Gospels would have been especially interested in those who were excluded from 'successful' and 'settled' parts of society. He would have known that, with these youngsters, it was bound to be a long time before they were likely to risk coming to church.

When George Burton died, no successor appeared for a year. The youth work was too important to lapse, so I took over as full-time youth leader myself. A gang of 'rough' young people at first seemed frightening. Was it possible to keep control? Would they speak to me? But, as I came – slowly – to know them by name, and to share experiences and stories of their world with them, they ceased to be 'Folk Devils', and became young men and women with fears and hopes like the rest of us. The degree of freedom George had allowed and the good team of helpers he had trained left us a model to follow. I was emboldened to take that risk, with the lively help of Rosemary Finch who kept her vision fresh of staying alongside youngsters who were socially excluded.

It was the most demanding and emotionally exhausting task I have ever undertaken. It made me understand in an unforgettable way how many mountains young people like that have to climb if they are to find a settled Christian faith. Their situation bore no comparison with mine as a teenager. I did not have to be taught that it was better to be reliable than to let someone down. It was part of my background. So was forgiving rather than holding a grudge. For many of our members in the club, each of these changes would have required a seismic upheaval. As my respect for many of them grew, there emerged also a fresh realisation.

There were parts of their culture that I could well learn from – solidarity with their mates, courage not to despair, given some of their experiences at home. These experiences in our Open Youth Club have left me certain that there must be the willingness for a long haul if the Church is to make space for young people like that.

The Sunday Group

The Sunday Group was built on the contacts that open youth work established. While there was no obligation to come to church in belonging to the Open Club, membership of the Sunday Group meant a commitment to come to the Sunday evening service and accepting that there would be some discussion about the Christian faith. The group had their base in George Burton's flat. In this picture of him, he was not moving around as in the club. He was lounging back in his armchair, while the group moved around him. Sometimes individuals came and talked. Sometimes they danced. We knew when that happened, as our flat was immediately beneath them! Late in the evening there would often be a discussion. There were also weekends, when Grace and I sometimes joined them, and a holiday week away together. The weekends did not have a tightly organised programme. They were a time of sharing a common life. Often it was quite late when a discussion started. It might then go on for two hours.

Members became used to George having a tape recorder running during many of these conversations. In 1968 I wrote four small booklets for the Scripture Union that were based on these discussions. My first step in producing them was to listen to forty hours of tape recordings of Sunday Group conversations. The booklets were a team effort, with pictures, artwork and text. Vic Mead, editor of Shell's company magazine, and his wife Barb were committed helpers at the Mayflower; they met regularly with the production team. Vic was responsible for the layout, pictures and artwork. Ted Lyons,[6] a Sunday Group member, produced strip cartoons with a modern setting of a gospel parable in each of the booklets. I was told that we sold 250,000 copies altogether of the four booklets, *Belonging, Loving, Working, Arguing.*[7] Each included one or more of the Sunday Group discussions – for example about some people's faith growing faster than others, ambition and jealousy in the workplace, and boy–girl relationships.

Leaders were emerging from the Sunday Group, with George Burton in the background encouraging and needling them. After I had 'held the fort' for twelve months following George's death, John Roberts was appointed senior youth leader. He had to win his way with these local leaders who had learned at George Burton's feet. A crisis that put this to the test occurred when a young man who was moving gently towards the life of the church assumed he could come into the Sunday Group. Membership had always been by invitation of the leader. John Roberts, having asked advice, said he could not come. The young man went off in a fury and told his brother, who was a church member of three years' standing. The brother came round, saying they would never come to the Mayflower again. John, the new leader, went to Jim Gosling, who might well have been jealous of him. Jim backed him up to the hilt. Each member of that group has made important contributions, either at the Mayflower or elsewhere. Doreen Turner played a key role at the Mayflower until her death in 1999. Jim Gosling and Ted Lyons are both clergymen, each in charge of his own parish. Most of the others continue to be strong members of the Christian community in East London.

Involvement with youth work and youth leaders stretched me. 'Youth Clubs as a Sphere of Christian Service' became established as a co-operative venture that ran a series of conferences. Because I had the backing at the Mayflower of a full-time and skilled secretary in Hilary Harman, I was able to play a part in organising these events; for two periods I was the secretary of the conferences we ran. The number attending grew substantially. We agreed to set up a new charity – the Frontier Youth Trust (FYT). Michael Eastman, a Baptist lay man with teaching experience, took up the post of development officer. For thirty-five years he made FYT a service agency offering training, fellowship and advice to a growing constituency. These conferences provided a context in which it was natural to raise complex issues – plural cultures, different sorts of intelligence, racial justice. There were always a number of clergy present, most coming from the similar background of evan-gelical colleges. In this world of open youth work, others were present who had learned in different disciplines, like teaching and social work. It was common ground between us to take the Bible as our first authority. There are those who assume that this would always bring with it conservative attitudes to all human questions. Jim Punton, who joined the FYT staff later, called that in question. He opened up many issues where the Bible took a radical stance. We 'young lions' argued fiercely about our differing approaches to youth work. It was hurtful for these youth leaders, bearing the burden and heat of the day, to feel their work was not appreciated. Many church members expected to see rapid results and did not appreciate the patient work that was needed.

It was an encouragement to me when, in a group at the Mayflower, Grace's father Bryan Isaac was asked how quickly in a frontier missionary situation we should expect steady moral and spiritual response from more than a few individuals. Speaking from his long involvement with overseas missionary work, he said 'in the next generation'. The youth leaders who met on Frontier Youth Trust occasions knew that the realistic timescale to anticipate lasting response from such youngsters might need to be measured in many years, if not in generations. This response needed a base to be established in which they felt something of the goodness of God's creation. The text for Christians in open youth work is the same as for all Christian educators: 'The earth is the Lord's and the fullness thereof.' It is a powerful motive to offer interest and positive approaches to life to young people who are in the habit of dismissing everything as 'boring'.

This involvement with youth work played a significant part in my own growth. I could not be satisfied with ministry confined within 'gathered' congregations. Youth work brought me in touch with many who had little in common with tidy church life. There must be good news for them too. That includes the news that God is a good and purposeful creator who cares about the quality of life for inner-city people. It must include, too, the belief that he is the Redeemer who understands and meets us where we are. The beginning of believing for the young people I have written about in this chapter would only come if they met Christians who were attentive and caring. That could then lead on to being ready to listen to the good news put into words. Too often the Church has relied on words, rather than living its life alongside people, although I continue to believe there is a place for putting the Gospel into words.

5

Evangelism – And a
Cricketing Sabbatical

In 1958, our first full year at the Mayflower, I joined with an ex-communist trade unionist, Charlie Potter, in a mission to Tate and Lyle's refinery in Silvertown, a mile down the road. We were given firm support from the management. In preparation I had visited each part of the refinery over a period of months. During the fortnight's mission, the two of us visited every department several times and held meetings to which all were invited. We showed a Billy Graham film, *Souls in Conflict*, at three different times to reach each of the three shifts. A total of three persons came to these showings who were not already members of the evangelical Christian Union who had invited us. For the final three evening meetings some thirty were present who were not members, but few if any were from the factory floor of two refineries that between them employed some 7,000 workers. Four or five people professed conversion during the fortnight.

I was eager to be part of effective evangelism. But the word 'effective' raised questions about what we did that week. Simply offering words seemed to leave the majority cold. One memory remains etched on my mind. In turn, Charlie and I stood on a soap box at an open-air spot where factory-floor workers regularly moved to and fro. Around us stood a circle of workers from the office. These were the members of the Christian Union, together with others from the office whom they had asked along. Just within earshot stood a small knot of factory-floor workers. This group kept changing. No one wanted to be identified too closely with us in front of their mates. Among them was one of our own club members, a lanky Sunday Group boy, who towered over everyone and bravely stayed there. Reflecting on that image of myself on the soap box surrounded by the office workers, I came to believe that we were making the test for those on the factory floor one of *courage*, rather than *faith*. It was as though we were saying to them, 'You must leave your mates and join that company of office workers if you want to follow Christ.' Though keeping up the visiting at Tate and Lyle's for some months, I was not aware of any visible results among factory-floor workers.

I still looked largely within evangelical circles for fellowship and fresh thinking. However, many clergy from within those circles seemed not to understand what we were trying to do at the Mayflower. We knew we were privileged in having a strong team, and felt for some who were ploughing a very lonely furrow. On two occasions Grace and I invited three other couples from inner-city areas to come away for forty-eight hours' reflection. In addition, we helped start a group of East End clergy and their wives to come together for a morning and a lunch. That met every six weeks. We also invited ministers from churches and missions in our immediate area to join us for three Bible studies each year, and then stay to lunch. Each of these groups provided mutual support and at times lively debate. This revealed different approaches among evangelicals.

At one meeting of the East End clergy couples' group I asked if the congregations the others served were all converted people. 'I certainly hope mine are,' came an immediate reply. My response was the hope that there was a growing core of deeply committed Christians among those who worshipped at the Mayflower. But I was glad that our congregation was 'ragged at the edges'. If the culture of a church was one in which it was absolutely clear that you were either 'in' or 'out' it would be more difficult for strangers gradually to find their way in. Another study in our group was introduced by a carefully constructed paper, in which the author was at pains to make it clear that he was not claiming that his was the only view about a controversial matter. It had been agreed that there should be two papers at the start. The second author introduced his paper by saying, 'This is not my opinion. This is God's word.'

Many evangelicals placed their main hope of winning those outside the churches in preaching, perhaps in large-scale public meetings. From the Mayflower, we ran coaches to the Billy Graham Crusade at Earls Court. Our experience – and that of other churches in East London – was that those who went forward and were lastingly changed were people who had previously known some real contact with the Christian community in the district. That crusade did not touch more than a small number of those who had grown up right outside the Church. They needed to see something of Christian love in action. Seed needs to be sown before there can be a reaping.

John Stott

One of the bodies that encouraged fresh thinking was 'Eclectics'. John Stott, Rector of All Souls, Langham Place, established this group about the time that I was ordained. Evangelical clergy under the age of forty were invited to day-long meetings and a residential week each year. Some had been trained in theological colleges where 'the evangelical party line' was strong. 'Eclectics' offered a culture in which honest debate was expected. Expansion happened quickly. John invited me to chair an East London Eclectics with some forty members, which had its separate meetings. We came together with groups from other parts of the country in the residential meeting each year. At his invitation I also joined 'Christian Debate' which met for an evening in All Souls Rectory. In the letter of invitation, he hoped the group would discuss 'Pressing problems which even five years ago we might have ignored'. My notes of subjects we debated include: nuclear warfare; the Christian doctrine of punishment; God's purpose in healing today; the biblical doctrine of work; the family in modern society; authority in ethics; homosexuality; the Christian citizen; the playboy culture and censorship laws; A just revolution? Divorce and remarriage; and in my last meeting before heading off to Liverpool the group discussed my book *Built as a City*.

John Stott's leadership has set many Evangelicals free to tackle contemporary issues with confidence on the firm base the Bible gives us. At one meeting of Eclectics he encouraged us to be 'Radical Conservatives – RCs'! He has been a valued friend to me, especially during my London years. In 1952, during my last year at Cambridge University, I had attended every night of the CICCU mission that he led. This was three years on from my own conversion during the Barnhouse mission. John's preaching and presence was warm and eirenic, where Barnhouse had been aggressive and confrontational. His influence on my generation of students made us cautious in studying theology, because dominant strands were assumed to be destructive of trust in the Bible and of a living faith.

Academic theology changed in much more positive directions in subsequent years. Stott himself had something to do with this, for his encouragement led many evangelicals to put away their fears, to wrestle with theology, and for some indeed to become academic theologians. Yet the distrust of 'liberalism' remained. Bishop Timothy Dudley-Smith's biography suggests that John regarded all who were not conservative evangelicals as 'liberals'. This was too simple at the time of his ordination, and it is too simple now. Dudley-Smith tells how John joined the retreat for those to be ordained by Bishop Wand in St Paul's, 'Conspicuous among them, if only for the suit of plus-fours he chose to wear for the retreat, made from Scottish tweed bought in the Hebrides.' It was his personal statement, 'Distancing himself from the formal and ecclesiastical atmosphere beginning to close around him.'[1]

That reminded me of my own feelings of rebellion against being caught up in a 'churchy' institution at my ordination retreat. But the black-suited priests who made up half the candidates from the London Diocese, were from the Anglo-Catholic tradition, who would have recoiled from being described as 'liberals'. It would have been woefully misleading to describe Bishop Wand as a 'liberal'. In his Lent addresses to the London clergy, when I was a curate, the scholarly and orthodox Wand insisted with passion that the heart of the gospel lay in the death of Jesus for sinners, on the cross.

I consulted John on receiving the invitation to become Bishop of Woolwich. He pressed me to insist that the title 'Woolwich' should be changed, because he believed John Robinson's ministry at Woolwich had been deeply damaging to the Church. He wrote to Mervyn Stockwood, arguing the point. Mervyn was not impressed, and I did not feel that fighting such a 'party' issue would enrich the life of the Church. As I entered more deeply into 'mainline' church leadership, labels like 'liberal' or 'traditional' seemed more and more misleading. They sought to squeeze everyone into one or other opposing camp, when the faith of many Christians had been enriched from different sources. The line between 'traditional' and 'liberal' often runs within the individual Christian's mind, and not always between church parties.

It was a member of the local church at the Mayflower who challenged me because I never invited neighbouring clergy to preach. Peggy Lyons said, 'I know that you go and preach in their churches. Why don't you invite them? Do you think you need to protect us from their ideas?' That was near the bone, showing how paternalistic that approach was. Our people were well able to think through differing views, just as I had as a brand new Christian in Cambridge when faced with contradictory statements from the college chaplain and the CICCU friend. From then on, I started to invite other local clergy to play a part in the Mayflower programme. For a long time I had counted Brother Bernard of the Franciscans at nearby Plaistow and Colin Marchant, the Baptist minister at West Ham Central Mission, close friends and allies.

John Stott must have made a deliberate decision that his leadership was not to be in the Church of England or in the 'mainline' ecumenical movement, but in the worldwide evangelical churches. While he would enter into dialogue with Roman Catholics, he did not see them as full Christian partners. Yet, his robust writings and teaching have brought confidence to evangelical Christians. That confidence, in turn, has provided a springboard from which many have felt able to move out and play a full part in the 'mainline' churches.

I felt his encouragement in the questioning the Mayflower was prompting. He understood the limitations that made running an inner-city parish different from All Souls, Langham Place, with its large congregations coming from all over London – and indeed from all over the world. His preaching – unashamedly for fifty minutes at a time – was no model for ministry in 'our' sort of area. Indeed, worshipping at All Souls more recently, I thought his sermon more of a lecture on the scripture, without any application to what we would face in our daily lives. During my Woolwich years, Peter Selby[2] described someone's preaching as 'only expository'. Stott's ideal to aim at was expository preaching, while he acknowledged that he was sometimes weak in 'application'.[3] Selby said that it should always be 'existential', bringing our living situation into the preaching. Since then, my goal had been that my preaching should be both expository and existential.

In one conversation with a small group of friends, among whom I was sometimes referred to as 'Sheppie', John Stott said, 'Of course Sheppie is not so much interested in theology. He is more interested in love.' I wasn't sure if that was a compliment! Yet, Christian love is surely the most theological property there is. As the subjects listed from Christian Debate show, John believed the Christian faith must speak to issues of social justice. When I was Bishop of Woolwich I was asked to speak at a conference on evangelism at Morecombe on the relation of evangelism to social justice. During my address, several people walked out. At the end of the week, Stott, who was the chairman of the conference, said, 'There was only one moment during the week when I was angry. That was when people walked out while David Sheppard was speaking. He gave biblical reasons for what he was saying. If you disagree with him, you should give biblical reasons for that.'

Cricket in Australia 1962–63

We took a sabbatical when I had been ordained for seven years. I had made a public promise when we first went to the Mayflower that I would stay at least ten years, and a substantial break helped make it possible to sustain a long-term ministry. Our sabbatical turned out to be rather unorthodox. It originated with a winter's day surprise. A message had been waiting on my desk, asking me to ring a Mr Robins at a London number. For some reason my mind had connected this message with a rather erratic man, who wanted to talk to me about something that was beyond my power to help. The week was desperately busy and I did not have time to ring. Our secretary had been ill and away for a week. When she came back, I said, 'Who was that Mr Robins who wanted me to ring back?' 'I imagined it was Mr Walter Robins,' she said. It showed how far removed my mind was from cricket that I had not linked the call with him at all. I duly rang Walter Robins, who was chairman of the selection committee that year. He said, 'If it's true that you are available for the Australian tour, it's the best news I've heard for English cricket in a long time.'[4]

Walter Robins spoke unguardedly in that conversation of my captaining the team. I had been through this before in 1954, when there was an approach that I should captain the team in place of Len Hutton. The advice I received then had been that it would have been right to break my theological training if I was being asked to captain the Test team, but not if I was simply to go to Australia for a second time as a player. That led to a summer of making no comment in the face of intense press speculation. This time it was clear that I must simply make up my mind whether to make myself available for the tour or not.

As we thought about it, what had been a crazy pipe dream started to look a practical possibility. However, major personal questions had to be faced. We had thought of a sabbatical in a quiet retreat in a country hideout. Grace had worked through nervous illness to the point when the doctors had encouraged us to try for a baby. She was pregnant now, with a child expected in March. The arrival of Jenny in the London Hospital was a time that drew us closer than ever to each other. We drove along the East India Dock Road very early on a bright spring morning. When, in the labour ward, Grace handed me this tiny baby, my feelings were full of wonder. Some fathers told me that it was some years before they found their child interesting. Not so with me. I kept Jenny's bathtime and bedtime clear most days, and found it a delight. Every day there were fascinating new responses.

As the summer wore on, the decision was made to make myself available for the cricket tour. Grace still found going out beyond her front door formidable. Now she would need to get on a ship for four weeks to come and join me on the other side of the world. Gradually she faced the adventure, decided to come with our baby, and joined us in time for the second Test, together with Jenny's godmother Hilary Harman. We claim that Jenny holds the world record for having watched fourteen days of Test cricket before the age of one – though it has not made her a cricket fan!

Once again, the press had a field day in speculation: who was to captain the England team – Cowdrey, Dexter or Sheppard? Some in authority in cricket were somewhat nervous of public comments I might make as captain of the England team in Australia. I had publicly refused to play against the South African team in 1960, in protest against the way apartheid brought injustice into cricket. Walter Robins asked me to meet him and Gubby Allen at Gubby's flat. Would I speak publicly against the 'White Australia' policy? They pressed the argument that more influence for good would come from playing together than making protests. I said it did not seem comparable to South Africa. There was no evidence that Australian policies had prevented players from being selected on the grounds of their colour.

Major demands would be made on my cricketing skills. To be useful to the team's balance I would need to open the innings, as I had during my four regular seasons of first-class cricket in 1950–53. It was nine years now since I had gone in first. There were batting lessons to learn all over again. In April I went across the river to Kennington Oval, where Surrey invited me to join with their team for a week's hard practice. I played half the season for Sussex, and for England in the last two Test matches against Pakistan – in which I scored 83 and 57.

In the event it was the fielding that came unstuck. Much of catching close to the wicket demands instinctive reactions. In my regular seasons I had become a dependable close-to-the-wicket catcher. This time some sharp chances slipped out of my hands. My confidence drained away, and I dropped two 'dolly' catches. Fred Trueman has made the most of these in after-dinner speeches! He says that when I dropped a catch off his bowling he told me he thought I should have learned more about putting my hands together. Peter Parfitt told me that the origin of Fred's remarks in fact went in my favour. Fred was captain of the 'Players' at Lord's that summer in the match against the 'Gentlemen'. Peter Parfitt hooked a ball off the middle of the bat, and I caught a very good catch at short leg. Peter went back into the dressing room and threw his bat down in disgust. 'Bad luck, Peter lad,' said captain Fred. 'The reverend has got a better chance than most of us, when he puts his hands together.' Clearly he remembered this when catches did not stick in my hands!

That match was the last Gentlemen v Players ever played. I had been one of those who had argued in committees that the distinction between amateurs and professionals should be abolished. Now it was clear that the time had come to say that all players were to be known simply as cricketers, with their financial arrangements a matter for them and their county. A short-lived arrangement was made for the 1962–63 tour. Those of us who had been amateurs could choose to receive payments that would make up what we were losing by coming on the tour – 'broken time' payments. When I told Billy Griffith, the Secretary of the MCC, the amount of my stipend, his jaw dropped. He had to calculate my 'broken time' for five months on tour – five twelfths of the diocesan minimum of Chelmsford Diocese, £1,100 a year!

I struggled to find good form as a batsman that summer. It was announced that the selectors would postpone their date for announcing the captain of the side. It was assumed that this was to give me time to start scoring some runs. The final gasp was to be that last Gentlemen v Players match. Finally I came good and scored a century. The following morning newspapers assumed that I would now be made captain for the tour. At the end of the next day's play I was sitting, very tired, in the dressing room. Two journalists asked if they could talk to me. 'What did I think about the announcement of the captaincy for Australia?' I hadn't heard anything. Ted Dexter had been appointed. That was fine, and we became good friends on the tour. But it wasn't the best way for me to hear. Walter Robins might have told me.

The Test series was a close one, ending one match all. Bobby Simpson, the Australian opening batsman, said to me at the end of the fifth Test, 'This has been the friendliest series I have ever played in.' For me there were many of the ups and downs of cricket. One match produced all of them – the second Test at Melbourne. In the first innings I was out for 0, leg before to Alan Davidson, one of the greatest fast bowlers I played against. The match swung this way and that. We led by 15 runs on the first innings. In the second innings, we had a real chance of dismissing them for a modest score. The last over of the third day was coming up. As Trueman was about to bowl to the often-immovable Bill Lawry, Ted Dexter said to me, as we stood in the slips, 'Come on. He's going to nick one to us.' That over Lawry edged one; I had to come forward with my left hand, got it into my hand, but dropped it. As we came off the field, I said to Ted, 'I'm going to get into this game sometime.' At the end of the next day we were left with 234 to win. The Australians had dismissed my opening partner Geoff Pullar for 0. We all remembered that they had bowled England out for 201 at Manchester the year before in a very similar situation. On the last day I played as well as I have ever done, scoring 113. Ted Dexter reminds me of the partnership he and I had that got our score moving. 'We ran them ragged,' he says. We seized every chance to run short singles and to press the fielders for an additional run. When all was going well, I called Ted for one short one too many, and he was run out. But Colin Cowdrey and I had a partnership with more short singles, until we won by seven wickets.

Ministry in Sydney

It was a salutary experience for me to go round Australia as 'an Archbishop's man'. It was widely known that Hugh Gough had been my chairman at the Mayflower. Now he was Archbishop of Sydney. During the tour Hugh and Madeleine Gough gave a dinner for the England cricket team. Madeleine had organised the evening meticulously. Small tables for fours and sixes had been set out. After each course we were to move to another table, so that we met a wider circle. 'No one's to sit next to anyone they know,' she called out. Grace's heart sank. She still did not find these occasions easy. Colin Cowdrey rescued her, whispering to her, 'Let's not take any notice'.

At the end of the cricket tour I joined Grace and Jenny in a rented house in Sydney. I worked for Sydney Diocese for six weeks, and then we took six weeks' holiday before sailing home on the *Canberra*. Six weeks of ministry in Sydney Diocese added another dimension to my reflections on the mission of the Church. There was a healthy acceptance of responsibility by Christians who had no ancient wealth or endowments to rely on. There were strong bodies of men – I was conscious of the presence of men – pulling their weight, not only financially but also in vigorous church life. There were well-organised Christian groups in schools, leading young people to Christian leadership. Time was being given to new migrants to Australia, to overseas students being brought there by what was known as the 'Colombo plan', and increasingly to the aboriginal people. There was social responsibility for individuals who were in trouble. These were the highlights.

There were 'lowlights' too. Part of the Church had grown over-respectable, more taken up with improving its own buildings or arguing about its organisation. The emphasis generally was on the 'gathered congregation' rather than the Church of England sense that we had responsibility for all who lived in the parish. Sometimes I felt that members blamed their unresponsive neighbours rather than reaching out a hand of unjudging friendship to them. Small priority was given to inner-city parishes. I had insisted that half my time in Sydney Diocese should be spent in inner-city parishes comparable with our own area in London. This helped me to come back to earth. Here were no vast congregations waiting breathlessly for what I had to say. Few working people from these districts would come to religious meetings at all. The strong parishes were in the suburbs and on the North Shore. Those who stayed in Glebe, Erskineville, Waterloo, Paddington, Woollomoloo and Redfern had in some cases never been across the Harbour Bridge to see how the other half lived.

Archbishop Gough invited me to deliver three papers to a clergy conference. I made points about the need to build bridges, establishing common ground through friendship, meeting human needs, respecting the different culture of inner-city communities and celebrating the good things about them. One questioner was a member of staff at Moore College, where most of the clergy of Sydney Diocese are trained. He said that he had formed the opinion that there was more response in the areas I spoke of when there had been faithful, expository preaching of the word. I had to reply that this had not been my experience. That told me that the long slog of patient building of relationships and trust was needed to prepare the ground for the preached word. One of the effects of those weeks in Sydney Diocese was that I concluded that a church that tolerated mixed traditions was more able to communicate the love of God than one that was uncompromisingly evangelical, in the party sense of that word.

When it came to the sea trip home on the *Canberra*, there was the problem of mastering my seasickness. Joining the army in Belfast had meant facing the Irish Sea. That had destroyed any confidence I might have developed. Could I at last enjoy a sea crossing? Jenny had celebrated her first birthday in Sydney. On the ship, she woke us up around 5 o'clock. I walked round the deck before breakfast and settled down to write the book that had been simmering for a long time – *Parson's Pitch*. Coming back into cricket for this tour seven years after my ordination made it possible to write an account of a Christian trying to work out his faith in the world of cricket and in ministry in East London. I started to feel that I had at last cracked my seasickness. As far as Melbourne, all was fine. But the Great Australian Bight was another matter. In the middle of the night Grace found me crawling on hands and knees into the shower. She rang the ship's doctor, but he said that he had already given me the last dose he could. The Indian Ocean was rather calmer. There on the radio we heard Ted Dexter playing a heroic innings in a famous Test match at Lord's against the West Indies' fast bowlers.

Staying in the inner city

At the end of the cricket tour in Australia and New Zealand, it was clear that there would be no further 'come-backs'. The last Test match in New Zealand was my final first-class appearance. For a few years there was occasional club cricket. If I had been vicar of Horsham – my first cricket club – it would have made sense to go on playing, for cricket would have been part of the life of that community. But there was no strong cricket club in the East End of London. I would have needed to go out to suburbs like Ilford or Romford to find one. Playing cricket there would have made little connection with our life in the inner city. My club cricket was reduced to four days in a season, while we were away on holiday. On the morning of one match, I caught myself out, not wanting to play. That seemed crazy for someone still passionately committed to the game. I decided there and then not to play again – and all the enthusiasm to be a *follower* of the game came flooding back. Today I read the scores every day and go to watch whenever I can.

I had found myself talking about life in the inner city sitting on the deck of the *Canberra* in the Indian Ocean on the way to Australia. In 1962 it was still regarded as a team-building opportunity to have time together on board ship. There was a compromise that did not survive for another tour. We flew to Aden and went on board the *Canberra* there. It was the last time a team travelled by sea, because of the pressure of many tours and many weeks away from home for Test players.

On the *Canberra* I met Father John Groser, who until then had been only a name to me among the distinguished Anglo-Catholic clergy of the East End. So there we were, out on the Indian Ocean, talking about inner-city London. He showed close sympathy with what we were trying to do. One tale he told stayed in my mind. He said, 'When I had been three or four years in Stepney, an intelligent docker said to me, "I suppose you'll be off soon, like all the rest." Along with other things this was part of God's word to me, that we must stay and bring up our children there.'

We realised there were hard decisions for us to make about Jenny's schooling. Several neighbours had said to Grace, 'You won't bring her up here, will you?' We believed that God had called us as a family to serve him, and that he would show us the right way through. Perhaps that belief made me too complacent. I did not feel she was facing more problems than other children in her early years. But Jenny's account of her own schooling is critical. Now that she has two small boys approaching school days, she is determined to give them a better schooling than she had. She went to local authority schools, both in Canning Town and in Peckham, when we moved there on my appointment as Bishop of Woolwich. She feels that the junior school failed her and other bright children in many ways. She was bullied, and in later years said that the teaching staff seemed oblivious to what was going on. Grace and I decided not to interfere, but to trust her to cope without our running to the teachers. Other parents had been despised by their children for voicing their complaints. We remember clinging to each other one morning as she left for school, praying that she could handle it. Jenny endured the bullying for over a year. She showed great courage, and eventually won through.

When she reached the age of eleven, the question of secondary education arose. As prospective parents looking at schools in the neighbourhood, we wanted, if it seemed appropriate for Jenny, to support the new comprehensive system. At a parents' evening at Peckham Comprehensive School, the head teacher kept me back to raise a separate matter. After this, I asked her a personal question. Jenny had been the only child from a professional family in the schools she had been to so far. Now she was starting to ascribe problems at school to her being different from the other children. How many children of professional parents came to Peckham? She said, 'There might be as many as six in an entry of 270.' Peckham received such a small number of girls from the many professional families within reach of the school because there were several selective schools, both independent and maintained, in the same catchment area. These were where the majority of children from professional families went. As Grace and I talked it through, we felt it was not right to ask one child to bear the burden of divisions in our society. She won a place at Haberdashers' Aske's, then a maintained grammar school in New Cross, a short bus ride away. Jenny says that the five terms she spent at this school were the happiest and most productive of her entire school career.

Years later Harriet Harman, as a minister in the Labour Government, was pilloried for 'hypocrisy' because she chose to send her child to a selective school in this same area. We knew the schools from which she had to choose. There is no hypocrisy in arguing that there should be a fairer system in schools, and at the same time choosing what you believe to be the best package that is available at the present time for your own child. However, the inequalities of selection came home to us. In the successor to the eleven-plus three girls at Jenny's primary school had all been marked 1.1.1. Two of them found places at Aske's. The third girl was given a place in the local girls' secondary school. The girls were indignant at being divided. As we shall see, the question returned when we moved to Liverpool, and she went to a comprehensive school.

Charismatic questions

Before going to Australia, I had made a tentative approach to Michael Harper[5] about the possibility of his coming to join us as the chaplain. I wrote to him from Australia, to 'keep the pot boiling'. In his reply he said, 'Something has happened to Jean and me that we should like to tell you about.' They came to see us a few days after our return. They told us about receiving a direct experience of the power of the Holy Spirit. They had been 'baptised in the Spirit'. A number of my friends at that time spoke of a new charismatic blessing. Some made me feel that obedience to God's promises should mean that I must enter this experience too. Others had a different approach that took away any sense of superiority and special knowledge for some. They were ready to say that the charismatic experience was a great blessing to them, but understood that God brought equally deep blessings by different routes.

With all this in the forefront of my mind I made it a matter of deliberate prayer that God would give me every gift that was in his plan for me. As far as I know, he has not responded by giving me those particular charismatic gifts. Listening to the Harpers talking of their experience I could not help thinking that we had been living with a parallel immediacy of God's presence and leading in working closely with George Burton. We saw in him instincts that seemed to have been sharpened by the Spirit.

Healing through prayer and the laying-on of hands has been one of the features of the charismatic movement. Certainly there are times when God heals in response to deliberate prayers. But the achievements of medical skill should also be lifted on to the level of God's gift of healing. That year, a close friend was desperately ill in hospital. It was proving impossible to diagnose what was wrong. I visited him lying unconscious, and prayed for him there. I heard a few days later that Michael Harper had prayed over him, and that he was wonderfully better. Privately I complained to God that my prayers were not being recognised, but might also have been effective! His wife said to me, 'God doesn't care about the diagnosis. He can heal him.' I admired her faith, but could not help thinking of all the intricate studies over a lifetime to produce an accurate diagnosis. God's healing hand is also to be found in patient research that leads to the conquering of diseases.

The charismatic movement's approach to healing presents a healthy challenge to the rest of us to expect that God sometimes acts directly. It doesn't help, though, if they only tell the success stories. It would make me believe it all more if they spoke of the times when there was no healing after believing prayer. When one of our Liverpool clergy was diagnosed with life-threatening cancer, there was persistent prayer from many of us, especially in his parish. He recovered, only to fall ill again when the remission ran out. I had to help him and his wife to talk truthfully to each other about his approaching death. When he died, there were some people in the parish who found it hard to accept that God had not answered their prayers in the way they had wanted.

There is a mystery about suffering which does not allow me to insist that there should be a healing whenever there is faithful prayer. Equally persistent prayer may be followed by healing in one case, and what we are tempted to call unanswered prayer in another. David Ford expresses what I believe: 'God is not a God of quick fixes, and easy, instantaneous solutions. Signs of hope are given, but God is above all concerned with love and long-term faithfulness, with healing hearts, minds and communities as well as bodies.'[6]

Evangelicals and urban mission

In 1966 the National Assembly of Evangelicals requested the Evangelical Alliance to appoint a Commission on Evangelism. It should 'prayerfully consider and recommend the best means of reaching the uncharted masses'. I was asked to join a reference group that met for four lengthy sessions in support of a working party, all of whose members were under forty years of age. They tackled the fieldwork and prepared the report, *On the Other Side*. The report had much to say about what we later called Urban Priority Areas. It admitted that evangelicals had fared as badly as most other Christians in their attempts at evangelism here. Such churches as had prospered tended to be preaching centres, to which adherents had travelled considerable distances. It commended 'involvement in depth, centred in a living community of Christians'.[7]

I became the chairman of a small project that gradually came together during these years, the Evangelical Urban Training Project (EUTP). In his history of the project John Hunter explained why we put the word 'evangelical' in the title; it was too easy 'To allow evangelism to be sidelined in favour of leadership training or training in understanding urban concerns'. The main contribution of EUTP was the giving of confidence to working people to speak about their own experience of God in their lives. Congregations, from being passive worshippers, were to be inspired and empowered to become active.[8] Over the years, Neville Black and Jim Hart maintained EUTP's 'day of small things' with training groups in churches of different denominations. More recently the project has taken a new name, 'Unlock' (with the thought of unlocking God-given talents), with Jenny Richardson as project officer.

The report *On The Other Side* was affirmed in a lively and realistic debate in the National Evangelical Assembly in 1968. It was a high point in support by the Evangelical Alliance for 'urban mission'. That has grown again with the leadership of Joel Edwards, and the presence of black-led churches. Yet, listening to the debate in 1968 I felt that, for all the sympathy, there were very few present who represented long-term work on the ground. I was clear that my first calling was to a ministry that sought to reach out to people in the neediest urban areas. That led me on to the conclusion that I should throw in my lot wholeheartedly with 'mainline churches', like my own Church of England. With all its weaknesses, the parish system brought commitment to every area in the country, and mutual support that would ensure that it lasted. At our best, that commitment doesn't stop at the boundaries of the Church. God calls us to look at the common good. I was soon to learn that this means we cannot shrink from involvement in public affairs.

6

Justice and Peace – A New Awareness

From the day I was ordained it was clear that there was likely to be involvement with the media – for better or worse. I resolved that it would be for good and for the Gospel. That would mean thinking through fresh ideas about communicating the faith. There was my weekly piece in *Woman's Own*, with the healthy discipline of writing 520 words in a language that was understandable to people outside the Church. Then there were occasional invitations to take part in radio or television programmes.

One more regular commitment in the early 1960s was with ABC Television in Manchester. In *Sunday Break*, young students from RADA came together for twenty-four hours to rehearse, perform music, dance and discuss. Each week someone was invited to be present the whole time, be part of the show, and play a central part in the discussion. The religious adviser was Penry Jones, later head of Religious Broadcasting at the BBC. Penry was a member of the Iona Community of the Church of Scotland. Long discussions with him introduced me to the commitment of Iona *both* to God's calling to worship and personal discipleship *and* to working it out in the world of work and community, reflecting his concern for justice.

We had many visitors to the Mayflower, some of whom brought important challenges to me. Justice matters were raised forcefully by Hugh Anderson, who came first in 1964 when he was sixteen. He saw me as very pale pink, and used his visits to sharpen me up! When he went to Cambridge he became deeply involved in student politics and was President of the Union the year before his early death from cancer at twenty-one. In my first meeting with Hugh Montefiore,[1] who was Vicar of Great St Mary's, the University Church, I said people spoke of Hugh Anderson as an outstanding president. Hugh Montefiore said, 'He was the best president in living memory.' I was asked to preach at a memorial service for Hugh in the chapel of Trinity College. In my address I spoke of his passion for justice for oppressed people. I referred to his 'basic lecture' that many of us had received about the shape of society. He said that there had never been a time when those who dominate have voluntarily given over power to those who are dominated. It had always been that the oppressed had taken power in their own hands and had forced changes. Hugh Anderson's 'basic lecture' stayed with me: society used to be shaped like a pyramid – with those at the bottom in the majority. One person, one vote, would then bring about change. Now society in this country was shaped more like a diamond, with the majority in the middle and having an interest in keeping the status quo. 'So now we have to do the impossible and persuade people to bring about a more just society against their own self-interest.'

Hugh Anderson came from a distinguished evangelical home, son of Professor Norman Anderson.[2] In my address I said that I believed Hugh's commitment to Jesus Christ remained all his life. He was often angry with the Church, though he told me he admired Archbishop Trevor Huddleston more than anyone in the world. He knew that, if the Church was true to its Lord, it could and should be a group setting the pace. Instead he so often saw it gathering up its skirts and sheltering along with the respectable and cautious-minded.

Apartheid and cricket

I too was influenced by Trevor Huddleston. In 1956 I received an invitation to hear him speak at the House of Lords. The meeting was a challenge to the worlds of sport and the arts to boycott South Africa. The Community of the Resurrection had just withdrawn him from his work there. He published *Naught for Your Comfort* that same year. After the meeting, Trevor walked me up and down the Terrace of the House of Lords by the river. He told me he thought nothing would jolt people in South Africa more than if the MCC were to refuse to send a team.

That winter a team did go to South Africa. At the end of the summer in which I had been brought back into the England team against Australia, Crawford White, then the cricket correspondent for the *News Chronicle*, rang up. He read me a piece he had drafted about why I was not going on the tour. 'Knowing you,' he said, 'I think that, when you saw for yourself how Africans are treated, you would quietly pack your bags and go home.' I said he had a perfect right to speculate. However, the reason for not going was a simple one: I was a curate in Islington with a job to do, and was not available. He duly wrote his piece. But what changed its meaning was the headline that put it on the front page. This said, 'I WON'T PLAY IN AFRICA.' When the tour was under way, there were injuries, and Peter May the captain wrote an airletter asking me to fly out for the last three Tests. By now, I was becoming cautious of the press. I cabled my refusal, signing it with a nickname he had given me at Cambridge.

In 1960 first-class cricket was no part of my plans. However, the Duke of Norfolk, our Sussex president, wrote, as he had in previous years, to ask me to captain his team in the opening match of the tour against our visitors – South Africa that year. By then I was clear that I would not play against an all-white team calling itself South Africa, and wrote, refusing. But now there were further questions to ask and answer: should I keep silent, or 'sing the song' about this great injustice that had intruded into the game of cricket, as into everything else in South Africa? I wrote to Joost de Blank, my former bishop when he was Bishop of Stepney, and by then Archbishop of Cape Town. Did he think it would help if I made my refusal public? He replied, 'It would do a tremendous amount for our cause here.'

Early in April, I wrote to Harry Altham, President of the MCC, telling him of my intention to make public my refusal to play. At the time, I was a member of the MCC Committee – the hosts to the South African team. We met, and Harry tried to persuade me to think again. My respect for Harry made me go over all the reasoning. Public protest would conflict with all my background as a sportsman – 'No religion, no politics'. And, surely, evangelical Christians stuck to personal discipleship. But I was learning that all over the continent African Christians were taunted that Christianity was the white man's religion, employed to keep white dominance. On 31 March 1960, sixty-seven Africans had been shot dead by the police at Sharpeville. Should a Christian cricketer go on playing with whites, as though nothing had happened? I had a breakfast meeting in central London, and drove up very early to beat the traffic. I sat on the Embankment and read the Scripture that was next in my regular lectionary. My mind was full of the question whether I should keep silent or speak up. The reading was Isaiah 58, verse 1: 'Cry aloud, spare not, lift up your voice like a trumpet; declare to my people their transgressions.' It went on that the prophet was to tell God's people, 'Loose the bonds of wickedness, to undo the thongs of the yoke, to let the oppressed go free.' That regular reading undergirded my decision to speak out.

Harry Altham agreed that before the event I should make my intentions known to the Committee. There was an immediate explosion from Lieut. Colonel R. T. Stanyforth. He said, 'Mr Chairman, I protest. We have just heard a political and religious statement that has no place here.' Harry rebuked him, and told him that I had a right to act according to my conscience, and to explain my actions to the Committee. I was grateful that, having tried to persuade me, he stood by me in that way. The massacre at Sharpeville meant that interest was at boiling point at

Never the fastest runner. In Carlyle Square, Chelsea.

With my parents, Stuart and Barbara, and my sister, Mary.
I'm passionate already for cricket.

My mother comes down to Sherborne for 'Commem' during
my first term at public school, 1942.

An off-drive off Vinoo Mankad brings up my first Test match
century, at The Oval against India in 1952. Pat Sen is the wicket-keeper,
Polly Umrigar is at slip. (Photo: Central Press)

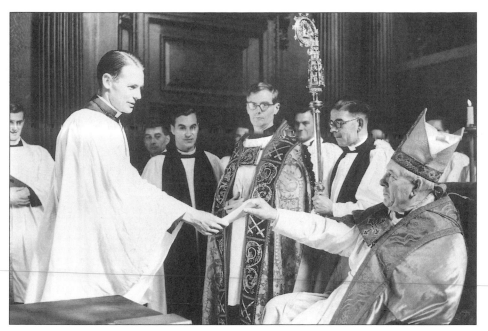

'I froze, because he did not let go' (page 29). Bishop Wand gives me my deacon's orders after my ordination in St Paul's Cathedral, Michaelmas 1955.

Pulling a ball from Richie Benaud to the boundary, when scoring 113 against Australia at Old Trafford, 1956. The wicket-keeper is Len Maddocks.

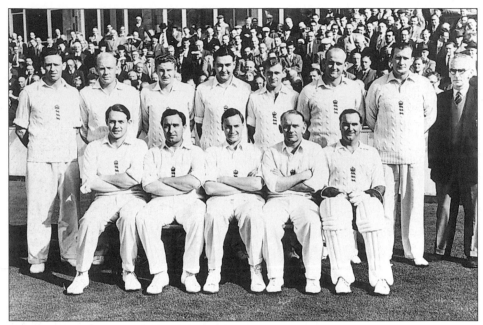

The England team for the match against Australia at The Oval in 1956.
Standing: Brian Statham, Tony Lock, Jimmy Parks (twelfth man), Colin
Cowdrey, Peter Richardson, Frank Tyson, Jim Laker, J. Tait (the masseur);
sitting: me, Denis Compton, Peter May, Cyril Washbrook, Godfrey Evans.

My wedding day with Grace at Lindfield Church, 1957.

George Burton (left) and Jean Hewitt with Colin Watts.

George Burton with young people at the Mayflower.

Being consecrated as the Bishop of Woolwich by Archbishop Michael
Ramsey, Southwark Cathedral, 1969. (Photo: George Konig)

A family lunch in Peckham with Michael Ramsey following
my consecration. With us, from the left, arc: Mary Maxwell (my sister),
Jamie Maxwell, Grace, Jenny, Sarah Maxwell. Ted Roberts and
Michael Green are in the background.

The Martin Luther King committee makes a presentation.
Wilfred Wood, later to be Bishop of Croydon, is on the right, with the
young sculptor standing behind his right shoulder.

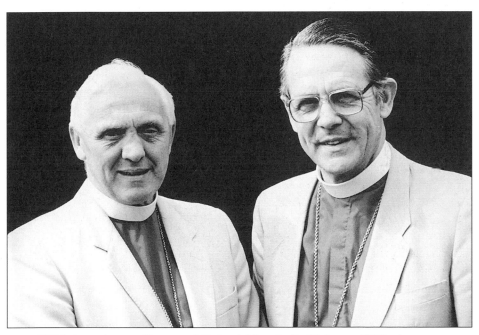

With my close colleague, Michael Henshall, Bishop of Warrington.

Church leaders join with MPs in a protest march against factory closures, 1976. With me in the front row, starting third from the left, are: Bob Parry, Eddie Loyden, Derek Worlock, Bob Wareing, Norwyn Denny.

the moment when the South African team arrived. The press got wind of my position on the eve of their arrival. I stuck to my brief statement, that took no more than a minute for the BBC *News*. It was the first item.

I had crossed a watershed. Now invitations arrived to speak to protest meetings about Portuguese oppression in Angola. A little flow of black, coloured and white South Africans came to see me. They talked about injustices there, and, as they asked about our life, it began to dawn on me that there were more parallels in Britain than I had liked to admit. It was a major lesson to grasp that helping an individual could only go so far. Having the right sort of headed notepaper might obtain a hearing from officials, but winning a better place in the queue for one person very likely meant displacing another. Loving my neighbour in respect of his housing or of his children's schooling would often require changing structures that shaped the lives of people. That started to bring unpopularity from those who benefited from the structures.

When I had wanted money to help the Islington Boys' Club, the *Daily Telegraph* had been glad to offer space. My open opposition to sport with South Africa brought their condemnation for getting involved in politics. Questions about sticking to spiritual issues rather than mixing them with the political came up in every interview over the years that followed.

The D'Oliveira affair

For me, 1968 was a year that brought together several steep learning curves. In August we went away with over a hundred people from the Mayflower to a hotel in Blankenberg in Belgium. There was a new manager who did not appreciate the noisy and untidy ways of some of our families. When a series of crises had been settled, we were summoned to be told that one of our men had been discovered asleep in bed with a cigarette burning the bedclothes. We were told this was 'the last straw' and we must leave. My rudimentary French rose to the occasion, and we won another reprieve. I came back to our bedroom, exhausted, after midnight, to be told by Grace what she had heard on the midnight news. Basil D'Oliveira, who had the day before scored 158 for England in the final Test against Australia, had been omitted from the team selected to go to South Africa. She tells me that I made her the butt of my anger, complaining that I now had no chance of any sleep that night!

By morning, I had determined to use every means at my disposal to find out what had happened and why. I was no longer a member of the MCC Committee. I had still been on their 'Cricket Committee', and had pressed in the winter that we should check with South Africa in good time that any team we selected would be welcome. I flew home from Blankenberg that morning, realising there were two clear days in my diary in which to do some detective work. I first rang Colin Cowdrey, a close friend, who had been selected as the captain of the team for South Africa, and asked if I could come and see him. Colin gave me what was plainly the official line. Basil D'Oliveira had had a bad tour of the West Indies the previous spring. We needed an all-rounder, and as a bowler, 'He couldn't bowl a hoop down a hill.'

There was much more to learn than that. So I went to Lord's, where there was a county match. I saw John Arlott, who said to me, 'You should know that there was a letter.' It occurred to me that there might be a source in D'Oliveira's county, Worcestershire. Viscount Cobham had captained Worcestershire years before and was a former President of the MCC. I found myself sitting next to Neil Durden Smith, who had been ADC to Charles Cobham, when he was Governor General of New Zealand. I asked if he thought Cobham would be concerned at what had happened. He thought he would be very concerned. Charles Cobham had been most welcoming to me on previous occasions. I pushed my luck and phoned him. More than once he had invited me to stay. Might I come for a night? Cobham was very hospitable. He was also wildly indiscreet. He told me he had been to South Africa that March and had seen the Prime Minister, Mr Vorster. He had asked him if D'Oliveira would be acceptable, if selected. Vorster had replied, 'Anyone else. D'Oliveira – no.'

A few days after the selection of the team, Tom Cartwright, a bowler, dropped out because of injury. The selectors, who had explained before that they had regarded D'Oliveira simply as a batsman, now picked him to replace Cartwright. Vorster said that this was not the team of the MCC but of the Anti-Apartheid Movement, and that therefore the tour was cancelled.

A member of the MCC put an advertisement in the personal column of the *Guardian*. If other members were as angry as he felt about the way the MCC had handled the affair, would they meet at his flat? I went along, not knowing what the response to the advertisement might be. Out of that meeting a small group was elected, and charged with calling for a special meeting of the MCC, which still ruled cricket in this country. As the public controversy developed, there were bitter comments. To begin with, I was the only Test player involved, and my name was at the centre of the criticisms. Our group developed remarkable personal trust through a campaign when some heavy flak was flying around. A few weeks later, Mike Brearley, then twenty-six, who had been a member of the last MCC team to tour South Africa, joined us.

We went through the process of formally calling for a Special General Meeting of the MCC. I met several times with the Secretary of the MCC, Billy Griffith, to talk about arrangements. He became profoundly upset by the whole affair. I feared that he might have a complete breakdown. I recalled that, when he was assistant secretary, he had said to me about Ronnie Aird, who was then Secretary, 'The great thing about Ronnie is that he's not very keen on cricket!' By contrast, Billy Griffith was far too keen on cricket! He became distressed about the conflict he felt was damaging the game he loved. The irony to me was that he had been one of the first to talk to me about the evils of apartheid as they bore on cricket. He had told me then that he had asked a senior and respected figure in South African cricket whether there were some good black players coming forward. The reply had been, 'Man, they're savages.' I could not help feeling that, if he were not Secretary of the MCC, he would have joined us. Some months after the Special Meeting was over, I told Billy how concerned I had been for him, and that I had prayed for him during those tense days. He replied, 'And I prayed for you too'.

Perhaps it was because Billy and I became too personally involved that we misunderstood each other about a meeting we agreed to hold. I reported to our group that three or four of us were to meet with three or four of the Committee, to make arrangements for the Special Meeting. When we opened the door of the Committee Room in the Pavilion at Lord's, we found not three or four members, but the full MCC Committee sitting round the room, including Sir Alec Douglas-Home, the leader of the Opposition and former Prime Minister. He said that he had flown down especially from Scotland, hoping to persuade us to call the meeting off. We made it clear that we had no mandate to do that, but agreed to enter into some discussion of the issues. Douglas-Home played a leading part in what followed, as it became plain that he had done in the MCC's dealings with South Africa. Repeatedly he said of the South African Government, 'You can't ask these people hypothetical questions.' My conversation with Charles Cobham had made it clear that the crucial question concerning D'Oliveira *had* been asked – and answered – but I did not feel at liberty to disclose that. I persevered in pressing that the MCC should have cleared the issue in good time before the selectors met. After long stalling, Gubby Allen, who was in the chair, said, 'Well, you may as well know that we did write, and we never got a reply.'

The Special General Meeting took place in Church House Westminster. It was the most fraught meeting I remember. I proposed resolutions regretting the Committee's mishandling of affairs leading up to the selection of the team, and calling for no further tours to take place until there was evidence of actual progress by South Africa towards non-racial cricket. Mike Brearley seconded the resolutions. Our group agreed that we must not attack any personalities. In contrast, the senior committee members persuaded Dennis Silk, without giving him all the information they had, to make an extended attack on my actions.

87

Thankfully, our friendship was restored later. Other members made personal attacks on me. I felt the pain that friends regarded me with such bitterness. Mike Brearley felt that bitterness too. At one moment, his body language said it. He turned in his seat as though protecting me from a physical attack. The only moment that lightened the debate was when an elderly member pressed on with a series of personal attacks that were losing his side votes by the minute. It had recently been announced that I was to become Bishop of Woolwich. The elderly member said, 'I don't know how the Bishop of Woolwich can wear his MCC tie.' A voice from the gallery called, 'Down the back!' The resolutions we proposed were defeated, especially in the votes recorded by post. In the hall, the resolution regretting the Committee's handling of the affair was lost, 386–314. The principles had been aired, and opinion within the cricket world gradually shifted.

Friendships were ruptured through this controversy. We had broken assumptions that sportsmen would get on with the game without allowing religion or politics to raise questions about what we were doing. Our campaigning group agreed that we should try to mend some fences, and invited a number of those who had opposed us to meet in our house. From my personal point of view the reply I regretted most came from Peter May, who had been a close friend in Cambridge days and since. He wrote me just two lines in response to my invitation, saying, 'I don't think we have anything to talk about.' His widow, Virginia, told Peter May's biographer, Alan Hill, that Peter was very upset with me over the affair. 'They were in two camps. My father and Peter sincerely hoped that all cricketers would support cricket. They saw this as a genuine option and the way forward.' Her father, Harold Gilligan, was in fact the representative for South Africa on the old Imperial Cricket Conference. Peter May's influence in cricket, as a player and as a captain, was wholesome, always promoting the best in the game. But he found it hard to forgive people who crossed him on various occasions. Other friends of his told Alan Hill that he was not easily dissuaded from his views once he had taken up a position.[3] Grace and I had been to dinner with Peter and Virginia just before he set off for his last cricket tour to the West Indies. He told us how hurt he had been by the press intrusions into his life during the Australian tour the previous winter of 1958–59. 'I will work with them,' he said, 'but I shall never forgive them.' I understood his pain, but was clear that an individual cannot hurt the press, though, if he tries to do so, he can be hurt himself.

Billy Griffith came to meet our group. He repeated the argument about building bridges – that continuing contact would help to bring about change in attitudes among South Africans. Mike Brearley had been a member of the last MCC team to tour South Africa, and Billy had been the manager. Mike reacted when the argument about changing attitudes through sporting contact was put. Mike said, 'Come on Billy. I remember the first meeting of the touring party, when you said that we should steer clear of talking politics. How were we to help change attitudes if we were not to discuss them?' In contrast to Peter May's refusal to talk, Dennis Silk responded readily. This came about through the intervention of Ted Dexter. Ted and Sue Dexter had become our close friends. Ted came to see me and said he felt saddened when two people he admired – Dennis Silk and me – were at odds with each other. I said that I would be more than glad to talk if he were willing. Dennis came down to the Mayflower without delay. He said he felt very badly about what he had said in the Church House meeting. He had no idea, for example, of what I now told him of my conversation with Charles Cobham, and what he had revealed to me. It meant much to me that this personal rift had been healed.

Much more recently, in 2000, Bruce Murray, a history professor at Witwatersrand University, came to see me. He shared with me an article he had written about the D'Oliveira affair. Cabinet papers of the South African Government were now available. These demolish Mr Vorster's claim that the rejection was because D'Oliveira's selection was an afterthought. That had allowed him to claim that the team was not that of the MCC but of the Anti-Apartheid Movement. Cabinet papers for 27 August 1968 – the same day the selectors met to pick the team – read, 'MCC. Kriekettoer 1968/69. As D'Oliveira gekies word is die toer af' ('If D'Oliveira is chosen the tour is off').[4] Bruce Murray also wrote of a revelation that damaged the reputation of the MCC leadership. Lord Cobham had passed on to Billy Griffith that Vorster had intimated that 'were D'Oliveira to be chosen, the MCC tour was most unlikely to take place'. 'Griffith consulted with Arthur Gilligan, the MCC President, and Gubby Allen, and they decided against conveying the information to the full MCC Committee.'

South Africa was due to send a cricket team to England in 1970. A strong protest campaign, 'Stop the Tour', led by the young South African Peter Hain,[5] had drawn large support and publicity in attempting to prevent the rugby tour in the winter. While it might be possible to protect a rugby match from interruptions, cricket was another story! I went to one of the 'Stop the Tour' meetings, at which ideas were being floated – like flashing a mirror in the batsman's eyes, and constant running on the ground by protesters. I argued against interrupting play, while identifying myself with those who would protest outside the ground, as I had done by marching with the protesters at Twickenham against the rugby international.

Some of us wanted to show that there was a wide band of supporters for stopping the tour, but who did not agree with interrupting play. We formed 'The Fair Cricket Campaign', which had a short and not very public life. I was the chairman; Sir Edward Boyle, formerly Conservative Education Secretary and Reg Prentice, then a Labour MP, were Vice-Chairmen. The secretary was Betty Boothroyd.[6] We set out to argue the case with as many as possible of those who might influence the decision of the MCC and the Government.

Edward Boyle played a major part. A person would be named that we might hope to persuade; the discussion would get as far as, 'Well they wouldn't listen to anyone from the Labour Party; and of course it mustn't be anyone from the Church!' Edward would then put up his hand and say, 'I'll go.' One of our small triumphs was when we targeted Geoffrey Howard, then secretary of Surrey at The Oval. We asked the head teacher of Kennington School to take some black sixth-formers to see him. Geoffrey told me afterwards that this meeting changed his position about the tour. The boys told him how they loved coming to The Oval, but would not feel able to enter the ground if an all-white team called South Africa was playing. Instead, they would be on the street outside, protesting. Pressure grew on the MCC, who tried with increasing desperation to carry the tour through. Eventually Jim Callaghan, then Home Secretary, summoned their representatives and requested them to call off the tour 'on grounds of broad public policy', and in the light of the threat of civil disorder. In his reflections at the age of ninety-one, Geoffrey Howard was asked if the cancellation had any effect: 'Oh yes. I think it was a great shock to the South African Government. I don't think they realised until then the strength of anti-apartheid feeling worldwide.'[7]

I could not have known then that this experience of feeling the heat in the kitchen of public controversy over cricket and apartheid would prove a valuable training ground for some of my future 'Steps Along Hope Street'.

Facing radical questions

Earlier in 1968, while I was still at the Mayflower, I took part in two conferences of a kind I had not known before. One was an Anglican-Methodist consultation on evangelism. Conversations were going on between our churches at the time that led to the abortive proposal for our union. The consultation saw some deep divides. However, the divisions were not between Anglicans and Methodists. They were between 'conservatives' and 'radicals' in both churches.

I admired Donald Coggan, then Archbishop of York, who was delivering Bible studies at the consultation. It was a shock to me when he came under fierce attacks from radical Christians with whom I was finding much fellow feeling about major issues in the cities. Joining in the discussions, I realised that the arguments were going on within my own mind. Both sides appealed to me. As I identified what was happening to me, it dawned on me for the first time that I might be regarded as leadership material in a church that needed to hold these two 'camps' together.

I had been sent a copy of Harvey Cox's *The Secular City* for review two or three years before. The radical American jargon defeated my undoubted interest. My efforts ploughed into the ground after forty pages, and writing a review was beyond me. It struck me that valuable ideas from writers and thinkers like Cox would defeat me unless I met Christians who thought and spoke like that. Hearing that Canon Stephen Verney was organising a conference in 1968 at Coventry, entitled 'People and Cities', I wrote to ask if there could be an invitation. This was the second conference that led me on to unfamiliar ground that year. There were 150 participants from 33 countries. It felt like breathing fresh air to be part of a company that shared the belief that large cities are part of the reality of the world, and that we need to make them places where human beings can flourish.

Preston Williams, a black Professor from the United States, gave us first-hand insight into black American anger and pride; he said that Americans had thought the job was only to rid individuals of prejudice and sin. 'Now we must attempt to think of structures of evil. The system must be reformed. Race relations are between communities, not just between individuals.' Richard Hauser, a gifted community development guru, spoke of 'The Invisible Community'; he said that communities went to pieces because they were deprived of the 'Single most important factor in the building of communities, human warmth . . . Human warmth cannot be bought. It cannot be legislated for. It can only be enabled.'[8]

'People and Cities' introduced me to the era of community development and planning. These were sometimes in conflict with each other. For example, we received a presentation of the 'Los Angeles Goals Project'. This was an ambitious joining together of 'inter-religious' groups to study the options for the development of the city. Huge decisions were at stake. The alternatives included whether the city should expand to 8 million, 12 million or 24 million. Should it develop along radial lines with fast public train services (still lacking in 2002) or in clusters around major shopping centres? When we were gasping in admiration at the quality of the literature, we realised that there would be a thousand different solutions from all the community groups. What expectations would be raised? Someone asked the question, 'After all that consultation, who will make the decisions about which option to follow?'

In my notebook at the end of the conference I asked myself, 'What will I try to do in the light of "People and Cities"?' I wrote down four points:

1 See what Richard Hauser has to teach us about tools to enable local groups and responsibility. Should the Mayflower seek to be a centre at which community happenings take place?
2 Try to decide what public policies I would support that might deal with social segregation: e.g. comprehensive schooling? Do I argue for integration or the solidarity of distinct cultures and groups, as Black Power is pursuing in the US? Do we insist on producing a housing mix by bringing owner-occupiers into the inner city?
3 Encourage the Mayflower to look at its neighbourhood, to see what God is wanting us to understand, to rejoice at, to challenge, to share in. I must try to produce a liturgy for the city.
4 Think through just what this tension between evangelical and radical theology implies for me.

It was a time of significant theological reflection in my life. A current radical slogan was, 'We must catch up with what God is doing in the world.' Malcolm Muggeridge had interviewed Simon Phipps[9] and me in a television programme. Simon said he believed that all the world was 'in Christ'. Muggeridge responded, 'If the whole world is in Christ already, what are you people bothered about?' I was coming to see that God, creator and sustainer of the whole universe, was indeed active everywhere. Sometimes he was present, inspiring new ideas and initiatives; and sometimes he was present, but ignored, or suffering at the hands of human sin. Radical theology in these two conferences was reacting against the emphasis on individualism and dependence, and the reliance on preaching by itself. Earlier notebooks of mine show that ever since going to the Mayflower I had been studying the relation of the group and the individual in the Bible. I accepted that it was healthy to speak of persons in community – in relation to other persons – rather than of isolated individuals, as though God meant them to develop apart from those around them.

There were sharp criticisms of Christian traditions that made for a wrong kind of dependence. My notes took seriously Bishop John Robinson's question, 'Is the Christian always to remain a child?' with his call to take up Bonhoeffer's phrase, 'man coming of age'. At this point, my notes contained a large 'but'. But Jesus is the Servant of the Lord. He prays 'Abba Father', and we are to learn to do that too. There is a right kind of dependence. The challenge to us 'to come of age' calls us to responsibility, and to a faith that is marked, not by calm and success, but by integrity and, perhaps, unease. Then there was another 'but'. The radical reaction against 'simply preaching' sometimes seemed to lead to conscious avoiding of putting the gospel into words. Donald Coggan's Bible readings on the Servant Songs of Isaiah accepted the ideal of John Robinson's 'Man for others', but supplemented it with 'Man with God's word for others'. At that Conference I agreed with Coggan that many cannot respond responsibly to the love of God unless they come to know the name of Jesus personally, and are able to know what that name Jesus carries with it.

After these conferences I started to think regularly of a 'both . . . and . . .' of sharing the faith. We were called *both* to name the Name, so that people might be changed from inside out; *and* to change unjust structures of society that were spoiling God's good world. In my attempts to produce a liturgy for the city, I started to write some 'Prayers of life' that we could use in our worship at the Mayflower rather after the style of the French priest Michel Quoist. One prayer reflected on living in the city:

Life for most of my neighbours
Means life in the great city, Lord.
I hardly dare pray to you about it,
Even though it's crippling them.
True prayer gets things changed, doesn't it?
Like sick people being made better;
And it's hard to believe
That, in this sick city, life can be made better.
They didn't ask our advice when they planned it.
They won't ask our advice when they knock it down.

There were hopes that tenants could be heard
Once.
A petition was got up
For a zebra crossing – with a lollipop man.
Everyone signed, except Mrs Holmes.
She was deaf;
Her son told her not to sign anything
When he came to see her twice a year.
The Tenants Association was strong then;
But no one heard if the petition was being considered.
There didn't seem any point in still belonging.
The crossing and the lollipop man
Appeared two years later.
No one remembered it was their petition that did it.

Then there was a youth leader.
Full of promises he was, Lord.
All the youngsters rushed home with their high hopes.
He's been gone a year,
Adding to a hundred broken promises the teenagers have heard.
Soon someone will say, 'You can't rely on these kids nowadays.'
He said no one on the Estate would help.
He hadn't learned that the Estate had never been asked to help
    before;
They'd ceased to believe that what they did could alter anything.
I feel for the youth leader, Lord.
He must have despaired
Just as the people he blamed did themselves.
Despair's a tyrant
Crippling our abilities.

Knowing all the immovable, despairing parts of city life
We need belief
That God's in the city,
That God made the people who make up the city;
That God has great purposes for each of them.
Prayer means listening to God,
Not just talking.
It means lifting up our hearts
To God's idea of how He wants it to be.
A Psalm has it;
Heaven, Moon, Stars,
Distant, vast, awe-inspiring;
Beside them
What is man that You should remember him?

It's the same in the great city;
Tower blocks,
Distant government Ministries,
House-eating urban motorways;
Beside them
What is man that You should remember him?
Your answer is that man is more important
Than all of them.
He is to be master over all Your creatures.
Man is to count, to matter, to be responsible,
Able to get things done.

When the great city destroys men's belief
That they can make choices
Which will bring about change for the good,
They can't believe that God is good.
God forgive us,
We run away so easily from the city.
You've given us responsibility, Lord,
To make our city,
Our corner of the city,
A place where people truly count.

It was October 1968 when Mervyn Stockwood, the Bishop of Southwark, asked me to go to lunch, 'to discuss sport and South Africa'. Half way through lunch he said, 'John Robinson is going to go back to Cambridge, and there will be a vacancy as Bishop of Woolwich. I would like you to take that on.'

7

Bishops and Bishoping

There were more 'walks with God' to help me arrive at a decision about becoming Bishop of Woolwich. We had planned a sabbatical year in Edinburgh, when I would try to write a book. We stayed a week in a hotel, close by the Forth Rail Bridge, looking for a house to rent, and a school for Jenny. So the walks took place, some of them alone, some with Grace, on winter mornings, along the shore of the Firth of Forth. The alternative to accepting the Woolwich appointment was an attractive one – a sabbatical year in Edinburgh and then a further period of years at the Mayflower.

Just as I had done when wondering whether to offer for ordination, I used the sequence for decision-making we had been taught in the army: object–courses–factors–plan. Reading now from the notes written at the time, two or three factors stand out. First, after eleven years, I was tired. It would be good for the Mayflower to have a new warden. When I told Grace, her response was, 'I didn't feel I could tell you.' Second, if we believed that the visible church is part of Christ's Church and one of his vehicles, we must want to make it more effective. So some of us must be prepared to work from within 'the Establishment'. Third, my usefulness was that, as far as was possible for an incomer, I understood working-class life. At meetings, I listened with my neighbours' ears. If being a bishop meant being cut off from such people, I would lose my usefulness. The deduction was that we must live in a working-class district, and have continuing contact with our immediate area.

While we were still sweating over the decision, Mervyn Stockwood suggested that we should go and see the play *Hadrian VII* at the Mermaid Theatre close to the Thames at Blackfriars. It was about the rapid rise of a priest to bishop and cardinal. Just before the interval in the play he was elected pope. Suddenly large figures came sweeping down the aisles beside us in the scarlet of cardinals, with incense swinging before them. Hadrian was enveloped by the cardinals. Grace said, 'I'm not sure I can stand any more of this.' In the interval we walked up and down the

Embankment, talking about our feelings. Was I going to be swallowed up by ritual, pomp and Establishment? Could Grace face being married to someone who was being swept into that? We just managed to return for the second act.

A Peckham home

The decision to accept was made. But where were we to live? The house where previous bishops had been required to live stood in an unmade-up road in Blackheath. My mind refused to work on being the bishop to all the inner-city parishes of South East London from that base. Bishop Mervyn Stockwood agreed that we could hunt for a house in the 'inner ring'. We found a house in Asylum Road, Peckham, just off the Old Kent Road. It had once been a doctor's house, and we felt it would give us an appropriate base. Many inner-city clergy told us that they valued the fact that a bishop was experiencing something of the life they knew. Works on the house were not completed by the time we needed to move in. So we started with no water or electricity, borrowing an old oil lamp from my mother. There was still no carpet on the stairs when Archbishop and Mrs Ramsey came to lunch following my consecration in Southwark Cathedral.

Grace had entered into the decision-making in Edinburgh, but found fresh fears rising up about coping with life outside the warmth of the community at the Mayflower. Out of the blue, a Morris 1100 came as a gift from a friend who was leaving for Africa – just when we had been scanning the papers for a second-hand car. It made a huge difference for Grace. She still had agoraphobia:

> I could not cross the road or walk far alone without needing to walk by a wall, or hold on to a person or pram. I would feel totally drained after each effort to push the boundaries, and often felt defeated. But the thought of driving made me feel safer. I visited friends and set myself journeys with a 'treat' at the end as a carrot.[1]

Living in our own house presented another raft of challenges to Grace. I was going to be out most days visiting parishes in the diocese, and Jenny was at primary school. No one came to the door as had happened in our Mayflower flat. Meeting new neighbours was a daunting prospect that could only be tackled by her. 'One day I opened the front door and began to brush the steps. It was the best I could do. I felt very unsure of myself, but I was determined not to give up. I had to begin somewhere.' From this beginning began a stream of conversations and contacts with passers-by and local residents, from pensioners to school children. She made the most of living within the limits that agoraphobia imposed. She learned do-it-yourself skills in the house, and kept a well-stocked garden in order. We also decided to entertain on a regular basis. Grace did all the catering, having put the years of isolation to good effect in learning cooking skills. One memorable evening I arrived home rather late for the party to see some thirty people in the room. 'We've asked next week's guests to come as well!' I said. We decided to come clean and admitted what had happened. Grace sent some of the guests out into the garden to pick some more vegetables. Others came into the kitchen to help put a sufficient meal together. Everyone responded positively and we remembered it as one of the happiest evenings. Sometimes a few friends would stay on after the majority had left. Often music became central at that point. I think that was how we discovered that Eric James had the marvellous social grace of being an excellent accompanist. Eric came for more evenings when he persuaded Grace to sing.

She joined the Parochial Church Council at St John's, Peckham, worshipping there with Jenny rather than coming round with me. She also served on the Parsonages Committee of the diocese, fighting the corner for clergy wives when the diocesan budget usually offered limited works on vicarages. She became involved in the community by joining an Asylum Road Action Group, set up to fight for the preservation of some fine houses, and in becoming a school governor of the comprehensive school that we faced across the road. The chair of governors, Jessie Burgess,[2] was in her eighties, still sharp in spite of moments when others were tempted to think she was asleep. She introduced a candidate for deputy head, going round the room of the interviewing governors; when she reached Grace, she said, 'And this is Mrs Bishop, the wife of the famous footballer!'

The solemnity of the consecration service in Southwark Cathedral produced a mixture of feelings in my mind. I felt awe at this calling to public leadership in the church; yet there was a strong conviction that God had indeed called me. With that came also a warm sense of the support and prayers of family, friends and colleagues. Archbishop Michael Ramsey agreed to my request that members of other Christian churches should be invited to receive communion – an invitation that was to become an official part of the canons of the Church of England within a few years. There were anxieties too. Would the Mayflower members there feel at home in the beautifully sung service with its immaculate ceremonial? Would they feel I had been taken over by the Establishment?

I came to love Southwark Cathedral, a beautiful gothic church just by London Bridge, smaller than vast buildings like St Paul's – or indeed Liverpool. Southwark had trains rumbling past its windows. We could never forget that we were worshipping in the heart of a busy city, with the borough market around us. The following year I led the Palm Sunday worship in the cathedral. We processed outside the west door. I spotted Jenny, determinedly pointing that my mitre was leaning over to one side. The problem for me was that I could not interpret whether it needed pushing over that way or pulling back! So I left it as it was.

The 150 parishes in the eastern half of Southwark Diocese, for which I had responsibility, covered the whole spectrum of the population of London. There were regular visits for patronal festivals, confirmations and institutions of a new vicar. Then there might be consultations over plans for reorganisation – not the occasion when the bishop was the most popular visitor. At Mervyn Stockwood's suggestion, like him, I made more extensive visitations at intervals. I would arrive at 6 p.m. on the Sunday, asking the parish to move their Parish Communion to that time, and stay until 10 p.m. on the Monday, with a carefully planned programme in between. I made these visitations to fifty-seven parishes during my six years at Woolwich. Churchgoing varied sharply, with social class a major pointer to how many were likely to be present in a church service. Southwark Diocese includes a great variety of communities – some rural, as well as the 'urban sprawl'. I made a study of Church of England attendance as a percentage of the population in the different parts of the area I regularly visited. It is an impressionist picture, but one that points in truthful directions:

Surrey	9%
Blackheath and Dulwich	4%
Outer suburban	3.25%
Inner suburban	1.8%
Inner city and outer estates	0.9%

The outer areas of Surrey

Visiting these parishes took me as far as the Sussex border. (There has been reorganisation since my time, with the Croydon area being brought into Southwark Diocese. The Bishop of Croydon is responsible for these parishes now.) There was a handful of small villages, still largely rural, like Tatsfield, Chaldon, Crowhurst and Outwood. There were large villages with a mixture of rural and dormitory population, like Godstone, Oxted, Limpsfield, Felbridge, Blechingley. Then there were suburban towns like Caterham, Purley and Coulsdon.

There was a new set of lessons for me to learn. One large village was described by its vicar as 'a village with a great many organisations in it – very few church-run organisations'. Members of the Parochial Church

Council (PCC) told me they hoped that church members were involved in all these village activities. The vicar in a parish like that can know and be known, with all the opportunities and the demands that brings. As the number of clergy has fallen, many village parishes have been joined with others so that the demand on the one vicar has grown.

In my report for Mervyn Stockwood about another village parish, there is a note that a good number of church people I met 'were involved with charities of one kind or another. In areas at this distance from London much of the commitment to Christian work was plainly outside the parish, and rightly so.' In another parish in this band round the outer edge of London there was pride that Desmond Tutu,[3] not yet a bishop, had been their honorary curate when he was working in London. There was serious interest in the needs of inner London. Cecilia Goodenough, a formidable figure in tweeds and woollen stockings, would drive up in her Landrover. She spent much of her time with the poorest families, who were living in what was then called 'part three' accommodation, and had questions to raise in smart Surrey about the inequalities she saw. She liked to needle people into thinking – not least bishops, who held no terrors for her. Having awoken that conscience, she challenged those living in these villages not to think that all their Christian responsibility lay in the inner city. She wanted to build on that, for it could open their eyes to needs which were also to be found in genteel poverty hidden behind lace curtains in their own community.

Not all our worshippers liked to be reminded of inequalities. 'We're getting a little tired of being called "the gin-and-Jag belt" by the Bishop of Southwark,' I was told in one parish. A friend of mine told me that he had stopped worshipping in another of these parish churches. He said it was because 'It was so left-wing'. I could not work out what had touched him on the raw, for the vicar was a most sensitive and thoughtful person, and the worship was always beautifully conducted. The penny dropped for me when I was told that Peter Selby, then the lay training officer, had run a course in the parish under the title, 'What is the village contributing to the death of London?' In another parish the vicar's wife asked me, 'What about all these marches you go on?' I had to tell her that the 'Stop the Rugby Tour' march that she had read about was the first and only march I had been on!

I asked a young clergyman who had done an excellent piece of work in the daughter church of an inner-city parish to consider moving to one of the villages in the loveliest part of Surrey. He came back to me and said, 'Please don't press me to go there.' I said, 'You'd better tell me about that.' He said that while they were looking round the parish he and his wife had been given dinner in the home of one of the two churchwardens, with the other churchwarden and his wife there too. Over dinner, he said, 'Several remarks were made about black people and the police that I knew were not true. They were such charming people that I don't think I could stand up to them.' If ministry in comfortable situations like those parishes had ever seemed easy, I never thought so again. It calls for courage and sensitivity – not to be cross with people for being well off, but raising some of the kingdom of God questions that can be uncomfortable. When I drove down into the leafy parts of Surrey, I myself was tempted to think this might be hostile territory. I needed to take myself in hand. These were brothers and sisters in Christ, and I could learn from them. They too had pains and pressures to face. Our 'inner-city' experiences should not be denied, but I must learn to share them with love and respect.

I was pleased that in my last year at Woolwich I was invited to lead studies every week in Lent in Godstone deanery, the 'leafiest' part of the diocese. My theme was 'God's dream and our reality'. In one study I consciously raised a sensitive subject, speaking of business life in the light of the kingdom of God. There was a tunnel the train came through on the commuters' way home from the office in London. They said that they breathed a sigh of relief as they came out of the tunnel. London and its demands had been left behind. I suspected that there would be two voices inside commuter Christians if a clergyman raised questions about business life. One would say, 'Don't you dare talk about a subject you know nothing about: and don't raise those awkward questions. I live in Surrey because I need to withdraw from the pressures of business.' Another voice would say, 'Please help me. The most anxious-making pressures of my life are to do with work. I wish I could see how the kingdom of God relates to my life at work.'

In that Lent course, looking at daily issues of living led us to question what the Gospel means for each of us. I made a point of talking about Jesus' parables of the lost things: the lost sheep, the lost coin and the lost boy – and the waiting father's joy at his being found. That brought forth the comment, 'I've always felt sympathy for the elder brother in that story.' There was a real divide between the ethic of hard work that would earn God's favour and the Gospel that speaks to each of us as a sinner who can know herself or himself forgiven. Gratitude for that costly forgiveness is the motivation for living for him.

Suburban parishes

A visit to a suburban parish might find different social groups living within the same neighbourhood. One All Saints Day I went to confirm in two churches dedicated to All Saints. The morning service was at All Saints, Carshalton. The reception afterwards had to be confined to families of those who had been confirmed, because otherwise there would have been too many to fit in the hall. In the evening I was at All Saints, Hackbridge, Mitcham Junction, not more than a mile away, on a council estate. There were six young candidates. None of them had any members of their family supporting them. The contrast was stark, and made clear that in the latter parish we were in the kind of missionary situation where there was little Christian background for young people who made their own choice to be Christian disciples.

I visited five parishes in Sydenham where these contrasts ran through each parish. My notes about one vicar read: 'Extremely thoughtful and able pastor and teacher. I met three adults in their thirties who had clearly experienced conversion in the last six months.' This was an evangelical parish, in which there was concern that the Gospel should be preached, together with the exercise of pastoral care for neighbours. The number that would have claimed the 'evangelical' label for themselves in the Woolwich area was 14 out of 150. The greater number came from the moderate catholic tradition; some counted themselves definite Anglo-Catholics. Worshipping in parishes of all the different traditions that the Anglican Church embraces was an enriching piece of spiritual stretching. I made it a particular matter of prayer that I would learn how to enter into worship in each of the traditions. In an Anglo-Catholic parish, in one of my earliest visits, the vicar took me to visit a man who was dying. His faith was rock-like. He told me how that faith had come for him, having grown up outside the Church. He said, 'It was in the Mass, Father, at the elevation of the host. I saw vividly what Christ had done for me on the cross.' I was face to face with an assurance of salvation as clear as any evangelical could wish.

The parish where we lived in Peckham was in the Catholic tradition. I shared some of my anxieties with the vicar Geoffrey Heal about wearing a bishop's mitre. I did not see this as an old argument about 'High Church' and 'Low Church'. Rather it seemed to me that it was triumphalist, as if I was declaring that the king was there with a crown on his head. Geoffrey heard me out. Eventually he said, 'When you come to St John's, I want them to listen to what you have to say to them. If you did not wear a mitre, that is the only thing they would talk about.' I was conscious that a bishop entered a parish on the backs of those who bear the burden and heat of the day. It would be triumphalist indeed to insist on wearing the robes I thought most suitable if they were alien to the people of the parish. I decided that I must learn to enter the tradition of each parish. Encouraged by Mervyn, I went to Stanley Ashby, an Anglo-Catholic vicar, for several lessons in 'how to sing and to swing'! I learned how to swing incense and to sing the variety of musical settings that different parishes used. One Sunday morning I realised that the music they expected me to sing in an hour's time was new. I rang Stanley Ashby with my problem. He sang the service down the phone to me, and I sang it back to him, until confident of my lines.

Among my notes on the visitations, a number of disheartened clergy appear: 'He's tired – seeing out his time.' Very occasionally I describe rogues or good men who have made shipwreck. But even with them I could in every case see why – complex as people are – they had once had the potential that brought selection for ordination. Much more often the comment is like this one: 'Good pastor, loved by his people. He enjoys the life of the community.' There is my concern too about overwork: 'They are a most engaging couple, very open to people, ready to listen and to learn, and full of life and fun. Quite how he is going to cope with the demands of this parish I don't know.' This vicar seemed to be 'running to keep up' – trying to visit before and after baptisms, funerals and weddings, doing all the pastoral caring he possibly could. I feared that he was leaving himself no room to give special time to those who might be 'the Twelve' who could build up some new work. In the Gospels I saw Jesus giving unequal time to those that he saw could be leaders in the Church he set out to build. And sometimes, in order to keep time to be still with his Father, 'He sent the multitudes away'.

Often there was a council estate in suburban areas, where people came to church from every part of the parish except the estate. In Blackheath Park I met a woman who was battling against the feeling among her neighbours that the church wasn't for 'people like us on the estate'. They had once had a group that met in someone's flat there, but this seemed to have lapsed. She could well have been a person with the drive and ability to get such a group going again. Such an initiative would mean the vicar taking some risks. I was told of the traditional training in a famous Anglo-Catholic parish in the diocese, where the vicar resisted the idea of groups run by lay people. He said, 'It might get out of control.'

Inner city and outer estates

These parishes made up much of the Bishop of Woolwich's area. Here, my years in unchurched Canning Town helped clergy and lay people to feel I understood what church life meant for them. My first institution of a new vicar was in a Walworth parish, near The Elephant and Castle. I went the previous evening to talk over the service with the two churchwardens and the young priest who was to be their new vicar. What did they want me to wear? 'I had rather wondered if you and I might wear a suit,' replied John Austin, the young priest.[4] The reactions of the churchwardens revealed two solidly traditional men. 'I think I probably should wear cope and mitre for this service,' I said. 'If you decide together that you'd like me to come in a suit on a later occasion, you tell me and I will be ready to do that.'

One remarkable ministry was that of Father David Diamond at St Paul's, Deptford. He was a firm Anglo-Catholic, unswerving in his beliefs and teaching. He thought much modern church questioning made it all too complicated. His was the inspiration of a Festival of Deptford that drew together crowds from the community. He mounted colourful traditional worship, supported by fireworks and parties that would have been fully recognised in the East End. It was the only parish in which I agreed to take a week's mission, believing that the vigorous community involvement of the parish meant that many 'stepping stones' were in place. It was an education to walk round Deptford with David Diamond and to be in many different homes, meeting a wide variety of people in his company. People knew him and had deep respect for him. He identified with Deptford in a considerable way. He had undoubtedly done a major job in helping people to stand up and be proud of their own neighbourhood.

We agreed that in the week's mission the parish would make a list of their 200 best contacts, and concentrate on inviting them to one event or another during the mission. There was to be no widespread publicity. I insisted that my name should not even be on the noticeboard. This was hard for David to agree to, for he was a brilliant publicist, gathering large crowds for special services, complete with royalty. The trouble was that, if there were large numbers from outside, they could take the attention away from local people. The only main services to which everyone was invited were on the two Sundays. At High Mass at 10 a.m. communicants were 105 and 94, the total attendance being nearer 200 on both occasions. The 'best contacts' were invited to meetings with me in 14 homes. Some 140 different adults came to these groups – possibly 4–1 being women. The normal weekly number of communicants, which I discovered by looking carefully through the service book, during the last year had ranged between 60 and 80. I include those figures, because other clergy were often told of the success of David Diamond in ways that made them feel failures. I admired David's work, but, like him, knew that there was a struggle to win people for Christ and the Church in his parish too.

David wrote to me after the mission:

I got quite a feedback in the High Street this afternoon, when some of the most unlikely groups of people spoke about your visit. It is obvious that we hit several nerve centres – and that what was said in the homes is spreading more quickly than we dared hope. We shall do all in our power to build on what has happened – and I feel sure that the house meetings are not only here to stay, but will expand.

He must have changed his mind about that. Rodney Bomford, then curate at St Paul's, wrote about me, that one of my dearest wishes was to see a group or groups in which ordinary people could become 'thinking Christians', informed and active in the faith:

> His initiative has had important and creative consequences. It began from an awareness of the cultural problem similar to David Diamond's, but the ambition was quite different: David Diamond wanted people to be 'unthinking Christians': their faith should not be a matter of earnest study or discussion, but rather it should be natural to them to practise the faith in prayer and sacrament – and of course in family and community... To invite people to become self-consciously 'thinking Christians' was likely to bring about a new alienation from their background.[5]

Perhaps it was David Diamond's respect for the office of bishop that he never brought himself to argue with me. Reflecting on this debate, I stand my ground in believing we should not underestimate the intelligence and gifts of working-class people. Visitors to the Mayflower frequently commented, 'How articulate people are here'. A gifted doctor came to talk with an adult group about some of the ethical issues raised by modern medical progress. At the end of an evening of vigorous questioning, he said, 'I was as exhausted as I am by my brightest students.' Maybe such 'adult education' as they had found through the 'talking groups' at the Mayflower added to the risk that they would feel alienated from their own community. But the future of our cities must call for the floor of educational questioning and achievement to be raised all round.

David Diamond was always in a hurry. Staying that week in the clergy house, I worried about the lack of anywhere for the priests to withdraw and feel that they were in their home. I encouraged David to furnish one of the upstairs rooms as a sitting room that would be for the clergy and their friends only. There was an atmosphere of busyness, 'success' and hurry in the house. One of the clergy was clearly more vulnerable to the pressure, but perhaps he revealed needs all of them had – to have interests that were nothing to do with their work. It was a question that arises again at the time of retirement with clergy who have made their work the sole purpose of their lives.

In the next-door parish, reflecting the varied traditions of the Church of England, was a conservative evangelical vicar, Bob Miles, who had been at St Nicholas for many years. He was a great personal worker, reminding me of the books I had read by George Dempster, like *Finding Men for Christ*. Bob Miles would go all over the country, finding individuals in great need. He prayed at the beginning of every conversation or meal, and sometimes right through the night. These 'brands plucked from the burning' were never likely to build up the congregation in Deptford, which remained small. He admired David Diamond, though he did not understand some of his ceremonial. Mrs Miles seemed, like her husband, to belong to a previous generation. Yet I was given a salutary and beautiful insight that told me that love and respect cross all the lines of 'traditional' and 'radical'. She told me that a homeless woman had come to the vicarage door. She took her across the road for advice about her housing to the Albany Centre, very secular in its approach. Her heart sank when she saw that the young man who was to deal with her was dressed in jeans, with an enormous shock of hair. However, she told me, 'He has been wonderful – treating her case with great care and perseverance.'

Living in Peckham, I came to know some of the local churches and wider community life better than most. I agreed to chair the Peckham Settlement, supported by UGS – United Girls Schools. John Lane, then the Methodist minister, was closely involved in its life, and later became the Warden of the Settlement. The Methodist church was being rebuilt, and during the rebuilding their congregation worshipped together with the Anglicans at St John's, Peckham, our parish. I saw genuine co-operation between the churches in Peckham, with Father Raymund at the Roman Catholic friary sharing in many joint Christian enterprises.

I was learning to look beneath the surface at parishes that statistics would dismiss as failures. One vicar, Percy Leach, had been at St Andrew's, Peckham, for over twenty years, after serving for many years in India. At first I saw him as a bumbling, gentle person. As I spent the day and a half of the visitation with him, my respect grew. He seemed to have the art of getting other people to do things for him. Percy wrote a play every year at Christmas time, getting thirty to forty people involved, both in taking part and in jobs such as an electrician's, in staging it. Local people built the stage in the hall. He clearly enjoyed the youth club, and was regularly there. He expected to recruit leadership from within the club, and succeeded in doing so. He told me that in one of his earlier years in the parish (which had a membership of six when he arrived) he visited a docker in hospital. The docker made one of those promises that if he got better, he would do something for the church. He brought his mates with him to be confirmed. Percy says that there was a confirmation that year of seventy-five people, of whom two-thirds were adult. Nearly all this gain of his earlier years was swept away by widespread demolition in the parish.

I visited St Luke's, Peckham, where the urban regeneration process was further advanced and the new North Peckham estate was emerging. This was to be regarded as a disaster estate thirty years on, when it received publicity as the scene of the murder of the small boy Damilola Taylor. One young couple I met in that parish had joined as the result of simple good practice. The very traditional vicar of their original parish had married them. On the following Monday he had commended them to Clifford Wright, the rather radical vicar of the Peckham parish where they were now going to live. He had visited them without delay, and they were becoming involved in the life of the church.

I also heard about a public meeting on the estate. It was to discuss the proposal to place there a hostel for adults with learning difficulties. There had been an angry, shouting meeting of 400 tenants. Clifford Wright's was the only voice raised in support. He got as far as saying, 'Are we a caring and compassionate . . .' before he was howled down. I was told about this by a man in front of the church group. He said he was now starting to come to worship because he had seen a church that really cared about the life of the community. I learned that he had resigned as chairman of the Ward Labour Party, because of what he regarded as the lack of integrity of the councillor. After the noisy meeting, people had been swung by quiet consultation to agreeing that the hostel could come, but the councillor continued to say a year later that he expressed the voice of the people on the strength of that one public meeting.

Going to a meal before a service with another clergy couple, I was arrested by a theological question as we went in to the meal: 'Do we *have* to name the Name?' asked the young vicar, with a heavy sigh. In my first round of clergy chapter meetings I had argued for the 'both . . . and . . .' that had become important to me. That meant *both* by deed and word reflecting the creator God's concern for right relationships and justice, *and* naming the Name of Jesus Christ as our saviour. Church party allegiances and conflicts had led him to reject the way some Christians appeared to live out their calling. He said, 'I know these Anglo-Catholics and evangelicals. They don't care about people's human needs.' From the other side of that fence, radical clergy were dismissed as being earthbound, without believing in the salvation that came through the death and resurrection of Christ.

Donald Reeves[6] was regarded as a leading 'radical' in the diocese. He ascribed the comparative strength of the parish to consistently generous staffing by the diocese. He invited me to spend an evening with the staff team. This was made up of stipendiary and non-stipendiary clergy and lay workers. That evening, we talked first about the factors that made for human warmth in the community and the part the parish could play. Then I said, 'Many people on the estate have grown up without any

Christian background. Do you believe it is laid upon you, by whatever means you believe will be most effective, to share your faith with them?' The firm reply was, 'Yes'. Meeting away from ecclesiastical factions, we were able to engage as fellow Christians who respected different priorities others had, and to agree about our responsibility to pass on the faith.

Another young vicar with radical views was Derek Jones. He was sensitive to local opinions and combative in fighting their corner. Derek expressed a belief in immanence in an extreme form. He said he could only meet God on the Roundshaw Estate. He was reacting against a view that saw God as always coming from outside. My predecessor at Woolwich, John Robinson, had written about God as 'the Ground of our Being', but also as 'the Beyond in the Midst'. I find it helpful to look 'in the midst' for the presence of God, yet also continue to search beyond the local. To say that one could only find God on the estate where one lived would be a denial that gifts can be creatively brought into a community from outside. Some community development workers were arguing that all the professionals should go away from working-class areas and leave development to local people. That would mean giving in to class and race divisions, when the transcendent God has created all people of one race.

Mervyn Stockwood

Crossing the river to the South Bank brought a steep learning curve for me. I was thirty-nine when Mervyn Stockwood approached me. I had first met him some ten years earlier when he rang me up to rebuke me! His first words to me were, 'David, you've been getting me into trouble! Here am I, trying to bring these Anglo-Catholics to order, and they tell me you've taken a wedding in a Baptist church.' I said, 'I'm very sorry. The bride is a close friend of ours. What should I have done?' He told me I could properly have preached or said prayers at the service. Then he said, 'I shall have to write and tell you off. Don't take it to heart too much. Come and cheer me up and have dinner with me.'

One of Mervyn's strengths was to cut through the politeness that muffled clear debate between different traditions. Over that dinner he probed my evangelical convictions. He told me that in the 1930s he was at a conference on unemployment; Bishop Christopher Chavasse, a great evangelical, had said, 'I have never seen a converted man unemployed.' I shared Mervyn's shock at such a limited view of God's love for his world. When we were starting to think hard about his invitation to go to Woolwich, Grace and I went out for the day with him. I told her that I needed to know whether Mervyn was a chameleon, who changed his colours for every situation, or whether there was a hard centre of his own convictions. We walked and talked through beautiful country, before enjoying a sumptuous lunch – the first of many walks, talks and good meals we shared. I came to see that he had entered deeply into the different religious experiences that made up the mixture he now embraced. His first upbringing was at All Saints, Clifton, in a decisively Anglo-Catholic tradition; the daily eucharist was always at the heart of his spiritual devotion. As a young man, he entered on a lifelong friendship with the great evangelist Bryan Green, who was then leading mission teams in which Stockwood joined. He loved to show evangelical parishes that he knew all the CSSM choruses he had learned then. Next, as a student at Cambridge, he fell under the spell of Canon Charles Raven, with his open and liberal approach to great world issues. Then came the years in an East Bristol parish, when he came to feel passionately about the effects of unemployment, poor housing and inadequate schooling on people he came to know closely. Those years made him a socialist. I came to believe that, underneath the showman he unquestionably was, there was a believing Christian who wanted to be true to the best of all these insights.

Most of all he enjoyed pastoral contact with clergy and lay people. He must have made 150 parish visitations in the same pattern as I have described above. He would have encouraged lay people to question him, and his public utterances would often have been raised. He stood up to be counted on some controversial subjects that tested their loyalty at times. Most people in the diocese respected his views though many, especially from the Surrey parishes, disagreed with his – or my – comments about public life. Some of the lay men that he respected most held different convictions about Church and State. Strong friendships bridged those gaps. They recognised the fairness he observed in dealing with parishes and clergy, his deep concern that the Gospel should be preached, and his pastoral care for the clergy.

Nicholas Frayling[7] told me of ringing him late at night – as he encouraged clergy to do in a crisis. Nick was invited to come straight round and talk about an unpleasant situation he was facing in the parish. At 11 p.m. Mervyn said, 'We'll go up to the chapel and pray about it. Day or night you can ring me. I'm at your disposal. Ring Mary (Mary Cryer, his secretary) and ask her to find a date when I will come and preach' – as he did. Nicholas said, 'We all felt we were special.' Robert Runcie, as Archbishop of Canterbury, preached at Mervyn's celebration of twenty-one years as Bishop of Southwark. In his sermon, he said, 'Southwark is special.' Even though the media constantly told us that the church was in decline, morale in the diocese was high. And part of that high morale was due to Mervyn's great capacity for laughter, fun and hospitality. Cheerfulness kept breaking in.

In spite of the flamboyant exterior, Mervyn was often vulnerable. Michael De-la-Noy's biography has a perceptive subheading, *A Lonely Life*. Mervyn told me that his mother, who lived with him until her death at eighty-seven, had never given him a single word of praise for anything he had done. He was deeply hurt by an article in the *New Statesman*, written by Anthony Howard, which included him in a series entitled 'The Defectors'. As a young man Mervyn had been an active member of the Labour Party in Bristol, chairing the Housing Committee. That had brought him close to Nye Bevan and Jenny Lee, and to Stafford Cripps, who invited him to stay in No 11 Downing Street when Cripps was Chancellor of the Exchequer. He lost some of that confidence in the Labour Party. He would regularly speak of Harold Wilson as 'Helpless Harold'. The theme of the *New Statesman* series was that some who had once been strong socialists had 'defected'. The article said that to many people Mervyn Stockwood 'seemed to have gone over to the enemy'. It cited his decision to go and support Dick Taverne (who had broken away from the Labour Party) at Lincoln. 'To some of his friends it appeared to mark the culmination of what had already begun to look uncommonly like a collapse with relief into the arms of the Establishment. The former turbulent priest, twice tossed out of the Bristol Labour Party for left-wing deviations, had long since ceased to remind anyone of a socialist firebrand.'[8]

He was bent on writing a furious reply. I pressed him that this would not help. I suggested it would be more effective if Paul Oestreicher, a vicar in the diocese, known to stand for radical causes, wrote a letter to the *New Statesman*, setting out some of Mervyn's firm and continuing commitment to social justice. After long arguments, he said that he wanted me to go and see Lord Goodman, the distinguished lawyer often consulted by the Labour Government. He would accept his advice. That led to one of my more bizarre duties as his suffragan bishop – breakfast with Lord Goodman. My instructions were to go to the ground floor lift, where I had been advised to press the unmarked button between the first and second floors. When the lift stopped there appeared to be no way of my opening the door. There was a spyhole, through which I presumed someone would look at the occupant of the lift and send him back down if he or she did not like the look of him! Lord Goodman appeared in dressing gown and gave me breakfast. I showed him the draft of what Paul Oestreicher had written. He said, 'Your friend knows how to handle invective too!' His advice to Mervyn was to leave the matter at that.

Mervyn Stockwood remained unpredictable. None of the apparent contradictions of his colourful lifestyle prevented him speaking out powerfully about racial justice, unemployment, housing, capital punishment or homosexual law reform. He said that what John Tindall had been saying on behalf of the National Front was 'An affront to Christian civilisation – no Christian person should have anything to do with him'. He said the lack of black people in many of our churches was a rebuke to our faith.

Mervyn risked being 'captured' by his socialising, but could laugh at himself. At the end of one splendid evening, wearing a silk purple cassock, fingering the decorated pectoral cross given to him by the Patriarch of Rumania, he said, 'I'm only the servant of a poor carpenter!' That lively sense of humour helped, but did not entirely save him. He allowed his judgment to be distorted by generous entertainment, for example by the Rumanian Orthodox Patriarch. He brought back accounts of the Church's freedom there, which were far removed from the facts of living under a brutal regime. From time to time he would repeat broad praise for the discipline that Marxist governments brought, even in Eastern bloc countries. At the other end of the social scale he enjoyed high society; inviting princesses, poets, writers and actors to good meals and fine wines at Bishop's House. We met an unusual circle there. Ned Sherrin often came, together with Caryl Brahms. She greeted me by saying, 'If you, a bishop, were to convert me, a Jewess, that would be nothing. But, if I were to convert you, that would really be something!'

Grace had been told that Mervyn could not get on with women. However, she found him very ready to meet and talk with her, interested in Jenny, and at times asking Grace to act as hostess for dinner parties. That was fine, except for the long delay after the women were asked to withdraw before the men appeared. He learned that she knew how to open oysters, so she was given the task of opening a hundred for a dinner party at Bishop's House – though she was not expected to eat any of them.

Before my appointment had been announced, an early arrangement for Grace to meet him highlighted the dramas that often surrounded him. To avoid press speculation and leaks, she was to come to the House of Lords to meet him. She was instructed to say that she was Joanna Martin. We discovered later that others were saddled with similar pseudonyms. While negotiations were going on with Michael Marshall, who was to follow me to Woolwich, he was to call himself Mr Pilkington, while Hugh Montefiore at a parallel moment was Mr Johnson.

Staff meeting was a great change from what I had been used to at the Mayflower, where more than half of those present were women. In the diocesan staff meeting all were men, observing seniority scrupulously. I told one friend that it reminded me of when I first played for Sussex. If we went to the cinema, we entered in strict order of who received their county cap first. All of us who worked closely with Mervyn found him infuriating at times, but also great fun. The parties were often uproarious. Alcohol flowed generously. His chaplains, who saw more than anyone, make it clear that he often drank a bit too much. But they also affirm that he was remarkably clear-headed the next morning. As this dawned on me, I would try to make sure that business that mattered most to me was dealt with before lunch.

As a rule drink did not affect his judgment. There was one unhappy experience, when I was staying at Bishop's House some time after I had moved to Liverpool. John Nicholson, a gifted lay man employed by the diocese, came in late at night to talk about the new management at Dartmouth House, then the Southwark Diocese's conference and retreat house. Mervyn had exploded when he discovered that the young men in retreat before ordination were, like it or not, being given vegetarian meals, and he ordered meat to be produced. John Nicholson came to defend the new management. This included criticising how my successor had handled this affair. Mervyn had heard enough of the case. He regarded the trust between himself and his episcopal colleagues as sacrosanct. He shouted, 'I'm the Bishop. I'm the Bishop. I'm the Bishop.' I felt helpless. There was no way the decision was going to be changed. Alas, the diocese would lose an able and loyal worker.

Mervyn was never good at admitting he was wrong or apologising. Another row led to two gifted clergy leaving the diocese. One believed Mervyn had made promises of responsibilities to him, when he recruited him to a senior post – promises that he then broke. The other challenged him about the injustice that he believed was being done. No response was forthcoming, and this produced a major rift in what had been a trusting relationship. At that moment I wrote identical letters to both of them, pressing them to meet and listen to each other. Such reconciliation as there was proved to be partial.

In his book, De-la-Noy made a great issue of Mervyn's sexuality. Undoubtedly he was homosexual in his orientation, but I was not aware that he was active. His approach as bishop echoed Pierre Trudeau's comment as Canada's prime minister that he did not wish the State to legislate about sexual relationships. He said he had no wish to peer through the keyhole of anyone's bedroom. Mervyn encouraged lasting and faithful relationships. He would add that they must be discreet. All that made me think afresh. The culture of evangelical church life at that time would not have given a homosexual man or woman the confidence to be open about a relationship, and I had never previously met anyone who was explicit about his or her orientation. Now Grace and I met couples who were plainly Christians, who believed that their best way to work out their calling was in a same-sex partnership. We came to believe that it was right to accept their invitation to a party, to welcome them into our home, and to make them know that we accepted them as Christian brothers or sisters.

Mervyn Stockwood did not argue that 'anything goes'. Faithfulness was part of Christian discipleship. He shared disciplinary matters with his suffragan bishops, Hugh Montefiore – who came to Kingston after I had been at Woolwich for a year – or me. Southwark had its fair share of scandals. Mervyn said, 'They'll never tell you the truth about sex or money.' Yet, if someone was truthful, he was ready to listen and, wherever possible, to reinstate. Years later in Liverpool I read and destroyed files of long-forgotten disciplinary cases of Clifford Martin, who was Bishop of Liverpool before my predecessor, Stuart Blanch. One told me about a priest who had been sent to prison for a year. Martin's notes described this as a savage punishment for a petty homosexual offence with another adult. When the priest came out of prison, Clifford Martin asked Mervyn, at the other end of the country, if he would find the priest a post. Now, more than ten years later, I knew this man well, widely regarded as a saintly priest, as he remained until his death.

Mervyn taught me how to be a bishop in the way that a good vicar trains a curate. I welcomed all the training he could give me. The Mayflower had taught me much about the Church serving the world of inner cities, but I knew little about the many traditions of church life. He was generous with his time for me. His priority was always that the Church – and he included churches of other denominations – should be effective in living and proclaiming the kingdom of God. I quickly learned that he was easily bored with church administration. He barely concealed his contempt for much of the General Synod's activities, believing that the best lay men felt themselves too busy to stand for election. He told me he wanted to cut it down to size. I felt he was wrong to distance himself from the General Synod and those who served the Church through belonging to it. In Liverpool, I invited our General Synod members to meet at Bishop's Lodge on the Sunday before the Synod week, so that we could look at the agenda together. Every other year, Grace and I entertained them to dinner during the London meeting of the Synod. In alternative years, they entertained us. That closeness between members served us well on one particular occasion, when our dinner was agreed for the evening of the day of the vote to ordain women. Friendships were strong enough to hold the group together, though members had voted in opposing ways.

Mervyn gave me great freedom. Some suffragan bishops feel that they are no more than episcopal curates, and are frustrated, having left major parishes where they had large influence. I never felt that. However, one of the words never to use with Mervyn, if I wanted his attention, was 'structures' – referring to the way the institution of the church was organised. There was no legally defined area for which I was responsible. That was to come later in Southwark, with 'area bishops' who have their own staff and clear boundaries of responsibility. In our day it relied on personal trust. Mostly that worked all right. I knew there was freedom for me to get on with the job. But there were frustrations. On occasions, having delegated responsibility to me, erratically Mervyn took it back. Nevertheless I preferred that erratic delegation to what was really abdication about other matters, in which he took no interest.

Central to the way he ran the diocese was to recognise openly the qualities different strands of churchmanship contributed, so that all felt they had an honoured place. There was a greatness about Mervyn, in spite of real flaws that were there too. As a young man he had learned much from Archbishop William Temple. For someone of my generation he provided a bridge. He communicated the policies and priorities that Temple had stood for – passion for social justice, a gospel available for all people in our nation, and ecumenical partnership. He encouraged me to build bridges both with Free Church people and with Roman Catholics.

8

Glass Partition or Brick Wall?

Ecumenical partnerships

In 1970, at the first ordination service in which I joined with Mervyn Stockwood, the preacher was a Methodist minister with whom Mervyn had worked in his Bristol days. The hopes for formal Anglican–Methodist unity had recently been dashed by the failure of the General Synod to deliver the unrealistic and special majority that had been set of 75 per cent in all three Houses – of Bishops, Clergy and Laity. But some of the momentum remained, and partnership with the Free Churches was welcomed on all sides. It came naturally to me.

What was new for me was to meet Roman Catholics on a regular basis. I was particularly interested in the strength of their presence in working-class areas, and wanted to learn from them. Father Charles Walker was chaplain to the Young Christian Workers in Southwark. He arranged for me to visit a YCW group in a back-street Bermondsey parish. Ten young people around twenty years of age were present (five men and five women). The curate was there, but said nothing unless they referred to him. The pattern was the regular YCW programme – first a 'Gospel enquiry', next 'Facts of the week', when members spoke about issues at work, and then discussed a youth Mass. They went on to review a dance run particularly for school leavers. The principles under each heading were – see, judge, act. I saw in that very articulate group familiar questions about church life in working-class areas: 'How can the Church present the challenge of Christ and the need to grow as a thinking Christian and still be – and remain – a Church of and for the district? How many of them were likely to establish their homes in Bermondsey?'[1]

I spent a day with Micky Bowen, then Bishop of Arundel and Brighton, who had been a parish priest in Walworth.[2] As we walked on the Sussex Downs, I asked him to explain part of Roman Catholic Church history to me. What was the difference between that church in the inner-cities in England and Scotland on the one hand and its presence in similar districts in France, Belgium, Italy and other European countries? In his studies of church-going practice in continental Europe in the 1950s, the French writer Boulard said that large towns everywhere presented a great problem to the church. 'Among certain social classes abstention from worship is almost unanimous.'[3] By comparison, surely church-going of Roman Catholics in English cities had held up rather well, hadn't it? Why was that? Without hesitating, Bowen replied, 'Because in England it's an Irish-rooted church'.

In Ireland poor people would not have blamed their bishops for their conditions. They would have blamed the English! The Irish poor who were sucked into inner cities in England and Scotland saw the Roman Catholic Church as a friend. It provided a rallying point – not unlike the role we were now seeing black-led churches play for a later immigrant group. When they experienced the harsh and erratic life of the inner city they would not have expected their leaders, lay or ordained, to have the power to do much about it. By contrast, in France, they would have seen their bishops and major employers among their fellow worshippers having easy relations with those in power – just as poor Anglicans did in this country. In both countries they would have resented the fact that their church could have stood up to social injustice, but had failed to do so.

The Archbishop of Southwark, Cyril Cowderoy, invited me to lunch at Archbishop's House. Courtesy reigned supreme. The nuns who looked after him produced a cake decorated with cricket bat and ball. As Bishop of Woolwich I chaired the Thamesmead Christian Community. Anglicans and Free Churches had agreed to share the same worship space. After the excellent lunch at Archbishop's House, I was able to raise some questions: 'Could we share in a new place of worship?' He said, 'Your predecessor sat in that chair and asked that. I'm afraid we cannot. We want to have our aids to worship around us.'

The Roman Catholics were not formal members, but the parish priest in nearby Abbey Wood, Frank O'Sullivan, entered fully into the team. Frank pressed me to go back to Archbishop Cowderoy and try again. He was sure that I had a better chance than he did! This further attempt received the same answer. The dotted line on the architect's plans must give way to a solid line – meaning a brick wall. Now he was instructed to produce plans that would allow as much shared worship with the Roman Catholics as possible. Ingenuity made more progress than I had feared was possible. When I came down from Liverpool for the dedication of the church, in which Micky Bowen, now Archbishop of Southwark took part, a shared baptistry was there in the middle of the whole building. It expressed the common baptism that Pope John had declared to be the basis of speaking of us as 'separated brethren'. On either side of the baptistry, where the dotted line had given way, there was glass above the brick wall, so that as members of each church we could at least see our separated brothers and sisters at our prayers.

The Thamesmead Christian Community taught me much about partnership that needed to be lasting and at the same time robust. I had to hold my ground in a tough bargaining session with the Methodist chairman of their national buildings committee about the commitments we had all made in Thamesmead. My Methodist opposite number, Norman Dawson, told me that my opposite number in the bargaining had been a Welsh rugby player. It certainly felt like a scrum! Inflation meant that we had to ask each denomination to increase the money they had promised. Norman Dawson had plainly been having a hard time keeping his own church up to their commitment. In the Thamesmead Ecumenical Council, he said, 'I have been wondering whether in the Church of the twenty-first century we should expect to have large buildings for worship.' Jim Thompson,[4] leader of the ecumenical team, said, 'That's all very well. But, while you maintain your 2,000-seater churches in Bromley, it is putting Thamesmead at yet another disadvantage, if you say we cannot have the sort of building for worship that other areas take for granted.'

That led to our having some sustained debates about what value we put on a place of worship. I had been reading the sociologist David Martin's, *Tracts Against the Times*, and asked members of the Thamesmead Ecumenical Council to read the chapter, 'Can the Church Survive?'[5] David Martin made the point that spiritual awareness can have a geography – more likely on the Brecon Beacons than in Birmingham. The growth of more and more Birminghams heightened the value of architecture, ancient or modern, that proclaimed the presence of God. We had to come to terms with inflation by reducing the proposed dual-purpose buildings from three to two. But we agreed to build the best we could for the town centre.

Bringing Jim Thompson to the diocese was one of the most valuable achievements of my time at Woolwich. I had come to know him in East London. When Grace was recovering in the London Hospital from the surgery for cancer, she told me about a curate from East Ham she had seen on the television: 'He was saying all the things we believe in.' We invited Jim and Sally to the Mayflower for an evening, and spent several days off together. On at least one of them Jim rejoiced in a Test match innings by his cricketing hero Tom Graveney. When we went to an evening meal with Jim and Sally in their rambling flat over the church hall in East Ham, I found myself locked in the toilet! I could neither undo the lock nor make myself heard round the different corridors of the hall. It was only when a search party came to find me that I was released. When he was appointed to the staff of Cuddesdon Theological College, I said, 'We'll get you back to the city one of these days!'

That cocky remark was made at a time when there was no likelihood of my ever having the authority to make it come about. When the need for a first team leader at Thamesmead came round, I remembered my boast. The post was advertised and I encouraged Jim to put his hat in the ring. The salary and the housing were provided for the Anglican team rector, but we agreed that an ecumenical panel should make the team leader appointment. I realised the sensitivity of my position in the chair if we were to offer the post to someone that I knew personally. That sensitivity was heightened when the appointing group began to discuss the three candidates we had interviewed. Before we had started to state the pluses and minuses we saw in each, a Free Church colleague pitched in, 'Well, I don't want Jim Thompson. I'm sure of that.' I suppressed a sigh and thought, 'We're in for a long afternoon' – for he seemed much the strongest candidate. The panel agreed to set out unhurriedly the strengths and weaknesses we perceived in each. Gradually it became clear that all the others supported Jim, young as he was at thirty-three. Then the objector said, 'Of course he's the best candidate for the job. I was just angry that, because of his public school background, he knew how to express himself so much better than the others.'

Good foundations were laid for a living church in Thamesmead as the plan on paper began to turn into real people. The ecumenical basis made for unfamiliar questions: new Christians could not see the point of being asked to become members of our different churches. Yet they were part of a mobile society. If they moved, they would be likely to live in an area where different denominations still had their particular disciplines. I found myself insisting that new Christians were brought into membership of existing churches, though they could properly have joint membership. Seeing this from the point of view of a bishop led me to believe that the cause of unity would not be helped by setting up, in effect, a new denomination.

Learning about 'bishoping'

There was much for me to learn about 'bishoping', and, at forty years of age, I took seriously the need to retrain. I went on a course for church leaders at St George's House, Windsor. Some of us were discussing what features we saw in those we regarded as good church leaders. We remembered bishops who knew the families of their clergy well. Then we asked ourselves whether, valuable as it was, it should be a bishop's priority. I felt that it was equally important for bishops to make it possible for clergy to think through their *work* and their own performance with them or with another appropriate person.

'Retraining' started with assessing my own strengths and weaknesses. A strength was the ability to trust those I appointed to get on with their task, without interfering. But a weakness was a failure to offer appropriate support, apart from coming to the rescue at crisis moments. The unhappiness of a lay leader at the Mayflower came to mind. She ran our children's church. Believing she knew more about her task than I did, I left her to it. She expressed her pain by saying, 'I didn't know what was expected of me.' This had gone through me like a knife, as a fair and sharp criticism of my leadership. But how to offer the right kind of support?

In spite of his distaste for structures, Mervyn Stockwood had accepted the offer of some money from Neil Wates,[6] then Managing Director of Wates the major building firm, to invite the Industrial Society to take a look at the way the diocese was run. The consultant they appointed was Eddie Smith, who was amused that, as a Quaker, he was being asked to advise an Anglican diocese on its organisation. The most specific recommendation that was implemented as a result of the study was to appoint full-time borough deans in each of the boroughs in South London. Eddie Smith wanted to look at the task of a bishop. It suited me well to have some sessions with Eddie. I asked how many people one person could properly supervise. He told me that in industry the answer would be eight. That figure influenced all my subsequent approaches to bishoping. It was clear that no one person could provide practical oversight to two or three hundred clergy. What mattered was not simply whether the bishop himself offered support, but whether effective support was given. With Mervyn's agreement, I began to offer a work review with the area deans of my area, and encouraged them to do the same with the clergy of their deaneries. I wasn't surprised that Mervyn was unwilling to offer such a structured review to me. Instead, he agreed that we should go for a walk to one of his favourite places on the South or North Downs instead, and talk about my work as we walked.

In the Bishop's Council, I put forward the idea of 'joint work consultation' for the clergy. Hugh Montefiore, by then Bishop of Kingston,[7] said, 'That would change the whole ethos of the Church of England. Don't get me wrong. I think it would be a good idea. But it would be an enormous change for clergy with their freehold, answerable only to God, to be expected to be accountable in this way.' That traditional independence of the clergy could of course be robust. It could also lead to despair, as clergy set themselves impossible goals and then whipped themselves for failing to achieve them. Setting achievable goals and then reviewing them each year became the heart of 'joint work consultation' that we eventually set up in Liverpool. It takes away the isolation that clergy have often felt. It turned out to be more of a 'loosing' than a 'binding' of burdens. Predictably, those who most needed support like that were often the most resistant.

Hugh Montefiore and Eliza were good friends to Grace and me. Over the years we admired the patience and commitment he showed when Eliza suffered from Alzheimer's. Hugh was a lively, thought-provoking colleague. In the 'three-bishops' days' we had in Southwark, he was often the one who made us stop and think, with decisively Christian insights about our work. Mervyn wrote about his coming to Southwark:

> I marvelled at Hugh's capacity for work. First and foremost he was a pastoral bishop. He knew his clergy and their parishes, and he understood the problems of both. At first some thought he would be too much of an intellectual for the people in the pew and for confirmands. But that was not the case. He had the ability to move from one wavelength to another.

This was what Bishop Colin Buchanan, his suffragan bishop when Hugh became Bishop of Birmingham, described as his 'roaming, restless, creative mind'. This could never have been confined to church matters alone. While we were in Southwark, he chaired an Independent Transport Commission, and wrote the report himself, published as a paperback book. I asked him when he had found the time to write it. 'In the middle of the night!' was the answer. While he was at Birmingham, he was made Chairman of the General Synod Board for Social Responsibility – a task that fell to me some years later. The Board secretary at the time, John Gladwin,[8] wrote of Hugh: 'It is the speed with which he grasps issues, reads documents and produces drafts, which is so notable. Hugh has been there and back before most have even begun.'

One of my tasks was to be chairman of the Diocesan Pastoral Committee, which had the responsibility of pastoral reorganisation. In the 1970s, Southwark Diocese faced substantial reductions in clergy numbers. There were legal thickets that had to be penetrated in order to bring about change. There was much pain every time we had to consider joining parishes and closing a church that had emotional family ties for many. Some were prepared to fight against every scheme we brought forward, believing that Christian witness was removed whenever a church building was closed. After one diocesan election I discovered that three people had been elected to the committee on the direct ticket that they would oppose all pastoral reorganisation. As we worked together, looking at the needs of the whole diocese, I was thankful that they too began to enter into the issues we faced. It was a valuable moment in our life together, when the whole committee spent a weekend in an inner-city area we were considering. We walked the streets and listened to local church members. Many of us came to see what it would mean for church people if we ducked away from the hard decisions. In his early years at Woolwich, Bishop John Robinson talked about 'mountains of masonry' that were tying down the energies of the few worshippers who maintained the life of the parish. I saw the point about buildings. If a tiny group used all their time in keeping the show going – with larger buildings and all the organisations that justified keeping them – they would have no time left to play a part in the wider community and witness to their faith.

In a parish visit in Greenwich there was a meeting in a mission hall on an estate to discuss the future of the church's ministry there. An elderly woman stood up to speak: 'Bishop, I have come as a visual aid of what you mustn't do.' Those who lived in the large houses in Blackheath Park had built this mission hall for the servants to go to. She had been recruited, because 'workers' were wanted. She saw clearly that, if there was to be a local church established, its leadership needed to come from the estate itself. It was perhaps significant that the previous evening in the question-and-answer session in the parish church the first question had been, 'Do you find that parishes are short of workers?' I tentatively suggested that the bold way forward might be to sell the church and the vicarage, which were now awkwardly placed, and share with the United Reformed Church and the Methodists in their modern church nearby. Then we might invite them to join us in building a new dual-purpose church on the estate. There was a moment's silence. Then the church-warden said, 'Your predecessor came here and suggested that ten years ago.' Change that involves the closure or demolition of a church building is painful. While the regular members of a church face realities of maintaining unsuitable buildings, often the opposition comes from those who do not belong now, but whose parents were married or buried from the church.

There were genuine conservation issues to be considered; fine architecture offers features that a community should not lightly lose. I was determined that the needs of the local church should come at the top of the list of considerations. Especially in inner-city parishes, congregations were likely to be small. They needed sustainable buildings that would equip them for worship and for serving the community. When he handed over to me, Bishop John Robinson said he did not think there would be any visible church in the inner-city in ten years' time! I made a mental note to do everything in my power to prove him wrong. I found that Christians threatened with the closure of their parish church could be as aggressive as community action groups – or MCC members! Plans that the diocese put forward were treated with acute suspicion. From the community work theories of participation, I learned that it was important to make clear what was on offer. The difference needed to be plain between providing good information, offering consultation, participation or shared decision-making. Frustration and anger were stoked up if people were led to believe that they were actually being asked to share in the decision-making, only to discover that this was never intended. The reality was often that in the end someone else had to make the decision.

Hugh Montefiore replaced Bill Gilpin, who had been Bishop of Kingston for seventeen years. Gilpin belonged to a 'no-fuss' regime that was out of tune with Mervyn's flamboyance. Communications between the two were nil. When he was about to retire, for the first time he accepted an invitation to lunch at Bishop's House. Across the table, Mervyn said, 'There's David over there, starting out on being a bishop. What advice would you give him?' Without a moment's hesitation Gilpin said, 'When I first became Bishop of Kingston, I thought that I must give up all my other commitments in order to be completely free for the parishes. It was a great mistake. You should keep other interests going.'

Community interests

I brought many community interests with me from my years in East London. Some chimed in with highly respectable occasions in community life, where a bishop's presence is welcomed. At my first meeting in Woolwich Town Hall, when I had been introduced as David Sheppard, the Mayor intervened to say, 'We always like to call him Dick!' I became used to this confusion with Dick Sheppard, famous for his broadcasting and the work of the Crypt at St Martin-in-the-Fields during the First World War and in the 1920s. Matching the Mayor's mix-up was that of an elderly woman, during my visit to a retirement home. I asked her where she used to live. 'Walworth,' she told me. I told her our home was in Peckham, not far from Walworth. 'Peckham?' she said. 'That must be a long way to St Martin-in-the-Fields.'

I had the hopes for the London of the future explained to me by the planners. That included going round the new and vast Aylesbury Estate with the architect, just before the first tenants moved in. He had thought deeply about the quality of homes he was designing on the Aylesbury Estate, reproducing terraced streets on each deck. In the event a major criticism of Aylesbury was to be that it offered escape routes to villains in too many directions. In thirty years time, it would be paraded as an example of our worst problems. Tony Blair chose it as the site for his first policy speech about plans to tackle urban deprivation, weeks after becoming Prime Minister. Most of all it was the inhuman scale that defeated all the careful planning of the Aylesbury.

We had a party at home soon after this visit. A local councillor came, who had a small business nearby on the Old Kent Road. The conversation turned to housing. He said he was a member of the Southwark Borough Housing Committee, and went on, 'We're not building anything higher than five storeys now.' I asked if it was the Greater London Council that was building the Aylesbury. No, it was Southwark. 'But', I said, 'I've just been all over it. It's eleven storeys high and a third of a mile long.' He looked bemused for a moment. Then he made a gesture of impatience, 'Those architects!' he said. Perhaps the explanation was that Aylesbury comprised not flats but maisonettes, each built on two or three floors. The architect must have told his committee that he was building five units on top of each other. Cardboard models, with puffs of cotton wool showing the trees that would be planted, could easily fool the inexperienced observer. They did not tell the story of the *scale* that might produce an inhuman environment.

The results of good planning appeared in another Walworth parish – St Peter's. After the service, I met a wide circle of people over a drink in the crypt. Everyone there seemed to have lived in this inner-city area all their life, and intended to stay there. Local people took their place naturally as the leaders of parish activities. I asked the vicar, Harvey Hinds, how he accounted for this unusual inner-city story. He said, 'It's something good the Ecclesiastical Commissioners did under the influence of Octavia Hill around the turn of the century. She said that it was as important how you managed a housing estate as how you built it.' She insisted that children born to couples on the estate should be offered housing there. When in turn their children arrived, larger housing must be made available. When they grew old and were on their own, smaller properties should be there for them. The estate was still there, managed according to her principles, and I picked up immediately the effect of her vision sixty years later. Hinds persuaded Evelyn Denington,[9] Chairman of the GLC Housing Committee to meet us, to discuss the continuing relevance of these principles. As I write, there is controversy about a proposal by the Church Commissioners to let these properties at high market rents now that the district has become more fashionable.

It was the length of waiting lists that dominated the thoughts of councillors in London boroughs like Newham and Southwark. I asked a housing director why they could not demolish and redevelop 500 dwellings at a time rather than 1,000. He said that only a rolling programme on that scale could both catch up and prove economic. Years later, as Bishop of Liverpool, I saw West Bank, part of Widnes, being successfully redeveloped by the new Borough of Halton. Fifty houses were being cleared at a time, to be replaced by building fifty. Everyone who wanted to stay in the district could return and was invited to choose which house they wanted. I asked how this could be economic and was told that they had no evidence that it was costing any more than redeveloping 500 at a time. I told the story to the Institute of British Architects who were holding their conference in Liverpool that year. Whole swathes of cities with their established communities had been demolished in the name of that faulty 'wisdom'.

Other involvements were not regarded as respectable places for a bishop to be. One example of a 'grass-roots' body was the 'Southwark Self-Help Housing Group' that I helped to form. Hundreds of properties were standing empty in Southwark, while thousands were homeless. Illegal 'squatting' was causing delays, because the council could not obtain possession when they were ready to redevelop. Our group was set up in order to make temporary use of those properties on a legal basis.

Housing the homeless was not always popular. One Southwark alderman greeted me at a reception for a new vicar, with the words, 'I hear you're in favour of the homeless.' It was stated as an accusation. A current part of the background to that remark was the story I heard repeated in East as well as South London; this alleged that other London boroughs paid homeless people their fare to go to those boroughs that made provision. There was a much older background too in the old concept of the 'parish of settlement'. The Poor Law made it possible for some people to move from their rural homes to the cities by giving some assurance that their parish of settlement would support them in times of hardship.[10] These settlement laws were also intended to protect provision for the poor of the locality against 'immigrants' from other districts. When the alderman attacked my soft-heartedness, generations of hostility to the 'feckless poor' lay beneath his resentment. They were thought to have made themselves homeless, and to be adding to the burdens on hard-pressed boroughs like Southwark.

A new style of voluntary movement had been emerging in the 1960s. Both supporting and campaigning bodies came into being nationally – Help the Aged, Child Poverty Action Group, Shelter, Campaign for Homosexual Equality, Gingerbread. The current talk of 'participation' encouraged local groups to emerge. Grace joined in an action group in our own road. It was dedicated to restoring a terrace of Victorian houses and keeping them for the use of local people – and was successful.

Community groups increasingly came into being in response to particular issues. Sometimes those that talked about community action became locked into the particular conflict issue. When that matter was resolved, or the action failed to change anything, the group quite often disintegrated. It was easier to bring a group into action to oppose a proposal than to bring new approaches into being. Protests were successful, for instance, in stopping the London Motorway Box from being built. That protected particular neighbourhoods, where it was possible to mobilise indignation. In the long term, it probably lost South East London many jobs, because transport systems could not carry the traffic that firms needed.

There was plenty of indignation around at a conference of community activists held in Manchester. I was asked to take the chair jointly with Geoff Shaw, a Church of Scotland minister who was now Leader of Strathclyde Council. It soon became clear why they had asked two church ministers. There were so many crosscurrents running between other groups that were present. The conference started with protests against the agenda and the organisation. 'A bishop in the chair for God's sake!' After a quarter of an hour or so, I said that in five minutes I would put to the meeting the question whether they wished to move to the first item on the agenda. That was clearly carried, and progress was made. The nearest to an Establishment figure to appear, though he would not have accepted the label, was Tony Benn. When he arrived he told us he was going to show slides for his presentation. That would mean putting the lights out. He had not been present to see what was going on in the hall. Geoff Shaw and I argued that this would lose him any semblance of the attention of the meeting. Tony was not to be persuaded. He kept going doggedly with his strong voice and his slides, showing the injustice of some multinational companies having larger annual turnovers than the GDP of many nations. Anarchy reigned in the darkness around him among much of the audience.

There were painful learning moments about community work. It hurt to hear one black community leader 'bad-mouthing' another black leader that I mentioned. He responded sharply to my protest that good people, trying to achieve similar goals, should run each other down. He said, 'It's all very well for you, coming from your smart public schools. For us it's different. When scarce resources are thrown to us, we're like dogs fighting for a share.'

Many self-help groups came into being from within minority communities. But supporting minority causes presented dilemmas. One vicar was a member of a tenants' association on a large housing estate. He told me he found it hard to know whether he should speak up for the gypsies, whom the majority of tenants felt strongly should be moved out. He knew he did not have the same pressures on him. He had only lived there for a few years. In another 'twilight' area a vicar supported a squatters' group who were using houses that were standing empty. The head teacher of a school there said he had never known his parents, black and white, so united over an issue as their hostility to the squatters.

They feared they might be 'jumping the queue' for housing. The view of the majority is not always right, but I learned that their sense that they too may be deprived needs to be openly faced – especially if affirmative action rightly gives fresh resources to a minority group. Then there are times when the just action must be defended against the anger of the majority.

The requests for public comment come without warning. If a Christian voice is to be heard, routines may have to be dropped. There must be briefing and action – or suggesting someone else. People inside the Church and outside were marvellously willing to make time to offer advice, and I learned to ask for it. Arriving home in the middle of one particularly crowded morning, I was told by my secretary that the *Sunday People* had rung. They were doing a four-page spread on poverty in Britain. What would I want to say? There was a moment of feeling helpless. Then my sermons about the gifts of the whole body of Christ came back to mind. I asked my secretary to ring one of three people in the diocese, all of whom were closely engaged with some of the poorest in London. Would they set out three points that they would like me to make? When I returned from the different commitments of the day, three points from the person at the top of my list were carefully set out on my desk. I was able to digest them, make points in my own way, and ring the paper. It seemed to me a good example of the role of a bishop making the link that made public the expert knowledge of someone the media had never heard of.

Taking on wider interests such as these brought a fear lest some might claim that I neglected the 'in-church' part of my calling. So the temptation was to try to outwork the most diligent of clergy. But this was not the way through. A bishop is necessarily part of the body, and the secret was to learn how to use my gifts in partnership with other members of the body. My picture of the body of Christ grew and grew from that time on; the calling was to be increasingly a team player, with colleagues and allies – the diocesan team, ecumenical partners, expert advisers, lay people at work and in the community, people of goodwill. Collaborative ministry made it possible to reach out beyond the boundaries of the Church in ways that working as an individual could never have done. Thank God, there were willing allies to be found, not least in the black community, as I was to discover.

Black and White Encounters

The experience of black people

A striking difference on crossing the river to South London was to meet a large black population, in contrast to Canning Town which was still mainly white at that time. Asylum Road, by the time we moved to Peckham, was fifty-fifty black and white. Neighbours were quick to blame black people for trouble. We learned that our popular 'beat bobby' had been beaten up and was in hospital. The story went round that he had been beaten up by black youths. The truth emerged that he had gone to arrest a man on the landing of a block of flats, and a group of white women had cornered him and attacked him, including putting a stiletto heel into his face. When gypsies encamped on some derelict land, the blame frequently switched to them. A neighbour said, 'That will give black people a rest.'

One of my earliest parish visits was to St Catherine's-on-the-Hill in New Cross. The vicar set up a whole evening's visit to 'The Moonshot Club', a black youth club. It was a shaking and converting experience. I walked into the clubroom, and then was compelled to stand motionless for two hours. Throughout that time a gradually changing circle of some twenty-five youngsters surrounded me. No smile was to be seen all evening. 'Would you like to tell us why you have come here?' I felt badly out of my depth, trying to find some ground on which I could stand, yet desperate to enter into the stories they wanted to tell me. To start with, I made the mistake of saying that I understood about disadvantage, having spent twelve years in Canning Town. They wouldn't have that. They insisted that I listened to their experience. They wanted me to understand that, though they shared deprivations with white working-class people, being black doubly disadvantaged them. Each fresh group that joined us repeated the anger and frustration.

Going back to the vicarage that night I was unsure whether any good had come from going there. However, next day a message came back that they had been glad that I had spent the evening there, and would welcome me again. The youth leader was a West Indian, Sybil Phoenix,[1] who became a friend throughout my South London years. Her office in the club provided a safe place for members to go. She offered much more than a shoulder to cry on. There was wisdom and practical advice. Sometimes she found the outpourings of anger she had to receive hardly bearable. Feeling the bad experiences of the young people so deeply, she felt her Christian faith under attack. She was a Methodist, clinging on to her faith by her fingertips.

I found many black people in parish churches. In one I received a series of conflicting reactions. Half the choirboys were black. There were a few mums, but no black men, and no black presence on the PCC. When I raised the question in the PCC, the response was like throwing a calming blanket of reason over this inflammatory issue. They explained that you needed to be known as a regular before you could expect to be elected. Those who might have been chosen had come very occasionally, or had stopped coming – just when they might have been elected. I started to wonder if there were many black people living in the district after all. However, the following morning at an infants school, I was told that 56 per cent of the children were black. A major reason why black Christians told me they withdrew from the 'mainline churches', to which most of them had belonged in the Caribbean, was that they found themselves just tolerated – so long as they weren't in the majority or in power. There were few exceptions to the pattern of church life in 1970 that decisions belonged to white people. Sometimes this exclusion led to a deeper rejection of what was perceived to be Christianity itself.

This kind of experience led some to reject the whole Christian faith. I drove three black workers home following a community meeting. One of them referred contemptuously to 'the Christian ethic'. After the others were delivered, and we were on our own, I asked what he meant by 'the Christian ethic'. 'All that about having a black heart,' he said. 'You know, you have a black heart, and must wash it in Jesus' blood so that it becomes a white heart.' In the car it seemed overwhelming to me that we must review our language, and be willing to put away fondly held pictures if they were so damaging to brothers and sisters whom we had never listened to before.

I met other black Christians who were in charge of their own church life – in independent black-led churches. For example, during a parish visit in Peckham, I joined in worship with a church which rented the parish hall. The singing was enthusiastic, repeating each chorus about nine times. Everyone grasped the words quite quickly. The themes of the choruses were either the love of Jesus or that God will bring me safe to heaven. The black-led church in Peckham was firmly in the pietist tradition that regarded politics as part of the sinful world to be avoided by Gospel-loving Christians. That faith in God's salvation in another world brought comfort and detachment from the affairs of this world, as it has for many people excluded from a proper share in good opportunities. Other black people in Britain were learning to react in the aggressive manner I had seen among American blacks, like Preston Williams at the People and Cities conference in Coventry. Years later, I wanted to preach about Martin Luther King, and asked some friends in the Liverpool black community to do some research among black young people on their attitude to him. The majority said that they regarded Malcolm X, who preached revolution, as the more significant figure.

In the year following my move to Liverpool, I went back to South London for just two meetings. One was on a Saturday morning, in Brixton, with twenty-five black pastors. They divided sharply over this issue of engaging with social and political matters. I argued from the Bible that we were called both to preach Christ as saviour, and to join in working for his kingdom of just and right relationships. Only then would disadvantaged people feel we had anything to say to them. One of their number addressed his brothers: 'You all know that you are losing the young people, who do not feel that the Church has anything to say to the realities that they are facing every day. Many of them are being kicked out by their own parents, because they don't understand what they are facing at all.'

The other occasion was, at Sybil Phoenix's request, to be one of a small number of church leaders from the different churches that a group of young black men asked to meet. It was a bruising twenty-four hours. They insisted that we should understand their bitter feelings about being shut out from good opportunities in education, employment, training for jobs, housing and the media. The meeting was firmly chaired by Trevor. He looked at us, and said to the young man, 'You know these powerful people. Why don't you tell them how it is for us?' Jim Thompson, then Bishop of Stepney, found it so painful that he could take no more, and went home; he then found fresh strength to come back next morning. Trevor said, 'It seems to some of us, looking up from below, that there is a network of people who make decisions. We should like to be part of that network.'

A later visit to The Moonshot Club was at their express wish that I see the members turning out at the end of the evening. I walked up to New Cross Road among a crowd of them, and stood at the bus stop with them. There was much cheerful banter, a bit noisy, but harmless. Suddenly, across the road, a police officer appeared, chasing and grabbing a member. Parties of police emerged from vehicles that had been parked in several side streets. They seemed to be everywhere around us. They said that there had been some bag-snatching and that one young man had been arrested.

I asked to see the Commander, who came to our home for a long talk. He said that there had been complaints from neighbours about the noise and disturbance when the club turned out. He owed it to residents to set their minds at rest. He seemed unable to hear what I had to say about such a heavy over-reaction to a problem, and the influence that would have on young British blacks towards police officers. In his eyes they were immigrants still, who needed to be taught to fit in with the ways of the host community. I was reminded of the incident when the report into the South East London murder of Stephen Lawrence was published in 1999, with its comments on attitudes within the Metropolitan Police.

Mervyn Stockwood invited some senior police officers to meet with a number of clergy working in inner-city areas. At the beginning there was some knockabout joking between the Brixton commander and Bob Nind, who was Vicar of St Matthew's Church in the centre of Brixton. As the general conversation developed, the police officer said, 'What I can't stand is people who know how difficult policing is and criticise us in public.' Bob had listened to this with his head held in his hands. Now he looked up and said, 'Hast thou found me O my enemy!' Bob went on, 'I think we have to understand that we come from different sides of the fence, and trust each other that we speak with integrity.' There were police officers, like Peter Marshall, Commander of the Community Relations Unit, who did understand, and believed in the priority of listening and building respect and trust with minority communities. There was an occasion when Mervyn believed that unwarranted criticisms of the police had been made in some work that I had authorised. He was angry and wanted it disowned. Eventually, at my request, Peter Marshall made it plain to Mervyn that he understood what was being said, and that there was no issue that the police wanted to take up.

During these Woolwich years I was Chairman of the Martin Luther King Foundation. We supported International Personnel, a training project for black young people, in Balham. Addressing employers and trade union leaders, I argued for two things: positive discrimination and keeping accurate statistics.[2] Good practice was the best argument to persuade other employers. In one firm it was established that the managing director had to be shown the application forms of all black people applying for jobs, whether they had been appointed or not. The personnel officers and recruiting staff soon recognised that the firm meant business, and was not just repeating that it practised no colour prejudice. We always made it clear that we were not arguing that people should be given a job or promotion simply because they were black, if they were not competent to do the work. But affirmative action was a necessary step on the way.

There was hostility among some employers and teachers to any whiff of 'positive discrimination'. We learned soon afterwards to talk of 'affirmative action', undoubtedly a better concept; but I never felt that those of us who knew how deep the disadvantages were should have been too coy about either phrase. 'Keep accurate statistics' could receive an equally frosty reception. A head teacher, when I asked how many black children she had in the school, replied, 'I don't know. I only have children.' No doubt she thought this was a step towards equal treatment and equal opportunities. But she did not give weight to the scale of disadvantage black children knew. There was no 'level playing field'. During my Woolwich years, a black researcher told me that she had visited one of the largest works in the London area. The managing director told her that there was no prejudice there, and that many black people were working on the factory floor. She asked, 'How do you get to do your job?' 'Probably you would join as an apprentice.' 'All right. Tell me about the apprentices you took on this year.' 'There were eighty apprentices.' 'How many were girls?' 'Four.' 'How many were black?' 'None.' Twenty-five years later, poor race relations in that firm became a public issue.

Wilfred Wood

I owe much of my own thinking about good race relations to Wilfred Wood, a black priest.[3] We had met through the Martin Luther King Foundation. When I moved to South London, I asked him to take me and educate me. That led to a day with him in the parish where he was then serving in Shepherd's Bush, West London. He took me into a number of homes of black people, and we spent the evening with a group of black community workers. I had brought a list of questions with me, but hardly reached any of them. The group insisted, before we could discuss anything else, that I listened for a full hour to what they wanted to say about relations with the police. At the end of a catalogue of resentments at insensitive policing and worse, Wilfred's white vicar made his one interjection. He said:

> It's like you want to talk to a man who lives in a great house about the use of his land. He sends the butler to get rid of you. And you're angry with the butler. You want to get to the people who make decisions in our country, but you never reach them. Like the butler in the story, the police are the part of the Establishment that you do meet, and you are

angry with them, as they prevent you from finding your way to the places where power lies.

I became keen to bring Wilfred to Southwark Diocese. Mervyn Stockwood had never met him, and I asked Wilfred to write something about himself that I could show him. He wrote of his training at Codrington College in Barbados, part of the Community of the Resurrection. Bishop Frank Weston of Zanzibar was quoted as a role model. Weston insisted both on the centrality of Christ in preaching and worship, and God's concern for justice for the poor. He told the Anglo-Catholic Congress in 1923 that they could not claim to worship Jesus in the tabernacle if they did not pity Jesus in the slum. 'If you say that the Anglo-Catholic has a right to hold his peace while his fellow-citizens are living in hovels below the level of the streets, then I say to you, that you do not yet know the Lord Jesus.'[4]

I described to Wilfred two possible parishes where he might serve as vicar, without disclosing their names. One was in the inner city with a large black population; the other was St Laurence, Catford, more suburban, where more successful black people were moving, and with Lewisham Town Hall in the parish. Wilfred had no hesitation; if he were asked his preference for himself, he would choose St Laurence, Catford. That led to eight effective years there. He said that we must not simply place black clergy in 'the ghetto'. They must be seen to take proper leadership roles in the whole Church of England.

Problems to do with race relations were not confined to the inner city. Bournemouth – and Southport, as I later discovered – were inclined to say they had no race relations problem. Yet I had already discovered through my own public involvement in the cricketing controversy over South Africa that the hate mail was more likely to come from Canterbury, Winchester, Chester or Exeter than areas where real black people were to be met and known. It seemed that this was driven by a fear of the unknown. Something called 'the British way of life' was felt to be under threat.

People in these 'white highlands' praised individual black people who fitted into the British way of doing things. They did not know or understand how large were the barriers that excluded minority groups in inner-city areas from middle-class life. When, some years later in Liverpool, I was writing my book *Bias to the Poor*, I asked Wilfred for his comments on what I had written about race relations. At one point I had written, 'It needs to be recognised that race relations are between communities. It is only individuals with exceptionally strong self-confidence who can cross these gaps by themselves.' Wilfred wrote a comment at this point: 'No individual can cross these gaps by himself.' He had underlined 'no individual' twice.

Enoch Powell

These fears that the 'British way of life' was being eroded seeped into the Church and its people. A senior clergyman in Southwark Diocese told me he thought that Enoch Powell was raising some important issues for the country. Wilfred Wood made me realise how Powell's speeches were heard within the black community. His young daughter, listening to one of these on the television, asked, 'Daddy, why do these people hate us?' Wilfred refused to soften his resistance to all that Powell said on race relations. He went on making us think about these uncomfortable questions. He said that among British Christians the 'nation thing' was always stronger than the 'Christian thing'. I believe that, when he weighed up a choice between his own career in the church and his solidarity with black people, Wilfred firmly opted for the latter. He was honoured in 2000 by being awarded the knighthood of St Andrew, the Order of Barbados.

I felt that Powell's speeches, whipping up fear and resentment against 'an alien tide', were calculated to make crude pub talk respectable. He issued apocalyptic warnings that 'whole areas, towns and parts of towns across England would be occupied by different sections of the immigrant and immigrant-descended population'. Less measured was the picture he drew of 'grinning piccaninnies'. At the end of 1969 I took part in a television programme about the 1960s. I was invited to take part as the newest bishop in the Church of England, alongside Archbishop Michael Ramsey. When we met to plan what we should discuss, I asked the Archbishop whether we should talk about Enoch Powell. 'Don't mention him', came the passionate response.

When Wilfred Wood went to be vicar of St Laurence's, Catford, one church member wrote to Mervyn Stockwood, saying that she could not receive holy communion from the hands of a black priest. She received a firm response, making clear that belief in one, holy, catholic Church crossed all race and class divides. One lay person in another part of the diocese asked who this Wilfred Wood person was who was always going on about race. He was told that it wasn't very surprising seeing that Wilfred was black himself, and exclaimed, 'What? You mean he's actually black?'

It was Ronnie Bowlby, Mervyn's successor as Bishop of Southwark, who appointed Wilfred as Bishop of Croydon, that area now having been brought into Southwark Diocese. He also took over the East Surrey part of what had been the Bishop of Woolwich's area. As the first black bishop in the Church of England, he carried high expectations. Other black people have told me about 'the stiletto effect'. Just as a stiletto heel bears the whole weight of the body on one small point, so black individuals who pioneer leading posts bear the weight of enormous – not to say impossible – expectations. Wilfred Wood has won many hearts and minds in the Croydon area, reflecting Bishop Frank Weston's double thrust of both the centrality of Christian preaching and worship and also God's concern for justice for poor people. At the same time he has stayed in close touch and sympathy with black people in the inner city. He wrote to me that 'the outstanding need in the black community was to adjust to a strong self-image. The outstanding need in the white community was to adjust to a proud black man.'[5]

The 1976 British Council of Churches published *The New Black Presence in Britain*. Its author John Davies said that the sentence in the report that brought the greatest hostility said: 'The basic issue is not a problem caused by black people: the basic issue concerns the nature of British society as a whole, and the features of that society which have been there long before the recent phase of black immigration: the black communities are holding a mirror to British society.'[6] Mark Bonham-Carter, Chairman of the Race Relations Board, said that black people were 'the barium meal' in British society. Barium meal simply introduces colour that reveals what is already going on in the body. In the same way black people's presence has not introduced problems that were not there before, but by the colour of their skin has revealed what is going on in the body of the nation.

Wilfred Wood said that 'black British' young people were surely the most alienated generation ever. The parents had pictures of the Caribbean islands on the wall, and many lived with the dream of returning one day. The children were British-born. The world of their parents meant nothing to them. In turn, their parents found it impossible to enter the children's world of school and the leisure interests they shared with other British teenagers. Wilfred was sceptical about how much the Church was prepared to give serious priority to black people in its life. But he gave us all his support when we tried to make some progress in the diocese. He said the first priority should be to try to reclaim those young people who were not too far away from the Christian roots they had been given as children.

Southwark Diocese and race relations

I chaired a small working party from the Bishop's Council that was charged with showing the full costs of all the ministries in the diocese. The background was that Anglicans were inclined to think that the only significant ministry was in their own parish. Resentment was often expressed at the share of the diocesan budget that went on chaplaincies in industry and higher education. Usually, in synod debates, what came from central sources towards the cost of paying the parish clergy was left out of any account of diocesan spending. That meant that posts such as the chaplaincies appeared to consume a disproportionate share. We tried to show the whole picture, including the cost of parish ministries. That revealed that the posts reaching out beyond the life of the parishes claimed only a modest part of the total cost.

In the diocesan synod in May 1974 we proposed eight new posts, mostly chaplains in polytechnics and further education colleges, two of them in the field of race relations. I could hardly believe it when the synod voted to create these posts, with the clear understanding that the money for them would come from reducing the number of posts in the parishes. I felt it was remarkable that church people accepted this costly vision. Many years later I was to see the fruit of this decision to create a diocesan team concerned with race relations. The Committee for Black Anglican Concerns,[7] set up following the report *Faith in the City*, invited every diocese in the country to send a delegation to a weekend conference at York University. There was a roll call of each diocese. Our little band of six from Liverpool duly stood up when we were called. (That different story of black people's experience must be told when I reach my Liverpool years.) When Southwark was called, my heart jumped. It seemed that everyone in the hall was getting to their feet. There were many young men and women among them, and I knew that there were many more behind them who had not come to York. It was the fruit of twenty years of patient ministry.

In 2000, the present Bishop of Southwark, Tom Butler, told me of his experience on moving from being Bishop of Leicester to Southwark; he was deeply impressed that many parish churches in South London now had strong black membership. Today, there are Anglican congregations that are 90 per cent black – often more West African than Caribbean. This more positive development has redeemed some of our failures of the 1960s – which had seen racial prejudice grow in Britain, alongside the new freedoms that other groups embraced.

10

Not Only . . . But Also . . .

I lived through the years of the 1960s in Canning Town, busy within our demanding, yet unsophisticated, circle. We enjoyed The Beatles' music. Somehow, Flower Power did not seem to fit with the East End. Increasingly I found myself wrestling with issues of social justice in our own inner-city world. Speaking out about apartheid and cricket brought me new allies and fresh awareness of racial injustices. On the world stage, the hopefulness of the years of John F. and Bobby Kennedy swept me along with it. After the terrible days of the murders of both of them, there was renewed hope in Lyndon Johnson's War on Poverty, soon to be shelved because of the war in Vietnam. I did not hesitate when I was invited to take over the chair of the Martin Luther King Foundation. He had been a heroic figure to me throughout these years, and the struggle for racial justice had become a priority for me.

'Permissiveness'

Those struggles brought new freedoms and questioning of unreasoning authorities. Now, moving to be Bishop of Woolwich took me into the heart of 'South Bank religion', where there had been much questioning of all sorts of authorities. Indeed my predecessor was John Robinson, whose book *Honest to God* had seemed to be pushing the search for freedom beyond some Christian boundaries. I missed the force of the immediate controversy around the book, because we were in Australia when it was published in March 1963. Soon, the Bishop of Woolwich had entered the demonology of evangelical Christians. Reading the book that summer, I felt that he had set up an Aunt Sally of a God 'up there' and 'out there', which orthodox believers were said to hold. Later I was to understand his motives in writing it. In his 1987 biography of John Robinson, Eric James was certain that he would not have written parts of *Honest to God* but for the pressures upon him as a bishop in South London. He was facing 'the all but total alienation of the urban working class from the institutional Church. John was aware that in Southwark he was experiencing *The Secular City* . . . as he had never experienced it before, not even in Bristol, and in complete contrast to the religious "boom" he had come from in Cambridge.'[1]

Robinson explained his motives in the *Sunday Mirror*: 'The traditional imagery of God simply succeeds, I believe, in making him remote for millions of men today. What I want to do is not to deny God in any sense, but to put him back into the middle of life – where Jesus showed us he belongs.'[2] He used Bonhoeffer's phrase that God is 'the Ground of our Being'. Sometimes I felt that John Robinson kept different parts of his thinking and theology in separate compartments, as though he was saying, 'We're doing the Person of Christ today. Yesterday it was the Doctrine of God.' Eric James' sensitive biography reveals a solid Christian faith, for example in the moving chapter about his last day before the cancer killed him. Ruth Robinson wrote:

> We said together the prayer we had used ever since we were first engaged: 'O God, the protector of all that trust in Thee, without whom nothing is strong, nothing is holy: increase and multiply upon us thy mercy; that Thou being our ruler and guide, we may so pass through things temporal, that we finally lose not the things eternal.'[3]

The explosions around *Honest to God* shifted after a few weeks to what it said about personal behaviour. It seemed to fit with The Beatles in their song 'All you need is love'. At the time I said, 'If I were clever enough and good enough, it would be right to say "Love is all you need". Because I'm not clever enough or good enough, there's a need of signposts to show that it is never the loving thing to go down particular paths.'

John Robinson welcomed the openness of the new generation to talk about sex and personal responsibility. This led him famously to give evidence for the defence against the prosecution of *Lady Chatterley's Lover*. He said that Christians do not make jokes about sex for the same reason that they do not make jokes about holy communion – not because it is dirty but because it is sacred. He claimed that by dragging this book through the courts, the prosecution had ensured that it received the maximum publicity. He denied that it was a dirty book. Some of his answers in court led to his being accused of saying that an adulterous relationship was the equal of holy communion.

In 1967, I agreed to give evidence in an opposite direction in the trial of another book, *Last Exit to Brooklyn*. I was much influenced at the time by reading Pamela Hansford Johnson's book *On Iniquity*. She quoted a friend who had been in Germany at the time when Jews were being publicly humiliated in the streets. The first time he saw this happen, he took to his heels and ran. The second time, he told himself that he ought to stay and see what was happening. The third time, he found that something in him was beginning to be attracted by what he was watching. When he became aware of this attraction, he took to his heels for the second time and ran. It was a time when we were being encouraged to rid ourselves of inhibitions. But some inhibitions need to be strengthened, not ditched. I was persuaded that, though censorship should be a weapon sparingly used, there were times when it made for health. In court I said that in *Last Exit to Brooklyn* at regular intervals of twenty pages there were accounts of sexual adventures with explicit sexual details. This seemed to me to play on titillation quite deliberately. The defence counsel pressed me that I did not seem to have been corrupted by reading the book. Therefore, he claimed, my experience was not showing that the book tended to 'deprave and corrupt'. My response was that I had not been left unscathed.

One Christian reaction to 'sixties permissiveness' was to support the Festival of Light. I was invited to speak along with Malcolm Muggeridge and others at its first rally in Trafalgar Square. Making the decision to refuse was another watershed for me. I wanted to fight for the strengthening of family life, but the Festival of Light seemed to identify Christian faith with a moralistic stance that was set over against society. There was a 'not only, but also' here – times when in the tradition of the prophets we would be right to challenge the culture of the day. But there were also moments when we were called to stand alongside puzzled people as they wrestled with new and difficult questions. I had met Malcolm Muggeridge at John Stott's suggestion, and read his autobiography in preparation. I told him that in the book his father was so attractive. Malcolm had rejected what he described as his father's hopefulness pinned in education. The Christianity he had come to defend seemed to me to be degenerating into no more than a code of laws, with pessimism about the world around.

'South Bank religion'

Following John Robinson was not entering such strange territory as some would have supposed. Our first meeting was in Cambridge, when I was a student. He wrote to me, asking me to come to lunch. He said, 'You go in first for England, and my sister goes in first for England. You must meet.' Mary Robinson was a distinguished part of the England women's cricket team. We enjoyed meeting and eating a good lunch together in the Robinson home. I attended John's lectures on the gospels, and was impressed by the parish communion service, which he had introduced at Clare College, of which he was Dean. When he started at Woolwich, and

I was at the Mayflower, he invited me to join a group to help him think through the pastoral task of the Church. I had therefore entered into the thinking that was going on about pastoral reorganisation in South London.

Part of the inheritance he left me was the Bishop's Council for Ministry and Mission, a 'think tank', bringing together those who had a training role. Reading the names of its members was daunting. I felt it would be impossible to keep up with 'all John's bright stars'. The list included Eric James, Peter Selby, John Nicholson, Douglas Rhymes, Peter Challen, Paul Oestreicher, Gwen Rymer, Cecilia Goodenough, Gordon Davies, Derek Blows, Leslie Walters and Frank Fisher. Others joined, like Ivor Smith-Cameron and Patrick Miller. It did not take long for my fears to melt. I learned much from them. At the same time I found that several of these gifted people were vulnerable too, and needed a champion to fight their corner in the diocese.

No one was surprised when I brought together a small group to discuss mission in the inner city. This brought different insights into collision. Cecilia Goodenough said, 'If I hear the words "Pastoral Committee" again, I shall scream.' Eric James retorted, 'Not to care about the Pastoral Committee is a failure of love.' Cecilia liked to describe herself as 'a wilderness person'. She gave me a lasting insight into the interplay in the Old Testament between the wilderness and the vineyard. The wilderness was the place of clear vision. There, God revealed himself vividly, with clear boundaries of right and wrong. In contrast, the vineyard is the regular picture of the settled life of the nation of Israel. When the people stopped wandering, and moved into towns and cities, civilisation took a step forward; ethical decisions about justice in the community became more complex, sometimes having to sort out the lesser of evils. Prophets, like Amos, were wilderness figures, who stumped in from the desert, to challenge the managers in the vineyard. The creative force of what was happening in the Old Testament was the interplay between the two.

There was another 'not only, but also' here. As a bishop it was undeniable that I was a vineyard person. So it became of first importance also to listen to wilderness people. Vineyard people are tempted to defend the status quo in church and in secular life. Religion can be no more than a chaplaincy to the vinegrowers, saying grace at their banquets. Or it can challenge them to listen again to God's clear word spoken in the wilderness. In their contrasting experience, wilderness people are tempted to freewheel, enjoying the luxury of pursuing ideas that are never likely to be implemented.

Cecilia treated everyone on equal terms. Much of her time was spent with families in the poorest estates. There was no condescension. One mother said to her, 'I won't let my boys play out in the yard with the others.' Cecilia came back with a challenge that I would not have dared put: 'Why does your group always think the others are stronger?' I noted that she was not abandoning the boys to have to fight all their own battles. She spoke of the mother's group, who could together offer support, if they stood beside each other. Reflecting on this, I realised that Christians too often think 'the others' are stronger, and lack the confidence to see how much we can bring about change if we stand together. Cecilia loved to say, 'Some of us like to think of ourselves as wilderness people.' She was fearless in challenging those she thought were too comfortable. When she was in her seventies, she said, 'Some of us have promised each other that we will never allow a racist remark to pass unchallenged.' She could be impatient at having to bother with church structures. But she made time for me. When I moved to Liverpool, my mother was still living in Sussex. Each time I came down to spend some days with her, I stopped in Camberwell to have a seminar with Cecilia. A bishop finds that there are few people who will challenge their ways of thinking. Cecilia had never been in awe of any bishop. It was rather the other way round. She kept feeding me with ideas from her searching theology of the Bible as the Word of God for today.

Industrial mission

One of my roles as Bishop of Woolwich was to be the bishop who related to the South London Industrial Mission (SLIM). I learned to think about the world of work from making visits with the SLIM chaplains to the places of work they visited regularly, and from attending their staff meetings. Some of the chaplains were ministers of Free Churches; when I visited with them, they introduced me as part of the one mission of the Church. The senior chaplain to SLIM was Peter Challen. I spent many hours talking with him. He inspired me in my visits with new-found courage to ask searching questions. He saw the role of industrial mission as being 'to hold up the mirror' to those at work to see what they were doing to each other. The presence of industrial mission should 'remind people of some forgotten factors'. Peter was inclined to use tortuous phrases that caused some to give up listening to him. I took him on about using 'jargon'. He said, 'It's not jargon. It's pushing the boundaries of thought!' I never resented time spent with him, and, for example, encouraged Caterham deanery synod to invite Peter Challen to an evening. The follow-up was that a group who lived in Caterham asked him to meet with them across the river, in the business City of London – outside the diocese, but within the context of their daily work.

Reflecting on the work of SLIM, it seemed more likely to win praises from those at management level than from those on the shop floor. Perhaps that merely revealed that fewer people on the shop floor were close to church membership and thinking. But there were places where SLIM's presence had made shop-floor workers aware of God's presence in the workplace and of his call to them. Managers told me that they valued the presence of a chaplain to whom they could open their heart. One said, 'I am conscious of the power I have, and of the powers to which I am subject.' Many felt they were caught between the fires. I was often invited to lunch with the management team; sometimes this would be together with the shop stewards; sometimes it would be a separate meeting. Examples of visits I made that followed this pattern were at Bankside Power Station, GEC/Elliott Automation and Sainsbury's at Charlton.

One of the SLIM chaplains took me back across the river to the *Daily Mirror*, where he was a regular visitor. The management team invited me to have lunch with them. It is easy for conversation on those occasions to probe no deeper than swapping anecdotes about the old padre they knew in the army. This time the chaplain waited for the meal to be served, then said to the managing director, 'The Bishop and I were talking before, and wanted to ask you: what are you in business for?' 'To stay in business,' came the immediate reply. We acknowledged the priority of achieving that, but pressed on with the questions. After a while the managing director looked across the table at a senior colleague: 'Shall we put our current problem to him?' They set out a major dilemma about the agreement they had in place that prepared the way for shedding staff, with their feelings for loyal workers who would suffer if they pressed ahead. I made it clear that it was not my role to produce answers from on high, but was glad to enter into the issues of productivity, humanity and justice that were being raised.

Peter Challen encouraged the idea of a social audit that a number of firms were exploring. Neil Wates, who sadly died in his forties, was determined to bring his Christian faith into his business decisions as Managing Director of Wates, the large building firm. He said they did not market just houses, but a community; therefore it was impossible for them to trade in South Africa, because the apartheid laws forbade what Wates understood by a whole community. He insisted that this was a business decision, made long before the boycotts of South Africa had become widespread.

Cecilia Goodenough was one of those who did effectively reach people on the shop floor. She told me of a lunch-hour meeting she had at Mullins factory in Bermondsey. She said she was trying to persuade them to do some Bible study on Ezekiel's chapter on the shepherds of

Israel who were not caring for the sheep.[4] They weren't taking it too seriously. One said, 'We don't have many sheep in Bermondsey.' Another said, 'I did see a sheep once on holiday.' But an older man, a shop steward in the Electrical Trade Union (ETU) said, 'It was the Annual Meeting of our branch last night. We have 1,000 members, and only three turned up.' Cecilia said she thought something was required of her, so she asked, 'Where were the 997?' 'They were straying on the mountains,' he said, 'and it's our fault for allowing meetings to become so dull.' He had understood that as a shop steward he was one of the shepherds of Israel, responsible for the care of people in his branch, and for 'stopping the fat sheep from butting the lean sheep'.

These were years when there was much talk of 'over-mighty union barons'. I have referred earlier to the series of talks I gave to (largely professional) lay people in Godstone deanery in my last months as Bishop of Woolwich. I said:

> My greatest criticism of powerful unions is their lack of concern for workers in the weakest bargaining position – or those who are unemployed: it needs to be said, when we raise questions of differentials and sectional interests, that we all have sectional interests. What has to be worked for is that each section should be heard, but heard along with others, and accountable to the others.

That made genuine consultation more important, respecting the intelligence of those on the shop floor. One of our clergy said that if people were made to feel like silly kids they would behave like silly kids. Then they would believe they would only be listened to, if they applied the greatest pressure in their power, by withdrawing their labour.

Local ministry

Questions about the ministry of the Church in working-class areas were arising on both sides of the river in London. Trevor Huddleston returned from Tanzania to be Bishop of Stepney. After his years in Africa, he never got over the shock of meeting the standards of affluence so much of Britain had attained. I felt closer to him than to any other bishop at that time. He had already played a significant part in my life by making me think about cricket and apartheid. I recognised in him the 'not only, but also' that had become a guide to me personally. He not only passionately wanted to keep Christ central in preaching and worship, but also equally passionately fought for justice for the poor of the world. 'Passionately' was the word with Trevor. He saw matters through the eyes of those at a disadvantage. We started to spend a day together at intervals, talking and praying together. He told me that the clergy that criticised him most were the Anglo-Catholics. My experience was the same – only the criticism was from evangelicals. Both of us sensed that those who had seen us as members of their 'party' were most aggrieved that we were glad to be serving all parties within our Church.

Trevor at Stepney 'was a tireless visitor to sick clergy, a relentless campaigner in committees whenever he felt the Stepney parishes were overlooked'.[5] Kate, the young daughter of close friends from our East London days, Ted and Audrey Roberts, was knocked down by a car and seriously injured. Trevor visited her in hospital most days when she was critically ill. He maintained the friendship over years, and later officiated at her wedding. Her story matched what Archbishop Desmond Tutu wrote about his illness as a child. When he contracted TB, Trevor drove him to hospital and visited him mostly once a week over the twenty months he was in hospital. Desmond wrote, 'What this said to me, a Township urchin, about caring, about gentleness, about being made to feel you really counted, is more than I can put into words. Maybe I hoped to emulate him one day. His affection helped me to exorcise a likely bitterness against and hatred of whites and made my future ministry more possible.'[6]

Trevor wanted to ordain six men from the Bethnal Green parish, where Ted Roberts was vicar.[7] As Bishops of Stepney and Woolwich, he and I agreed to set up a joint working party to look at the questions raised by the proposal to ordain local working-class men who would stay local. It was a strong group, representing all traditions. Our report, *Local Ministry in Urban and Industrial Areas*, was published in 1972. We said our thesis was that 'There is indigenous leadership with intelligence and ability which cannot be easily measured by academic yardsticks'.[8] We argued that a local ordained ministry was desirable. It needed to emerge from a movement that should be largely lay. Thirteen years later, the *Faith in the City* report was to make substantially the same points. We said the crucial question was not about ordination but about whether we believed that a locally rooted, responsible Christian Church could be established in these areas. We made a judgment between two possible reactions to such ordinations. One would be that some might say, 'If he's the clergyman, I'll leave him to get on with it.' On the other hand, others might say, 'If *he* can be ordained, then perhaps *I* could join the neighbourhood council/take charge of the visiting programme/run the play group/lead a discussion group in my home.'

We made it clear that we did not want dull men to be ordained, who could not handle ideas. But academic achievement and intelligence are not the same thing. Children from working-class homes frequently did not achieve the potential their intelligence called for. There was a revealing clash about social class within the working party. One day Trevor Huddleston exploded: 'I find all this talk of class terribly English. In South Africa, with all the wicked divisions of apartheid, the Church has reached across the much bigger racial divide.' John Rowe, a priest-worker in Stepney retorted: 'They are not bigger divides. When the racial barriers in South Africa have been removed, there will still be the subtle divisions of class in this country.'

Trevor ordained the six men from Bethnal Green, asking me to lead their retreat before the ordination. Ten years later, when the Archbishop of Canterbury's Commission on Urban Priority Areas visited the Stepney area, Eric James and I spent a Saturday morning with them. As we walked away, Eric said, 'That experiment is talked about as a failure. What we have seen this morning includes a lot of pain; but it's been no failure.'

Built as a City

My book *Built as a City*, published in 1974, provides a measure of how much I had been influenced by 'South Bank religion', and how much I continued to draw from evangelical roots. Bruce Reed, Director of the Grubb Institute, wrote me a letter with some penetrating comments about *Built as a City*:

> It comes across as a pastor's note book – for himself and his colleagues – highlighting in an intensely human way the plight of those who live in inner-city areas. But there is insufficient room to get at the fundamental policy issues, from which the truly awkward questions come. My chief criticism is not that you set out to explore these questions and failed to do so, but that the size of the book makes it appear that you did, and consequently it disappoints people like me.

My letter in reply says that the more I worked at the book, the larger the task transparently became: 'It is an interlocking and very confusing set of causes that makes so many people powerless, and feel unable to make any choices for themselves. I would claim that some fundamental policy issues do emerge in the book, but certainly accept the criticism that I haven't got my arms round the barrel.'

In the last section of the book, 'The Gospel for the City', I tried to pull together the best of what I had been learning from radical theology with the great themes of evangelical belief that remained central to me. One of the radical challenges was to say that the movement of God's activity was not always God–Church–World. I wrote that if we rejected that order of activity, we were in danger of replacing it by saying that the movement must always be God–World–Church. The living God would not be tied down to either formula. He might inject new ideas or action first through the existential situation which the world's agenda brought to us; or through the corporate learning experience within the church fellowship; or through new understanding brought through exposition of the Bible.[9] Some Christians said we had to tackle personal and interpersonal problems first. Others exactly reversed this and said it was a waste of time 'tinkering' with personal problems unless we first changed the structures of society. But salvation is *not only* personal *but also* corporate.

It is of the nature of city life that we are all involved together in the bundle of life . . . That is bound to mean politics at a local or a wider level, though not necessarily party politics. Many Christians say that they are apolitical. This probably means that they think politics is a dirty game in which their hands would be bound to get dirty . . . In many Shop Stewards meetings or Board Rooms or Town Hall committee meetings it will be the layman who speaks the prophetic word – or keeps silent. Often he doesn't speak up, because he feels so alone, or because he's never been given the chance to thrash out the issues with other Christians . . . in the context of a brotherhood that is strong enough to cope with disagreements . . . Christians often fear that public disagreements will damage the Church's witness. But there is no one clear Christian viewpoint on thorny public issues. This leaves two alternatives. One is that Christians enter the public arena locally and nationally, and sometimes disagree with each other with the pain that brings. The other is that we keep silent. The voice of Christian prophecy is then silenced . . .

The preaching of the Gospel of the Kingdom calls men into personal relationship with Christ. Its challenge does not stop there. It is to lift up our horizons to what God wants the world to be like, and what He wants us to be as His responsible partners. If a man dares to join Him in His work of overcoming and casting out whatever hinders God's purpose for the world, 'Then he will discover how much there is in himself from which he needs to be cleansed and set free'.[10] Man only realises that he has a great need to be forgiven, when it dawns on him that God is truly good and calls him to use to the full the gifts he has in responsible service. Then he understands what it is to come short of the glory of God . . .

I sat in a juvenile court while Tony aged sixteen stood in front of the magistrates. The way the clerk asked him if he pleaded guilty or not guilty left him confused. 'Yes', he said. Eventually it was agreed that he was guilty of taking and driving away a scooter. They dealt with him in a kindly fashion, and lectured him about the seriousness of the offence in a language he clearly did not understand. But how could they know that his mother who sat there helplessly was ill, and would be dead within a year; that his father had already given up, and would soon be

£150 in arrears with the rent, that nobody bothered to get Tony and his brother up in order to go to work? They knew a bit on paper, as I knew it, but how could they, or I, feel what new actions were really possible for a boy like that?

We see a new kind of authority on the Cross. It is no longer distant, bound by a set of rigid rules, emerging from the world of the powerful. It has become personal in Jesus . . . The one who hung on the Cross is the only Person who can understand what is possible and what is not possible for someone like Tony. He alone can justly judge – and can therefore justly forgive. Like anyone who has been wronged and seeks a personal reconciliation, He bears the pain and the loss Himself.[11]

At about this time I went to preach in the chapel of my Cambridge college, Trinity Hall. In welcoming me at the start of the service, the dean said, 'David Sheppard won't know this, but the following conversation took place over a meal in hall the other evening. One said, 'If it wasn't for the CICCU, David Sheppard wouldn't be where he is now.' 'Yes,' retorted his friend, 'in Trafalgar Square with the longhaired lefties.' I broke a lifetime's rule never to be side-tracked from my prepared talk by a chairman's remarks. This time, in my own college, it seemed right to put my notes away and speak about the journey that had led me to the 'not only, but also' position in which I now found myself.

My friends in Christian Debate decided to discuss *Built as a City* at my last meeting before I moved to Liverpool. I said that the kingdom of God in the Gospels was not a tidy, western idea. Yet it was the central theme in the teaching of Jesus. We could only grasp its meanings with the help of studying the Old Testament prophets, in whose writings he had soaked himself. The prophets had two great themes. One was the knowledge of God in the heart. The other was God's concern for justice, especially for the poor. The kingdom was not the same as the Church, which is called to be its servant. It was an elusive, eastern idea, treated in different ways in the Gospels. It was God's reign in his world that was 'at hand'; it was 'just round the corner' too; it was also coming in power when all things were to be put under God's feet.

Oliver Barclay, Secretary of the Inter-Varsity Fellowship, cross-questioned me about what the phrase 'the kingdom of God' meant in Scripture. His questions seemed to be tempting me to produce a tight logic, arising from the one text that entering the kingdom of God required us to be born over again. That seemed to lead to equating the kingdom with the Church, understood as the invisible company of true believers. In my reading of the Gospels, I did not feel that tight logic was helpful in understanding the truth they contain.

In the debate that followed there were members who took positions close to mine. But I knew I did not belong in that group of friends as had once been the case, accepting what now seemed tight boundaries to the searching we should attempt. It felt painful, for I owed them much. But surely the life of faith meant obeying what I understood to be God's continuing call to search for him in the urban world of today, even if that became a lonely journey at times. It was a painful watershed in my pilgrimage, preparing me for new challenges as I moved to Liverpool.

11

Southerners Go North

I was in the garden of my mother's Sussex house on a post-Christmas break, when the telephone rang. It was my secretary telling me, 'There's a letter from the Prime Minister!' We had been living with months of rumours that I might be appointed to Liverpool. It was indeed that invitation. My mother, who was recovering from a broken hip, burst into tears. Her first reaction was that she would never see us again if we went off to the North! Grace joined in the tears – 'a mixture of empathy with her and relief that the time of speculation is over'. To me, going to Liverpool seemed like a straight line from serving in East and South East London, so there was none of the long questioning that had taken so much time before agreeing to go to Woolwich. That was all very well for me. For Grace and Jenny, the move to a new city was a leap into the unknown. And we were not at liberty to look at the house before the post was accepted and had been announced.

The public announcement was soon made. When I came home from a press conference, my secretary had placed on the top of a pile of greetings a telegram from the Roman Catholic Archbishop of Liverpool, George Andrew Beck. It was quickly plain to me that Protestant–Catholic relations were going to be more important for me than they had ever been.

Another issue soon became plain. A few days later we went up to Liverpool to stay with the Suffragan Bishop of Warrington, John Bickersteth, and his wife Rosemary. On the first of many train journeys on the West Coast Line I woke up from a good sleep as we crossed the Runcorn Bridge over the Mersey into Widnes, and entered the Diocese of Liverpool. A forest of chimneys added to the murk of a foggy day. It felt like the Lowry paintings of the industrial North. But all those chimneys were to be demolished within twenty years. The year 1975 saw unemployment figures climbing. The issue of unemployment was to fill the foreground for us – with Merseyside showing double the national count.

Our Liverpool home

When someone becomes a diocesan bishop, the Church's Establishment is involved. Within a day or two of moving to Liverpool, I was back on the West Coast Line, in order to 'kiss hands' with the Queen, before my appointment could be confirmed. I allowed an extra hour for the journey, to ensure reaching Buckingham Palace in plenty of time. But there had been a train smash at Nuneaton and we were rerouted through Birmingham. Soon after that, we came to an indefinite halt – beneath the motorway, where we could see traffic racing in both directions. Eventually the train moved on, but we were going to pass through Rugby about the time I was due at the Palace. Somewhat anxious, I told the guard my problem, and he passed a message out at Rugby for the official at the Home Office who was responsible for the arrangements. I did not mention this to anyone else, but soon everyone on the train seemed to know. One of the catering staff said, 'Tell her to send your head back, and we'll stick it over the altar!' At the Palace all was calm, there was something to eat, and the ceremony was rearranged at a time when Roy Jenkins, the Home Secretary – who had to be present – could return.

There was some nervousness that this new bishop with his inner-city passions would not accept the housing arrangements, following our insistence on changing houses in Woolwich. I was to be only the sixth bishop since the Diocese of Liverpool was formed in 1880, and there had already been four houses. Bishop's Lodge is a large house, built for merchants, standing in two and a half acres of terraced garden in the pleasant suburb of Woolton. Later, I came to believe that there was a strong case for moving to a more modest and less demanding house, but there was no time for a new bishop to have that debate before settling into a base for his work. I was persuaded that most people in the diocese saw it as a working house: it was easily accessible from the motorways. Our predecessors, the Martins and the Blanches, had been happy there. In contrast to what I faced when I went to Woolwich, this time the Church Commissioners would have had to be persuaded. And their costs would soar if every bishop insisted on different arrangements. I had to laugh at myself, remembering that they said of Mahatma Gandhi's insistence on his lifestyle that it cost a great deal of money to keep the Mahatma in poverty.

Grace brought an artistic eye to the garden. We welcomed several bodies who used it for special events. Grace herself ventured into organising an 'Open Garden' day each summer for the Liverpool branch of Family Service Units (FSU). (There will be more about FSU in subsequent chapters.) She recruited and held together a volunteer team of men and women who discharged their various tasks with commitment

149

and enthusiasm. Hoping for a thousand people for the first opening, it was salutary to register just 127 visitors. Undeterred, the team continued until the third year, when there was a breakthrough. Just over 900 turned up. The numbers grew to 2,000 in the years that followed, with people expecting it to be an annual event. There was always a game for the children, planned by one of the team of helpers. One year, we helpers had to dress up as characters from Alice in Wonderland. I was the Mad Hatter. Another year we were the 'Mister men'. My role was to be 'Mr Silly'. That involved wearing one black shoe and one brown one. Some adults found that quite difficult to handle: 'Do you think he knows he's wearing odd shoes?' The children had no problems at all, and entered into the game.

Thirteen was not an easy age for Jenny to make a move. On a visit to Liverpool before making the move, we looked at a church grammar school and at Gateacre, our local comprehensive school. This had a catchment area that made a reasonable social mix possible. A large mixed school had a formidable feel after the girls' grammar school where she had spent five happy terms. After our visit, Grace suggested that Jenny and I should walk back up to Bishop's Lodge on our own. Jenny said, 'You want me to go to Gateacre, don't you?' I said, 'I think most people in the country will go to comprehensives. If you can manage it, I think you'd learn to meet all sorts of people. But not unless you feel happy about it.' We were all so exhausted that afternoon that we decided to 'switch off' the subject and play cards on the train back to London. We had further unhurried discussions. Jenny said she was happy to go to Gateacre. We believed she had the strength of character to cope. Her description now is that Gateacre did not build on the good progress she had made at Aske's. Rather, she says the poor teaching and lack of personal guidance made her very frustrated, and led her to make poor decisions regarding higher education. She is very understanding of the motives that made us choose as we did. She concedes that it laid the foundation for a broad experience of life, and she obtained a university degree. But she is determined that her boys should have a better education. My feelings about the price she paid are tinged with regret that we may have put too much on her shoulders in asking her to make the decision. They also include admiration that she made the most of what was a broadening but testing experience.

We loved the house, and in Liverpool we were quickly put at our ease, with humour never far away. At the Town Hall, the police band played 'Amazing Grace' as we went up the stairs. There were one or two awkward moments. At Anfield football ground, the chairman John Smith led me along the corridor, expecting Grace to follow. He paused to say, 'Oh, Mrs Sheppard, you're in there', pointing to a door to one side. With some trepidation, Grace opened the door, to find a room full of women, still kept separate from the males! Later, John Smith became a firm friend of hers. At the welcoming press conference, with her customary openness, she answered a question by saying that she wasn't very keen on opening garden parties. Perhaps that reported remark inhibited people from inviting her to events, but it left her free to find her own interests and causes. The friendship that our neighbours, Chris and Anne King, offered two doors up the hill was crucial in those first years. During that time, Donald Gray, Rector of Liverpool Parish Church, persuaded Grace to join the local committee of the FSU. That led to a demanding and fulfilling involvement.

During our first year, a BBC *Anno Domini* film was made about my going to Liverpool. Two features stood out. One was meeting a group of dockers: they asked me how much I earned. I had the answer ready in weekly wage terms, and asked in turn, 'How much do you earn?' They weren't prepared to say. Afterwards the shop steward who had made it possible for us to have the interview said, 'We couldn't tell you how much we earned, because we are in dispute with the Seaforth dockers (lower down the Mersey) about rates.' Predictably, much feedback concentrated on that exchange.

But far and away the most comments I received were about the interview with Grace. Knowing that she was battling with agoraphobia, the producer, Bill Nicholson, asked to meet her, after he and I had agreed several venues for filming. Grace agreed to a trial meeting. Bill sat very still as she responded to his questions. Clearly moved, he turned to me and said, 'Looking at the surface, your life looks like constant success. If Grace were willing to talk about her fears, it would help people to see deeper issues you and she have had to face.' Grace was impressed with his sensitivity and integrity, but was reluctant to 'go public' on such personal issues so early in our time in Liverpool. Bill Nicholson then suggested to Grace that he could prepare an alternative clip that would exactly take the place of her interview, omitting her contribution at the last minute if she rang him to say she wanted to pull out. He promised to change that section right up to the time of transmission of the programme. She never made that crucial call.

Nothing in which I have ever been involved has brought so much response as Grace's contribution to that programme. We received over a thousand letters from men and women; strangers stopped us – on the train, in social conversations – for years afterwards. My interpretation of why it touched so many feelings is that assumptions are often made that a Christian leader – or any devout Christian – should be above such emotions. Her honesty and her account of her vulnerability brought Christian faith within reach for many. Years later, with Grace's confidence restored, we went to see Bill Nicholson's play, *Shadowlands*, in the West End of London. Afterwards, we climbed on a bus and went to supper with him and his wife in Islington. Grace reminded him of the promise he made her. Bill Nicholson's approach to her story had a major part to play in her healing and subsequent ministry.

She wasn't out of the wood yet. Liverpool Cathedral presented her with a particularly formidable challenge: she had come to acknowledge the fact that agoraphobia was the fear of public places. She determined not to make a fuss when she was asked to sit in the front row. But, as she wrote later, 'This massive Cathedral was one hell of an open space!' During the next seven years she sat in her appointed place at every service, pinching herself till it hurt under a purpose-bought cloak of warm green woollen cloth. The pinching helped divert her attention when feelings of panic arose. In *An Aspect of Fear*[1] Grace described how, with professional help, she gradually learned that it is all right to be afraid, but it is not necessary to be driven by it. She learned to manage the fears. It took years, but gradually she was able to put the phobia behind her and live a varied and fulfilling life, playing a full part in public life. Living alongside her, as she worked through this, I admired her courage and perseverance greatly. And I also learned for myself that part of being truly human meant acknowledging feelings – which is not the same as parading – and not hiding them, as my childhood had trained me to do.

Completing the cathedral

The cathedral presented some immediate questions. There was some nervousness that, with my concerns about poverty, I would not be willing to support the further appeal for £400,000 to complete this 'largest Anglican church building in the world'. The Building Committee was a lay men's body, but naturally wanted the bishop as a member of the committee and his support for the task. One older vicar told me it had felt monstrous to him in the 1930s, when he was working in Toxteth amid extreme poverty, that this vast new cathedral was being built at the end of the road. But that wasn't the question being asked in 1975. It would not have done any favours to Liverpool to leave it as a half-built tower, with its temporary wall and tarpaulins flapping. It was immediately clear to me that a wide range of Liverpudlians were very proud of this great building. Part of the argument used against putting money into buildings was to say it would be better used in funding projects for poor people. I said that cities knew too many projects that started with high hopes, but collapsed when the going became hard. The dean, Edward Patey, never ceased to remind us that worship in a beautiful building could provide a springboard for service in the community. He told me that he spent longer in his own prayers before a meeting of the Merseyside Community Relations Council, of which he was the first chairman, than before a meeting of the cathedral chapter. I quickly recognised in him the 'both . . . and . . .' of commitment – *both* to personal discipleship *and* to social justice – that had become so important to me. I decided to support this appeal – and two years later another for a further £400,000 – before the cathedral was triumphantly completed in 1978 without any debt outstanding.

Liverpool Diocese: the Lancashire parishes

Liverpool itself has a history comparable with what I had known in East London. Both grew around the docks and the commerce attracted by them. But Liverpool Diocese also includes industrial towns, like St Helens, Warrington, Widnes and Wigan – and rural and coastal parts like Ormskirk and Southport. The Lancashire towns have histories that are in sharp contrast to what I had known in London. In offering a glimpse of church life, I describe parishes in these towns and in Merseyside's outer estates rather than those that are comparable with what I had known in the Woolwich area. Towns like Wigan were new territory to me, and I needed to listen attentively to understand church and community life in them. My first chaplain, Alan Ripley,[2] knew the diocese well, having been diocesan youth chaplain before joining me. He alerted me to avoiding stereotypes of 'owner-occupiers' as being necessarily middle class, as we might have expected in the 1970s around London. The Lancashire coalfields in Wigan and St Helens had provided rows of terrace houses in small communities, bought by miners who would not have seen themselves as middle class.

There were strengths in the stable communities and social mix of these towns. Those who achieved well in school and had the confidence to organise institutional life had not moved right away, as so many had in large cities. This resource made it easy to miss the real poverty that was also to be found in the old industrial towns. The decline of a specialised industry on which a town had depended – like the glass industry in St Helens – hit people hard who had been less used to changes than city-dwellers.

In Wigan, heavy industry stood next door to the fields of a working farm. The town had experienced the worst of the 1930s slump, when it had depended exclusively on coal and cotton. Since then, its industry had diversified, and Wigan survived the unemployment of the 1970s and 1980s better than much of Merseyside. Church membership was relatively strong in Wigan. Round the fringes of church life, 'folk religion' was alive and well. There has always been a danger in assuming that church life 'works' in an area, because of the momentum left by the faith of previous generations. As elsewhere, churchgoing has declined in Wigan, but it still produces comparatively large congregations, particularly for special occasions. Accepting the need for change has been particularly hard in such parishes. One Wigan parish, Christ Church, Ince, called in an outside adviser to consider whether it was right to continue to run two mission churches in addition to the parish church. The population of the parish had dropped markedly. Housing developments that had been anticipated had not materialised. It made good sense to concentrate the work in the parish church, and the decision was made to do so. That was brave – and painful – because a number of loyal members saw their church commitment as being to their particular mission hall.

Many Wigan clergy ascribed the strength of churchgoing to the presence of church schools. Lancashire has the largest number of Church of England schools in the country, and in Wigan almost every one of our parishes had its own church primary school. I saw church schools in a different light from what had been told me in South London, where they were sometimes accused of serving only the 'nice' children. Most children from these primary schools were able to find places in Deanery High School, the largest church high school in the North West. Deanery High was originally formed out of four secondary modern schools, rather than grammar schools, as critics sometimes assume to be the background of church schools.

Liverpool Diocese never had the large clergy staffs that London had known. That was a factor in the vigorous lay leadership many of our town parishes possessed. Part of that leadership was the ministry of trained and licensed Readers. There were 200 in the diocese in 1975, increasing to over 300 now. The Readers were the spearhead of active lay membership. Wigan parishes sent a strong contingent of lay members every June to the 'Lay Swanwick' weekend. Some 300 lay people would meet with the bishops and our wives, filling the Swanwick Conference Centre. These conferences were enormous fun. They kept space for relaxing unhurriedly over meals and walking in the grounds. The Saturday night entertainment, with its impromptu performances, allowed us all to let our hair down. They were organised with professional skill by volunteers – in our first years by Erica and Ian Hague from an Everton parish, and later by Audrey and Jack Moss from Wigan. We rang the changes of subjects: part of the challenge of running these weekends was to encourage church people to look outwards at a needy world; if the title for the weekend highlighted prayer, the spiritual life or healing, there would always be a full house. If it was about the third world or the 'world of work', it would take harder recruiting to fill the centre. The membership of the conference showed a gentle turnover from year to year. Generally two-thirds of those present had been to a previous Lay Swanwick. The diocesan training team prepared the ground thoroughly, with twenty-five group leaders meeting for training before the weekend. This weekend was something to look forward to each year, and it provided a powerful resource for an active and thoughtful laity.

Confirmations in Wigan parishes often produced a full church. Many extended families came in support of candidates. When Bill Flagg joined us from South America as an assistant bishop, he put down as a subject for discussion at one of our 'three-bishops' days', 'Wigan confirmations'. He was concerned that sometimes the candidates were the whole of the top form of the primary school, and seemed unlikely to have made a personal response. I said, 'If I am going to take on Wigan, it will be on ground where there is some possibility of success! There's no point in picking a fight with the whole tradition of these parishes.' I felt that it was right to 'go with the grain' of folk religion, believing that confirmation in these circumstances was a proper introduction to the worshipping community – a step along the way. The challenge to more mature commitment can still be made within the life of that community. In 'folk religion', unknown faces present themselves, expecting the church to be there for them, without accepting any regular responsibility of membership. That is very demanding on clergy and regular worshippers. However, I believe the cost is worth paying. Only God knows how deep occasional contacts with the church go.

Bill Flagg[3] gave us eight years as a colleague, with an assistant vicar in his parish to set him free for his ministry as an assistant bishop. He accepted the philosophy of 'going with the grain' where there was a background of folk religion, and encouraged gentle persistence with the claims of the gospel. He also agreed to chair a 'healing panel' that brought accountability and support to different initiatives in the diocese. A positive result was that regular healing services became increasingly part of 'mainline' parish life, rather than being regarded as wild enthusiasms on the margins of Anglican church activity.

Church people knew each other in Wigan across the lines of denominations. I stopped one Christmas time for a pub lunch. We were on what I called 'the chocolate run'. My colleagues and I would take a box of chocolates to clergy widows in the diocese each Christmas. The man sitting next to me in the pub, a Roman Catholic, said, 'You'll be visiting Rector Cleugh'. Norman Cleugh, one of our clergy, was very ill, and I was indeed about to visit him. Where else would the health of a vicar be common knowledge to members of other churches? The difference between urban and rural life emerged on another chocolate run. Ian

Jones, a young man from Liverpool, who had worked in Church House, offered to drive me for these visits around the diocese. One year we were driving through our most scattered parish, Scarisbrick. 'I shouldn't like to live out here,' said Ian. 'What would you do if you got yourself barred out from the pub – and it was the only one in the village?'

In a long-settled community like Wigan there were sometimes defensive attitudes against the world 'out there'. One extended parish visit I made was to St John's, Hindley Green. On the Sunday night, the elderly churchwardens came into the vicarage for a drink. Telling me about the parish, they started to speak of the 'Hindley Greeners' and the 'Liverpudlians'. If I had shut my eyes, all the issues surrounding immigration were brought up. Some remarks betrayed underlying prejudice, others welcomed the variety that newcomers brought into community and church. As I went round the parish with the vicar, Derek Clawson, on the following day, I learned who were regarded as 'Liverpudlians' in that community. I realised they might come from Bolton or Atherton or Hindley – anywhere but Hindley Green. In effect 'Liverpudlian' had become a word for 'immigrant'! In another vicarage conversation, newcomers who were indeed from Liverpool were identified; the vicar's wife said, 'They're taking our jobs.' Another vicar told me that in his parish a substantial number of people from Liverpool had settled in new estates, and several had joined the church with potentially great gifts. He said that the defensiveness of an 'old guard' in the parish regarded these newcomers with fear. So, when there was a task to be done, he had to receive a refusal from every longstanding member before he could feel free to approach the 'Liverpudlians'.

Alan Ripley's briefing had told me of young people from Wigan going away to university, but coming home again within a term, unable to adapt to such a foreign world. Over twenty-five years, I believe that fear of mobility has changed for many young people. My most recent visits to Deanery High School made it clear that youngsters there were being stretched to experience a wider world and the need for changing skills.

Mobility varies greatly from parish to parish. One St Luke's Day, I preached at two churches dedicated to St Luke, perhaps ten miles apart. In the morning I was in the Lancashire town of St Helens, at St Luke's, Eccleston. There was much of the stability there that Wigan knows. At coffee after the service, it was fascinating that everyone I spoke to seemed to have lived all their lives within a mile or two. That evening, I started a parish visit on the coast in Formby, much of which was commuter-land, with people travelling in to Liverpool to work. In the church school in the morning, I asked the senior class how many could visit a grandparent the same day. Six hands went up out of thirty-six. There were different problems here in attempting to minister among a transitory population. I was told that many deliberately did not involve themselves in the community, or make friends, because they did not want to experience the pain that moving on again would bring.

When I had come to understand parishes in leafy Surrey, it was clear that they offered no easy ride for clergy. That was equally true here in these more affluent areas. Janet Eastwood wrote to me when she was a curate in seaside suburbia;[4] she said that so much importance was laid upon the security that came from material possessions, with the need to keep up appearances. Beneath those appearances, she saw problems like stress coming from a father working all hours to pay for his children's education and a large mortgage; worry, because, though the new house was larger than the old, it still had to be paid for; loneliness of mothers tied to their homes with small children, or because a marriage had split up. 'These are the things we see. Under the surface are the problems of the incest victim, the woman with a history of mental illness. In the suburbs we just don't see them for the pristine facades these broken people present to the world.'

One parish near Ormskirk contained much that might be called 'affluent commuter-land'. The curate, who had grown up in Speke, told me that a parishioner said to him, 'You've done well, lad, making it up to here!' After his apprenticeship there, I suppose he came down again in that parishioner's eyes, because he went on to become vicar of an inner-city parish. However, commuter-land also included many who were ready to fight for the cause of the inner city. In a later chapter I write about these 'gatekeepers', who saw the influence they could have in opening or shutting gates of opportunity for those at a disadvantage.

Liverpool Diocese: outer estates

Another difference from my London experience was the proportion of the population of Merseyside who lived in large outer estates, mostly established after the Second World War. The Inner Areas Study report, published in 1977,[5] said that twice as many 'inner-city' people lived in Merseyside's outer estates as lived in the physical inner city. Michael Plunkett, Vicar of Cantril Farm, a large outer-estate parish – later to become Stockbridge Village – wrote me thoughtful letters. He saw the Church as 'a centre of resistance' to despair. He pressed me to stop talking about the 'inner city', because people living on the outer estates felt their needs were not being noticed. His repeated pressure to find another way of description led to some of us coining the phrase 'Urban Priority Areas' (UPAs) – clumsier, but inclusive. After the report *Faith in the City* was published, the Church of England designated UPAs, using a formula of deprivation. In Liverpool Diocese the proportion was high – 80 out of 220 parishes were counted as UPAs.

The first major parish appointment I had to make was that of team rector of Kirkby, the largest of the outer estates. Driving out in good time to meet the lay representatives from the parish, I sat for a while, drinking in first impressions. In London, we had felt the constraints of space: if only there had been enough space for the development of estates, we thought they could have provided a much better quality of life. By comparison, Kirkby housing developments were spacious. Yet every empty house or flat had its windows broken. In several streets empty houses had their roofs smashed too. Most shops did not go in for glass, but had metal shutters. Understanding that community would require taking a careful look at the long and painful history of Scotland Road and other parts of the North End of Liverpool, from which people had been moved to Kirkby.

In our first year in Liverpool, we went to see *Love and Kisses from Kirkby* at the Everyman Theatre. We saw the first residents insisting that everyone take off their shoes before entering the spanking new homes that were replacing their old terraced houses. And then we saw the disappointments follow – no repairs, no jobs – that spoiled the dream of a New Jerusalem. Terry Gibson, the new team rector,[6] told me about mass youth unemployment striking Kirkby. He had been youth leader of Centre 63 as part of the parish team when Selective Employment Tax (SET) was introduced in 1966 by the Labour Government. Lord Kaldor, the Government's economic adviser, described SET as 'the perfect tax'. He hoped it would squeeze labour out of service industries and into manufacturing, and yet raise productivity in both. But the fixed charge per head bore especially hard on the more unskilled or older or handicapped workers.[7] Ruffwood School deservedly had an excellent name in Kirkby; but in 1976, only about half of its school leavers had obtained jobs by the beginning of the new year. By the beginning of 1981 the situation had greatly worsened. Of 350 leavers just 49 had found jobs. Anthony Hawley succeeded Terry Gibson as team rector. Anthony has kept the morale of the team and its four congregations high through demanding years. He has strengthened co-operation with the other churches, voluntary bodies and the local authority – Knowsley. Anthony's wife, Rosemary Hawley, has played a major role in Merseyside's health authorities.

In that context the Church was indeed called to be a 'centre of resistance' to despair and cynicism. I took a sabbatical leave after Easter in 1981, planning to work on a book – *Bias to the Poor*.[8] Christopher Smith was coming to the end of seven years as team vicar of St Andrew's, Tower Hill, in Kirkby.[9] He agreed to 'debrief' on his years there, to help me in preparing material for the book. He said: 'I'd hope more than anything, that people's confidence in themselves and in God should grow against all the odds. The odds include lack of confidence, anger, the risk of mental breakdown and the shortage of money.' There were small but resilient congregations in several of these estates, determined not to give in to vandalism. For example, it was standard practice in a number of parishes to mount guard over any cars parked outside the church while a service was going on. That wasn't always effective protection. Our diocesan working party on UPAs held one meeting in Everton. We came out to find that one car had received a direct hit from a defunct TV set, heaved over the balcony of a tall block of flats. Understandably, some church congregations did take on embattled attitudes, but I was impressed by the many in which members were involved widely in the life of the community. These outward-looking attitudes were to be strengthened by grants from the Church Urban Fund after the *Faith in the City* report in 1985.

During a parish visit to St Aidan's, Speke, they told me about a kind of mobility that was hard for the parish to sustain. I was told that forty young members of the parish had moved away when they married, and were worshipping in suburban churches. Good memories were also cherished at St Aidan's; when Graeme Spiers was rector,[10] he and Ann had a son called Peter. Peter was a thalidomide victim. An older member of the parish told me that Bishop Clifford Martin came to take the baptism service. After the moment of baptism, Clifford Martin carried Peter down among the congregation, and said, 'This is a very special baby.' I asked, 'Did you know that Peter Spiers has been ordained?' She did not, though she had prayed for him over many years.[11]

Being a bishop meant relating to 'UPA people' and those who lived in suburbs, towns and villages – to people up the hill and down. I gave a Granada Lecture on television, in which I spoke about 'Up the Hill' and 'Down the Hill', contrasting the experience of life people had within one mile of each other. I described Netherley, a large estate built at the foot of the hill where we lived in the pleasant suburb of Woolton. A neighbour, who eventually became a good friend, angrily told me that people in Woolton had problems too. I tried to listen carefully to some of the demanding issues our near neighbours undoubtedly faced, but poverty, often based on unemployment for three generations, was crushing the spirit of too many in the outer estates.

Links between a parish like St Peter's, Woolton, and Netherley have proved creative – with the gain not always in the direction that is assumed. In 1981 I made a parish visit to St Peter's. The last event in these visits was always to meet with the PCC and other leaders. When the subject of finance arose, one member said, 'Of course, we have to support all these inner-city parishes.' I had briefed myself very carefully, and responded, 'You do know, don't you, that you at St Peter's are net receivers from the diocese, not net givers?' This was received with disbelief, but I produced the figures that showed St Peter's receiving larger grants towards their two curates than the whole sum they were giving to the diocese. The parish had inherited some endowments, which meant they had never needed to increase their giving in order to pay their way. The new rector, John Roberts, made a point of teaching regularly about giving as a part of Christian discipleship. My challenge may have helped, but another event shook any complacency out of the parish. Woolton's new church school was burned down in an arson attack. Christ Church, Netherley – 'down the hill' – heard of this and donated the whole of their Christmas market proceeds to Woolton for the school. Whatever the reasons, the giving at St Peter's rose dramatically, until it was giving more than any other parish in the diocese.

For a clergy family, serving – and living – in UPAs, especially in monochrome outer estates, often seems one challenge too far. Meeting with a group of clergy wives, I said that there was an unspoken career structure: you messed about in UPAs when you were young, strong and free, but hoped you would move on to what was sometimes called a 'thoughtful ministry' – in other words, a parish where people came to church in substantial numbers. A senior clergy wife said, 'It's not unspoken. Bishop Stuart Blanch asked my husband to move to another UPA parish from the one where he had served some years. I received phone calls from other clergy and wives, saying it was disgraceful that he was being asked to go to another council estate parish and he should refuse it.' Later I asked Martin Hunt to consider moving from Christ Church, Southport, where there was a substantial eclectic congregation, to St Luke's, Princess Drive, a large council estate parish in Liverpool. He told me, 'They thought I'd been a naughty boy!' In fact he said going to St Luke's brought the greatest personal growth he had known.[12]

Across the diocese the balance of church traditions was markedly different from what I had known in the Woolwich area. The proportion of evangelical parishes was higher in Liverpool than in any other diocese, and the number of decisively Anglo-Catholic parishes was in single figures. Many parishes did not fit these party categories; there were many that would have answered to 'Lancashire low' and to 'Lancashire catholic' that were firmly Anglican. Thankfully, party squabbles seemed to happen less. The human needs we were all facing in Merseyside were so demanding that Christians looked outwards more and were more conscious of the need to join hands with other Christians.

Michael Henshall

When I received the January letter from the Prime Minister inviting me to become Bishop of Liverpool, another letter was enclosed from Colin Peterson, the Patronage Secretary. He said that he would be willing to come and give me a rundown of his two-day consultations in Liverpool, if I would welcome that. I rang to ask him to come. My first question was, 'Am I going to lose John Bickersteth?' John was the Suffragan Bishop of Warrington. 'He probably will be appointed to a Diocese, but I don't think that will be for some years,' he replied. Colin's forecast proved mistaken. In July, when I hadn't been in post for more than three weeks, John came to see me: 'I'm terribly sorry,' he said, 'but I've been asked to go to Bath and Wells.' That seemed plainly right.

So I had to find a new colleague. It was clear to me that he should be a northerner, and that he should belong to a different tradition from mine – therefore I was most unlikely to know him, having been there no more than five minutes. How to find him? For some years now, there has been a full-time appointments adviser to the archbishops, who provides thorough briefing when a new bishop is needed. In 1975, I was simply told there were lists of men recommended by their bishops for consideration for such appointments. For the only time, I broke my holiday and spent a hot August day at Lambeth Palace, going through long lists of names and references. Donald Coggan's senior chaplain, Douglas Cleverly Ford, drifted in with a cup of tea at intervals, and stayed to make a comment that turned out to be of first importance to me. He said, 'If you are going to be able to have the public ministry that you should, you need a colleague who will be glad to tackle the 'in-church' business of diocesan committees.'

Further crucial advice came from my episcopal neighbour, Patrick Rodger, then Bishop of Manchester. I rang him and said, 'Help! I've made a list of fifteen names – five of them are in your diocese – and I don't know any of them.' He kindly came and spent an afternoon working through the names with me. Gradually the name of Michael Henshall came to the top of the list. He was Vicar of Altrincham, a son of Chester Diocese, in church tradition a moderate catholic. I wrote to ask him if he and his wife, Steve, would meet Grace and me for lunch and then spend an afternoon together. The appointment that followed led to partnerships and friendships that have proved supportive, challenging and creative.

Michael and I built into the diary a 'two-bishops' day' three times a year, and separate annual days when each of us in turn gave account to the other of our performance in ministry that year. In these joint work consultations, we helped each other set and review achievable objectives each year. Later we added an 'appraisal in ministry' every third year. We

161

developed a pattern at the end of the day, when the appraiser would offer three 'affirmations' and pose three more critical questions to the one who was giving account of his year's ministry. In my notes of twenty years, these 'affirmations' of Michael appear that I played back to him:

> He has put his stamp on the Diocese and the Ecumenical partnership as architect and promoter of a line of projects which have had lasting influence . . . I trust my colleague in handling complex, sensitive pieces of work and taking people with him . . . He is a selfless supporter to me, a key sustainer of clergy and households which are under unprecedented strains – taking proper pride in thorough attention to appointments – 'extra-miling' and not wearying with clergy and parishes . . . He is trusted for having a professional knowledge and a pastoral understanding . . . I see energetic spotting and attending to the weaknesses and the potential of a wide variety of clergy . . . I celebrate his ability to rise above the swamp of administration with a sense of transcendence that shows in awareness of fresh possibilities and initiatives . . . His courage in taking people on, when others keep silent . . . He is a whole-hearted Christian and it shows in enthusiasm and resilience in serving the Lord . . . he lives with gusto for God and His creation . . . He is greedy for knowledge, inquisitive, fascinated by a high ideal in the Lord and His saints.

To round this picture of a remarkable colleague, some of the sharp questions follow that I put to him on those accountability days:

> Is he sometimes too quick to show his hand at the beginning of a discussion or interview, inhibiting what others might want to say?
>
> Does he sometimes miss out on establishing that others are on secure ground before engaging in robust argument?
>
> Is he at times not listening when charges are made about 'top-down' decision-making?
>
> Does he at times allow himself to be 'caught in the stampede' of busy-ness?
>
> Can he stand back and let go?

Perhaps there were times when my style seemed too laid back and tolerant to Michael, drawing forth sharper attitudes than he might have shown on his own. But in general, I believe our contrasting gifts made an effective team.

Steve Henshall shared Michael's faith and loyalty to the Church. She made Martinsfield, their house, a warm and welcoming place. I sometimes said their home was like an extension of the sixth form at Manchester Grammar School, where their two sons followed in Michael's footsteps – their daughter also joining in lively controversy and debate. Steve always gave high priority to the family. Over and above that, she was 'much given to hospitality'. She had her own ministry – very effectively in her leadership of the diocesan Mothers' Union, which I found to be stronger in Liverpool Diocese than I had known in the South. Steve proved to be an effective writer and broadcaster. She was indignant at those who saw clergy families as being hard done by, and wrote *Not Always Murder at the Vicarage*.[13] In another book, *Is It a Daddy Sunday?* she looked sympathetically and realistically at family breakdown.

The working parties Michael chaired have left a lasting mark on the church in Liverpool. He was the prime architect of great diocesan occasions that lifted morale. Liverpool Cathedral cries out for colourful services, and Michael's flair has left me with memories of champagne moments in each of them – balloons descending from the roof, handbells brought to ring, rockets set off from the tower. At his own farewell service, Michael himself vigorously crashed cymbals borrowed from the Liverpool Philharmonic under the precentor Mark Boyling's orders. He led the way in large financial appeals, for the Church Urban Fund and for church buildings in the diocesan centenary in 1980. We used a centenary prayer that year: I never asked Michael who wrote it. I did not need to; it breathes his style of faith and Christian leadership:

> Almighty God, we pray for our Diocese and Your rich blessing on all our Centenary plans. We pray for a new and urgent sense of renewal, commitment, discipline, zeal and endeavour in Your splendid service. We ask for the conquest of meanness in our hearts, and for the enthroning of gospel generosity and total self-giving: for vision in evangelism and for courage in mission. Above all we ask for a constant, daily, hourly sense of Your risen, glorious presence in all our worship, work and leisure, through Jesus Christ our Lord.

Michael 'delivered the visions' we had – seeing to it that good dreams, ecumenically as well as diocesan, were not left in a siding. Ecumenical developments that I shall go on to describe, like the Assembly and Liverpool Hope College, owed much to his skilful work behind the scenes.

12

'A Matter of the Affections, as well as the Intellect'

A bitter history

In 1998, the 'thirty-year rule' released Cabinet papers for 1968. Harold Wilson as Prime Minister had been asked if royalty should be invited to the consecration of the new Roman Catholic Cathedral in Liverpool. Wilson, himself a Liverpool MP, opposed this. He said that relationships between Protestants and Catholics, though they had calmed down, were too fragile to risk a royal presence at such a public Roman Catholic event. A long history of sectarian suspicion and, at times, of violence lay behind this.

Sometimes I was asked if Liverpool was 'getting back to its former glory'. That often referred to the years when it was claimed that the city had more millionaires than any other city apart from London. The decade of the greatest wealth was the 1900s – during which the building of the Anglican cathedral began. But that was also the decade with the worst record of sectarian violence.

The year 1909 saw the climax of sectarian violence. In contemporary language, 'ethnic cleansing' happened on a large scale in north Liverpool. 'Houses were marked to denote the creeds of their inhabitants and beatings and looting ensued as partisans aimed to enforce in the Netherfield and Scotland Road areas a monopoly of faith.'[1] Priests at St Antony's on Scotland Road knew 157 Catholic families (833 individuals) who fled from 'Protestant' streets. On the other side of the fence, 110 Protestant families left the parish of St Martin's-in-the-Fields. These bitter years had left gut feelings about the 'other' community that died hard. One of our clergy described growing up in Wallasey. When she was five years old, her mother told her about their next-door neighbour, 'You must never trust Mrs Murphy, because she's a Catholic.'

I was told all these bitter stories of the past. There were other tales that showed how Liverpool's famed sense of humour had lightened some experiences. A great elderly woman, Elfrida Cotton,[2] used to have a story ready for me whenever she saw me. My favourite was of a visit to a home in Scotland Road. It was plain that this was a mixed marriage: on one side of the fireplace hung a picture of the Pope, while on the other side was an equally large picture of King Billy – the Protestant hero of the Battle of the Boyne. The visitor asked the wife how it all worked out. 'Oh, it's all right,' she said. 'When my husband's in a temper, he takes the Pope down, takes him out and pawns him. What do I do? When my husband's out, I takes King Billy down, and pawns him. And with the money I gets, I redeems the Pope.'

On arrival in Liverpool, I made a point of asking advice about ecumenical partnership. The most frequent advice was, 'Do be careful. Don't rock the boat.' But surely, the Gospel was at stake in building bridges between Christian churches, and every opportunity should be seized to act in partnership with Roman Catholics.

'Call to the North'

At a personal level there were friendly relations between the church leaders, some continuing from 'Call to the North', which Donald Coggan had led when he was Archbishop of York. John Hunter was diocesan missioner in Liverpool; he had been seconded to work for Call to the North, and made sure the diocese knew about these initiatives in collaboration. George Andrew Beck, the Archbishop of Liverpool, was by then a sick man, but gave me time and a warm welcome. He and Stuart Blanch had established a warm relationship. The principals of our Anglican and Roman Catholic colleges of education, St Katherine's, Notre Dame, and Christ's, told me they wanted to build closer relations with each other in the 'federation' they had established. Beck agreed with this, but, by way of caution, added, 'Our schools must have confidence in these colleges.' I asked him if he thought we might work towards joint schools; he thought that was going too fast. One of our clergy in St Helen's rang me to say that there were bad feelings aroused because we proposed to appoint a former Roman Catholic priest, now an Anglican, as vicar of a parish in the district where he had formerly served. I immediately rang Beck and said that, if he felt this would threaten good relations, I would withdraw the appointment. He thought for a minute, then said, 'No, you don't need to. They must learn to live with it.'

During these first months, the Lord Mayor of Liverpool, Owen Doyle, a Roman Catholic, invited me to meet him to discuss how we might respond to the Call to the Nation, which Donald Coggan, now at Canterbury, had issued. I responded that I would be delighted to come, if he would invite Archbishop Beck at the same time. As a result, Owen Doyle called a meeting of all the mayors and chief executives of the Merseyside boroughs to which the church leaders would come. We agreed that Edward Patey should address the meeting. Edward was not among those who had warned me against pressing forward with ecumenical partnership – quite the opposite. He chaired the Merseyside Ecumenical Council that had been established, with a part-time ecumenical officer, David Savage, a Baptist minister, serving it. Another enthusiast, on the Roman Catholic side, was Peter Ryan. He was curate of St Helen's in Crosby, and invited me to preach at the January 1976 united service during the Week of Prayer for Christian Unity. I asked him if a meal would be possible before the service. This caused great embarrassment. The housekeeper in the clergy house said that she would not produce a meal for me. However, the reason was not what we feared. It was *bishops* that she could not stand – not Anglicans! So instead, I went to a fine meal with Peter's mother.

Norwyn Denny comes: Free Church leaders

Three months after my arrival Norwyn Denny was installed as Methodist district chairman. He quickly became a firm friend and ally. I met with him regularly over a working lunch every six weeks, as I tried to do with each of the other Free Church leaders throughout my time. The support that Norwyn and the other Free Church leaders gave to ecumenical partnership has never been given sufficient acknowledgment. When Derek Worlock and I began to speak and act together in public, I grew nervous that the place of the Free Churches was in danger of being ignored. Norwyn encouraged me to go ahead, telling me that I spoke for them. Trevor Hubbard, the Baptist superintendent and John Williamson, the United Reformed Church moderator both stayed in office for the first ten years after the year in which Norwyn Denny, Derek Worlock and I arrived – a gift of continuity we could not have organised. There will be much more about Derek Worlock in subsequent pages.

Most of the church leaders went on the youth pilgrimages we led every four years. We took fifty young people from our different churches. For the first pilgrimage, we travelled by coach to Taizé, the ecumenical community in Burgundy. Near the end of a long drive, we stopped in order to allow a photograph beside the road sign for Taizé. Norwyn Denny told us that the conversation at the back of the coach had started to become uncomfortable; the original politeness had given way to sharp questions, including, 'Surely you don't believe that!' It was one of the gifts of spending a week together that there was time to work through honest disagreements and listen to the convictions of others who became friends. That went for the church leaders too. One of the values of the pilgrimages was that we listened to what was important to young people. Spending that week together, praying and living close to one another, drew us close early in our years together.

I made it an absolute priority to be present at church leaders' meetings; the others teased me as a diary freak, when I pressed them to agree dates a year or more ahead, before other commitments squeezed them out. The subsequent Free Church leaders, Eric Allen, John Newton, John Taylor, Graham Cook and Keith Hobbs, have continued the commitment to partnership between the churches. The senior Salvation Army officer regularly attended the church leaders' meeting. He or she covers an enormous area, of North Wales as well as the North West as far as the Scottish border, and found it difficult to take as full a part. Major Douglas Rayner in particular played a full part in the life of our church leaders' meeting. As well as six business meetings in the year, we started to keep two evenings free for a longer time together. This would include a discussion on a subject on which we were not all likely to agree, and then a dinner together, generally in Bishop's Lodge or Archbishop's House. Good storytelling was mixed with party pieces that some performed. Eric Allen left his mark literally on Bishop's Lodge. His party piece after one of these dinners was to flick a postage stamp on to the ceiling, where it stayed for years.

When the Ecumenical Assembly (MARCEA) was brought into existence, the Free Churches decided to elect one of their church leaders as Free Church Moderator for Merseyside. This made it possible for three of us to stand and speak together for the 'mainline' Christian churches. The media were still inclined to focus on the Bishop and the Archbishop; one photograph appeared from which John Williamson, the Free Church Moderator, had been cut off. After that we insisted that he stood between Derek Worlock and me for press photographs. When John Newton succeeded Norwyn Denny, and was elected Free Church moderator, he joined Derek and me in many engagements – several in Northern Ireland, as well as in different parts of England. For example, we preached in Exeter Cathedral when the church leaders in Devon signed a covenant for unity; we were introduced as 'The Liverpool Three' – echoing some famous groups who had recently been released from prison after unsafe verdicts had been overturned in response to public campaigns.

There were other Christians, Independent Baptists, Brethren, Pentecostal Churches and House Churches, who did not feel able to join in ecumenical bodies or services. Our growing links with Roman Catholics contradicted much of their history, though some of their ministers began to attend ministers' fraternals. I tried to make personal links wherever possible, but realised that, for some of them, bishops were not part of how they believed God wanted his Church to be. The Merseyside Christian Fellowship invited David Watson, Vicar of St Michael-le-Belfrey in York, to lead a preaching mission. I had kept in touch with David since our meetings during Cambridge days. He was to die tragically young. He made it a condition of his coming to Liverpool that Roman Catholics should be involved in the planning and in the follow-up. That was too much for some of the Independent Baptists, who withdrew from the fellowship.

David Watson had become an outstanding preacher, recognised as a leader among Anglican Charismatic Christians. He was keen to hold evangelistic preaching alongside the healing ministry and a concern for justice in the world. There were natural bridges between charismatic Christians in the different churches, including the Roman Catholic Church. He built on that, but was glad that Bishop Tony Hitchen was willing to bring the archdiocese's more formal support to the planning body.

Some years later Billy Graham came for a preaching crusade at Anfield football ground. All the 'mainline' church leaders went along together to show our support at the opening night. I greeted him in their name. Later that week someone described this meeting. He said it was difficult to hear some of what was said, because they had not worked out the loudspeaker system properly: 'There was first of all an American voice; then there was what sounded like a sort of cultured Merseyside voice.' Perhaps that marked acceptance as part of Liverpool life! A later set of Billy Graham relay meetings raised the old spectre of co-operation again. The Southport committee insisted that 'enquirers' should only be put in touch with churches who were participating, and not with their own churches, if they were Roman Catholics. Holy Trinity, Formby, had entered into a local covenant with local churches, including the Roman Catholic parish. They saw the Southport committee policy as a breach of the trust implicit in entering into a covenant, and withdrew their support from the relay meetings.

Derek Worlock

Towards the end of 1975, George Andrew Beck resigned as archbishop because of ill health. Mervyn Stockwood asked me if I would welcome being invited to dinner together with the Apostolic Delegate, Archbishop Bruno Heim. After dinner, Heim and I were duly left alone together for an hour, and I was encouraged to speak freely about Liverpool, its churches and our needs. That was the method of the old-fashioned, 'old-boy network'! Twenty years later, when Derek Worlock's successor was being considered, I was invited to the Nuncio's[3] home for an unhurried discussion, including being encouraged on this occasion to name names.

Nine months after my arrival, Derek Worlock came to be the new Roman Catholic Archbishop of Liverpool. When we were both serving in the East End of London, we had spent a long evening together in his presbytery in Stepney, finding much common ground. His account of arriving in Liverpool is that I rang the doorbell as his first visitor, carrying a bottle of wine to greet him. Within a few days, we were talking about working together more closely. We knew that our predecessors had been good friends in private. We hoped we would repeat that. But also we agreed – in spite of the warnings not to 'rock the boat' that both of us had received – to look for public occasions when we could offer a firm lead towards ecumenical co-operation. Good Friday fell within three weeks of Derek's coming to Liverpool. He said that he was finding it increasingly difficult to hide his sense of bereavement from the Diocese of Portsmouth. That evening, I rang, making it clear that there was no business agenda. Rather, I wanted to share our reflections about the Lord's death as two disciples. We made a point of meeting in this way every subsequent Good Friday.

He became my closest ally and friend, and a major influence on my life. Reflecting on the twenty years we worked together, I recognise some common features about Derek that were present in the other partners who were closest to me in my adult life. They were different personalities in many ways, but sharing characteristics that influenced me: Grace, my closest partner; George Burton, unconventional but a huge influence on me in our Mayflower time; Michael Henshall, my partner in the diocese. All these three were, like Derek, quick to notice potential dangers, aware of possible implications of crossing the bridges that lay in front of us, attentive to the 'minute particulars', sensitive to atmosphere, spotting what another might be feeling. By comparison, I am more a 'broad-brush' person, with a wide vision of where God may want us to go, sometimes stumbling into commitments and then having to stay with the demands they make. Partners who see what is coming have prepared me for challenges I would not have identified on my own.

Derek Worlock was shorter than I, slim, with an ascetic look. At first glance his expression could seem lugubrious, but enlivened quickly with his sideways smile. Black-suited, slightly balding, thinning hair brushed back, he wore glasses and held his head bent to one side. On the face of it, he seemed still to be what he had been as a young priest – 'God's civil servant'. He was an astute politician. That was part of his training and part of his personality. He had his antennae finely tuned to spot possible threats. He was suspicious, feared sometimes that he might lose control, at times saw enemies where I would have wandered on: 'He/she's poison!' he'd say of a journalist of whom we must be wary. He was conscious often of his weaknesses. That helped produce an empathy with other vulnerable people. Clifford Longley, his biographer, comparing Derek with Cardinal Basil Hume, saw in the Cardinal a relaxed, warm personality, at ease with Church and society around him. Derek was more thin-skinned, prickly at criticism, finding traps of which to beware. Clifford Longley rightly says that the calm personality does not necessarily prove the finer Christian. Indeed, being able to cope with fears and threats and still to handle public life can be – and was – a powerful witness to God's grace.

Derek was endowed with a phenomenal memory for people and capacity for work, reading papers meticulously, including the small print. He always wanted to know what was happening ecumenically in parishes, so that he could not be caught unawares by questions. Indeed he often told me pieces of news about the Church of England that I had not yet caught up with. He was always in the 'engine room' of the Catholic Bishops' Conference, when there were papers to be drafted or redrafted – often into the small hours of the night. I soon found myself joining with him in such drafting. In 1977 the Labour Government published an Urban White Paper, following the Inner Areas Study, which had included Liverpool in its detailed account. Each church leader received a copy of the White Paper, and was asked to offer comments on the policies contained in it. We brought together clergy and lay people from all our churches, who had first-hand experience of the inner areas, to identify the points we might want to make. After that the church leaders sat down to consider our responses. Derek Worlock insisted at this point that we should make one agreed submission rather than five separate ones. We got so far, but time was running out. Norwyn Denny said to Derek and me, 'If you can agree a text, then go ahead and send it on behalf of all of us.' That week we were both staying at Scargill House in North Yorkshire as part of the Northern Church Leaders' Consultation. Drafting the joint response meant a very late night. It was the first of many texts that we worked at together. He taught me much about taking trouble over a press release, cautious about how a phrase would be read.

Vulnerable to criticisms himself, Derek was sensitive to wounds that others might feel. Anne Robinson, cutting her sharp teeth that were later to be demonstrated in the television game *The Weakest Link*, was a reporter for the *Liverpool Echo*. She wrote a 'hatchet job' on me. She had been annoyed that I had offered her a date for an interview that was the other side of the summer holiday: I had just had an operation and was catching up on engagements. So she wrote the piece anyway, without ever meeting me. One of her comments was that a vicar 'in one of the plushier parts of the Diocese' had said of me, 'if you're not poor, black or unemployed, he doesn't want to know you!' A friend said, 'That sounds like a good reference!' I was away from home when this piece was published, and Derek rang Grace to offer his support at a moment when he sensed we might both be feeling sore. On another occasion, when I had been the object of a public attack in a national newspaper, he rang me and said, 'I know you're a brave soldier, but these arrows hurt, and I wanted you to know that I totally support what you said.' As the story of our Liverpool years unfolds, it will become plain how much our close partnership meant to me when we walked through some fiery days together.

Grace and Derek understood each other well. She said, 'It takes one to know one!' when his sensitivity and awareness of how another was feeling became apparent. Meals in each of our homes drew us closer, as did the three of us sitting beside the fire in our drawing room, seeing the New Year in together. One year, Derek invited us both to join him and his chaplain, John Furnival, for a fortnight's holiday in his favourite places in Italy. Derek's barber, a devout Roman Catholic, paused for a moment when Derek told him we were going to go to Italy together, then said, 'I suppose it's all right!' Liverpool had not been used to living with the barriers between Christians so openly removed. Derek consulted Grace about his ideas for refurbishing his sitting-room at Archbishop's House, which had not been decorated for years. His artistic sense was also plain in the reordering of the chapel there – and in the commissions for bringing beauty to the chapels that ringed the circular Metropolitan Cathedral.

Our daughter Jenny became a Roman Catholic – both by conviction and to share the faith with Donald Sinclair when they married. The marriage service held painful possibilities of the two families feeling divided: Jenny and Donald, very conscious of this, worked out a plan with the guidance of Father Michael Hollings, their parish priest. This was intended to accommodate, as far as was possible, the needs of all concerned. Their solution involved the two of them attending church three times on their wedding day. The couple alone would receive communion at a nuptial Mass at St Mary and the Angels, Notting Hill. Michael Hollings was open-hearted in his welcome to people from every walk of life – and to Christians of other churches. Grace's father, an Anglican vicar, was invited to join in the blessing, while I gave Jenny away. In addition, earlier in the day, Jenny and Donald would attend a Mass at which Donald's family would receive. Thirdly, they would attend an Anglican service at the nearby Anglican parish church, at which I would celebrate communion. I told Derek Worlock about their plan. After a few moments, he asked if he might attend the Anglican

171

communion service. He would move his commitment to be in York that day in order to be with us in London. Michael Hollings and Sister Marie Towey, Jenny's sponsor, joined us too. They each followed Derek in coming forward for a blessing. Jenny became very close to Derek, particularly during his last two years. They enjoyed each other's company, and built up a strong friendship. His death – and that of Michael Hollings – proved a great loss to her.

Derek told me that the Second Vatican Council of the early 1960s was like a conversion to him. Clifford Longley shows in *The Worlock Archive* just how far he moved theologically during the Council. He was like the best civil servant in his Westminster years, offering his skills and his loyalty to his cardinal master. He went to the Council as Cardinal Godfrey's secretary. *The Archive* – his diaries that he kept all through the Council – shows him strongly defending the most conservative positions of Godfrey and his allies. Longley suggests that Godfrey's death freed Derek Worlock to be more his own man.

> It is as if his loyalty to Godfrey had held him back from entering fully into the rhythm of Vatican II. Even at the end of the first session, he was still calling Cardinal Montini of Milan, the future Pope Paul VI, 'an extreme leftist gentry'. But within a few months he had become a Montini enthusiast – who would continue the direction chosen by Pope John.

Clifford Longley compared the ways in which Basil Hume and Derek Worlock saw the effects of the Second Vatican Council:

> Worlock thought it was a new way of talking about the Church. In fact, as Basil Hume intuitively understood, it was a new way of talking about God. Talking about the Church was what Worlock was good at: talking about God was what Hume was good at . . . Worlock exemplified a man in love with the Church; Hume, a man in love with God.[4]

There is some truth in this comparison, yet it misses deep realities about Derek. He told me of his colleague in his parish in Stepney during those Council years, 'who taught me to pray to the Father' – as he always did extempore in my presence. He now determined to study a scripture at the daily Mass, and either he or John Furnival invariably gave a scriptural homily when I was present. Central to the close relationship that Derek and I developed was my recognising in him the 'not only . . . but also . . .' that had come to be so important to me – not only Christ changing people from inside out, but also his concern for justice in the world. Derek liked to repeat Pope John Paul II's address to the European

Bishops' Conference: 'We need heralds of the gospel who are experts in humanity, who have shared to the full the joys and hopes, the anguish and the sadnesses of our day, but who are at the same time contemplatives in love with God.'

In 1994, I was invited to speak at the dinner at which Derek celebrated his golden jubilee as a priest, with priests of the archdiocese. The island of Iona had been much in the news because the leader of the Labour Party, John Smith, had died young the week before and had been buried on Iona. George Macleod's words about the island had been quoted in national newspapers: 'Iona is a very thin place with only a tissue paper separating earth from heaven.' At the jubilee dinner, I said:

> Let me draw a picture which has come to my mind of Derek on Iona during one of our youth pilgrimages. I see him walking slowly but steadily round that island, where St Columba landed, aware of centuries in which people have worshipped there and when Iona has been a springboard to serve the Lord all over Europe, or in modern times in Glasgow. If Iona is a thin place, perhaps I may say that Derek is a thin man for whom there is a tissue paper separating earth from heaven. Worship lifts him up to God and at the same time thrusts him out into a needy world, indignant at the way disadvantaged people are treated so often.

When Derek talked to me about his Westminster years, I noticed that all the characters he mentioned to me were Roman Catholics. As secretary to Cardinal Griffin in Westminster (within a year of his being ordained), he believed that the battles they had to fight were to strengthen the position of the Catholic Church. In 1950, Griffin responded to a lengthy correspondence in *The Times* on 'Catholicism today'. He wrote: 'To us reunion can only mean the resumption of that unity which was destroyed at the Protestant Reformation. A call for reunion means an invitation to all non-Catholics to join the one, true Church. It means in other words submission to the Holy See.' This would have confirmed what Derek's training in seminary taught him, as he described it at the beginning of our joint book, *Better Together*:[5] 'As a small boy I had been told off for always having an answer. Now I learnt the vital importance of knowing the Church's answer on every question, and above all of winning the argument, even if it meant demolishing your adversary (in the nicest possible way) in the process.'

The barriers were not all erected on one side. Years later, at George Carey's invitation, Derek and I addressed the Nikaean Club Dinner at Lambeth Palace. Derek delighted in telling a story about an earlier visit to the Palace he had made. Archbishop Geoffrey Fisher had insisted that at an inter-denominational meeting in the Albert Hall the whole of the Lord's Prayer be said by those present – and aloud. Roman Catholics had been taught to pray 'Our Father, who . . .' rather than 'Our Father, which . . .', as Anglicans did, and omitted 'For Thine is the Kingdom . . .'. Cardinal Griffin had recently died, and Derek was sent by the senior archbishop, William Godfrey, who was to succeed Griffin, to ask that the Our Father might be said in silence, so that conscientious differences might be observed. 'Fisher exploded, saying that this request from Archbishop Godfrey was monstrous. "Haven't you Romans lived long enough in this country", he demanded of me, "to know that we are the establishment and you must toe the line?" He led me to the top of that formidable staircase at Lambeth Palace, and as I descended with as much dignity as I could muster, I heard him calling after me, "Aggression. It's Roman aggression." '

That would have hurt Derek more than Fisher knew. His parents had both been converts from a high Anglican tradition, his father's side of the family having no less than twelve ancestors in holy orders in the Church of England in the previous 300 years. When he offered for the priesthood in the Diocese of Portsmouth, the bishop, Timothy Cotter, a Cork man, had made it clear that he would not consider a candidate from such an English background. Most of his priests came from Ireland.

All this personal history accounts for the quality of gratitude I received from Derek, at my invitation to him to join in responding to an offer from the Queen to spend an afternoon with the church in Liverpool in 1978. She had agreed to be present in the morning at the dedication of the last two bays of our cathedral. When I received the offer, I sat down to think what was my 'doctrine' of a visit from the monarch. Such a visit should mark significant developments in the community. The most significant development in the life of the church in Liverpool seemed to be the growing partnership and trust between the churches. So I asked Derek and Norwyn Denny if they would meet with me to see if we could agree a possible programme to put forward. We learned an important principle for ecumenical partnership that day. Sometimes one church would make a plan and then invite the other churches to join in. That was not true partnership of equals. Equal partnership meant going back to the baseline together and discussing what we might jointly plan from the beginning.

We agreed to invite the Queen to follow her formal visit to the Anglican cathedral and lunch at the Town Hall by meeting Christians from the different churches who were working in co-operation in the community in the inner city. This would take place in the Roman Catholic Parish Church of St Mary's, Highfield Street, which already had a close partnership with the Anglican Liverpool Parish Church. After that, we would invite her to ride out on the newly opened Merseyrail line to the largest of the outer estates, Kirkby, and meet a similar group in the civic suite there.

We learned later that the message from the Palace had assumed that I would invite her to visit Anglican church work. In the event, the Queen welcomed the opportunity to meet such a wide range of Christians involved in 'grass-roots' work in the community. We were told that this was the first time a reigning monarch had entered a Roman Catholic parish church in England. Derek frequently referred to my readiness to share our visit from the Queen – not least when he insisted that his invitation to the Pope in 1982 should be to come to both cathedrals. It mattered to Derek that he was an Englishman, and that his faith made him a loyal citizen.

In Clifford Longley's interpretation of history, Derek had grown up in a Counter-Reformation church. Vatican II changed all that for him. It looked at the other Christian churches with wholly different eyes, and saw the calling of the *whole* Church to serve the *whole* community in which it was set. Longley says of Derek that at the end of the Council, 'For him the Counter Reformation was over'. Coming to Liverpool led him to work this out on the ground. Increasingly, he was concerned for the whole and not simply for 'our' people. He told me that he had been the only Roman Catholic in the room, when we had met with the council of the Merseyside Chamber of Commerce. But he seemed to notice such distinctions less as time went on. He obtained an invitation for me to address the Roman Catholic bishops at their January meeting, when they gave time to explore ideas rather than be tied to a business agenda. I talked about urban mission. George Patrick Dwyer, the Archbishop of Birmingham, kept silent for the first half of the evening. When he entered the conversation, he took centre stage for the rest of the discussion. He said, 'You must give the Anglicans credit that they set out to serve the whole community and not just their own people.'

After Derek's death, an article in the *Tablet* by Rupert Shortt quoted 'a senior Anglican source' as suspecting 'that, at the end of the day, Ecumenism for Derek meant Anglicans becoming Roman Catholics'. I am sure this 'senior source' was mistaken. In 1994 we wrote *With Hope in Our Hearts*, looking back over nearly twenty years together in Liverpool. Sometimes friends thought they could guess which of us was the original author of different parts of our joint writing. Derek took a mischievous delight in proving them wrong. We described John Newton becoming Free Church Moderator for Merseyside and Region making up 'The Liverpool Three' rather than the Two; we went on, 'In one sense that has been the most significant development of all.' It was in fact Derek who wrote those words about the significance of the Free Church

presence. He repeatedly said in meetings when we were questioned –
sometimes by fifth or sixth formers – that ecumenism was not about
'ecclesiastical take-overs': the goal, he would say, was 'not of uniformity
but of legitimate diversity'. He and I both believed that we should not
give up on the goal of visible unity that would leave space for that
diversity.

At times, on pilgrimages, we were pressed to concelebrate. We never
did, believing we should do more harm than good by breaking the
rules. On the last day of the ecumenical youth pilgrimage in Iona, we
planned carefully how we could celebrate the eucharist. The young
people planned and led the Ministry of the Word jointly in the youth
camp. Then we processed to the abbey, singing a hymn. In the abbey
we parted to left and right; I led the Eucharistic Prayer for Anglicans
and Free Church members in one chapel, Derek for the Roman
Catholics in the other. We then met back in front of the high altar for
the greeting of the peace and the blessing. Derek said to me, 'I could
hear you saying virtually the same words as I was. We must make more
progress.' That has remained in my mind, so that I think of him when
we pray in the eucharistic prayer:

> Send the Holy Spirit on your people
> and gather into one in your kingdom
> all who share this one bread and one cup.

He never used the title 'Catholic Church' in my presence, but always
'Roman Catholic', realising the hurt that other Christians might feel,
when one church called itself 'the Catholic Church'. In turn, I regularly
used the title 'Anglican', sensitive that some Christians felt that in
speaking of 'the Church of England' we were making an over-large claim
too.

At Pentecost 1985, the Merseyside and Region church leaders signed
a Covenant for Unity at a service started in the Metropolitan Cathedral
and completed in the Anglican after walking the distance in between –
along Hope Street. I was to greet everyone as they arrived in our
cathedral. I asked Canon David Hutton to listen out for what people
were saying as they walked. He met me at the west door: 'They're saying,
"If the church leaders wanted to turn back now, we wouldn't let them." '
This two cathedrals' service and walk became established as a Pentecost
event every two years. It fulfilled dreams that some of our predecessors
had expressed. A woman of ninety-five wrote to tell me of an address
Bishop Albert Augustus David had given many years before: 'He said he
visualised in the future a walk from each of the cathedrals, meeting in
the middle of an open road and exchanging the kiss of peace.'[6]

In subsequent years, we attended the signing of fifteen local covenants between groups of churches. There were careful consultations about the commitments such a covenant would involve before the signing. Indeed we were encouraged when one or two backed off, because one or more congregations did not feel ready to enter into such an agreement. It showed that churches did not enter lightly into the covenant relationship. Other local links were formed when churches entered into local ecumenical projects, and in some cases – two between Anglicans and Roman Catholics – where we built a new, shared Church.

In these situations, consultation with the partner clergy was crucial before fresh appointments were made. There were occasions when the archdiocese went ahead without full consultation, and there was a key church leaders' meeting when Derek was challenged about this. He explained the tradition that, if a parish priest died in office, ideally his successor should celebrate the Mass there the following Sunday. But he agreed that there must be proper consultation, accepting that there would be a longer delay than he would have liked. The rest of us agreed that others must be prepared to drop engagements in order to be available for this consultation with the priest who was being asked to consider the parish. There were other, informal partnerships that we tried to take note of too. Derek had told me of the death of a young priest. The next day, meeting Peter Jordan, the vicar of the local Anglican parish, I mentioned what Derek had told me. Peter, a firm evangelical, said, 'That priest was my brother in Christ!' They had developed a close and trusting partnership. I told Derek of the conversation. He clearly had not known of such informal ecumenism there. I could see the brain working fast. He said he would withdraw the appointment that was planned, and find someone who could be expected to continue that relationship.

I tried to encourage personal relating across denominations. One of our most active clergy told me he had never spoken to a Roman Catholic priest, when I consulted him about an invitation to me to visit a Roman Catholic church in his parish. A year or two later, he told me he had been meeting his Roman Catholic neighbour. Every other year we called a two-day ecumenical consultation for clergy. We kept seventy places each for Free Churches, Roman Catholics and Anglicans. We made a point each time of inviting a good number of clergy who were not among the 'ecumenical enthusiasts'. On several occasions we agreed that one church would celebrate the eucharist, and the others of us would be asked to attend. One year it was to be the Mass. I received a letter from one of our evangelical clergy, who was making heavy weather of the invitation. He wrote saying that he was due to go into his parish church school that morning – what should he do? I wrote, suggesting that he could offer an alternative date, since it was his own church school. He duly came to the ecumenical consultation, and I ran into him just after the Mass. He was in tears. He said, 'I had no idea it was like that', and spoke of how full of Scripture he had found the service.

On the national stage, Derek was the leader from the Roman Catholic side in the negotiations that led to Churches Together in England (CTE) and the Council of Churches for Britain and Ireland (CCBI). Decisions had to be made at a conference of representatives from the churches, held at Swanwick Conference Centre in 1987. Derek gave me a bulletin each morning about progress. Most mornings he expressed frustration that Basil Hume had produced yet one more obstacle. We saw the strength of their partnership at the end of the conference: the more cautious Basil Hume came on board, his objections finally answered. Speaking slowly, every word carefully chosen, he threw all his authority behind a decision to go forward. It was time, he said, to 'move from co-operation to commitment'.

John Newton echoed those words at the launch of the Council of Churches for Britain and Ireland, which was held in Liverpool, using the two cathedrals and the walk between them along Hope Street:

> We meet in hope, and we meet in Liverpool. At one time to mention Liverpool and Christian unity in the same breath would have seemed a sick joke . . . There are still a few contemporary ancestors who have not heard that peace has broken out . . . but the great majority of Christians on Merseyside have moved from rivalry to co-operation, and from co-operation to commitment . . . We are *Churches Together*, not yet fully one, but to a wonderful extent reconciled.

An example of the practical working out of Derek's commitment to the witness of the whole Church came in a phone call; I was off work, having had a hip replacement operation. A pressing message came through, Derek insisting that I came to the phone. He told me there was to be an event in the city next day, at which it was important that all the churches should be represented. He had learned that Michael Henshall was away, and that there was likely to be a gap where there should be an Anglican representative. Young Derek Worlock at Westminster might have chalked that up as a bonus for the Roman Catholic Church – that they were involved when the Anglicans weren't. But Derek, having spent seventeen years in Liverpool, did not want to win any of those skirmishes. He told me about the meeting, and rang Bob Metcalf, the Archdeacon of Liverpool, briefing him about the meeting, when I said he should be our representative.

Derek brought an earlier commitment with him to Liverpool – releasing the gifts of lay people. In his Westminster years he was 'let out of school' from his duties as secretary to the cardinal, to encourage what he referred to as his 'team' of lay people – often members of the Young Christian Workers. I was introduced to the network of ex-YCW members at the ordination of Derek's first new auxiliary bishop, Tony Hitchen. Tom Casey was a trade unionist with whom Derek had often stayed when he came to Liverpool in earlier years. At the reception after Tony Hitchen's ordination, Tom Casey took me by the hand and led me through the crowded crypt to meet one former member of YCW after another. I said it was like an underground mafia! The 'team' of lay people like Tom remained Derek's model that he hoped to extend. He often returned to YCW's 'See–Judge–Act' pattern of study on the world of work. That might be with a group of trade unionists or with the senior management figures that he and I brought together over breakfast from 1984 as 'The Michaelmas Group'. This group will play a significant part in later chapters.

I tried unsuccessfully to persuade him to appoint a priest to the Liverpool Industrial Mission team. He believed that such an appointment would obstruct rather than enable lay people in their apostolate in industry. I believed that this depended on the quality and approach of the clergy concerned. Tom Casey and others in that ex-YCW network found the availability of our industrial chaplains a resource they were glad to make the most of. I was pleased when Archbishop Patrick Kelly, Derek's successor in Liverpool, appointed a member to the Industrial Mission team (by then renamed 'Mission in the Economy').

Soon after arriving in Liverpool, Derek introduced his 'Twelve Apostles' plan, calling on every parish to choose twelve lay 'apostles'. He introduced this plan in an early visit to the inner city of Liverpool's North End, together with the idea of something like a team ministry for the parishes. These had lost membership drastically through bombing and slum clearance. Tony McGann, a local man, who saw this as taking resources away from a needy area, shouted him down. Tony was later to become the most loyal protagonist for the archbishop and the bishop, because of our support for 'the Eldonians' and their fight to stay in the area against the Militant-led council's plans for demolition.

In 1980 the National Pastoral Congress was held in Liverpool. The idea had been put forward by the National Conference of Priests (NCP), at which Derek was the regular representative of the Bishops' Conference. He became the driving force that produced a superbly organised Congress, in which vigorous ideas and questioning abounded. I was made a full member, and attended group and plenary meetings. Among the 2,000 participants who were billeted in Liverpool homes, two stayed with us at Bishop's Lodge. The Congress raised great expectations. A survey was published showing that the membership represented a fuller cross-section of the population than the Anglican General Synod did. Basil Hume and Derek Worlock flew to Rome with a copy of the Congress report, *The Easter People*, to present to the Pope, together with the invitation to visit the United Kingdom in 1982. Michael Gaine wrote in his obituary of Derek Worlock in the *Tablet*:

> For tens of thousands of Catholics throughout the country there had been, for a short time, a sense of genuine consultation and involvement in the life of the Church and a new spirit of religious enthusiasm. The disillusion was the greater when it became clear that *The Easter People* was not going to become the blueprint for change which many of its participants had envisaged.[7]

Clifford Longley says the most likely reason *The Easter People* went no further was the fear that such 'progressive' ideas might bring down the shutters on all attempts of the English church to move forward. He describes a meeting Hume and Worlock had with leaders of the National Conference of Priests: the NCP leaders expressed misgivings that the bishops had moved away from some of the resolutions of the Congress, and were too willing to give way to the Roman Curia. Hume and Worlock told them that if the English Roman Catholic community was to hold on to what progress had been made so far, it was going to have to proceed very carefully in future. Already there were signs that their own positions were under attack.[8] Certainly the National Pastoral Congress has never been repeated.

Derek told me that attacks were made in the bishops' meeting on 'the Hume–Worlock axis' by one or two fellow bishops. When we were preparing for the Pope to come to Liverpool, the diplomatic bag from Rome told him that there had been 400 letters of complaint against him. And all the complaints had to be answered. There were influential lay Roman Catholics who saw Derek as a traitor to traditionalist ways. He had been 'their young man' when he was at Westminster. Now, he was the toughest promoter of the changes of Vatican II.

The Pope's visit

Derek managed to hold together complete loyalty to the Pope with absolute distrust of the Vatican! To prepare the way for the Pope's visit, Archbishop Paul Marcinkus, later head of the Vatican Bank, was to come to Liverpool. Derek warned me that he might arrive with little notice and at an awkward time; would I arrange for the cathedral to be open?

He duly rang me, and I arranged for the dean and precentor, Edward Patey and Gordon Bates, to be there to meet him. Already on the way from Liverpool Airport, there had been an awkward moment: Marcinkus had said to Derek, 'I'm staying tonight with Father X.' Father X had told Derek he would destroy him. He had been one of those who wrote letters, informing against errors he believed the Archbishop was encouraging. Derek replied to Marcinkus, 'You are making an official visit to the Diocese. You are staying with me.'

Entering the Anglican cathedral, Derek fell in order to draw Gordon Bates alongside him, behind Edward Patey and Archbishop Marcinkus. He said, 'If this man asks for a copy of the service, for goodness sake don't give him one at any cost.' When they reached the front, Marcinkus asked if he might see what was planned for the service. Edward Patey asked Gordon if we had copies of the service. Gordon's reply was that 'They were not yet complete, and therefore not yet available'. That produced a warm 'Well done!' from Derek afterwards. Marcinkus' next question was, 'Dean, what would you say, if I said that the pressure on His Holiness's time was such that we must make some cuts in the service?' Edward replied, 'Well, we've got over a few problems in the last 400 years. I think we could manage that.' Then Marcinkus said, 'Dean, what would you say if I told you that there was not enough time for His Holiness to come to your cathedral at all?' Edward drew himself up to his full height and said, 'Quite frankly, I would not believe you!'

In the event, I was glad that Marcinkus was present with the Pope. When I welcomed him to our cathedral, there was an explosion of cheering and applause that went on and on. I interpreted this as Liverpool's relief that the old bitterness was well and truly banished. Afterwards, I watched the film of this moment, and saw the Pope's eyes tracing the massive Gothic arches of the building: 'You have a wonderful cathedral,' he said to me. As we moved towards the west doors, the enthusiasm was such that I began to worry whether he would be able to reach the outside safely. I was glad to see the burly shoulders of Archbishop Marcinkus, once an American football player, firmly holding the way open in front of the Pope.

In the 'Popemobile', travelling along Hope Street through the crowds, John Paul II, clearly moved by this reception, said to Derek, 'Ecumenism is a matter of the affections as well as of the intellect.' Putting that in street parlance, 'gut feelings' influence our attitudes to other Christians. Liverpool had lived too long with 'visceral' comments like, 'You can never trust a Catholic!' – or its reverse. For a while, I had been somewhat coy, when people said, 'Of course you and Derek Worlock are friends.' Being friends didn't sound very weighty or theological. On reflection, I came to believe that theology rates friendship very highly indeed. And I realised that our being seen to be friends was touching popular gut feelings. One of our clergy in the worst of the old 'Orange' and 'Green' areas told me, 'The fact that you are seen to be friends gives us permission to be friends too, without being accused of being disloyal to our history.'

The Pope's visit was a golden day. I believe painful experiences during the preceding winter cleared the way for it. The sharpest of these was when Robert Runcie preached at Liverpool Parish Church during Lent. He had been preaching for three or four minutes, when members of the Orange Lodge stood up, put on their sashes and interrupted the sermon with shouting and jeering. It became clear that they would not allow him to complete his address. He went and knelt at the altar in prayer. The noise continued. Eventually, he walked out of the church. Grace was seated behind a woman who stood, screaming at Robert. He stopped and said, 'Don't be afraid. There's nothing to be afraid of.' Outside the church, George Walker experienced our car being rocked by Protestant protesters. It was a rude introduction for him on his first day in this new job, as our gardener/chauffeur. That evening I visited one of our clergy in hospital. He told me that everyone in the ward had seen the Archbishop shouted down. And everyone was furious. After this, the extremists knew that Liverpool was no longer on their side. When the Pope came, they stayed at home.

Soon after Robert Runcie had been shouted down, the Grand Master of the Merseyside Orange Lodge came to see me. Before we had sat down, he said, 'We're afraid'. I asked what they were afraid of: 'We're afraid that the Pope is going to become the head of the Church of England, the Queen will have to move over and our constitution and liberties will be lost.' I said, 'If you're right, I will join you at the barricades. But it is not like that at all.' Also that week I was the next preacher in line following Robert Runcie. I have never been so well prepared for a sermon. In case I was interrupted, there was a five-minute version, a seven-minute version and a fifteen-minute one.

The longer-term hopes stirred up by the National Pastoral Congress were not to be fulfilled. For example, there was no requirement on bishops to implement the recommendation to form a council in each diocese and parish. Like some other bishops, Derek created an Arch-bishop's Council and encouraged parish priests to do the same in every parish. Those who saw how that worked out in practice wondered whether there was a contradiction in his make-up. Michael Gaine wrote that 'Worlock's vision of a responsible laity never dimmed'. Yet he liked to keep control. Some of his priests say that he would correct an account of what had happened at a meeting, to chime in with the wishes he had expressed himself. Michael Gaine commented that Derek rarely, if ever, delegated genuine decision-making powers. For example, the archdiocesan pastoral council was never invited to discuss the future of Upholland College once the seminary there closed down.

Derek was never more fulfilled than when he made time to be with his clergy or those training in seminary – which meant a drive over to Ushaw, near Durham, each term. I saw his eyes sparkle when he told me of a day spent with a group of clergy. Equally, I saw his personal distress at the death of a priest, or when one was in trouble. Michael Gaine wrote that priests who approached him in difficulties testified with gratitude to his practical sympathy. Those closest to him knew of his concern for those who had left the active ministry. Michael went on to make the point that, 'As elsewhere in the English-speaking world, however, during his time in Liverpool the number of secular priests dropped by more than a quarter, and those who remained were an ageing group.'

Some clergy criticised him for being away on national concerns, when they wanted him to be there for them pastorally. I knew comments like that were made about me too. How much more when celibacy heightened the feeling that the diocese was a priest's first family! Derek created high expectations by his regular visits to Ushaw, and the way he talked about his care for clergy. I was briefly tempted to try to outwork him. Then I took myself in hand. He was called to be celibate and my calling was to be married as well as to be a bishop. So it would be quite wrong for me to vie with his working hours.

From the beginning Derek made it known that he had been given a 'double mandate' by Pope Paul VI: this was to 'address people's social and material needs and to ensure that Liverpool did not become another Belfast'. We were quickly to see the growth of social and material needs, as factory closure followed factory closure.

13

Staying with the Struggle

The story of Liverpool has consistently been 'a tale of two cities' – 'Enterprise City' and 'Hurt City'. In the 1990s there were many encouragements in enterprising developments. But, arriving in 1975, I entered into a city's struggle for survival. In East London I had avoided describing people as 'poor'. In 1960s London, it was possible for the vast majority to obtain paid work of some sort. Now, in Merseyside, I was in no doubt that there was poverty that crushed people's spirit. Nor did I doubt that a bishop should make this a matter of major concern. In the consecration service, the archbishop includes in his charge to the bishop, 'You are to have a special care for the poor and needy'.

Unemployment fills the foreground

In 1975 the post-war confidence was evaporating. International events broke the fragile structure of prices and incomes policy that had been propping up manufacturing industry. In 1974, the international price of oil had leaped up fourfold. Entry into the European Economic Community in 1972 had brought what many hoped would be a wake-up call to British industry. In the event, this smashed the deal that had bought wage restraint by controlling profits. Inflation accelerated. The Labour Government led by James Callaghan introduced strict controls on spending. The harsh measures associated with 'Thatcherism' were starting to bite then. Reducing inflation, rather than preventing unemployment, became the priority. The national figures of those out of work rose to 5 per cent each year until 1979 – double the level in any year during the 1950s and 1960s. Unemployment hit Merseyside harder than anywhere – averaging more like 10 per cent. For the least prosperous estates, the figures doubled again: sometimes they were as much as 50 per cent. A long line of closures began: in the first ten years after I arrived (1975–85), a *net* 10,000 jobs were lost each year in Merseyside.

The ability to resist these closures was weakened by the departure of head offices for the South. This had been taking place over decades. Once large firms were controlled from outside the region, they became increasingly vulnerable to cutbacks or closures. We found ourselves on the wrong side of the country. The market for Europe had replaced that of Empire. Air travel had taken over from the great passenger liners that had tied up at the Pier Head in the heart of the city. Undoubtedly the reputation for 'bloody-mindedness' of Liverpool dockers turned away some would-be employers and investors. Dockers fought to keep jobs in what was a declining industry from 1919 until its revival in the 1990s – when a larger tonnage than ever was turned around, though with a small fraction of the labour force once employed.

The Liverpool Industrial Mission team invited me to join them for a presentation by Bob Houlton on the 'Merseyside worker'. To understand the Merseyside worker, we needed to grasp the 'culture of the Dock Road'. Long-held bitterness at the casual method of hiring and firing men – 'standing on the stones' – had built up over the years. Houlton said that you would stop drinking with your mate if he obtained a job as a trade union official. You would have assumed he had gone over to the other side, the side of the institutions. Many of the strikes of the 1960s and 1970s were unofficial disputes, led by local shop stewards. National officers had limited authority in these matters, especially in the climate of fear that growing unemployment bred. If you lost your job, where else would you find work?

I stood in my study with the managing director of a large company that had announced its closure. He said, 'Our workforce are good lads. They are being led by the nose by four or five wreckers.' I asked him what the employment climate must be like, if thousands of 'good lads' could be led by the nose. Powerful fears of unemployment were driving workers to fight last-ditch stands against closure or cuts. Those attitudes changed as the harsh climate of the 1980s forced more co-operative approaches to the fore. Increasingly, firms learned that a good living could be earned here, with noticeably lower costs than in the South.

In 1976–77, with the help of the Liverpool Industrial Mission, I ran two weekends under the title 'Work or What?' It was encouraging that a strong group of lay people and clergy linked with industrial mission – and other employers, trade unionists and local government officers – came together to think about the subject. The chief planning officer for Merseyside County Council, Audrey Lees, produced figures that showed the region moving into recession more quickly and emerging more slowly than others. She said that unemployment in Merseyside was 'chronic' not 'cyclical' – long-term, not simply due to 'boom and bust'. These weekends led me to a conviction I held for twenty years, that full employment was not going to return. I continued to believe that until the 1997 report, *The Churches Enquiry into Unemployment and the Future of Work* converted me to the view that full employment was a practical goal, if the nation really wanted it.

An opportunity came to me to make a contribution in this field. In planning my diary, I realised the folly of trying to take on every commitment. But I reckoned also that one substantial secular involvement would bring a healthy balance into my life. I refused four or five secular commitments during my first two years in Liverpool. In 1977, an invitation came to chair the Area Manpower Board for Merseyside of the Manpower Services Commission (MSC). I hoped that the temporary programmes the MSC was introducing might offer good training, and might also – just possibly – be allowed to develop into some 'real jobs'. I chaired the board, with its monthly meetings, for eight years. Much of the MSC's training has been criticised: it was generally judged by the yardstick of whether it led to a 'real job' or not. But that depended on the availability of 'real work' in that particular area. As the years went by, the approach of funding by 'outcomes' meant that we were forced to close many of the more local training bodies – kicking people in the teeth without whom we could not have run the programmes earlier. That made many voluntary bodies suspicious of entering into partnership with government programmes again. In areas that seemed like industrial deserts, the Youth Opportunities Programme (YOP) often provided training that changed a youngster's attitude to service for the good of the community. Supervisors were often grandfatherly figures who had been made redundant, but passed on positive approaches to time-keeping, reliability and care for needy people.

The balance in the diary that I sought included meeting and listening to those who are outside the circles of power. To further that, I set an objective to spend 50 per cent of my 'beyond-the-church' working time in their company. That annoyed some who complained that the bishop 'wouldn't come to their dinners'. In fact I did go to a number of dinners. Hard as I tried, that 50 per cent objective was not achieved. To make up the shortfall in first-hand meetings, I made time to listen to 'interpreters' who could bridge the gap and help me to understand what was going on in working-class life – and among poor people.

The gap that needed bridging was sometimes very wide. In one factory visit with an industrial mission chaplain, I had an hour's discussion with the shop stewards. Some of them attacked the Church: 'We don't think your track record is too bad, but the Church is hopelessly compromised. Bishops sit in the House of Lords. All twenty-one bishops voted against the Government on the Dock and Harbour Bill.' I said so many bishops were unlikely ever to have been present at the same time, because of their longstanding engagements in their dioceses. However, I would write to find out, and let them know what I discovered. (I had not then been introduced to the House of Lords. That came in 1980, when I had been in Liverpool for five years.) My research told me that, out of many amendments to the Bill, there was one on which one bishop, then Chairman of our Industrial Committee, and therefore likely to be well briefed, had voted against the Government. How that had been converted into 'all twenty-one' perhaps showed the persistence of folk memories. (There was one occasion when the whole Bench of bishops had voted against a Government Bill – the Great Reform Bill – but that was in 1832.)

The Winter of Discontent

The number of days lost through industrial disputes shot up in 1977, stayed up, and in 1979 produced one of the worst years of the century for industrial unrest. The Winter of Discontent of 1978–79 brought to a head the feelings that the trade unions were too powerful and were holding the country to ransom. I met with groups of trade unionists; some were ready to talk practically about protecting jobs by work sharing or banning overtime. No one on Merseyside then believed that full employment would return. I discussed the Bullock Report with one of these groups soon after it appeared.[1] It recommended that worker participation should be required, some being taken on to the boards of companies. I felt profound disappointment when Christian trade union-ists told me they preferred to stay their side of the table to keep their bargaining rights. In any case, a colder wind soon blew, and the Conservative Government chose not to pursue Bullock's recom-mendations.

In the Winter of Discontent, Derek Worlock and I made a statement highlighting the hurts that lower-paid public workers were bearing. In February 1979, we said that powerful groups both in management and in the strongest unions seemed to have assumed that the Government's pay guidelines were binding on everyone else except themselves. Those who had broken through the guidelines – whether quietly or aggressively – bore as much responsibility as those on the picket lines for the damage to industry and the distress of individuals which the disputes were causing. We wrote, 'It is the proud boast of the Unions to have concern for the poor and the low paid. The poor include those who are not sitting at the bargaining table at all, because they are unemployed.' In the early Thatcher years, Eric and Doris Heffer[2] came for a long Sunday evening with Grace and me. Towards the end, I asked him, 'Why don't the unions fight for the poor?' Eric paused. Then he said, 'Damn it!

They've beaten us! Our people have been taken over by ambition for personal profit.'

Thatcher Government policies

In 1974, Sir Keith Joseph had challenged the accepted commitment to full employment. He said that this commitment was the error from which the whole drift towards ungovernability flowed. When the Thatcher Government introduced its tough monetarist measures in 1979, both ministers and the economists they followed believed that any rise in unemployment would be small and short-lived. They also believed that a return to mass unemployment would be a political death-knell for the party. When, as MSC board chairman, I went to see Jim Prior as Employment Minister, I found a sympathetic ear. He and others in the Cabinet, like Sir Ian Gilmour, wished to work with the unions. Sharper teeth took their grip in 1981, when Margaret Thatcher appointed Norman Tebbit in Prior's place.

The 'New Right' succeeded in putting the supporters of wide provision of public services on the defensive. Freeing enterprise would strengthen initiative and personal responsibility – ridding us of 'the Nanny State' by 'less government'. Feeling guilty at being better off should be put away. It was argued that society was like a marching column. If the front ranks pressed forward, they would draw the back ranks with them, and the poorest would benefit. Many of us never accepted this trickle-down theory.

An economist who was a protagonist of the New Right, Professor Patrick Minford, came to Liverpool University. I invited him to come to the annual day conference held by the MSC board. Complete with graphs on a blackboard, he expounded his theories. Unemployment was not the result of Mrs Thatcher's policies. It sprang from the inefficiencies of the labour market, especially the trade unions and the provision of income support for the unemployed. It was high wages that put people out of work. A trade union leader, Dave Gough of the AUEW, was the first to respond. He said he understood well what was being expounded – *slavery* could mean that everyone would be in work! I whispered to Minford that this was the leading right-wing trade unionist in the region. Minford later conceded that what in fact brought down inflation was the unintended deflationary shock. The decline of industrial output between June 1979 and December 1980 was the fastest in recorded history.

The political disaster that had been expected for a government that presided over such a steep rise in unemployment did not happen. Several reasons accounted for this. The Labour opposition fell into disarray, with the election of Michael Foot as leader, the breakaway of the Social

Democrats and the activities of Militant, which was to play such a significant part in Liverpool. Newspapers like *The Times*, acquired by Rupert Murdoch, were happy to give a platform to the Militant leader, Derek Hatton, and the miners' leader, Arthur Scargill. The paper's vitriol was turned on 'wets' like Ian Gilmour, who would have shown that there was another debate to be had. For, if the debate really lay between Thatcher and Scargill, then every *Times* reader would have agreed with Margaret Thatcher's slogan that 'there is no alternative' to her policies. I myself felt angry at what was done to *The Times*. I had loved the paper, and read it – together with the *Daily Mirror* – every day while we were in East London. Rupert Murdoch was alleged to have said he wanted *The Times* to 'be an ordinary newspaper'. My personal reaction was that he had succeeded beyond his wildest dreams!

At a demonstration at Liverpool's Pier Head, I heard a call that 'we must oppose the deindustrialisation of Britain'. Productivity of those in work increased in the Thatcher years, but at the cost of a massive loss of jobs in manufacturing industry. Unemployment in the City of Liverpool rocketed upwards. The overall figure for the whole city climbed from 10.6 per cent in 1971 to 20.4 per cent in 1981 and to 21.6 per cent in 1991. The Merseyside Churches Unemployment Committee made a study of 300 workers made redundant. It showed that those who found work had in every case gone 'downmarket', earning less than they did before.

Attitudes to unemployed people could be harsh. I found myself engaged in a sharp disagreement with the Duke of Edinburgh at a glittering function in Liverpool. The Royal Yacht Britannia had tied up at the Pier Head for the royal visit to mark the Queen's Jubilee in 1977. Grace and I helped someone up the stairs to the upper deck for the beating retreat by the band of the Royal Marines. Rather breathless, and arriving last, we made for the least crowded part of the ship's rail. Before we reached it, we realised – only too late to go elsewhere – that this was where the Queen and the Duke were standing. While the band was playing, the Duke turned to acknowledge us, helping Grace into her cloak that had slipped off her shoulders. Then he launched into critical remarks to me about Liverpool, including the statement that 'Anyone can find a job if he wants to!' I disagreed firmly, and our half-whispered conversation must have sounded like a series of hisses. Grace was embarrassed, when the Queen turned round and beckoned me. She thought I was about to be sent to the Tower! What she actually said, with a twinkle in her eye, was, 'Don't you think it strange to have written a piece of music for a celebration in a minor key?' She had been listening all day to a piece written for the children to sing for her Jubilee by the Master of the Queen's Music, Malcolm Williamson. She may not have appreciated the music, but had delighted in seeing Hope Street crowded with children from all the city's primary schools on this hot summer's day.

Harsh criticisms of jobless people also came from some who were nearer to the world where mass unemployment was to be found. One of our clergy was dismissive of unemployed people, until his own son found himself without a job. That was in the later depression at the end of the 1980s. This struck deep into parts of British life that had not known unemployment at all, bringing sympathy more widely. Many church members in Liverpool Diocese had seen this as a priority concern much earlier. In 1975, at my first Lay Swanwick, I was a member of a small discussion group. A mother told us of her fears for her son. She had shown him an advertisement for jobs in the local paper, only for him to throw it back across the room. He had applied unsuccessfully for more than fifty jobs. She said, 'I'm terrified he's going to go and become a mercenary.'

Margaret Thatcher frequently referred to the threat of a 'brain drain' from this country. It seemed strange that she could not understand our concerns that there was a 'brain drain' from cities like Liverpool. In the 1980s, Norman Tebbit's notorious remark that his father had 'got on his bike' to go and find work, led to the naming of the early train to London on Mondays and the 6 p.m. train returning on Fridays as the 'Tebbit Express'. An additional train had to be run at those times to handle the large numbers going to London in search of work. We were glued to the television for Alan Bleasdale's play, *The Boys from the Blackstuff*. This portrayed vividly the desperate search for work of a group of roofers, and the pull of family and community that brought them back again.

Merseyside had a fragile economy because of the shortage of skills. Liverpool had never been an industrial city like Manchester. It was a commercial city that developed around the docks, with disproportionate numbers of semi-skilled and unskilled workers. In 1980, Mrs Thatcher told young people in South Wales that they ought to 'get mobile'. Derek Worlock and I wrote a letter to *The Times*, saying that the Prime Minister's call to young people to get mobile should be contradicted, whether in South Wales or in Liverpool. Down the years there had been many forces that had encouraged the 'get up and go' young people to leave.

If areas like the Inner City are to live again, we need more mixed housing policies and the creation of jobs in private and public sectors, so that there will be an incentive for the adventurous to stay. The alternative is an increasingly cynical community of the left behind, who may feel their voice can only be heard by saying no, whether to new technology or by violence. We want to say to many of the most adventurous young people, 'For God's sake, stay!'

Derek and I believed it was impossible to stand for justice without taking sides over some political issues. As far as we could, we tried to avoid adopting a party political stance. Inevitably, fighting for Liverpool's cause led some of our critics to say we were involving the church in party politics. The two of us were invited to address the trustees of the Roman Catholic journal, the *Tablet*, and then stay for dinner with them. One senior trustee said, 'We like what you do in bringing our churches closer together. But we think you're rather lefty!' Another trustee said from the end of the table, 'If Jesus had been around now, I think he would have been a bit lefty!'

Just before the 1987 election, the *Sunday Times* published an article on its leader page by Brian Walden. It was in step with the line the newspaper had been following for some weeks. It had advocated tax cuts and asserted that there was no such thing as the 'North–South divide'. Brian Walden wondered what they should say to me, because I had argued for tax cuts to be withheld so that more money could be spent on the poor of the inner cities. 'The Bishop is a good man. So I am reluctant to tell him that sizeable sums have been spent already . . . What is needed to release the Bishop's flock from unemployment and comparative poverty is mobility . . . Some of Liverpool's unemployed have jobs waiting for them in the south and east.'

He mentioned me by name eight times in the course of the article, and I felt there should be some right to reply. I telephoned the paper, and talked to the acting Features Editor. He said he would be interested to see a piece from me. When it reached him a day later, he said he could not promise to print it, but that he liked it very much. Two days later, he informed me that the editorial conference had decided there was no room for it, because of fresh news items that had come in. He hoped that next Sunday there would be the space. During the following week, we had a further conversation, agreeing some minor changes. Nothing followed, until I received a one-line message that they would not be using my material!

Norman Tebbit was now 'our minister' for MSC training matters. We had invited Tom King, whom he had succeeded, to address a special synod, drawn from all the Merseyside churches, on the subject of employment. He had now been moved to the Northern Ireland Office. We tried to pass the invitation on to Michael Heseltine, but Norman Tebbit, as Tom King's successor, said he wanted to take it on. His visit to the synod was combined with meeting the MSC board and other visits. So I had been his host throughout the day, and longed for him to engage with real needs at this unique synod. We had agreed that he would respond after listening to a debate. I was proud of the Church, as speakers from all our churches, clergy and lay, showed how deeply involved they were in practical employment programmes. They were raising the most sharply relevant questions. Norman Tebbit rose to reply: 'You haven't told me anything,' he said. That was the only memory that was carried away from what he went on to say. Afterwards, a few of us took him out to dinner. By the end, he was agreeing with what we were saying – perhaps out of sheer exhaustion. Some weeks later, both Derek Worlock and I received a personal call from him. He said: 'What you said to me about the indignity of unemployment got to me. I want you to be the first to know that I'm launching a new scheme, that I think of as the Liverpool Programme.' This was the 'Community Programme'. He was as good as his word, and the Community Programme offered substantially more temporary jobs.

There were other contacts that helped me to learn how life was experienced 'outside the circles of power'. Grace had joined the local management committee of the Liverpool Family Service Unit (FSU). In 1982, she became its chairman. She showed her grit in staying with struggles that voluntary bodies know so well: tensions between national and local committees, patiently handling a 'grievance procedure' in the staff; raising the core funding in an erratic period for local authority and government grants. She signed endless letters and made many visits asking for support. She and the unit organiser once drove across England to brief an employer in the South, who had expressed interest. In near-biblical words, speaking of his firm in relation to poor people in Liverpool, he said, 'Our welfare lies in their welfare'. He gave generous support on a regular basis, making an additional staff post possible. Through Grace's interest, I became drawn into the life of FSU, and served as national president for twelve years from 1985. That gave me the opportunity of seeing Units in needy areas in other cities, through a 'president's visit' each year – and a further chance of seeing life 'from below'.

FSU was founded in Liverpool during the Second World War. Nationally, it now supported twenty-one or more Units. Statutory social workers often referred families to FSU, knowing that, as a voluntary body, it could offer intensive time that, with their huge caseload, they could not. Families could refer themselves. Sometimes parents in difficulty feared falling into the hands of statutory social workers, because their children might be taken away. With FSU they could 'sack' their social worker if they wanted to.

It has been astonishing that the voluntary movement has remained so vigorous over these years. When the Militants took over Liverpool City Council in 1983, some prophesied that the voluntary sector would be reduced to no more than half its current size. Grace remembers a visit from Derek Hatton to FSU, when he put her on the spot – to persuade him that the Unit should not be municipalised. A robust account of what the Unit was providing – and the cost the city council would have to find if they took over this work – staved off the threat of extinction. Grants from the council were already as low as 20 per cent of the Unit's costs. In subsequent years, severe restraints on local government spending have hurt FSU nationally, causing the closure of some Units. It was a heartening measure of the renewed value the Liverpool City Council placed on FSU's work that in 1997 grants or service contracts met 70 per cent of the Unit's costs. But uncertainty about support remains.

Seeing life 'from below' made me feel keenly the effects of some government policies. The 1980 Budget made me feel ashamed to be British. It cut taxes for those who were best off and maintained tax allowances, mainly benefiting those without children to support. At the same time, it reduced the value of most of the benefits for working families. Child benefits, free school meals, educational maintenance allowances, grants for clothing were all falling in real value.

Many debates now took place about poverty – whether it existed at all in Britain – or how seriously 'relative poverty', in contrast to third world poverty, should be regarded. Going around the UPAs of Merseyside, I saw for myself how 'relative' poverty hurt. The marching column of the successful pressed forward the living standard of the majority. And those who couldn't keep up felt the hurt of being excluded. So, for example, living in a flat without an efficient washing machine had become unthinkable. Television was the only window on the world for poor families. High-pressure TV advertising screamed at children that all the goods being promoted were necessary parts of normal British life. If you couldn't have them, you felt you didn't belong. Christians were sometimes reminded that we admired poverty when we saw it in St Francis – without distinguishing between *choosing* a lifestyle, as St Francis did, and having it imposed.

I learned much from the writings of Professor David Donnison about the reality of poverty in wealthy Britain. Donnison was Chairman of the Supplementary Benefits Commission from 1975–80. In 1982, while those years were still fresh in his mind, he wrote with passion, 'I am disgusted by the depression, deference, fear, jealousy and supercilious contempt – all the sick human relationships that fester around poverty. And when the plight of the poor is contrasted with the wealth and the massive productive capacities which could so readily put things right, I am enraged too.'[3]

The Liverpool black community

Moving to Liverpool from South London, I was surprised that black people were conspicuously absent from the mainstream of life in the city. More than in any other city in Britain, the Liverpool black community was confined to a few streets, in Liverpool 8 – part of Toxteth – largely around Granby Ward. Here the great majority of black Liverpudlians lived, often in once-fine houses, now divided into flats. There had been little recent migration, because immigrants knew there were few jobs available here. So, to a large extent, this was not an immigrant community. The Revd Sam Pratt reversed the pattern of migration that took so many gifted young people away from Liverpool, by coming back to the city where he had grown up. He later served a distinguished and lengthy chaplaincy at the Royal Liverpool Hospital. Sam told me his grandfather came to Liverpool in 1894. Others spoke of settlements 200 years old, probably made up of travelling seafarers. The stories of slaves being sold in Liverpool are contested, though Liverpool was extensively – and shamefully – involved in the slave trade.

During 1975, black people picketed the city centre stores, complaining that they were never offered jobs there. Several employers undoubtedly tried to respond to this, but reported that over the years no applications came from black people. A vicious circle developed. Euan Gilhespie, the youth leader at the Methodist Youth Club in Princes Road, told me of pressing a young man to go after jobs. His reply was, 'You not only expect me to be twice as good as white people, but to go where no one else from our community has gone before.' There was undoubted fear of venturing outside the streets where other black people were to be seen. Stories were repeated of violence and abuse of those who had tried to move out to the suburbs. They had then returned to the security of known streets in Liverpool 8.

That summer, I opened the Caribbean Centre in Upper Parliament Street. I had to pass a picket line of young black men. I stopped and asked what their complaint was. They said that the centre was run by older people who had migrated from the Caribbean themselves, and looked back nostalgically to life in the islands: 'It's not for the likes of us. We're Liverpool blacks.' In a session with the fifth form at Paddington Comprehensive School, an inner-city school that white parents were inclined to shun, a black girl asked why black people had not obtained jobs on the buses in Liverpool. She said, 'Black people drive buses in London. I know. I've seen them.'

The black churchwarden of the small congregation at one inner-city parish, St Bride's told me, 'We feel God has deserted us.' After an overnight parish visit to St Margaret's, Princes Road, I wrote in my notes,

'I have never known the pall of defeat hanging so heavily over an area.' The vicar, Colin Oxenforth, who had also moved from South London, was shocked by the local situation of massive unemployment. He saw 'depression and a rather tired anger at being neglected or patronised'. A visible difference from Southwark Diocese was the small number of black people worshipping in any churches. The history of black migration to Liverpool was altogether different from that in London. The shortage of employment in Liverpool in the 1960s onwards meant that there had been little fresh migration in the period when black-led churches were being established in London, Manchester and Birmingham. It followed that we saw little of the vigour of black-led church life in Liverpool – though one such church has grown strong over subsequent years. The pattern of settlement of what was largely a long-established black community meant that few lived outside particular streets in Toxteth. Young ordinands, asking about possible parishes in which to work, told me they would like to work in a multi-racial parish. We had no more than three parishes that truthfully answered that description. While black children attended some churches, few who were born and brought up in Britain were to be found as adult worshippers.

In my first year, I kept a commitment in Brixton, staying there for a night or two. In Brixton, I was staying in a community where black people were in evidence at every turn. In the train back to Liverpool, the strong impression suddenly came over me, that there weren't any black people in Liverpool. They were invisible! The significance of that description was born in on me in 1977, when I went to the United States as a representative of the Church of England at the Episcopal Church's Partners in Mission consultation. Before the fifteen-day consultation in Louisville, Kentucky, I spent a week staying with Paul Moore, the Bishop of New York, visiting inner-city parishes and projects. In Harlem, I described the Liverpool black community. A black American rector told me I should read the classic *Invisible Man*.[4] The thrust of the book was that in the northern cities of 1950s USA, where there appeared to be none of the overt racism of the South, black people became invisible. The point was that they were invisible not only to white people, but also to themselves. As a result, they did not expect to find any place in the front ranks of American society.

Soon after moving to Liverpool, I was asked to write the Foreword to the British Council of Churches' report, *The New Black Presence in Britain*. I sent the draft of the report to Father Austin Smith, a Passionist priest, who made his home in Liverpool 8. The black experience in Liverpool was so different from what I had known in London. So, was it appropriate for me to commend this report? I was to learn much at Austin's feet over the years. He said he thought the report was highly relevant to Liverpool, and I duly wrote the Foreword. He wrote me a note at the same time about the Church's presence in inner-city areas: 'The Church has certainly been present in all these areas, but I question whether it has been present in a listening kind of way.'

Bill Sefton, Labour leader of Merseyside County Council, publicly attacked me for what I wrote in the Foreword.[5] He said that Liverpool was a tolerant, cosmopolitan city, in which there was no racial prejudice. Most people of goodwill believed that, until the explosion of the Toxteth riots in 1981 shattered the illusion. One result of the invisibility of the black community was that the history of race relations in Liverpool had been suppressed. Few people in the city knew of the race riots of 1919. After the end of the First World War, thousands of black men were looking for work in the ports of Liverpool, Glasgow and Cardiff. Many had served in the forces. Others had worked in munitions factories in Manchester and elsewhere. Seamen on ships requisitioned by the Government for transport service were paid off in Britain. Thousands of demobilised white men also made their way to these ports. Over two million 'other ranks' were demobilised in the space of four months.

The worst riots were in Liverpool and Cardiff. Recently I was told in Cardiff that, before the riots, black soldiers had been excluded from the victory parade through the city. It was as though they had played no part in the war. In Liverpool, there was wide destruction of black people's property. Dozens of people, black and white, were wounded. The title of The Charles Wootton Centre, a further education college in Liverpool 8, preserves a bitter memory from the 1919 riots. Charles Wootton, a black man, was chased by a white mob to the docks, where he drowned. Official accounts of the disturbances, like that of the 'Head Constable' were far from even-handed. That spoke of 'the arrogant and overbearing conduct of the Negro population towards the white, and by the white women who live or cohabit with the black men'. Hundreds of black families were evacuated from their homes into 'protective custody'.

The stereotype of black men was that they were seamen. A later Liverpool study, in 1939, of 220 black heads of households showed unemployment of 74 per cent.[6] The comment then was that no seamen's jobs were available. The Second World War, like the First, produced a call for help from the Commonwealth. Skilled technicians were wanted. The first group arrived in Liverpool. The warden of the hostel in which they were housed described these volunteers coming with a real sense of patriotism to the 'mother country'. They were shocked by the 'colour bar' they experienced in factories, dance halls and hotels.

I was told by a West Indian, Denis Maloney, of his experiences on arrival in England in the 1950s. He had sought jobs in Exeter without success. Coming to Liverpool, he applied for a job with the fire brigade.

He was turned down. They told him that in the smoke he might not be visible to his colleagues, because of his dark skin! He was a practising Anglican, and went to two parish churches in the area. At each, someone took him on one side at the end of the service, and said, 'We think you would be happier if you went to worship at the African Church Mission, down the road.' He did not give up. He worked for British Rail, becoming an inspector, and became churchwarden for many years at St Margaret's, Princes Road.

Racial prejudice caught me by surprise in the middle of a pleasant Sunday lunch in suburban Liverpool. I felt our host was setting out to needle me on various issues. At last, he told a story about an insulting piece of behaviour by a black railway porter. I said, 'Would you have told us that the man was white if that was the case?' I felt very angry, and found myself spontaneously getting off my seat – feeling unable to stay any longer. His wife grasped quickly how upset I was, and pleaded with me not to leave. Grace said to the host, 'You said you wanted to hear forthright views from David!' Somehow lunch settled down again. Like other issues, race relations had to be worked out both in public and in private.

Some Christians objected to the Church involving itself in matters that were not 'spiritual'. The more I saw of the effects of unemployment, the more I believed that there were indeed spiritual issues underlying what might seem to be social and political matters. Who was going to say that despair, low self-esteem and wasted gifts were not spiritual issues? Black or white, the proportion of those excluded from decent opportunities was far too large. Staying with the struggle and the hurt is unavoidable, if we are to become instruments of change in our community.

14

'Costly Openness'

'It's been a bad year for Liverpool, between Government policies, closure of firms, Militant council elected in May. Grace has felt very heavy burdens in threats to voluntary bodies from unpredictable cuts in grants. We have both been very aware of poor people's exclusion from opportunities and of judgmental attitudes of successful Britain. It hurts to be Bishop of Liverpool – and it ought to!' These reflections come from my joint work consultation in 1982.

One of the fulfilling parts of being a bishop was that so many doors of all kinds in the community came unlocked, if I was ready to push on them. Some label these openings as 'secular', but they affect body, mind and spirit. Being open to these opportunities meant time spent outside the church structures, with the temptation to crowd more and more engagements into the diary. I recognised the dangers in this, and determined to keep time for leisure – 'creation time'. That meant there were lessons to learn about managing the diary.

In 1981, I had enrolled in a bishops' training course. William Temple College in Manchester and the Urban Ministry Project (that I had chaired in Woolwich years) jointly made this the most serious piece of in-service training that I experienced. It was disappointing that it did not become a regular resource for bishops. First, we kept a work diary for three months. Each of us was expected to recruit a 'reference group' – whose main function, I concluded, was to make sure we told ourselves the truth about how we spent our time! One member of this group was Sir Stanley Holmes, who had recently retired from being Chief Executive of Merseyside County Council. He began our meetings by saying that he did not understand the ins and outs of church organisation. He then produced the sharpest comments about them. When I had let the group see my three months' work diary, Stanley said, 'Bishop, these pressures you feel – would you say that some of them were . . . self-induced?' I said, 'I know what you mean, but if you champion groups who feel no one stands by them, you cannot lightly put those commitments down.' The most heartening comment from Stanley Holmes came later. He said: 'I left the Church, because I thought it was not living up to its calling to stand for justice for those at most disadvantage, as I felt its beliefs called it to do.' He then said softly, 'I've come back now.'

We remained enrolled in the bishops' training course for a full year. One project was to write an analysis of our own work diary with our comments. These were to be presented under the headings 'It delights me . . .', 'It is acceptable . . .', 'It bugs me . . .'. There were many entries under 'It delights me . . .' I enjoyed being a bishop, and always saw it as working with a team – in the diocese, with ecumenical partners and with other bishops nationally. For example, I wrote:

> It delights me that I have never failed to look forward to fresh support as I come to Staff meeting . . . to feel understanding and support of the Bishop's Council over a sensitive issue like the projected Law Centre in Liverpool 8 and close understanding between ecumenical leaders in this possible project . . . to be able to share my priorities in Christian mission with younger clergy and with theological students . . . to feel close allies among the bishops concerning urban and race issues.

Most of the daily demands that came my way I found *acceptable*. I knew that structures had to be attended to, if clergy and church members were to know they could rely on the diocese. I did not resent the time these demanded.

Managing the desk

Several issues emerged under the heading 'It bugs me . . .'. One pressure point was about managing the desk: 'It bugs me to have allowed the diary to become so full that time for desk has been eroded. I have still not kept abreast of a relentless post. I think I need an actual 16 hours a week at my desk.'

There were times when there were real feelings of fear that I would fail to 'keep up' with the demands that seemed relentless. Soon after arriving in Liverpool, I learned that CORAT, a church body that helped with organising skills,[1] had made a recent survey – before my time – of the bishopric of Liverpool. I wrote asking if I could see their report. Peter Rudge, Director of CORAT, responded by saying he would bring it to me. In this survey, he had looked at four bishoprics. One was Durham with Ian Ramsey as bishop. He had a very wide-ranging ministry, and was struggling to keep up with the correspondence that flowed. The most dramatic part of the survey was that CORAT were trying to help him organise his days better, and were negotiating with the Church

Commissioners for further staff to help him, when he died. Peter Rudge clearly admired the style of my predecessor in Liverpool, Stuart Blanch, because he kept time for study. The story that the diocese enjoyed about Stuart was that a curate rang him one weekday at 11 a.m. Stuart answered the phone himself, and said, 'I'm just studying my Hebrew Old Testament.' The curate said, 'Yes, sir, that's just what I wanted to ask you about.' But Stuart did not have a wide public ministry. The survey showed that Ian Ramsey had more than double Stuart's correspondence. I found that at the beginning of my ministry in Liverpool, I was already receiving the same volume of post as Ramsey. It was a cautionary discovery, and I took serious note of what Peter Rudge had to teach me about making the best use of staff and of my time. Others should answer the telephone. I should never open my own post. My secretary should be given time to sort it into priorities and obtain a brief from appropriate members of the staff, before it was put in front of me.

Time for reflection

Closely related to that piece of 'bugging' was this: 'It bugs me that I failed to guard Quiet Days I had planned.' Unrelenting programmes all too easily crowded out reflection. The notes from my first joint work consultation in Liverpool record 'Feelings of relief when a big event is over. I "switch off". Is this a "safety valve"? Without reflecting on the experience, I press on to the next event.' Grace observed that it was in my nature to 'put my head down, and keep going'. Grasping how easily times for reflection were eroded, I insisted that such time apart was given priority when we made up the diary. In later years, my secretary for my last twelve years, Margaret Funnell, and I told each other that there was a special angel who arranged cancellations, when the programme became too full.

Michael Henshall, Grace and our close staff met for two 'date-making days' in May/June for the following year's programme. First into the diary went holidays, then reading weeks, quiet days, two bishops' days. When I realised that my daily times for prayer and study were limited, I determined to block off 'chunky' times in the diary. A lifeline was to keep two regular reading weeks in the year. Going away to a religious house – together with Grace when Jenny left home – helped these weeks to have something of the character of a retreat. During each of those weeks, I set out to read one big book and think about it. We lapped up the quiet.

When there had been days away in London at boards or synod, it felt that I had fully come home when I was back at morning prayer in our chapel with Grace, our chaplain and George Walker, our chauffeur/

gardener. Each of us took it in turn to lead. We borrowed an idea from Mervyn Stockwood to keep Christmas cards in the chapel and pull out four each day to add to our prayers – as we still do. One fruit of our 1981 sabbatical was that I established an early morning walk, that has remained part of my pattern of living: these 'walks with God' include explicit prayer – and sometimes explosions of indignation to God about injustices that are ignored or frustrations that I cannot resolve.

I planned to write a book on that sabbatical, but those three months offered space for varied interests. Grace asked me what gaps in my life might need filling during these months. I had not given serious attention to my approach to preaching for twenty years. So I enrolled with Douglas Cleverly Ford, now retired, who had led the work of the College of Preachers. He promised me six sessions, and asked for the text of some of my sermons before we met. When I came home after my first meeting with him, I said to Grace, 'He's rumbled me!' He had said, 'You don't seem to care whether they like you or not.' I had always liked to plunge straight in with my theme, but now realised that establishing common ground with a congregation was a necessary step in winning their assent to engaging with my thoughts. Douglas also persuaded me of the value of working at discovering an image that would convey the central theme.

We achieved balance and variety in that sabbatical in a flat in North London. Weekends and evenings were free for the two of us to be together. I kept weekdays clear for writing the book *Bias to the Poor*, from 9 a.m. to 6 p.m., with a generous lunch and siesta break of two hours. The pattern held good except for one lunch break: I switched on the Test match at Headingley at almost exactly the moment when bookmakers announced odds of 500 to 1 against England. Graham Dilley had just joined Ian Botham. There was no way I could tear myself away from our portable black-and-white set! I saw the rest of Botham's 149 – and next day compulsively watched Bob Willis's storming bowling and England's most improbable win.

Sabbaticals have been valuable times of refreshment – two and a half sabbaticals during my twenty-two years in Liverpool. I made a point of making that known in the diocese. This was a deliberate step, in order to establish this novelty – as it seemed to many – in the minds of clergy and of their Parochial Church Councils, as a normal part of clergy life. I was encouraged when our director of continuing ministerial education told me in 1997 that over half our clergy had now been away for at least one sabbatical of three months.

In the analysis of time spent in my work diary for the bishops' training course, 'Resources' was a heading under which all these times for prayer, reflection and study fell. I also saw meetings with other bishops as a resource – the more formal House of Bishops, the twice-yearly meeting of North West Bishops and Wives and the informal group of Urban Bishops and Wives. I never resented time given to them, or to the Ecumenical Church Leaders Group in Merseyside and the 'North West Triangle' meetings for twenty-four hours twice a year in Belfast, Glasgow and Liverpool for four or five church leaders from each of our three cities. Church leaders share with each other some pressures that are not always understood by other people. However, it is also true that bishops can become isolated from people outside hierarchies, so when we arrived in Liverpool, Grace and I repeated a step we had taken at Woolwich: we helped form a group of six couples, clergy and lay people, who met for a meal every six weeks. It was not programmed, but developed into a 'safe place', in which each could share experiences and raise questions in the company of friends. These groups provided resources from which I learned much and a firm base in which to feel understood.

Bringing about change

Another pressure point was, 'It bugs me to be powerless to shift the ground in situations which are breaking clergy; and when those who most need support push away every offer.' Pastoral reorganisation that would create the support of a team was often resisted by clergy and lay people who wanted to hold on to the independence of solo parishes. Team ministries were often criticised. However, I saw morale sustained and continuity maintained in some of the most difficult areas by teams. My predecessor, Stuart Blanch, was the least dogmatic of bishops. After my appointment, I pressed him that we should have time to discuss the diocese. The only way we found uninterrupted time together was for me to join Stuart, now Archbishop of York, for a train journey from York to London. During the journey, I asked him where he thought the best forward-thinking was to be found in the diocese. After a long pause, he said, 'in the team ministries – yes, in the team ministries'.

Synodical government produced a significant example of an initiative starting from the 'grass roots'. The inner-city deanery of Liverpool North brought a motion to the diocesan synod, asking for fresh help to be given where the struggle was hardest. In response, the Diocesan Synod set up a two-year 'Urban Priority Areas (UPAs) Working Party', which I chaired jointly with Graeme Spiers, the Archdeacon of Liverpool. One far-reaching recommendation of our report was to change the system of financial quota (based on what a parish had raised in the previous year) to 'quota by potential'. I shall describe that in a later chapter. We also recommended that clergy should never be asked to serve without a colleague. That meant giving some priority to UPAs in staffing, and raising serious questions about the possibility of joining parishes together in group or team ministries.

Many of those plans were frustrated because of opposition bred from old loyalties in long-established parishes. I valued the careful way in which Michael Henshall approached proposals like this, with colleagues in the Pastoral Committee. On many occasions, it meant accepting that proposals we had hoped to carry should be dropped, rather than riding roughshod over local objections. We still pressed clergy and parishes to learn more about working collaboratively. Our predecessors had already done much of the unpopular work of closing parishes.

I was grateful to those who had tackled pastoral reorganisation drastically in the 1960s in areas where the population had declined dramatically. In some cases, for example in Liverpool's northern inner city, it had fallen to as little as one-tenth of what it had once been. Demolishing churches is never a popular activity. But it made it possible for the diocese to put good resources into new parishes in the outer estates to which twice as many people had moved as stayed in the inner city. When team parishes were established in post-war outer-estate areas, they did not have to overcome long-standing loyalties to old parishes.

Offering support to 280 stipendiary clergy could only be done by sharing the load with the diocesan team. I tried to give unhurried time when clergy faced crisis moments, but had to learn to hand on to others who could stay with problems over a period. We introduced joint work consultations (JWCs) along the lines I had explored in Southwark Diocese. We appointed consultants from within each deanery. Some years later we introduced appraisal in ministry, which was held with the area dean, a key member of the diocesan team. Canon Owen Eva said of JWC, 'It bridges the gap between indifference and interference'. Of our clergy, 50 per cent used annual JWCs. A much larger proportion used the three-yearly appraisal, which was expected of everyone.

The role of women

The role of women in the Church was to become a major point of controversy for the Church of England. At this early time in Liverpool, I wrote:

> It bugs me to be conscious that women in ministry are anxious about whether there will be jobs for them, that they need to have some sort of career structure with more responsible posts. I feel frustrated at being unable to widen the scope of women's ministry, so that the Church's ablest women would offer in greater numbers. I can't help feeling the actual pressure points concern the ordination of women.

Deaconess Lena Prince came to see me soon after I arrived. She had been elected to the General Synod as a member of the House of Laity. She told me she had decided she must resign, because she found herself thinking as though she was a member of the House of Clergy. Like many others, she believed her calling was to be a priest. Deaconess Thelma Tomlinson came back from a visit to the Episcopal Church in the USA, where she had met some of the women who had recently been ordained. She told me she did not want to be an extremist. 'All right,' I said, 'be a tough moderate.' Personally, I became steadily convinced that the ordination of women to the priesthood was God's will for his Church.

When Derek Worlock and I wrote our first book, *Better Together*, we agreed that it was important to show how we handled matters on which we disagreed. We each set out our views on the ordination of women. I said that true ecumenism was not helped forward by holding back from actions we deeply believed to be right. Looking at the biblical evidence, it was true that Jesus chose all males to be his Apostles. I made the point that he also chose all Jews and all free men. The great promise in St Paul is, 'There is no such thing as Jew and Greek, slave and freeman, male and female; for you are all one person in Christ Jesus.'[2] It took the Church eighteen centuries to break down the barrier between slaves and free men. Perhaps it was not surprising that it should have taken even longer to break down the barrier between male and female.

When firm proposals were brought to the General Synod, the 'ecumenical argument' was often brought in as a reason why we should not go forward. Opponents said it would make unity with Rome impossible. One of many joint trips Derek and I made to Ireland was to the college at Maynooth, where most priests for the Roman Catholic Church in Ireland were trained. We were asked to address the John Paul II Society. In my talk, I made the point that the ecumenical movement was between all the churches. There was something arrogantly Anglican to think that it was just between Canterbury and Rome, for Rome was in conversation also with the other world-wide churches – Lutheran, Methodist, Reformed, Baptist. The fact that these other churches had ordained women had not stopped all partnership and serious conversations with Rome. After the meeting, a woman came up to me and said, 'I'm so glad you said that. I'm a Lutheran priest, and I'm studying here at Maynooth.'

November 11, 1992 was a memorable day, when the decisive vote was taken in the General Synod, agreeing that the Church of England would now proceed to ordain women to the priesthood. I felt deeply the rightness of what we had done. Joining in a vigil in Westminster Abbey the night before, and sitting through the debate in the synod, I was in no doubt about the honest – and passionate – convictions held on both sides of the argument. That underlined the pain for those who believed we made the wrong decision. I realised also that Derek Worlock might well be pressed to comment, and rang him immediately after the vote to tell him its result. He issued a statement in which he deeply regretted the additional obstacle it constituted to the fullness of unity he earnestly desired between our two churches. He went on:

> But I know also the conscientious urgings felt by Bishop David and others to an extent that could not be ignored. The final rule for ecumenical dialogue is that when all else fails, all we can do is to offer our endeavours and hurt to God. This we must do by prayer and sharing in the work of the Gospel: by building on the Christian friendship and partnership, which in Merseyside has replaced the sectarian hatreds of old.[3]

Marriage

Another pressure point was around marriage. 'It bugs me that people who talk a lot about marriage break-up do not support a programme to help couples in their marriages . . . It bugs me when a clergy marriage breaks up.' I made various attempts to bring people together to think about marriage – clergy and spouses in particular. Dr Jack Dominian came to speak to ecumenical events and Lay Swanwick. One of my objectives in opening up this subject was to help create the atmosphere in which Christians would feel able to shout for help. Too often people felt this would be an admission of failure that faith should have overcome. I gave wholehearted support to an ecumenical resource for counselling – COMPASS[4] – that was established in Merseyside during these years, with the leadership of John Williamson, the United Reformed Church Moderator. COMPASS sustained training and counselling that included help for marital problems.

One year, as part of a three-day visit to each deanery, Grace joined me for meetings to which couples were invited from each parish. In our joint presentation we tried to make it plain that we had known 'bumpy' days in our own marriage, and had obtained – and valued – help. One discussion began with a question from the floor: 'Is there a particular problem in the Church about marriage? We don't have any problems in our parish!' In the same meeting, I was attacked fiercely by one man for not stating moral positions more firmly. 'You ought to be giving us a lead!' he said. Grace made a point of sitting next to him and his wife over teatime. It emerged that they had just discovered that their own son was homosexual, and they could not come to terms with this. In their confusion it seemed that they were looking for church leaders like me to make hardline statements that might remove the pain they were feeling.

Being able to shout for help can be especially hard for clergy spouses. If there is hurt and the other partner is the vicar, she or he can feel trapped, fearing that all routes to God are blocked. One of the fears is that going for help to someone in the diocese might cost a vicar his or her job. At the suggestion of Michael Baughen, the Bishop of Chester, we set up an Inter-Diocesan Counselling Service (IDCS) that was available to clergy and partners. I made a point of 'topping and tailing' separate letters to every clergy spouse as well as all clergy, telling them about the resource. Telephone numbers are listed for counsellors in each of the five dioceses in the North West. That encourages clergy and spouses to feel free to contact a counsellor outside their own diocese. As bishops, we provided expenses for IDCS, and knew the substantial number who used it each year; but we made a point of not knowing any names of those who had gone to this source for help.

Public/private tensions

Grace and I knew the tension between 'public' and 'private'. The balance was sometimes difficult to achieve. She was the daughter and grand-daughter of clergymen, knew the demands of clergy life and made me know that her support was firmly there. She had given up her career to marry me. Many in her generation of married women were now pursuing their own callings. The rightness of assertiveness in its proper place challenged some of the attitudes that had forbidden clergy spouses to speak up for their own needs. It allowed women to pursue the develop-ment of their own gifts. In a marriage this inevitably leads to changed priorities and redistributing some responsibilities. I was proud when Grace launched out into a new calling as a writer, and her writing led on to speaking engagements and broadcasting.

Entertaining at Bishop's Lodge strengthened many creative links in the diocese and in the wider community. Some meals supported my calling as a bishop – lunches for staff meeting, for area deans, dinner for ecumenical church leaders. The ordinands' party brought together perhaps sixty people in training when they were home for Christmas. In addition, we tried to make the most of meeting people from different walks of life. We had frequent evenings for fifteen or sixteen guests for a buffet meal and lingering conversations. At first Grace did all the catering. Later, we had help, leaving us free to host the various events.

A great deal is expected of bishops' wives. In our early years in Liverpool, a group of them were discussing their lives. Disconcertingly, one said, 'You know we all hate it!' Grace worked her way through, until she felt positively about it as a calling. At the request of the Archbishops'

Adviser on Appointments, she wrote a 'Jackdaw Kit' for wives of bishops. In this she tackled practical – and painful – issues for wives, with humour assisted by cartoons, as they sorted out their modus vivendi with – or in spite of – their husbands!

Keeping a balance between public and private required my supporting her, as well as expecting her to support me. It always seemed to her that my calling must come first, though I banned work from days off and holidays. The day off had always been sacrosanct, and – since the doctor tackled me in Mayflower days – so had six weeks' holiday. One day, Grace came into my study – which she rarely did in working hours – and said, 'I'm taking my cards!' There was a staff crisis at Bishop's Lodge, and I had left the management to her. She had been holding the fort for some difficult months, with no back-up. At the end of our first sabbatical from Liverpool, she told me of her dread of coming back to Bishop's Lodge. We had known such freedom in communicating with each other during that three-month period: now it felt to her that it was all over. I knew that her misgivings were not just about the details of time given to the home, but also at a deep level about my whole attitude. Work commitments sometimes built up to such a degree that personal and family issues were left until we were both tired – often after 11 p.m. or even days later. That had to change. Some modest adjustments to the timetable would be a sign. Reflecting on this change of gear, we both acknowledged that our renewed commitment to keeping some 'prime time' for each other stood the test through some demanding periods. I tried to pass on these hard-won lessons. We gave newly ordained clergy written terms and conditions of work: all clergy were expected to take two hours 'creation time' each day – this was for single people as much as for married – a regular day off each week, and six weeks holiday in the year.

Using the Bible

These issues arose in the bishops' training course. Looking back at my papers from the course, I do not find any account of what now seems a significant 'moving on'. Perhaps it was the case with me, as I read in a description of someone else, that 'imperceptibly he had left fundamental-ism behind'. I asked Canon Basil Naylor, responsible for in-service training of the clergy, if he would give me a seminar on how we treated the Bible. He brought Julian Thornton Duesbery with him. Julian had been Principal of Wycliffe Hall and had retired in Liverpool. We agreed that the New Testament must always be much more than the first chapter of church history. It must always be our first authority – though Julian said, 'I'm so thankful that the Holy Spirit did not die at the end of the

New Testament years.' I was happy as a member of the House of Bishops to agree a report on *The Nature of Christian Belief.* It said: 'The Scriptures, both Old and New, must always have a controlling authority. We need to place ourselves continually under the Scriptures if we are to draw on the grace of that truth of God which brings salvation, and to grow in Christlikeness.'[5]

I saw the calling of the bishop to be not only the guardian of the faith, but also the guardian of the exploration that God encourages his people to attempt. Scripture provides the foundation documents for the Christian Church, against which all our explorations must be tested. But I found myself unwilling now to accept that, if something was 'biblical', this by itself gave it authority. For example, I looked at the Bible's teaching that forbade usury. Nothing has been more influential in the impact of religious teaching on the world than the setting aside of the teaching that forbade usury; for the whole structure of capitalism and of personal investments rests on the acceptance of usury as a moral way to use money.

Professor James Barr correctly described the way in which evangelical Christians, like those of other theological schools, pick out from the mass of biblical writings the material that they see to be the core of the Christian message, and leave other parts on one side. James Barr expresses how it is possible to keep the Bible as our 'controlling authority', having set aside the approach that a teaching is true simply because 'it is biblical'. Key tests would be that the core message we preach fits with the way God has turned towards us in Jesus Christ, that it embodies truths that would be ruined if diluted by other religious views, and that it speaks to human need and experience. 'Any of these arguments – all of which are continually to be heard from evangelical pulpits – are perfectly respectable and supportable views. But they are essentially theological argumentation and cannot be settled by mere appeal to the Bible as a whole.'[6]

Christians often express a longing for clear answers to the complex matters we face in human life. However, over the years among our ordinands, I met a steady trickle of men and women who were moving both from the Roman Catholic Church and from the newer independent house churches to the Anglican fold. They told me that the authoritarianism they had met no longer squared with what they understood the Bible to reveal about Jesus and his teaching. Several times, I tried to share some thoughts with ordinands about why I am happy to be an Anglican. One answer involved going to a cupboard in my room to find a paper delivered to the 1988 Lambeth Conference by Elisabeth Templeton, a Church of Scotland theologian. She told us she had been struck by the best generosity within Anglican life, which 'insisted that across parties, camps, styles and dogmas, you have need of one another'. She said she was saddened to feel that we were 'under some pressure to renounce this remarkable openness of being, to tighten up the structures of dogma, ministry, pastoral discipline'. She regretted this, she said, 'for I find your costly openness a gift to the other churches and a gift to the world'.

Bias to the Poor

Among the issues that bugged me most continued to be the realities of life in UPAs: 'It bugs me to realise the frustration of youngsters going back on the dole after twelve months with the Youth Opportunities Programme . . . to see a black community leader torn in half, feeling part of his community and also being embraced by "establishment people" who don't understand.'

The idea of another book, written from within the struggles of Liverpool, was growing in my mind. I was invited to deliver the William Barclay Lectures in Glasgow. Our two cities had much in common, and preparing these lectures seemed to me to be an appropriate first step towards a book. I went up to Glasgow for a two-day reconnaissance. There were visits to Easterhouse, Drumchapel, Black Hill, Andersonstown – inner- and outer-city parishes of the Church of Scotland, which were facing comparable problems to those that were familiar to me from London and Liverpool. William Barclay should have been present, but sadly died in the months before the four lectures on 'The Divine Bias for the Losers'. I had learned the phrase from a Mexican-American Presbyterian in my visit to New York in 1977. He spoke to me about the days of the Civil Rights marches, when Christians of all churches came together behind the leadership of Martin Luther King – and, he said, people saw 'that strange divine bias for the losers'.

I reworked the lectures for the Extra Mural Studies Department of Liverpool University. In a seminar following one of them, Don Bullen, a Methodist minister, said he heard me say nothing that rejected my Cambridge University, evangelical, Anglican background. I was grateful, having at times been accused of working out my guilt at having been given a privileged start. I saw my calling to be a bridge person, trying to hold together that background with what I had seen, heard and felt in urban priority London and Liverpool.

The next steps towards writing the book were to invite a small group to a two-day seminar at Bishop's Lodge. That was a sympathetic group that had first-hand knowledge of Liverpool UPAs. We were helped by the more detached voice of a theologian in John Baker, then a canon at

Westminster Abbey.[7] It was important for me to listen to some less sympathetic voices, and I read the *Daily Telegraph* for a year before putting pen to paper. In it I sometimes came across attitudes that mirrored what one Glasgow minister had said: 'In my opinion, some of these areas would be better described as areas of depravation rather than areas of deprivation.' Harsh judgments surfaced within our churches too. In a visit to Hindley prison, I ran into two volunteer visitors that I had met on visits to their parish. They told me that members of their congregation had told them they were wasting their time: 'You shouldn't bother with scum like that.' And there were those who blamed people for being unemployed – or poor.

In *Bias to the Poor*, I wrote:

> This is not to say that poor people are no more than cases with no responsibility for their actions. 'Where a man has been given much, much will be expected of him', said Jesus. The implication is that where a man has been given little, little will be expected of him. But it would never be right to go on and say that anyone has been given nothing. No one is to be treated as a 'case', as though nothing could be expected of him. The good news for the poor is that Christ meets people where they are; He understands the place where new beginnings are possible. His call to follow Him from that place may be difficult, but it will be realistic.[8]

I tried to show that UPAs present challenges to all citizens and in every part of our lives; Christianity is rightly concerned with wholeness of life. That includes both human hearts and social structures. We do not accept that life is made up of a series of compartments, each having its own autonomy.

> As the urban and industrial world developed, the Christian Church shrank from bringing these matters on its agenda. So whole areas of life in industry, technology and scientific thought slipped out of reach of the prayers and understanding of Christians. Neither with penitence nor with joy could men grasp the spiritual implications of the world they were so swiftly building.[9, 10]

> Our experience has for so long been in a Church which is divided denominationally and ethnically that we can scarcely think in terms of one Church. We take for normal what should be a scandal. The fact that we have for so long tolerated denominational differences and lived in separate Churches has a major influence on our inability to allow people of another culture and colour to share in the decision-making and shaping of 'our' Churches.[11]

Derek Worlock spent a whole afternoon and evening with me, working through the draft I brought home from the sabbatical. When he told a senior Anglican bishop that my book was going to be entitled *Bias to the Poor*, he said, 'He's not going to call it that, is he?' I believed that underlying the title was a debate about what kind of justice God stands for: 'The great prophets of the Old Testament, like Isaiah, Amos, Micah and Jeremiah, spoke about God's concern for righteousness or justice (*tsedeq* in Hebrew). *Tsedeq* "topples over on behalf of those in direst need". This justice is not the same as fairness, as though everyone started from the same line.'[12]

In the last month of our sabbatical, Toxteth had flared up in riots, leaving more than 700 police officers injured. Derek Worlock rang me each morning to keep me posted about what was happening in Liverpool. I went back for one day and walked the streets with him during the third night of the riots. Eventually we decided that we should cut short the sabbatical. We went home, giving me several days in which to listen to the stories that were emerging from Liverpool 8. Here was a fresh challenge to work out a bias to the poor.

15

Listening to the Cries

The Toxteth riots and their aftermath

On our first evening back at Bishop's Lodge a week or two after the Toxteth riots, there was a ring at the door. It was Father Austin Smith. He had not known we had still been away, and wanted to talk. For the next two hours we dropped everything to hear his story and interpretation of the events that had gripped the city and the nation. Austin needed to talk that evening and we needed to listen.

From my first year in Liverpool, I had regarded him as a key interpreter of race relations in the city. His religious order, the Passionists, had given him permission to live, together with another member of the order, in a basement flat off Granby Street. Looking for flickers of hope in Liverpool 8 meant opening the eyes to 'the day of small things'. None of us was going to win any medals there for success stories. Austin talked to me about 'a creation thing' that was going on: if someone was enabled to take control over some aspect of their own destiny, God's creation was becoming fruitful, 'even if it was a tiny acre'. Later, he wrote about the pain: 'The pain comes from the efforts being made by a friend or friends, those I love, to walk but one yard in asserting human dignity . . . Why should my black brother or sister have to fight for equal acceptance in a world boasting equality for all?'[1]

I did my own listening wherever possible during those diary-free days at the end of my sabbatical. However, it was in partnership with Derek Worlock that much of my involvement was now worked out. In July, I had gone back to Liverpool for a day from our sabbatical. Derek and I walked the streets on what was the third night of the riots, and found ourselves taking an unlikely go-between role. A huge police presence and large crowds, including white and black people who had come from other parts of the city – and from other cities – meant that there was something like a 'front line' between them. Wally Brown, then the first Liverpool-born black person to be in the chair of the Merseyside Community

Relations Council (MCRC), sent us a message, asking if we could bring him some megaphones, so that he could tell the crowds to go home. Where were we to find megaphones at 10 o'clock at night? Eventually we went to Hardman Street Police Station with our unexpected request. The duty officer asked what we wanted them for. We said it was to help the leaders of the black community address the crowds and persuade them to go home. 'Who would take them?' We would. 'Could we guarantee their safe return?' No, only their safe delivery. Eventually the duty officer returned from extended consultations. It would be all right if we signed the book for the two megaphones. We duly signed, and made our way to the Community Relations Council office. As we approached it, we were told by two aggressive black men – who had come across from Manchester – to get out. Across the road from the office, we felt it might not help Wally to be seen with us. We gave the megaphones to two small boys and asked them to take them to Wally Brown. A few moments later we heard his voice carrying across the waste ground to the crowd: 'Go home. You will be better there. There is no need for you to be out tonight.'

Lord Scarman asked to see Derek and me on his visit to Liverpool. He had been appointed by the Government to enquire into the Brixton riots that had exploded in April. Now he included Toxteth in his enquiry, and listened with the concentration that impressed so many of us. Leslie Scarman was accompanied by his secretary for the enquiry, Philip Mawer, who was later to become the gifted Secretary General of the General Synod and then of the Archbishops' Council.[2] Lord Scarman distinguished between underlying deprivations – extreme as he found them to be – and the flashpoints that sparked the riots both in Brixton and Toxteth. The flashpoints sprang from relations with the police. Scarman regarded 'Operation Swamp' – to enforce law and order by a massive police presence in Brixton – as the accelerator event which triggered actual violence. Four days later, there was 'a spontaneous act of defiant aggression by young men who felt themselves hunted by a hostile police force'.[3] The sequence of events in Toxteth was very similar. Wally Brown said the Liverpool black community had long experienced mass unemployment. It was the sense of hostile policing that triggered the riots.[4]

Dick Crawshaw, MP for Toxteth, told me that he had been to see William Whitelaw, the Home Secretary, several months before the riots to warn him that an explosion would take place unless policies were changed. After the riots, Dick said that there was a genuine belief that the enforcement of law and order was not even-handed.[5] The Sunday after returning, I asked if I might come and preside at the eucharist at St Margaret's, Princes Road, in the heart of Liverpool 8. Regular members of the congregation – white and black – told me they had been upset by some police behaviour they had seen: 'Why do they have to swear at black people like they do?' (I was told that, after the Brixton riots, Liverpool police had taunted young black men by saying, 'You haven't got the guts to "do a Brixton".')

Reconciliation with the black community and the police

Over the previous years, there had been several meetings between church leaders, the Chief Constable, Ken Oxford,[6] and senior officers. Relations with the black community had been discussed openly, with Edward Patey, Dean of Liverpool, who was then Chairman of the Merseyside Community Relations Council, taking the lead. There was honest talking between the two groups, who realised that we clergy were stereotyped as 'soft' and the police as 'hard'. Both groups rejected such assumptions, and were ready to look at the other's point of view. Ken Oxford found this subject overwhelming. During one conversation I had alone with him, he said angrily, 'Why can't these people who come to our country learn to fit in with our ways?' I was shattered that he had not taken into his thought processes the fact that Liverpool black people were not immigrants. The great majority had been born here. The riots and their aftermath were devastating for Ken. I believe he went through a breakdown. Parts of the black community launched and sustained a campaign for his dismissal, and some vowed they would never sit in a room with him. Actually, the Deputy Chief Constable, to whom Liverpool owes much, Peter Wright, was meeting quietly with black leaders throughout this period, when publicly there was understood to be no contact at all. It was tragic that, as Chief Constable of South Yorkshire, Peter Wright later found himself held responsible for one of Liverpool's greatest disasters – the crushing to death of ninety-six football fans at Hillsborough.

Margaret Simey chaired the police authority and engaged in a running battle with Ken Oxford – sometimes in public. She insisted that policing must be held accountable to the community the police serve:

> The law-and-order school would have us leave it all to the police, gladly endowing them with all the additional powers and resources they see fit to demand. Such an abrogation of responsibility is bred out of fear. That way, to quote Scarman, 'Is a staging post to the police state'. He asserts, 'There has to be some way in which to secure that the independent judgement of the police can not only operate within the law but with the support of the community'.[7]

The Church found itself at the centre of a public storm when the Community and Race Relations Unit (CRRU) of the British Council of Churches gave a grant of £500 to the 'Liverpool 8 Defence Committee'. This committee was set up in the days immediately following the first riots. Its main purpose was to arrange transport for families to visit those who were held on remand at Risley Remand Centre, which was an awkward journey from Liverpool for those without a car. The majority of members were housewives. However, newspapers like the *Daily Mail* pursued conspiracy theories about masked men on motor bikes inciting attacks on the police and 'the man in the white Rolls Royce'. The committee did itself no favours by allowing Michael Showers, who was indeed the man in the white Rolls Royce, to give interviews on television. They told me he had no authority from the committee to do so, but they seemed unable to stop him.

Newspapers attributed the making of the £500 grant to 'the churches', assuming that Merseyside church leaders had sanctioned the grant. In fact we had neither been consulted, nor forewarned of the announcement of the grant. But we respected the CRRU staff and were clear that we must stand by them. Norwyn Denny, Derek and I issued a joint statement. We reaffirmed our condemnation of violence, but asked for understanding for this gesture of help towards groups which were an authentic expression of some strongly held feelings. These resulted from the experience of years of massive deprivation.

It was an uncomfortable time. Derek Worlock and I received fierce criticism in public and in personal letters from police officers. A group of his clergy pressed Derek that he should not go out alone, because of their fears of what the police might do. I received strongly worded protests from suburban parishes; one insisted that, if church money was given, it should be channelled through local churches. One suburban vicar told me that there was real fear in his parish that rioters might come down their streets. In the middle of angry correspondence like this, I was grateful to receive a letter from Martin Hunt, vicar of a large outer-estate parish. He said that a police officer, a member of the church, had been injured. They were supporting him. At the same time he said how thankful he was that church leaders were trying to stand beside those who had been so deprived.

One member of the small group of couples with whom Grace and I regularly met was Canon Neville Black, team rector of an inner-city parish. He and Val lived close to the scene of the rioting. They asked the group to discuss how we felt about it. They said they did not agree with the use of violence, but believed that the police had picked on people in their neighbourhood over years. Two other members, Canon Owen Eva, Team Rector of Halewood, and his wife Joy then told us that their policeman son had been permanently scarred in the face by a brick thrown on the first night of the riots. There was no escaping the acute discomfort of being wedged between two sets of people, knowing that we belonged to both.

At the end of September I addressed the diocesan synod. I told them of spending a morning in the previous few days with the Toxteth clergy chapter: 'I was a little fearful that we might tear ourselves apart. For there are such different communities and attitudes within Toxteth. Churches naturally reflect these different communities. I was very thankful that, though different opinions were strongly held in that chapter meeting, there was a great deal of love and readiness to listen among the clergy and lay workers of the area. I hope that this may be true of the debate in the diocese.' When Robert Runcie came to preach at Liverpool Parish Church the following Lent, I went with him to have breakfast with the Toxteth clergy and their families. We were aware that those in the immediate area had faced special pressures.

Earlier, while Grace and I were still on sabbatical in London, the phone in our flat went at breakfast time. It was Derek Worlock: 'She's here!' he said. We had known the Prime Minister might visit Liverpool, but understandably security ruled and no announcement was made until she arrived. She wanted to talk with the church leaders, and I asked Michael Henshall to take my place. A crowd had learned that she had come and 'was baying for her blood' outside the Town Hall, where they met. She asked, 'Why is there such hatred?' Derek and Michael talked about our role in working for reconciliation with parts of the community that had been left out of good opportunities. Michael then spoke of the need for compassion. Denis Thatcher, who had come to stand by his wife, said to her, 'That's not one of your words, is it?' She replied, 'I find it so condescending.' They tried to explain that true *com-passion* meant 'suffering with'. Derek pressed the needs of Merseyside and asked that she consider appointing a Minister for Merseyside with a place in the Cabinet. Michael Heseltine soon appeared in that capacity, to Liverpool's considerable advantage.

In our attempts to work out the role of reconcilers we were on occasions attacked from both sides: attempts to move towards those who felt deeply alienated often met with suspicion or anger. And from the other side we were accused of being soft and of undermining society. Surmounting suspicion and anger felt in the black community sometimes took perseverance. In 1978, encouraged by some black Anglicans, I had brought a proposal to the General Synod that the Church of England should raise a special fund to make grants to self-help groups. I went over to Manchester to ask a group of black community leaders from Liverpool and Manchester whether they would welcome such a fund being established. A solid wall of suspicion met me: 'Why is the Church of England wanting to help just now?' Representatives from the two cities seemed to outbid each other in tough talking. I thought that this would give way, after the toughness had been established, to discussing practical means, but it did not. I stayed on for a drink, again hoping that informally there might be positive overtures. There were none. In the morning I rang a close ally in the black community: 'What was I meant to hear?' He said that control was the key issue. I was meant to hear that they would not accept grants that had strings attached, but that several younger people who had been present were very upset at the rejection of what I was suggesting. They would have welcomed such a fund.

The Bishop of Ripon, David Young, then Chairman of the Church of England Board of Mission, took the proposal forward, that the money raised should be given to the Ecumenical Projects Fund of CRRU, which already had experience of vetting and supporting self-help groups. The Synod voted to call for dioceses to seek to raise £100,000 a year for self-help groups in inner-city areas. When we brought the proposal to the Liverpool diocesan synod, Canon Malcolm Forrest moved an amendment from the floor that this should be placed on the diocesan budget. As Rector of Wigan, he was well placed to propose this amendment, as he was unlikely to see his own parish obtain grants from this Fund. Including it in the diocesan budget, rather than leaving it to a yearly appeal, meant that the Liverpool contribution was sustained, when others dropped off – especially after 1986, when the Church Urban Fund (CUF) appealed for large sums to be raised in each diocese. CUF gave substantial money to the Projects Fund.

After the riots in Toxteth, leaders in the black community approached Derek Worlock and me. Would we support their wish to set up a law centre? It would take some time to research ways and means. An American Episcopalian, Anne Exley-Stiegler, gave her skill and commitment full-time and in a voluntary capacity. She served a joint working party with colleagues put forward from the black community and from the Liverpool Law Society. Through the winter of 1981–82, they brought us a report each month; the five leaders of the main Christian denominations sat across the table from a changing group of black leaders. Gradually suspicion gave way to trust. At one meeting, Peter Bassey, who was to become the first chairman of the Liverpool 8 Law Centre, described how hurt they had been at the crude attacks made in the press, revealing past police records of some. Then he looked across the table at us, and said, 'And you took some flak too!'

Derek Worlock said to me, 'You and I must go round to see everyone who is likely to shoot from the hip.' We did that – also to see those we hoped would support the centre. David Alton, who became a trusted ally over many issues, expressed serious doubts, when he came to a working lunch in our kitchen with Norwyn Denny and me.[8] We argued that it would be a significant step forward for many in Liverpool 8 to believe that the law could be a friend and not a foe. At the time there was no black barrister, solicitor or solicitor's clerk in Liverpool. Over the years there has been small but significant progress, so that black barristers and solicitors are now working in Liverpool. One of our hopes was that the law centre could be a stepping stone towards the possibility of lawyers emerging from the black community. The Liverpool Law Society agreed to put forward a nominee, Laurence Holden, to serve on the management committee, alongside three representatives that the church leaders would nominate. Lord Scarman gave firm support. Lord Hailsham, then Lord Chancellor, and Home Office Ministers raised no objections. Peter Wright, the Deputy Chief Constable, saw the point of the law centre, and supported our involvement through thick and thin.

Reconciliation with the police received an important boost, when Peter Wright's successor, John Burrow,[9] took the initiative in launching a Church–Police Liaison scheme. This encouraged honest criticisms to flow in either direction. We nominated a threesome – Free Church, Roman Catholic and Anglican – in every police district, while the police put forward an officer to meet with them. Each year there was a lunch to which the new Chief Constable, Jim Sharples, always came, as we church leaders did. He was a man of very different stamp from Ken Oxford. He was open to discussion and honest criticism. The healing of personal relationships allowed trusting conversations on many occasions. It meant much to me, following the bitter times of 1981, for Grace and me to be given a dinner by Jim Sharples and his senior colleagues on my retirement, at which they presented me with one of the traditional Merseyside police measuring sticks.

In 1989, Jim Sharples got off to a very unlucky start. An independent enquiry made by Lord Gifford, published its report within days of Sharples taking up office. Lord Gifford said he had heard deep criticism of policing in Liverpool 8 from a number of witnesses, including 'priests, lawyers, shopkeepers, fire officers, academics, lay visitors, magistrates, councillors, social workers, as well as many ordinary people, black and white, old and young'.[10] Derek and I asked clergy in the area what they made of the report. Our area dean, Simon Starkey, said it 'did not go over the top. It seemed to tell things just about how they were.' It would have been hard for Sharples to accept these criticisms as his first action. He dismissed the report as being unofficial, that it had not taken evidence from most police officers, and was not to be relied on. I sympathised with the position in which he found himself – succeeding Ken Oxford, who had been described as 'Mrs Thatcher's favourite policeman'. Jim Sharples needed to win the confidence of his officers; yet the stance he adopted meant that many in the black community dismissed the possibility that he would ever understand them.

In October 1985 there had been serious disturbances again. Twice during the evening, leaders at the law centre asked Derek and me to come there to see what was happening. The area was ringed by a large police force. We kept in touch with the Deputy Chief Constable who was in operational control throughout. All seemed to have calmed down after a while. But at about 10.30 p.m., we received another request to come to the law centre. Local black community leaders took us to the main area of disturbance. One said, 'This is about territory. Granby Street is the heart of our territory.' When we arrived there, we saw rows of police vehicles, filled with officers in riot gear. Walking down Granby Street, we saw not more than 150 largely local residents, the biggest group numbering no more than 30 or 40. We asked the Inspector in charge whether, in the light of what the Deputy Chief Constable had said to us, it would be possible to withdraw the vehicles and especially to stay out of Granby Street. He assured us that his intention was to do just that. A moment later the vehicles revved their engines, drove straight through our group and, with sirens blaring, raced into Granby Street. It was obvious that something had gone wrong with the command structure. Drivers were receiving orders that contradicted the Inspector on the spot. We walked back down the street, hoping to be able to calm some tempers. Some ten police vans were now parked in the street. Then two Landrovers, with strong spotlights and sirens going, swept on and off the pavements to scatter those still gathered there. At one stage we both had to flatten ourselves against the wall, as a Landrover came on to the pavement between a lamp-post and the wall of a house. One of its side mirrors passed just beneath our faces. Eventually most people were persuaded to go inside or leave Granby Street. The community leaders continued to act as a restraining influence and dispersed some youngsters who were trying to set fire to a property. Fire engines were now able to come in without difficulty and the police pulled back from the immediate area soon after 1 a.m. The next day we did a complete debriefing session with John Burrow, who publicly expressed his thanks to the law centre and the community leaders.

I was asked to walk down Granby Street again some years later. Margaret Simey came on the phone. There had been a shooting in the street the previous day. She said, 'I want you to walk down Granby Street to show that it is perfectly safe, and that normal life goes on there.' I agreed, subject to two conditions. First, I needed to receive a request from local people. Second, I must be able to find a church leader of another denomination who would come with me. Within ten minutes I received a call from the chairperson of the local community group asking me to come. She would meet us and walk with us. Graham Cook, the United Reformed Church Moderator, came with me. Among other visits, we went into the 'Cop Shop' that had been established in Granby Street, as part of the extension of 'community policing'. I regarded that 'shop' as a brave symbol of firm intent that the police should be accessible to the community – repaired following an occasion when it was rammed by a vehicle. On my visit to inner-city churches and projects in New York, I had seen what happens if foot patrol community policing is abandoned. I was on the sidewalk with two black clergy from St Philip's, Harlem, when a voice boomed over our shoulders, 'Keep walking': it was a police car, crawling along the road with a loud hailer on the roof.

Since 1989 the Merseyside police have undoubtedly tried to make themselves more accessible and to build up more trusting community relations. An increasing number of voices from the black community have insisted that they genuinely want good communications with the police. When joy riders killed two children in the streets of Toxteth, mothers banded together to barricade whole streets and demanded greater presence and protection from the police. In a recent letter to me, Merseyside's Chief Constable, Norman Bettison, wrote about 'the feeling of condoning criminality that may have predominated a few years ago'. He believed that this attitude had now 'been reversed to the extent that people feel encouraged to assist us in ridding their communities of criminals and drugs'. Much crime in Toxteth, as in other parts of Merseyside – and of the country at large – has been drug-related. Most local people now would neither condone nor cover up the presence of the drug dealers. In a recent operation, the police provided a very visible presence, and also issued leaflets to residents, explaining their actions.

Progress in the key issue of recruiting black police officers in the Merseyside police has been slow, but significant. In 1987 there were 13 police officers from ethnic minorities. In 2001, there were 82 – exceeding the Home Office target for Merseyside (just over 2 per cent of the economically active population). We found senior police officers were increasingly ready to see that they had a part to play, if there was to be reconciliation with alienated communities.

It was part of our role in the 'reconciliation business' to engage with both sides. Some partisans of 'liberation theology' had the attitude that we should 'shake the dust off our feet' against all Establishment structures and authorities. Had not Jesus told his followers to do this, if people would not listen to them? But before believing that might be our calling, surely we must make every effort to call them back to their proper role. The anarchist does not explain what he or she would put in their place.

The Marxist looks to the triumph of the proletariat, but does not explain how such new masters would be less oppressive than other tyrants would.

In 1981, Alan Taylor was my adviser on race relations: he had served as a curate at St Margaret's, Toxteth, and was now vicar of another inner-city parish. The night the riots blew up, Alan went to see what was happening, and to report to me. Sometimes the violence that night was described as 'mindless'. That was not always quite true. Undoubtedly some attacked the police in the belief that they were part of an oppressive authority. Others insisted that they should be selective in what was attacked. Alan heard discussions among the rioters about which buildings they should burn: the Rackets Club was described as an intrusion into their area by another social class. The furniture store in the former Rialto was held to have been a poor employer. They decided they should not burn St Margaret's vicarage and church, because they offered service to the community. Locals restrained outsiders from burning down Princes Park Hospital. Alan's clerical collar enabled him to mix freely with all concerned, especially when he helped to evacuate the hospital, and stay behind, holding the fort until the following morning.

Liberation theology has pressed some sharp challenges to the Church. One is the need to see things 'from below'. Professor Bonino, an Argentine Methodist, said that the liberating Church does not impose a system from above – as in colonial Christianity. 'It accompanies the people, speaking the *kerugmatic* word' (the word for Christian proclamation).[11] That means standing alongside poor people when we believe their cause is just. It also means challenging them when the Christian word questions the methods they use and the attitudes they hold towards others.

I was embarrassed when, at one of the monthly meetings about the proposed law centre, Michael Showers (the man in the white Rolls Royce) appeared. Later, I was even more embarrassed that he was elected vice chairman of the law centre. We came eyeball to eyeball in the centre one day. Michael said, 'I hear that you don't think I ought to be vice chairman.' My reply was, 'I want the law centre to flourish, Michael, and I think your presence doesn't help.' 'What am I supposed to have done?' he asked. I said some people were afraid of him. 'I've never done anything I would be ashamed of my children knowing,' he said. I looked him in the eyes and asked, 'Drugs, Michael?' He was subsequently sentenced to twenty years for drug offences. Even in my meetings with Michael Showers, I was made aware of God's presence in unlikely places: one day, I brought him greetings from a Quaker prison visitor, who told me that, having visited him in prison at an earlier time, he had invited him to his home. Michael Showers' tone changed: 'That man is a beautiful person,' he said. And when Derek Worlock was gravely ill, he was surprised to have a letter from Michael. He wrote from prison, 'I don't know whether God hears the prayers of someone like me, but I am asking Him to help you.'

The law centre has had its ups and downs, including struggles to sustain funding. The City Council provided some grants, but these rarely felt secure with pressures on local authority funding. There were also cutbacks at times in legal aid payments to the centre's lawyers. Money from charities played an important part. In particular, John Moores Junior[12] told me that he and his wife Jane had determined to 'bleed themselves', if necessary, to make sure the law centre survived. I greatly admired their use of their part of the Moores' family fortune in supporting some of the neediest, but also most unpopular, causes. Derek Worlock and I continued for some years to show our support by writing a foreword to the law centre's annual report. I regretted the centre's continued policy of refusing entry to the police. But a wide range of people, many of whom had never thought the law could be a friend, have found sensitive and professional advice there.

The most painful moment for me was when Wally Brown came to tell me that he was pulling out of Liverpool. I had felt anxious for him when I saw him on television, emerging from meeting the Prime Minister in Liverpool Town Hall. Now he felt torn in half. Chairman of the Community Relations Council, he found himself being embraced by the Establishment – with the risk that his own people would distrust him. Serving on a management committee, he found other local black members discovering pressing calls on their time, when there were disciplinary matters against a black member of staff, leaving him alone to vote for dismissal. Years later, he told me how much he had valued being able at times to come and talk to me. But it didn't prevent his pulling out of Liverpool then. Perhaps he needed a 'breather'. He was to return later as Principal of Liverpool Community College.

Minister for Merseyside – Michael Heseltine

In the aftermath of the riots, Margaret Thatcher responded to the request to appoint a Minister for Merseyside in the Cabinet. As Secretary of State for the Environment, Michael Heseltine was given this responsibility. He immediately came up to Liverpool and spent fourteen days in the area, listening and seeing for himself. He described his first meeting with community groups in Liverpool 8 – boycotted by leaders of the black community. Afterwards, he was told they would only meet him if he came on to their ground. So, the next meeting was arranged there with leaders of the Liverpool 8 Defence Committee.

It was made clear that only my political colleagues, my officials and I could attend. The police had to remain outside . . . We descended into a basement room, sat with our backs to the window, as far from the door as it was possible to be. The room was packed. It was the most demanding meeting I have ever chaired. It was not ill-tempered, just extremely brittle . . . Slowly the tension subsided. The same issues came up time and again. I explained once more that I was there to listen, hopefully to understand, as a senior representative of a government that took their concerns seriously.[13]

That meeting lasted two hours. The word went around that Michael Heseltine was ready to listen. Meetings with other groups followed. He made no secret of his shock at what he saw – not only in inner-city areas like Toxteth, but also in outer estates like Croxteth and Cantril Farm – which he said was 'a disaster which looked beyond retrieving'. He came to talk with our group of church leaders during his fourteen-day walkabout. I asked him if he was willing to risk giving money to projects in deeply hurt areas, where perhaps 50 per cent might be wasted. He replied that he was willing to take such risks – provided the press did not make the position impossible. In the event, the ground rules for government grants usually ruled out major risk-taking.

He went to the Cabinet with requests for substantial increases in spending. When this was refused, he put all his energy into making the most of programmes that were already in being. He established a Government Office in Merseyside that brought together civil servants from different departments. This had the intention of producing what was later to be called 'Joined-up Government', with antennae listening for the effect of policies in the area. His enthusiasm boosted the Merseyside Development Corporation (MDC) and the plans for an International Garden Festival, that would regenerate a rubbish tip, preparing part for housing, as well as giving us the opportunity for a festival that would bring 3 million visitors to Liverpool in 1984.

Michael Heseltine introduced competitiveness into bids for public spending. One of his successes was to break a longstanding deadlock about the public or private use of the land below our cathedral. A councillor had said to me, 'We will stop them developing the land around the Cathedral,' as though an open space like a park would benefit the cathedral. I replied that the great Gothic cathedrals had been meant to rise up out of a jumble of roofs, and this vast building could look after itself. I always wanted there to be a buzz of life with people around it. Michael Heseltine set up a competition for the best architect's plan for a development that must include a mixture of public (housing association) and private housing. Architects entering it must have a developer's commitment in their pocket. The firm Brock Carmichael, who made major contributions to community-based architecture in the city, duly won the competition. Major hurdles still had to be overcome to produce the private housing. This was largely the achievement of the dean, Derrick Walters, as I shall describe in a later chapter.

Different programmes now relied on competitions. Perhaps the most effective was City Challenge, in the 1990s. The advantage was that it concentrated resources on carefully chosen areas. The damaging part was that competitions meant there were losers as well as winners. A major factor in a Minister's decision about which district won was the amount that could be 'levered in' from the private sector. The public money was 'top sliced' from the urban programmes of fifty-seven urban areas – in effect from the losers. One year, Knowsley, top of most league tables of need, took the bidding process for City Challenge very seriously. There was a high level of community participation in the preparation of the bid. When it was learned that they were not among the winners, there was a deflating sense of having been let down. To add insult to injury, Knowsley's own grants were among those 'top sliced' to provide City Challenge money for the winners. Later, they were to do much better with the European Objective One programme.

The largest of the Michael Heseltine interventions was the trans- formation of a 1970s estate, Cantril Farm, into Stockbridge Village. Heseltine brought together a consortium of major private sector companies, and backed them with public money. The phrase 'pouring money in' was used too often in journalists' accounts of government help. For example, when Meadowell estate in Newcastle exploded in the 1980s, a broadsheet newspaper said that £1 million had been 'poured in' only a year before. That would have amounted to about £100 per resident. But in Stockbridge Village, at a cautious estimate, £27 million of public money, together with major contributions from the private sector, was injected. Ten years on, Richard Evans and Hilary Russell reviewed the effects. The housing problems, which had seemed the sharpest, had been reversed to a remarkable extent. Tenants had been desperate to obtain a transfer out of the estate – some set fire to their own flats in order to do so. Now there was a waiting list of 700 to obtain a home in Stockbridge Village. However, the review showed that problems remained despite the evident relief of housing distress. On a number of indicators – unemployment, car ownership, single-parent households, eligibility for free school meals, clothing grants and housing benefit – Stockbridge Village's socio-economic standing relative to the rest of Knowsley had remained constant or even declined. 'It puts a question mark against an urban renewal strategy based solely on housing.'[14]

Jim Lloyd, the leader of Knowsley Borough Council was determined to bring about changes to what he once described as an 'anarchical' workforce. The first time I had met him was when he came with the Chief Executive, Mr Wilgoose, to calm down a row that had erupted. In a community newspaper, one of our most able young clergy, Dave Thomas,[15] had written sharp criticisms of the borough's housing policies and practice in Kirkby. The local Kirkby housing sub-committee had been angered by this and minuted that 'Rev Thomas be reported to the Bishop'. Mr Wilgoose regretted that he had not heard in time, or would have prevented them from passing this resolution condemning honest criticism. He then used circuitous language to describe the problems the council was having with its direct labour force. Jim Lloyd broke in to say, 'You know the truth is that we are facing anarchy!' When he became leader, Lloyd set out to make Knowsley, firmly left wing as it was, efficient and co-operative. Michael Heseltine recognised someone he could work with. However, he received a message by a round-about route from Jim Lloyd: 'Would Mr Heseltine please refrain from calling him Jim, as it was damaging his political credibility locally!'

Private-sector management

Michael Heseltine challenged the private sector to reverse its desertion of the inner cities. Famously in 1982, he took a busload of directors from the City of London round parts of Merseyside, pressing them to come and invest. Two years later, Derek Worlock and I invited a senior management group of Merseyside businessmen to meet in Archbishop's House on Michaelmas Day. There seemed to have been little response to Michael Heseltine's challenge, despite the private sector's desire to help. We agreed that those of us on the spot needed to see *our* responsibility and possibilities that lay with *us*, before asking outsiders to come and rescue us. We formed the Michaelmas Group, which met over breakfast each month from then on. It brought together senior management in the private and public sectors. I was asked to take the chair. The group flirted with some entrepreneurial ideas about mounting a 'Made in Merseyside' exhibition, but decided that we should not enter such territory. We became a group where 'Chatham House rules' prevailed: opinions were freely expressed without fear of leaks. Hard information was shared. Between the members of the group, we could feed positive ideas for the regeneration of the city into strategic places. When Derek and I were asked to talk to government ministers, we went well briefed.

In my first year in Liverpool, I had asked Alfred Stocks, Chief Executive of the City Council, if he would welcome meeting privately. He agreed and we met every six weeks – as I did with Peter Bounds when he became chief executive. During the years of confrontation between the Militant council and the Government, Alfred agreed to look at the text of any statement I planned to make. Occasionally that meant meeting before breakfast. He did not necessarily agree with my opinion, but made sure that I knew the facts as he saw them.[16] Belonging to the Michaelmas Group meant that we received advice from senior voices in the private sector as well. At the same time, I hoped to reflect how life was seen *from below* – through the contacts I have tried to describe earlier in these chapters.

Nicholas Barber, senior Merseyside director of Ocean Transport and Trading, was a founder member of the group, and made sure it was professionally serviced by seconding Roger Morris to be our secretary. Nicholas was promoted, and, as so often happened, had to move to the London office. I introduced him to a group that the Dean of St Paul's, Alan Webster, had brought together in the business City of London following the publication of *Faith in the City*. Nicholas wrote to me, describing his feelings on joining this group. He said the membership fell into two parts: these had decisively different approaches to what the private sector could offer in response to *Faith in the City*'s account of the needs of people in Urban Priority Areas. One part assumed it was all about how firms could help church and community projects with charitable giving. The other part agreed with that, but argued that the way in which a firm operated in its mainline business life could have even greater effect on people in poorer parts of a city.

Sir Hector Laing[17] was chairman of United Biscuits. He had close church links, and pressed me to invite him to address senior businessmen in Liverpool about his 'One per cent Club'. Joining this 'club' meant a commitment to giving 1 per cent of a company's profits to charity. I saw the substantial contribution this could make, and duly arranged a dinner. A good number came to listen. What was unfortunate was that many of them suspected that United Biscuits, a major and traditional employer in Liverpool, was about to pull out of the city. It was hard for employers like David Booth of BICC – who told me he had spent all his working life trying to keep the company invested in the North West – to listen to Hector's call. Within weeks after this dinner, the announcement was made that United Biscuits was closing in Liverpool, with the loss of over 4,000 jobs. My own feelings can be imagined when Hector Laing told me that he could not have closed it before, 'because of Douglas'. Douglas was Sir Douglas Crawford – of Crawfords Biscuits – who was Lord Lieutenant of Merseyside in the 1970s. While he was alive, Hector Laing did not feel able to close the Liverpool operation of their firm. I could not help comparing the personal influence of respect for one senior man with the effect of redundancy on two generations of families. Derek and I visited the factory at the request of the management after the announcement of the closure. We met five workers from one family, among the thousands who were losing their jobs.

In 1981 Tate and Lyle had closed their sugar refinery in the North End of Liverpool. Fifteen hundred people were made redundant in an area where unemployment was already 46 per cent. Derek and I went with a delegation from the city to argue the case for British sugar manufacturing with the Minister of Agriculture, Peter Walker. Then we made one last attempt by asking to see the chairman of the company, Lord Jellicoe. Early on a cold morning, we sat in the reception area at the company's London headquarters near Tower Bridge, waiting to be summoned to the chairman's room on the top floor. The receptionist was a young woman. She said, 'I know why you're here. I'm a Christian too, and I'll be praying for you when you're up there.' As we went up in the lift, I said how encouraging it was to think of her prayers supporting us. Derek said, 'There's a lot of it about!' We made the case, but, as was generally the reality when a closure was announced, the decision had been made – perhaps years before – when it had been decided not to reinvest in new technology.

In the Liverpool Bishop's Council, I was asked how successful we felt we were in our protests against closures. 'Very unsuccessful!' was the reply. I was very grateful to John Stanley, Vicar of Huyton, for what he said next; 'You may have failed, but it has meant a lot to people who are suffering that you have stood with them and been seen to fail with them.'

The question of insurance cover was raised with me when I met the senior men of the Indian Workers Association, on a visit to Southall. They were the shopkeepers of Southall High Street. Some told me that they had been refused cover; others that the cost charged for premises in their postal code made insurance prohibitive. As it happened, I was invited to have dinner later that week with a small group of senior bankers and other business leaders. Their other guest was David Young, who was then Secretary of State for Employment. I repeated what I had been told about these small businesses, and said to David, 'These are the hope of the side – especially the hope of your side!' Mrs Thatcher's Government had constantly spoken of the key significance of small businesses in regenerating inner cities.

The difficulty of obtaining insurance was an issue in UPAs all over the country. Clergy found that insurance on cars or vicarages soared if they were located in postal codes where risks were regarded as high. I was nearly shown the door by the angry managing director of a major insurance firm. I had suggested that something like 'redlining' was going on (American banks sometimes admitted that they would draw a red line round districts where bank loans would not be given). He denied that anything like that happened here.

However, years later I asked Merseyside Broad Based Organising whether they understood that insurance was a problem. MBO brought together members of religious bodies who would identify 'actions' that were needed in their community. An 'action' would set out to persuade authorities or companies to tackle unmet needs. They brought a group largely from Kirkby to Bishop's Lodge. They told me that few people they knew felt they could afford to insure their homes. One told me her brother was a plumber and spent Christmas mending people's burst pipes 'for free', because none were insured. When a friend from the insurance industry brought a colleague from the Association of British Insurers to see me, he acknowledged that when he started, his company would run a door-to-door campaign every year to sell insurance. Now it was largely left to people to approach them by telephone. The result was that basic services like insurance – and banking too – were not to be found in areas like the large outer estates. Rather than argue for priority treatment, in these circumstances we wanted to obtain the normal services that the rest of the country took for granted.

A journalist asked me if I was not risking my spirituality by getting so involved in secular issues. I said that these involvements often took me out of my depth. And the knowledge of being out of my depth drove me to take hold of spiritual resources. It never occurred to me that fighting their corner would bring hurt people straight to personal believing or into membership of the Church. Those who stand right outside the Church generally need to believe there is a good and purposeful creator, before they can start to think that Christ might be for them. These matters of social justice were 'kingdom of God issues' – or 'creation things' as Austin Smith taught me to say.

16

Confrontation

By the end of the 1970s, partnership between management and labour seemed doomed to failure after governments of both major parties had tried to work incomes policies by consent. Polarisation became the order of the day. Margaret Thatcher took advantage of unemployment as a weapon to bring the unions to heel. She described Arthur Scargill's National Union of Mineworkers as 'the enemy within'. She saw Liverpool City Council in similar terms, and in Liverpool the enmity was whole-heartedly reciprocated.

Michael Heseltine told me in a brief aside that Merseyside County Council was 'extreme left wing'. He was wrong about that. In the House of Lords debate on the Metropolitan Counties Bill at the end of June 1984, I said that the proposed abolition of Merseyside County Council was a tragedy at a time when there was an urgent need for reconciliation. 'Alongside the bitter divisions of politics which have long dogged Liverpool City Council, the County Council is a body in which there is that old and valuable habit of reaching out beyond the boundaries of one political party.' An example of this was when I seized an opportunity at a reception to ask Keva Coombs, then leader of the County Council, to consider a possible resource for voluntary bodies. He drew the Conservative and Liberal leaders over to discuss the matter. There had then been consensus. But all the debate centred on Ken Livingstone and the GLC, and the other metropolitan counties were swept away without any serious hearing.

The Militants

The extreme politics were not to be found in Merseyside County Council, but in Liverpool City Council. A Labour council was elected in 1983, with a strong hard-left element, a vote brought about by feelings that the city had been deserted. Then the Militants had taken over control of the Liverpool Labour Party. To start with, they had a broad raft of support.

At least they were standing up for Liverpool against a Government that did not seem to care. But, from the beginning, I was anxious about how the Militants might damage the city. Even so, it was right to work collaboratively wherever possible. They had been duly elected.

This raised harder questions for local government officers like Alfred Stocks, who sadly died within three years of retirement. Alfred served political masters holding very different convictions and ideologies. He saw his role as a public *servant* indeed. He offered robust advice in warning. But he believed deeply in democracy, the ballot box and local government, and he served the elected authority with loyalty and integrity. He talked to me about the young deputy leader, Derek Hatton, and encouraged me to meet him on a personal level. Derek had energy and an attractive manner. He could be good company. But when he drank in the heady mixture of power – speaking to large crowds and believing that he was fighting for the working classes of the city – he ranted the slogans that would keep the crowds behind him.

Margaret Thatcher's Government had cut expenditure on public housing, so that it was almost impossible to build new council estates. Now, the Militants deliberately courted confrontation with the Government on housing. They produced an urban regeneration strategy, which developed good council building – widely referred to as 'the Derek Hatton houses'. When the whole story emerged, we learned that money earmarked for other causes had been diverted to these. For example, the day after the Militant councillors were barred from office, I met the new chairman of the Housing Committee and the chief housing officer. They told me that, good as the 4,000 or 5,000 'Hatton houses' were, no budget had been allowed for keeping them in good repair. And the money for repairs for the 60,000 dwellings for which the corporation was responsible had been siphoned off to spend on building these comparatively few estates. The leader of the council, who had succeeded the Militants, Keva Coombs, came to speak to the Michaelmas Group. I asked him whether it was true, as I was informed, that there was at least twelve months delay for any housing repairs. Keva replied bitterly, 'We don't *do* repairs!' That was part of the legacy left by the Militant years. Part was also – as it was intended to be – that the new estates established a strong political base for Militant in parts of the city in which they might expect to win seats on the council.

The power behind the throne in the Militant council was Tony Byrne, who eventually became leader in their last days in power. Tony was a man of absolute convictions. He believed that municipalised housing or social services would always serve people better than private sector or voluntary bodies could. We had a long talk alone in my study one day. I had supported the development of housing co-operatives. Tony said, 'You

don't know where housing co-ops come from. They are a Liberal policy.'
I said I did not much mind where the idea came from. They seemed to
me to offer good homes and a stake for people in managing their own
housing. But ideology was crucial to Tony Byrne. He told me firms had
blacklisted him as a militant shop steward. He had then moved into the
field of housing for homeless people. He was alleged to have told Mother
Teresa that he had done more for the poor than she had! He did not
approve of the voluntary basis of the work her Sisters did in Seel Street
when they came to Liverpool.

Part of the Militants' urban regeneration strategy was to clear a large
area in the North End of the inner city. It was to form a new, large,
Everton Park. One morning, I received a phone call with a request from
Jane Corbett, wife of the Rector of St Peter's, Everton. She and Henry
Corbett played a vigorous, but self-effacing role in supporting local
people's growing confidence, knowing when to stand back from interfering with local leadership in the West Everton Community Council. The
request was that I should come down immediately and stand with them
in front of 'good four-bedroom houses' that the council had ordered to
be demolished – to make space for Everton Park. I was told that local
people did not ask for the Park, and that the council leaders had said
that consultation was 'a bourgeois exercise' that was unnecessary, because
the councillors knew what was best. I agreed to come, provided a Roman
Catholic priest from the area – where the old sectarian conflict had been
strongest – would come with me. Derek Worlock was away that day, so I
rang Monsignor Jim Dunn, who came and stood with us, protecting the
houses. In fact council workmen were already on the roofs, where they
received a powerful mouthful from a local member of the church, telling
them their work was not appreciated! While we were there, we heard
that Mark Hedley, later Judge Hedley, had won an injunction in court,
restraining the council from the demolition until consultations had been
held. The houses still stand.

Jim Dunn was parish priest at Our Lady's, Eldon Street. Derek Worlock
frequently looked to him for advice on inner-city matters. It seemed
sensible for me to listen to him too, and I valued his advice. Jim had
come into my office some years before, to show me the plans they had
for housing on the site of the demolished Tate and Lyle refinery. Now
the Eldonian Housing Co-operative was determined to put those plans
into bricks and mortar. They took on the council. Offers of housing
elsewhere in the city were made to members of 'the Eldonians'. But they
refused them, determined to stay together as part of the 'Eldonian
Village' of which they had dreamed. Jim Dunn stayed in the background,
believing that local leadership was crucial. Tony McGann, who had
shouted Derek Worlock down when he first came and promoted his

'parish plan', became the chairman of the Eldonians. I first met Tony when he showed a small group round a housing estate on Shaw Street, built within the last ten years, and now shot to pieces by vandalism. We asked him what answers could be found. He said that the council had placed people in that new estate, simply taking names from the city housing list. This policy had healthy origins – to break up the sectarian divide of the North End of Liverpool – but taking names from all over the city that happened to be on the waiting list produced strangers next door. No one knew or trusted their new neighbours. The only answer to vandals was if people had enough confidence that neighbours would stand with them.

The Eldonians would not just build houses, but a community of people who would know each other and fight for each other. This has been one of the success stories of inner-city Liverpool. Perhaps they received disproportionate support, as some other local groups felt. They won influential backers, in part because of their open conflict with the Militants. Their confrontation with the City Council went to court, and Derek Worlock gave evidence against the council's plans to disperse residents. I became involved as well, commending the Eldonian cause to government ministers and private-sector employers. The village was built. Derek and I were invited to various openings. At one, we were greeted with a banner stretched across the road, which read, 'Thank you Archbishop Derek. Thank you Bishop David. Thank you to all our friends. We did it Better Together.' Derek said, 'There's the title for our book!' When this joint book, *Better Together*, was published, I said we must have a service in Our Lady's, Eldon Street, on the same evening. This should be part of the book launch, in recognition of the source of our title. I wrote to our parishes in the neighbourhood, asking them to come and support me. A good crowd of Anglicans responded, and the mixed congregation needed to stand all round the walls in order to fit everyone in. I felt a mixture of amazement and fulfilment that we were worshipping together in the heart of Scotland Road, where none of my predecessors would have set foot, and where joint services had been unknown.

I had a later experience that made me aware that our battles against sectarianism were not necessarily over; it was the day Derek Worlock died. I was asked by BBC2 to film a piece about him. It was agreed that the interview should take place with the street sign in the background, reading 'Archbishop Worlock Court' – part of the Eldonian Village, which also has a Bishop David Sheppard Court. The cameraman had just switched off, when an egg thrown with great force hit the man on the chest who had been holding the microphone over my head! None of us saw where the egg came from. Perhaps it was a reminder that not everyone welcomed ecumenical partnership.

The Militant leadership believed they knew better than local people in their dealings with Liverpool's black community, just as they had over Everton Park. Long debates had at last brought the agreement to appoint a race relations adviser within the City Council. A short list of five was drawn up. Three were local black people with experience in race relations. But the councillors on the appointing body held a majority of votes and all of them voted for Sam Bond. Sam Bond had no such experience. His qualification appeared to be that he was a member of the Militant Tendency, working in the London Borough of Brent. Leaders in the black community came to Derek and me, asking us to join them in demanding that the appointment be reversed. At 9 a.m. the next Monday, the two of us met John Hamilton, the leader of the council, Tony Mulhearn, the chairman of the Party in the city, Derek Hatton, Tony Byrne and Alfred Stocks. We pressed the importance of healing the relationship with the black community. At one moment, John Hamilton suggested very mildly that perhaps they could allow some delay before confirming the appointment. But no ground was given.

The following morning, I met John Hamilton on the train to London. He said, 'I was rapped over the knuckles at the Party Caucus meeting last night for suggesting that we might question the decision.' He was only the leader of the council! John was not a Militant. He was a Quaker, a schoolmaster and an old-fashioned left-wing socialist. He thought – mistakenly as it turned out – that he might be able to 'ride the tiger' and moderate their policies. He wrote to me in 1997 that it had been hard to know what decision to make for the best during those difficult years. 'It was made even harder not having people around me in whom I could confide my thoughts. I did appreciate the help and friendship which both you and the Archbishop gave me when I turned to you for friendship and guidance.' John Hamilton never used an official car when he was the leader of the council. Partly this was due to his modesty. Undoubtedly it was also because he did not want anyone to check up on where he was going. It was standard practice among the Militants that a 'minder' should go with you, lest you step out of the party line.

As the row rumbled on with the black community leaders, Derek Worlock and I were present at a meeting – held at the request of both parties in the Roman Catholic Cathedral House. Derek Hatton – plus 'minder' – met with several black leaders. He offered them two additional appointments the council would pay for, if they would accept Sam Bond in his post. They refused all offers and arguments. Ideology played an important part in the row with the black community. The Militant Tendency followed Trotskyite dogma. It was *class* that caused all injustices, not race. So affirmative action programmes for ethnic minority groups, like monitoring housing provision, were dismissed.

There were three moments when the crisis in the city seemed so intense that as church leaders we issued a special call to prayer for Liverpool. One was 29 March 1984, when the Militants had called for public demonstrations against the Government's treatment of the city. There were two more occasions in 1985. Both these were at times when the city was sliding towards bankruptcy and the collapse of services. When we criticised the council's policy of confrontation with the Government, Tony Byrne challenged Derek and me to inspect the books. We said we were willing to do this, provided he agreed to leave us alone for part of the time with the treasurer. Tony said to Derek and me, 'If we were in South America, you would be telling your priests to get on the streets with us.' I said, 'As it happens, we both went to South America a year or two ago, and we saw what happens next after such protests. The extreme right-wing backlash there hasn't benefited the poor.' Did Tony Byrne hope that the revolution was about to start? Was Arthur Scargill trying to keep the miners' strike going in the hope that cities like Liverpool would come out on the streets too? It certainly dragged on long after the miners might have hoped to win on their own.

As we approached the first of those three flash points, there was great anxiety around. Just a few days before, I preached at a lunch-hour service at Liverpool Parish Church. The City Council was required by law to make a rate no later than 29 March. There was talk of a 60-per-cent rate increase for a standstill budget, or a 175-per-cent rate increase for some growth in jobs and housing renewal. There was also talk of making 4,000 council employees redundant, or of refusing to make a legal rate, with the highly uncertain consequences which might follow. I said, 'Some of us are trying to persuade people not to abandon the rule of law and peaceful processes of change. But, if we are successful and they pull back from the brink, what will happen then? Will prosperous Britain heave a sigh of relief and forget about Liverpool again?'

The Dimbleby Lecture

The following month, during Holy Week, I delivered the Richard Dimbleby Lecture on BBC Television. The title was 'The Other Britain'. I spoke of 'Comfortable Britain' to which the majority of us belong, and said there were two Britains today, damagingly divided. Setting out to persuade viewers to stand in the shoes of people in 'the other Britain', I was given an unplanned personal insight. Grace and I drove down to London at the end of our day off. As we unpacked, we discovered that, being in day-off clothes, I had forgotten to pack any black shoes to go with my suit. Grace rang the producer at midnight to tell him that he had a lecturer safely arrived, but could he find a pair of size eleven black shoes? When I arrived for the lecture, three pairs of shoes were waiting from which I was to choose. I felt it fitting that I should deliver this lecture on 'The Other Britain' standing in someone else's shoes!

In the lecture I said there was a series of doors clanging shut that added up to a poverty that imprisons the spirit – unemployment, neglected housing, lack of good opportunities at school, poor services in health care, transport and leisure facilities. Together these locked doors made very large numbers of people feel powerless and unable to make any real choices about their destiny. The poverty of 'the other Britain' was a priority concern for all of us, and especially for Christians. This priority concern for the poor was not an expression of off-beat radical theology. It sprang out of mainstream Christianity.

It was often suggested that to intervene in political or economic matters was a new stance for the Church to adopt. But down the centuries, the Church had intervened in some significant ways. It was heavily involved in the campaigns that William Wilberforce led against slavery. Further back, in the Middle Ages, it consistently condemned usury. When theologians found ways of saying that usury was not in itself wrong, the way was opened for the rise of capitalism, influenced by the Protestant work ethic and the individual drive that followed from it.

There was a great temptation for the Government and management to 'put the boot in' to the unions and local authorities at a time when their power was weakened. That could create longstanding bitterness. 'Cuts to local government and voluntary bodies weaken the hands of those moderate-minded men and women who work their hearts out to serve people in cities like Liverpool. If the capacity to deliver the goods is removed, no one should be surprised that some of those who face long-term deprivation should turn to those who offer more extreme policies of confrontation.'[1]

Government ministers

Derek Hatton's slogan against the Government was that 'They've stolen our money'. There was a certain basis to his claim that Liverpool had been hard-done-by: the Rate Support Grant (RSG) was calculated from a base year when an unusually low rate had been set by the Liberal council then in power. They had cut expenditure in order to prevent any increase in the rates. Before all this, Alfred Stocks had told me, 'We have actually been very mean in Liverpool – compared for example with Manchester – in what we have spent on housing. It's been less than the amount the Government has recommended each year for several years.'

Derek Worlock and I tried to keep in touch with whichever Minister was designated Minister for Merseyside. It was frustrating to have to start again with a new contact almost every year, after having established an understanding relationship with Heseltine's successor in 1983, Patrick Jenkin, and then with Kenneth Baker, who followed him. We met Patrick Jenkin on a number of occasions. He listened to the city's case, and tried to find some way of channelling additional resources to Liverpool. The reward he received was that Derek Hatton exploited what was seen as weakness, publicly claiming 'victory'. He said that Margaret Thatcher and Patrick Jenkin had 'bottled out' of the confrontation with Liverpool: 'There is no way even Thatcher can take on the might of the working class in this city.' It was widely held that Hatton 'danced on Jenkin's political grave'. After that ministers were not prepared to risk tangling with the Militants. According to the Chief Constable, there was one twelve-month period during which no minister visited the city at all.

The arguments that went on throughout these years about the increase or decrease of government funding were often confused by the concentration on the figures for 'Urban Programmes', as though they stood by themselves. The 1977–78 urban policy had been to 'bend' the mainline programmes in favour of the cities and 'top up' with the Urban Programme. It was to be 'the icing on the cake'. When the Archbishop of Canterbury's Commission on Urban Priority Areas (ACUPA) visited the Department of the Environment, I told colleagues that the only thing I really hoped to learn from that visit was the size and growth or decrease of the Rate Support Grant. It was never mentioned. We were simply given a presentation on the Urban Programme. Sometimes the complexity of computing the RSG was traded on. The joke civil servants liked to hide behind was that there were only two people in the world who understood how it was done, and the other chap had got it wrong. Such smokescreens do not advance intelligent democracy. After all, the RSG was the big money that local government relied on. When we made this point to Patrick Jenkin, he arranged for Derek and me to be given a full afternoon's presentation on the RSG. So, for a brief period, we were among the world experts on this mystery! In 1995, Professor Michael Parkinson delivered a lecture to the Department of the Environment to celebrate its twenty-fifth birthday. He showed that the major sources of funding for cities were still the RSG and the Housing Investment Programme (HIP): they had been substantially reduced during the 1980s – from up to 90 per cent of expenditure in larger cities in some cases to 70 per cent of local authority expenditure.[2]

The year 1984 was not all doom and gloom. The International Garden Festival (IGF) brought millions of visitors to the city from all over the world. It transformed what had been a vast rubbish tip, preparing part of

it for housing development after the festival ended. The City Council
would have nothing to do with it. Their reasoning was understandable.
No revenue money was on offer to maintain the gardens at a moment
when their grants had been cut back. But they misjudged Liverpool
people's enjoyment of the Garden Festival, which councillors mocked as
Heseltine's answer to urban needs. Modest charges were introduced to
allow families to spend a day there. There were days when Liverpool felt
like a village in which the whole community of all ages came out together.
In many ways it gave us a golden summer. The churches combined in
services to celebrate the beginning and the ending. Grace went more
than twenty times, often taking friends and visitors. On the last day
there were emotional feelings around. She talked to one of the gardeners
who had been given a job for the duration of the festival. Like others we
met, he approached this temporary job with pride and commitment.
Now, he took off his IGF jacket and, ignoring Grace's protests, insisted
on giving it to her. She still proudly wears it when gardening.

The happy days of what was in many ways a golden summer masked
the seriousness of the plight of the city's finances and services. The
threats by the City Council of breaking the law led to discussions about
putting Commissioners in to run Liverpool in place of the elected
council. Soundings were taken of some people to see if they would be
willing to undertake such a task. I feared that it would play into the
hands of those who wanted to take the conflict on to the streets. Un-
elected commissioners going to work would have been targets for protest
and violence. However, not everyone shied away from the idea. At the
opening ceremony of the Garden Festival, a junior government minister
said to me, 'We could achieve so much, if we could appoint commissioners
to run the city.' Derek Worlock and I met privately with Mrs Thatcher
soon afterwards. The suggestion of putting in commissioners came up.
Derek said, 'I think there's only one word I need to mention – Stormont.
If you take over the city's government, how do you ever withdraw and
return to an elected council?' Northern Ireland provided a sharp warning
that it had been easier to take power away from Stormont and locally
elected leadership than to give it back. Mrs Thatcher agreed, and made
it clear that she was not prepared to take the idea any further.

We never pretended to be negotiators between city and Government.
We tried to interpret what was going on to parties who were not speaking
to each other. There were occasions after meeting with ministers when
Derek congratulated me for having been 'on my white charger'! There
was one when he breathed out a deep sigh of relief. This was after we
had visited Nicholas Ridley, who followed the short period of months
when Kenneth Baker held the office. Derek Worlock drafted our account
of this meeting, and I saw no reason to alter it:

Nicholas Ridley rose, and, wreathed in cigarette smoke, demanded of us, 'How do I know which of you is which?' We each identified the other and were asked what we wanted. 'We want to ask you,' said Derek, 'whether you are in fact the new Minister for Merseyside whom the Prime Minister has promised us.' 'Well,' Ridley said slowly, 'I understand I am responsible for every town, village and hamlet in this country, not to mention every butterfly and dog licence, so I don't see why that should not include Merseyside.' Then David took over a conversation that was not proving promising. 'I read in the *Guardian* a few days ago that you had expressed doubt about any particular commitment to Merseyside. Do you accept that we do have special needs?' With that Nicholas Ridley rose from his chair in angry protest. 'I regard that remark as quite unacceptable. It's moral blackmail.'

I said we had been advised that he liked forthright speaking. The conversation lasted a little longer, but clearly was not going to produce any benefit for Liverpool.

In 1985 there was plenty of bad news. Liverpool Football Club, which had given the city reasons to be very proud during the years that both Shankly and Paisley were the managers, played Juventus of Turin in the European Cup Final in the Heysel Stadium in Belgium. Fighting between rival fans broke out, a wall collapsed, and many Italian fans were killed. We shared the sense of shame that hung over the city. As churches, we responded, as we were to do four years later after the Hillsborough disaster. There was a Requiem Mass in the Metropolitan Cathedral, and a service that followed a week later in ours. Thousands queued for hours before and after that service to sign a Book of Condolence. Derek Hatton then showed the imagination that could have been a positive influence in many more situations. At his suggestion a delegation from all parties in the city, the football clubs and the church leaders went to Turin to express our sorrow and penitence. The Chairman of the City Council, Hugh Dalton, led the Liverpool party. The Militants had abolished the post of Lord Mayor. It was to be resurrected when they had been removed. Hugh Dalton, who carried himself with great dignity in that office, wrote to Derek and me after the visit, thanking us for our part. He concluded: 'Perhaps the most unforgettable part of the whole visit was the service in the evening attended by so many thousands of Turin citizens. The fact that our two bishops from Liverpool were able in a spirit of cordiality and friendship to take part in the service together made, I am sure, a profound impression.'

In the morning we had gone to Turin City Council Chamber in an atmosphere of respectful formality. In the afternoon a small crowd outside the ground greeted us, when we visited Juventus Football Club. Hugh Dalton was right that the largest welcome was at the ancient

Shrine of Our Lady Consolata. The Cardinal Archbishop of Turin came back from visits in the diocese in order to be with us, and invited Derek to celebrate and preach at the Mass. I was invited to give an address at the end of the Mass, and the Cardinal then invited both of us to join him in blessing the congregation. By the end the whole congregation seemed to be waving or applauding. Even the most reluctant of the Militants, recovering from his shock at being firmly clasped and embraced by several Italian women during the exchange of the sign of peace, entered into the spirit of things and remarked on how the Roman Catholic Church had changed since last he had known it.

We made a great mistake in thinking we could carry that atmosphere forward into the next season. The Liverpool chairman, John Smith, asked us, with the Free Church Moderator, John Williamson, to lead a short service at the start of the new season at Anfield. It was agreed that we would lead from the centre of the pitch with a battery-operated microphone. Just before the start, we were told that the microphone had been left on all night and the battery was flat. We would have to use the police dugout at the side of the pitch – where, of course, we were invisible. Foolishly, we agreed to go ahead. Our short introduction, printed at the front of the match programme, was heard in silence, but, when we tried to lead the hymn 'Abide with me', the Kop decided they were going to sing 'You'll never walk alone'. The prayer at the end was inaudible against this competition! We learned some valuable lessons that day, which stood us in good stead when the club asked us to lead worship in another tragic context after the Hillsborough disaster.

We had tried hard to persuade council and Government to reach out to each other. When it was plain that confrontation was the only order of the day, we wrote a joint letter to *The Times* on 1 October. We expressed our concern that the case for Liverpool and other urban areas did not seem to have been heard in Whitehall:

> But Militant's intransigence and unwillingness to engage in serious dialogue creates divisiveness and uncertainty in which the most vulnerable elements of the community suffer, usually schoolchildren and elderly people unable to cope with a reduction in services ... Faced with such difficulties, a great city needs to bring together all the resources which people of goodwill can muster. Our Christian teaching is that we are members one of another. The dogmatic, divisive policies of the Militant leadership reject this. Very significant resources are being ignored or damaged.

This appeared in *The Times* on the morning of the Labour Party Conference at Bournemouth, when Neil Kinnock was to make his speech as leader. Alongside meetings with government ministers, we had kept in frequent touch with Jack Cunningham, Shadow Environment Secretary, and met Kinnock soon after this. He told us he was grateful for our piece. 'That morning, I read what you had written. And then I was filled with the spirit!' He made the speech attacking the irresponsibility of the Militants which had ended in 'the grotesque chaos of a Labour council hiring taxis to scuttle round the city, handing out redundancy notices to its own workers'. This marked a watershed in the Labour Party distancing itself from the 'hard left'.

Back in Liverpool that day, Alfred Stocks came on the phone. He said that Tony Byrne, now leader of the council, had stormed into his room, brandishing a copy of *The Times*. 'You are to ring them and invite them to come and address the Finance Committee.' Together with John Williamson, Derek and I went, each of us with a carefully prepared five-minute talk. While one of us was speaking, some councillors started to talk at the back of the Council Chamber. Tony Byrne rapped on the table, and said, 'They are here as my guests. You will give them a fair hearing.' His leadership was authoritarian. Councillors had an uncritical faith in his ability. We were told that he 'had the best financial brain in the North West'. Trusting in that ability, they ran on down the slope that led to their being held personally responsible for the city's debts. Some of these councillors, who had given fine service to the city, were not Militants, but went along with the policies in the spirit of solidarity. Soon, they were surcharged and then disqualified for five years from holding public office.

Confrontation between hard-line convictions in Westminster and Liverpool did lasting damage. The collapse of local government finance left little room for local councils to take initiatives – or to do anything that local people would thank them for. Why would the ablest citizens want to serve as councillors or as local government officers, if all they were able to do was manage cutbacks? These were questions that affected the whole nation.

17

A Postcard from Spain

The idea of a commission

Soon after Robert Runcie's death, Eric James showed me a postcard he had received from Robert, written in Santiago de Compostela. It read, 'Bought a *Times* today, and saw Clifford Longley on the inner cities. It calls for a substantial letter from you. Nobody else knows so much about it all.' Eric duly wrote to *The Times*. In his letter he said, 'I should like to see the immediate appointment of an Archbishop's Commission.' He pressed the Archbishop for a reply to his suggestion.

Robert Runcie asked an informal group of urban bishops to advise him. The first membership of bishops was Ronnie Bowlby (Newcastle), David Young (Ripon), Stanley Booth-Clibborn (Manchester), David Sheppard (Liverpool), Kenneth Skelton (Lichfield), Hugh Montefiore (Birmingham), John Trillo (Chelmsford) and Jim Thompson (Stepney). Robert Runcie asked the group to put up draft terms of reference. One of the crucial questions we wrestled with was whether the Commission should be ecumenical. At its meeting in our home, the group was joined by Derek Worlock, and discussed an ecumenical enquiry as a serious option. The histories of the different churches in the inner cities were decisively different from one another. We concluded that it would let the Church of England off the hook, if we attempted to include all the churches. In the light of this decision, the other churches were wonderfully gracious in supporting *Faith in the City* so wholeheartedly. Robert bounced our first attempt back to us, but accepted a second draft that we submitted of terms of reference: 'To examine the strengths, insights, problems and needs of the Church's life and mission in Urban Priority Areas and, as a result to reflect on the challenge which God may be making to Church and Nation: and to make appropriate recommendations to appropriate bodies.'

Robert asked me to join the Commission and to work together with his Public Affairs Secretary, Michael Kinchin-Smith, in making suggestions for its membership. I consulted the members of the urban bishops' group about names at each stage. The Archbishop kept closely in touch with the whole process, putting forward some names himself and examining its shape in terms of a spread across the nation and across theological schools. My greatest contribution was to suggest the name of Sir Richard O'Brien as the chairman. I had come to know Richard through the Manpower Services Commission of which he had been the national chairman. Richard was a thoughtful Anglican, bringing wide experience in industry from Wakefield, Birmingham and nationally; he was still chairing the Engineering Industry Training Board. He asked me to be his vice-chairman. He was determined from the outset that we should present a unanimous report, and deployed his pastoral skills in helping the Commission to see each other as 'members one of another'.

A good proportion of the membership of the Archbishop's Commission on Urban Priority Areas (ACUPA) had first-hand experience of living or working in UPAs. Others represented management, trade unions and academic studies. Eleven were lay people and seven were clergy. Though the majority were Anglicans, Robina Rafferty, Director of the Catholic Housing Advice Service, and Linbert Spencer from the Salvation Army joined ACUPA. In addition, Michael Eastman, a Baptist, came as one of four 'resource points'. Each of these brought skilled advice. The Department of the Environment agreed to second John Pearson to work full-time as the secretary of the Commission. He brought outstanding skills and commitment to the task.

Two years of *Faith in the City*

It was agreed that, in addition to regular meetings in London, the whole Commission should meet over a number of weekends, both to make visits to five major conurbations and for a series of residential meetings. Smaller groups to which each of us belonged submitted drafts. One looked at the history and reality of the church presence in UPAs, at worship, patterns of ministry, church buildings, training and finance; others studied urban policy, poverty and employment, housing, health, social care and community work, education and young people, law and order.

For our first weekend, it had been agreed that we should discuss the theology of urban mission. Several of us came with our best statements polished up for a theological disputation. But a significant challenge was introduced to that approach – and carried the day. We were asked how we could agree on what we should say about mission, until we had shared common experiences in the context of UPAs and UPA people. Such a method inevitably meant that our critics, who wanted precise statements, pronounced the chapter on theology weak. We said we had started a process and pressed them to join us in thinking the theology through.

The first of the visits of the whole Commission was to Merseyside. On the Friday evening, as in each of our weekend visits, we split up into three groups, inviting anyone to come and tell us their experience. The three hearings took place in Toxteth, Everton and Kirkby. I chaired the group that went to Kirkby. One woman told us that her husband was a gifted man; but his gifts needed opportunities. He had been out of work for ten years. Benefits were just enough to keep the wolf from the door, provided nothing went wrong. What happened if there was an unforeseen need, or the children's feet grew too quickly, or for birthdays or Christmas?

For the most part, our role was to listen. That had to be set aside, when Kirkby people realised that David Booth was a director of BICC, an employer in Kirkby as well as in Prescot, just down the road. He was pressed to comment on recent reports about possible loss of jobs. One man stood up and said, 'Are you going to press Maggie to invest in Merseyside – Yes or No?' David Booth asked, 'Do you want the good news first, or the bad news?' 'Let's have the good news first.' 'The good news is that we are going to invest millions into the plant' (he gave the actual figure). 'The bad news is that this will mean the loss of hundreds of jobs' (and again he gave the figure).

The Londoners present that evening in Kirkby expressed astonishment at the comparatively calm manner with which people spoke of the dispiriting effects of unemployment. They said that in London there would have been a riot in the same circumstances. This was felt still more in the visit to Tyneside. Indeed, several of us thought that, by comparison with Merseyside, people were fatalistic about the situation, as though nothing could be done about it.

These visits showed us faith and courage in local Christians that humbled us. We saw that church members in many UPAs gave more money per head than others, in actual figures, let alone in proportion to income. Church members were often deeply involved in the life of the whole community. One stay that remains fixed in my mind was on Low Hill, an estate on the edge of Wolverhampton. I stayed with a family next door to a vandalised house. That first-hand experience led me to say that, rather than describe such estates as 'hard-to-let', we would do better to call them 'hard-to-live-in'. It also gave me face-to-face knowledge of lively faith that approached life there with positive attitudes. This stay in Low Hill turned statistics about the collapse of manufacturing industry in the West Midlands into the experience of real people. The head teacher of a Midlands comprehensive school told us, 'Unemployment has dealt us a stunning blow . . . there is little motivation . . . truancy is high.'

During our visit to Bow in the Bishop of Stepney's area, a woman said to me, 'The terrible thing about youth unemployment is that going to work was the way you joined the adult world.' In a real sense, unemployed youngsters never grew up. The contrasts that were sometimes found side by side were reflected when we met the other London bishops. The Bishop of Kensington, Mark Santer,[1] said there were districts with great needs in his area – and also 'pockets of extreme and insolent wealth'.

In the Commission's visits members stayed in local homes. Some of these were in vicarages, giving an insight into the life of UPA clergy and their families. In the first visit, Richard O'Brien found himself staying in the vicarage of Cantril Farm, not yet transformed into Stockbridge Village. He saw for himself the pressures the clergy family knew. Living there was like being in a goldfish bowl, overlooked by high-rise blocks, since demolished.

We commissioned Gallup to do a survey of Church of England clergy, with particular reference to comparative differences between Urban Priority Areas and elsewhere.[2] This showed that clergy in UPAs were more satisfied with ministering in their particular type of parish than those in other areas. They found high job satisfaction in working where they did, in spite of many disadvantages in their environment. That was not always what we met. I went with one other member to visit a parish in North London. It had been selected for us, so that we could assess the value of dual-purpose church halls and worship centres. The vicar started to open his heart about his own discouragement. I asked if he minded if we stayed with him rather than visit others. He said that he had given up going back to his old theological college for their celebrations. This was because the talk there was all about success, and his life seemed to him to be full of failure. The same feelings kept him from spending time with a Christian couple who lived nearby, but travelled to worship in a central London church where they saw large numbers gathered. As he talked, the conviction grew that I was hearing about faithful ministry, in which there were signs of God being at work. But he was losing heart, because he was measuring his achievements by a yardstick that was not appropriate.

A vicar in Manchester told us, 'It is difficult to avoid the conclusion that one is living in an area that is being treated with hostility by the rest of society.' Even so, there were flickers of hope in the most pressured situations we saw; the headmaster of a comprehensive school in a most disadvantaged area wrote of the value of what the Church offered by way of quiet friendship, prayer and patient support of those in the firing line. He said he had been greatly heartened by the public pronouncements of leaders in the Church of England on industrial strife and unemployment. 'They have contributed to the morale of many Christians and others in the field, who can all too easily feel isolated.'

Lasting friendships were built in the Commission, which reached a deep consensus, based on what we saw and experienced together. Robert Runcie kept close to what was going on. One Commission weekend was held at Canterbury, so that he could have a morning with us. He told us a story of an earlier Archbishop, Frederick Temple (William Temple's father). On a holiday Sunday, he worshipped in a parish in the diocese, and heard a disastrously ill-prepared sermon. At the door at the end of the service, the vicar said, 'Your Grace, I took a vow that I would always speak without notes.' The Archbishop drew himself up to his full height, and said, 'We Frederick James, by divine permission Lord Archbishop of Canterbury, do absolve you from that vow.' After a few moments, Archbishop Robert came to the point of meeting with us. He said, 'I hope you will forgive me that I have not been able to read all your papers.' Ron Keating, trade union member, called out to Richard O'Brien. 'Go on Richard. Do it properly. I Sir Richard do absolve you.'

At our last full weekend the Commission agreed unanimously to the report. We thought we must live with a functional, but flat title. However, two members, Canon Anthony Harvey and Professor Ray Pahl, introduced another proposal on the last day; they said the report should be called 'Faith in the City'. The Commission acclaimed this; it had the right mixture of concern, reality and hope that arose from our enquiry.

Recommendations to the church

The Report made thirty-eight recommendations to the Church of England and twenty-three to the nation.[3] As the only bishop who belonged to the Commission at the start of its life, I felt I should serve on the section concerning the structures and policies of the Church of England. At parish level, we set out proposals for a parish audit. This was used very widely in locally adjusted forms – in Liverpool Diocese we called it a 'Mission Assessment Programme' (MAP). This would set out to produce an accurate picture of the parish – mapping where worshippers actually came from, and giving an account of local people's views. It proved an effective tool in encouraging parishes to look outwards – alongside gathering information about the congregation, its buildings and finance.

We had a lot to say about laity development. We noted that Christians from UPAs had frequently been overawed by finding themselves in a tiny minority on educational courses run by the church; often they had either withdrawn or had been absorbed into styles of church life which had deskilled them for their own area. We argued for a 'Church Leadership Development Programme' – locally based, yet wider than any one parish. It would be designed locally, and would seek to develop existing skills and introduce members to new ones directly related to local leadership needs.

We had much to say about the training of stipendiary clergy; submissions we had received had questioned the adequacy of preparation for ministry in UPAs. Indeed, some claimed that their training 'has not been simply inappropriate, but in many ways had positively unfitted them for the urban ministry to which they find themselves committed'. Many clergy were called to live and work in the middle of cultures (ethnic or working class) and religions, that were strange to their own background. Their training should help them take a 'serious look at the Christian religion from outside the traditional perspectives of academic theology'. We acknowledged with admiration the extent to which many theological colleges had found means of incorporating some form of 'urban studies' in their already crowded programmes. Some ran specific courses in college. Others included extended placements in urban areas.

Finance was frequently at the centre of UPA anxieties. What caught the imagination of many church people was that we recommended that a Church Urban Fund (CUF) be set up for the UPAs. That would mean a one-off heave to raise a large sum. Some critics said that CUF was the only product of the report. They missed the more long-term proposal that diocesan quota schemes should take 'potential' into account for each parish's share. Most dioceses have subsequently made that change. It has meant large increases in the contribution from parishes with greater potential. Since these are increases sustained every year, they amount to much more than the capital sum raised for the CUF.

The Commission was clear that issues to do with race relations were not concerns 'out there'. The church itself had painful questions to face: we were pressed that the Church of England must 'make space' for – and so better receive the gifts of – black Christians. The report said the church must make a clear response to the alienation, hurt and rejection experienced by many black people in relation to the Church of England. There were specific proposals for 'making space' in the central structures of the church: for example, we proposed the establishment of a Committee on Black Anglican Concerns.

The text we most frequently quoted to each other during our two years was from St Paul: 'We are members one of another.' That made us look for mutual giving and receiving between churches in contrasting parts of the country – perhaps in 'twinning' between parishes. We said we must not assume that it was the wealthier and more powerful members of the church who were always the givers, and the residents of inner cities always the receivers. 'We have again and again found evidence of a vitality and generosity in church life in deprived areas, which is a challenge to more affluent congregations.' The church needed to attend to the voices, the experience and the spiritual riches of the 'poor' in its midst. We said we had seen how the gospel, when faithfully proclaimed in word and deed, effected a transformation of individual lives, of families and of communities.

We recommended establishing a post for an Archbishop's officer to follow up the report – faithfully filled by Prebendary Pat Dearnley.[4] One of his tasks was to develop a system for designating UPA parishes. This needed to win enough confidence to be accepted throughout the church for priority in staffing and finance. Robert Runcie appointed an advisory group to support Pat Dearnley. It produced a progress report, *Living in the City*, in 1990.[5]

Challenge to the nation

On public policies, we said, 'It is our considered view that the nation is confronted by a grave and fundamental injustice in the UPAs.' We said that it was now the large housing estates in the inner ring or on the fringes of the cities that presented the most pressing urban problem of the mid-1980s. The report said that, as the national church, the Church of England had a particular duty to act as the conscience of the nation. It was right to question all economic philosophies. Some of these had 'contributed to the blighting of whole districts, which do not offer the hope of amelioration, and which perpetuate human misery and despair. The situation requires the Church to question from its own particular standpoint the *morality* of these economic philosophies.' The main assumption on which present economic policies were based was that prosperity could be restored, if individuals were set free to pursue their own economic salvation. We said that too much emphasis was being given to individualism, and not enough to collective obligation.

We said that wealth creation must be supported wholeheartedly. We shared the view of Business-in-the-Community that the principal way businesses could help was to stay in business and secure a healthy economic base. And we agreed with the way they continued, 'But it is fanciful to think that the results will trickle down to deprived areas to make a significant and self-sustaining effect.'

There was a thorough analysis of housing. The government strategy relied heavily on home ownership. Ian Gow, the Housing Minister then, had claimed it had opened up choice, saying, 'Choice is at the centre of liberty.' We said that for most low-income city residents, promising freedom of choice was a cruel deception. We recommended a major independent examination of the whole system of housing finance, including mortgage interest tax relief, to give most help to those in greatest need. We argued that it was unjust to tell those in bad housing that we could not afford to do anything for them, and at the same time give subsidies to those on middle and high incomes. We quoted the Building Societies Association projecting an expansion of home owner-ship to 72 per cent of the population by the year 2000. That projection went on to say that, once the council house sales boom died down, there would be little opportunity for low-income households to become owners. Decent housing for those in greatest need required more public finance. We recommended an increase in real terms of the resources allocated to Rate Support Grant, together with a greater bias to the UPAs.

Other parts of the report foreshadowed debates that are still live issues as I write in 2002 – care in the community, what schools offer black youngsters, the youth service, prison regimes. We said that the concept of 'care in the community' must be backed up by adequate resources. If the old mental hospitals were to be closed, smaller centres of care needed to be provided and staffed. We called for locally based support services for people (especially women) caring for vulnerable and disabled people.

We quoted concerns that 'institutional racism' in schools contributed to the poor level of attainment of black young people. One young black person said to us, 'I felt put down at school. I felt I could not excel at academic subjects . . . my teachers used to tell me not to bother too much with lessons and homework, but to concentrate on sport and athletics.'

On the youth service, we shared the views of the Thompson Report presented to Parliament in October 1982. Now, three years later, those in Government had still not grasped the degree of alienation with which most of those who worked in the youth service in UPAs were only too familiar. Being a discretionary service, the youth service was part of 'education' in which schools dominated. There was the feeling that the youth service was the Cinderella.

The draft of our report on prisons said that rehabilitation was officially no longer part of the purpose of prisons. When that came to a meeting of the Commission, I said, 'We can't say that.' The members who had spent a day at Strangeways Prison replied that this was indeed what they had been told. They were not expected to make provision for useful work or vocational training. The report therefore said that we saw a recent and officially sanctioned retreat from the objective of rehabilita-ting offenders. Of course we recognised that there was limited success in rehabilitation, but it was still our Christian duty to attempt it.

'Rubbishing'

I still have my copy of *Faith in the City* with the 'Embargoed – for use after 2100 hours 03 December' notice stuck on the front of my copy. On the Sunday, two days before that date, I walked down the hill to collect a paper. I bought a copy of the *Sunday Times*; the banner headline across the front page read, 'Church report is "Marxist" '. As I spread the paper on the kitchen table, a service was being broadcast on Radio 4. A reading from the Old Testament prophets said, 'There shall be integrity and truth in the land'. I exclaimed out loud, 'Oh Lord, how long?' The *Sunday Times* report quoted a 'senior government figure' saying that sections of the report were 'pure Marxist theology'. The *Financial Times* leader dismissed this as wholly untrue. Robert Runcie said that it would need 'mental acrobatics' to find any section of the report of which that could be a true description. The 'senior government figure' never broke cover to claim responsibility for the quotation.

We had expected sharp criticisms – perhaps personal ones. *Private Eye* was running a series about several bishops. I guessed that it would be my turn in the week that the report was published. The piece duly appeared that week, signed by Lucy Fer! She said that she had danced with me at a Young Conservatives' Ball at Petersfield in 1952. That seemed so precise that I wracked my brains to see whether such memories had been suppressed. But the truth is that I never belonged to the Young Conservatives, nor went to any of their balls. Dances were no part of life in that Puritan period that followed my conversion. And 'Lucy' rang no bells at all! The 'rubbishing' that the report received did not bear much more relation to the reality of what it contained than *Private Eye* did about me.

Grace and I drove down to London that Sunday evening, arriving at the flat where we were staying, just as the *Ten o'clock News* headlines were being read. It was a warm evening and people had opened their windows. From all round the courtyard, we heard reports of government ministers and supporters attacking the report. I rang Richard O'Brien, our chairman. He had been an infantry officer in the war. Towards the end he had become personal assistant to Field Marshal Montgomery. So I asked him, 'What would Monty have done?' 'I shall have to give some thought to that,' Richard replied. We agreed that evening that we should stick to our plan – which is probably what Monty would have done – and only speak to the report at the arranged press conference on the Tuesday morning. On Monday morning, there was a long succession of press calls. They said, 'You are allowing them to slay you, and you're saying nothing!' Eventually we agreed that we must respond. Grace's account is that I said with a glint in my eye, 'I'm going into battle'. Perhaps Monty was still on my mind! At the BBC's *World at One* studio, I had never known the media so supportive. Several expressed anger at what was being done to us. I was allowed to use their studio and phones for interviews with independent radio and television, and was still there at 5 p.m.

Government attacks made *Faith in the City* famous! The story continued to have front-page treatment for four days. I heard Kenneth Baker say in a radio broadcast that we had attacked mortgage interest tax relief – a policy, he said, that was 'overwhelmingly popular'. He did not say whether it was just or right, nor which part of the electorate it was that found it overwhelmingly popular. The most extended interview I had, and the sharpest, took place on Channel 4 *News*, with Norman Tebbit. He did not engage with the content of the report, but spoke of his own youth on a London council estate, claiming that he understood better than someone with my background what was needed in urban priority areas. I said that London had changed a great deal since then, not least with the growth in the numbers of black people. He then angrily accused me of suggesting that he was putting forward racist views. After the programme, we went back to the hospitality room. He claimed that the Archbishop's Commission had been unbalanced in its membership, with no one properly representing right-wing views. Norman Tebbit then revealed that he had asked to be supplied with a dossier on members, and read out what it said about members of the Commission, including reference to 'the personal problems' of one named member. There was sucking of teeth around the Channel 4 staff at that point. When I listed members who were in management or with conservative views he dismissed every name. By then I was angry, and foolishly said that it was difficult to find thoughtful Christians on the right who knew about urban matters. At that point, Norman walked out. The following morning I wrote in a letter to him that I regretted saying those words. My letter said, 'If they had stood by themselves, I would wholly disown them. I think you will agree that they did not stand by themselves.' We arranged to meet later, in order to understand each other better. By the time our agreed date came round, he was Chairman of the Conservative Party, so I went to Party headquarters. Jeffrey Archer, his number two, met me with an apology that Norman was delayed. We talked for a good half hour about Somerset cricket and other matters. He said he was surprised that I had lost my temper. 'Norman Tebbit's fuse blows several times a week,' he said. 'I should have thought yours blows very rarely!'

The debate that followed

The rubbishing approach was by no means universal among Cabinet Ministers. In the first week after the publication, the Leader of the House of Commons, John Biffen, stood in at Prime Minister's Question Time. He said the report was a serious, well-researched and solid document that ought to be studied. Privately, some Ministers made it clear that they disapproved of the attacks. I had sent a copy of the report to each member of the Cabinet that I knew. Peter Walker had been at Environment in Edward Heath's Government. He had then set up the Inner Areas Study that lay behind the urban policy the Government set out in 1977. In opposition he wrote a book about urban issues. As part of his study, he came up to Liverpool to spend half a day discussing matters with me. His reward, when Margaret Thatcher came into power, was to be made Minister of Agriculture! But, no doubt, he was regarded as a 'wet'. Peter Walker now wrote to me:

> I naturally regret the absurd outbursts by a number of my colleagues who obviously have not read the Report. The only satisfaction from their efforts is that it has probably aroused even more interest in your Report than would otherwise have been the case. I can only express my own gratitude to you for all you have done in this sphere and only hope it will meet with success.

The Archbishop stood by 'his report' through thick and thin. One of the ACUPA weekends had been held in Canterbury, so that he could spend a morning with us. Richard O'Brien as chairman, and I as vice-chairman, had tried to keep him posted about the directions the report was likely to take. I booked half an hour to ask him whether he felt the proposal to establish a Church Urban Fund was likely to be acceptable. He encouraged me that we should go ahead. As we shall see in a subsequent chapter, the fund made major contributions to needy areas. When all the flak from government ministers and their supporters was flying around his head, Robert never backed away from 'owning' it. He liked to speak of it as 'my report'. Adrian Hastings concluded in his biography of Robert Runcie that *Faith in the City* was, 'The most important venture of his whole archiepiscopate, the enterprise in which he affected the most people, was most attacked and most justified, the venture for which he is in the long run likely to be most remembered'.[6]

Early in January 1986, Robert Runcie told me that Michael Heseltine had come up to him at a Christmas party, and said, 'Your bishops have got it all wrong. Things are much *worse* than they say! I should like to meet with some of them.' That month he famously walked out as Minister of Defence over the Westland Affair. I was given a private telephone number to ring. Michael Heseltine came on the line himself. I said that the Archbishop had told me he would like to meet with some of us. He said, 'You realise that my circumstances are changed.' Yes, but some of us believed he cared very much about the cities when he was Minister for Merseyside. He replied, 'I did, and I do. I should very much like to meet with you. I would like to write a paper that we could discuss.' The paper duly arrived and he spent a morning with six members of the Commission. I still have the paper he wrote in March 1986. He wrote that he had never understood the view that the Church should keep silent about conditions of human life. He welcomed our focus on urban priority areas. 'They not only contrast unacceptably with those enjoyed by the vast majority, but also harbour and promote levels of crime, violence, human hopelessness and fear that are visibly rising with every new round of statistics. And in the end, damn the statistics; just go and look! Of course there are clear moral issues involved in the political challenges we face.'

He argued that bringing national commitment to the rescue of those areas required three preconditions. The first was that local politicians of whatever parties should show a real willingness to attempt to work together. The second was 'that we accept that the private sector cannot play the prime role; only public funds can buy out the accumulated legacy of decay and dereliction'. The third was to pursue policies that would make deprived areas attractive enough to bring investment and people back into them.

Of course, he wrote these words when he was out of office. Subsequent policies, even when he came back into government, never matched what he wrote in the crucial second of his preconditions. The House of Lords gave time to a debate at the Archbishop's request, in February 1987. Lord Scarman introduced it. In my speech, I quoted what Michael Heseltine had said to us about the scale of need being far beyond what the private sector could meet without the injection of major public funds. I said that at the time of the launch – or the pre-emptive leak – of the report *Faith in the City*, I had been confronted on television with a costing which had been made of all the recommendations in the report. The figure was revealed as if no sensible person could possibly argue for it. It turned out to be an increase of 4p in the pound on income tax. Of course no account could have been taken of the increased earnings resulting from a healthier, more productive, back-at-work and more united nation. I said, 'My response is that if the running sore in the side of our nation of massive unemployment and urban deprivation could be healed for only 4p in the pound on income tax, we should thank God and get on with it. Indeed 4p in the pound is exactly the amount by

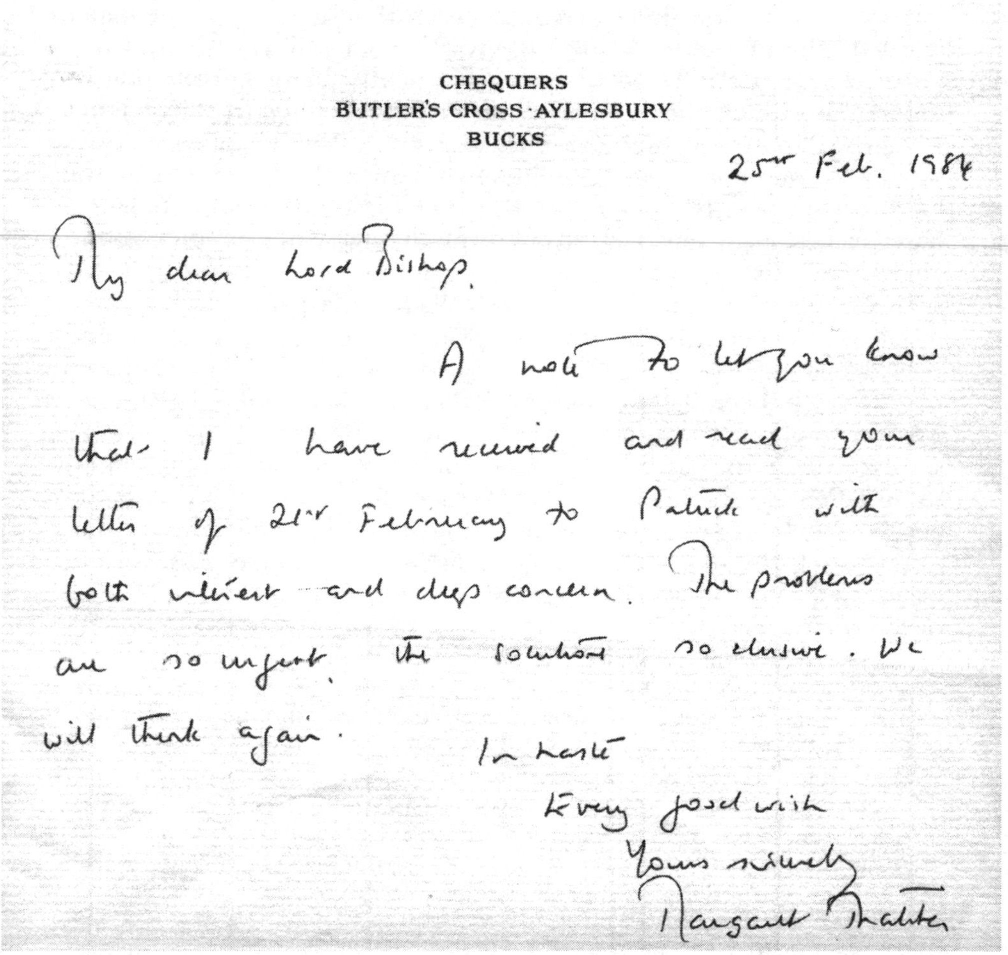

CHEQUERS
BUTLER'S CROSS · AYLESBURY
BUCKS

25ᵗʰ Feb. 1984

My dear Lord Bishop,

A note to let you know that I have received and read your letter of 21ˢᵗ February to Patrick with both interest and deep concern. The problems are so urgent, the solutions so elusive. We will think again.

In haste

Every good wish

Yours sincerely

Margaret Thatcher

which some people are urging the Chancellor to reduce the standard rate in his forthcoming Budget.'

Mrs Thatcher

The Prime Minister was generous in giving unhurried time to Derek Worlock and me on three occasions, each time overrunning the hour allotted. The first of these meetings was in February 1984, with Patrick Jenkin sitting in. Derek and I tried to paint the picture of the effect of the more confident moving away from a city. I managed to ask a question when there was plenty of time for her to answer: 'Prime Minister, knowing what we know about new technology, what three things would you hope for over the next ten years? I'm thinking of communities where men have been able to sell their strength or their willingness to work in a gang.' She started to answer immediately. Then she stopped. A long silence followed. Eventually she said, 'Well, I despair.' I recalled that moment on several occasions when her public statements were so full of confidence.

A fortnight later, I was sitting with other members of the Archbishop's Commission at the hearing in Kirkby, which I described above. For the second time in my life, a local person looked at me and said, 'You know these powerful people. Why don't you tell them how it is?' I could not avoid thinking of our recent conversation with Mrs Thatcher. So I wrote in my own hand to Patrick Jenkin, asking him if he would pass the letter on to the Prime Minister. My account of the hearing ran to seven pages of foolscap. I wrote:

> I wished you both could have been present at the Open Forum we held in Kirkby. Unemployment filled the foreground throughout – very long-term unemployment... I said the other day that the Community Programme is a small acknowledgement that unemployment is not a temporary phenomenon. But it is very small. In Merseyside we receive something like 6,800 places, when we have 150,000 unemployed... I am very conscious of adding to the burdens which you bear: I also have a strong sense of how difficult it is in Westminster and the City of London to understand how life is experienced in the 'Northwest triangle' of Belfast, Glasgow and Liverpool.

Mrs Thatcher replied by return in her own hand: 'A note to let you know that I have received and read your letter to Patrick with both interest and deep concern. The problems are so urgent, the solutions so elusive. We will think again.'

We raised specific issues on each of our visits to her, briefed by the Michaelmas Group (referred to in the chapter about the Toxteth riots).

Mostly we never knew whether our arguments for Liverpool resulted in any change in policy. But one attempt of ours did seem to have produced a surprising result. We had been briefed to make the case for Liverpool to be allocated one of the Freeports that the Government had decided should be placed in a limited number of seaports. Mrs Thatcher took careful notes of what we said. As we left 10 Downing Street that day, we saw ministers entering for a meeting that we were told would decide where the Freeports were to be. Later that day we read the announcement that Liverpool was on the list. We were also told that when a senior civil servant heard this, he refused to believe it, because he knew that Liverpool was not on the recommended list at all. The Prime Minister's intervention in this case had positive effect, because Liverpool has been the most successful of all the Freeports in Britain.

After *Faith in the City*, the bishops of the Church of England were widely seen as being in conflict with the Government. In 1987, the Archbishop and the Prime Minister agreed that there should be a meeting at Chequers between Mrs Thatcher and a dozen bishops, at which we would try to understand each other better. My train to London was very late, so the plan that I should travel with the Archbishop fell to the ground. He had to set off from Lambeth before I arrived. Lindy Runcie lent me her car. I arrived late for the lunch and was received with special courtesy by Margaret Thatcher, sympathetic at train delays. When the conversation got going in the afternoon, she made a sharp comment about *Faith in the City*. As the only member of the Commission present, I said that Lord Scarman had said it was the best analysis yet made. She said, 'I prefer what the Chief Rabbi said.' Immanuel Jacobovits, in commenting on our report, had spoken of how the Jewish community had lifted itself up by enterprise. I pressed on with some of our challenges. Now Margaret Thatcher repeatedly interrupted. It was like being heckled. Indeed my mouth went dry as I remembered it doing once when facing Lindwall and Miller! But I kept going. I told Derek Worlock how different this experience had been from the very open way in which she had spoken with the two of us. He said, 'She has to be seen to win when there is a number of people present.'

Critics of Margaret Thatcher have consistently acknowledged her personal interest and care for individuals. My experience echoes that. She had written, formally inviting me to become Bishop of Oxford. For one brief evening, I could just see reasons why that might be God's calling. But, in the morning, the reasons had floated away, and I felt that Liverpool was still his place for me. Later that year Mrs Thatcher came to our cathedral for the service to mourn the ninety-six spectators who had been killed at the Hillsborough football disaster. She ran into me after the service, which had been both moving and appropriate.

Immediately she said, 'I can see now why you didn't feel you could go to Oxford.'

On the day of her 1987 election victory Margaret Thatcher said, 'And now for those inner cities!' 'Action for Cities', the Government's programme then introduced, was mainly a capital spending programme intended to improve buildings, rather than help with social and community needs. A review by a group from Manchester University found that smaller cities benefited more from the programme than the seven largest cities, where there had been 'an intensification of economic distress'. It also showed that total government expenditure on cities was relatively limited.

Mrs Thatcher determined to find a foolproof system of limiting local authority spending. This led eventually to the introduction of the poll tax. 'The Third Wave' of Thatcherism for the 1987 election intended to impose the elected national Government's will on local affairs. During the election, she described the poll tax as 'the flagship of the Thatcher fleet'. In the event it was to be the torpedo that sank the fleet. Widespread protests revealed the unfairness of its demands on poorer people, and soon its unpopularity convinced the Government that it must be dropped.

After John Major came into power, slowly co-operation replaced confrontation. Michael Heseltine returned to the DoE. He had always attacked irresponsible spending, but regularly argued for a constructive role for local authorities. Now in his first speech to the Commons on returning to office after Mrs Thatcher's fall in 1990, he said that there was the chance for a new, constructive phase in the development of local government. 'Some of the greatest moments in British history have coincided with the times of resolve, civic pride and municipal initiative in our great towns and cities . . . The country wishes us to try to identify a stable and just basis for the future development of local government and the provision of local services.'

So, was the Archbishop's Commission worth having? What did it contribute? When Lord Scarman, whom the Government had appointed to enquire into the 1981 riots, introduced a debate on inner cities in the House of Lords in 1987, he said *Faith in the City* was 'The finest face-to-face analysis that we have yet seen. In the long run it will take its place, I believe, as a classic description of one of the most serious troubles in British society.'

The very public debate started by the report – enlivened by the attempts to rubbish it – played a considerable part in bringing the needs of the cities to the attention of the nation. Politicians could no longer brush them aside as matters of no interest to the majority of voters in 'Middle England'. In the Church, the report became a rallying point.

A Postcard from Spain

Often a report is damned with faint praise by those who might have been expected to support it. That did not happen with *Faith in the City*. Even though it was a Church of England report, Christians of all churches used it as a stimulus for action. The tonic it gave to parishes in UPAs encouraged many to be more outward-looking in their communities. Now there was the challenge to 'get *Faith in the City* into the bloodstream of the Church of England'.

18

Handling Disagreements

The North–South divide

It has often been denied that the 'North–South divide' in Britain existed. Having lived on both sides of the divide, I never doubted its reality. That did not involve supposing that the entire South was prosperous. East London was too much part of my life to think that. London's inner city did not share the wealth that much of the South East knew. It wasn't until 2000 that official figures for unemployment separated inner London from the South East. They then showed inner London's unemployment to be the same as South Yorkshire's. My first FSU President's visit was to the East London unit, in The Highway, Stepney. On this misty November day, the North–South divide could not have appeared more starkly – there in East London. On the south side of The Highway vast new buildings rose out of the murk: this was Wapping, part of the London Docklands development, bringing offices and expensive flats along the riverside. On the north side of The Highway were inter-war estates, 70 per cent populated by Bangladeshi families. Life was a struggle for many of these families. The contrast could not have been sharper.

While acknowledging contrasts like this in London, I still believed the geographical North–South divide to be true and destructive. Department of Employment figures showed where jobs were lost between 1979 and 1986: 6 per cent of jobs were lost in the South, where 42 per cent of the population lived; that meant that 94 per cent of jobs lost were in the Midlands and the North.

The House of Commons held a debate on Church and State in 1989. John Patten, a Home Office Minister, spoke for the Government. He was widely quoted as saying that the Church needed to develop new theologies for a largely successful nation. It would not have been new for some churches to preach a 'prosperity gospel'. For myself, I could never grasp how followers of Jesus, who came to his victory by way of shameful rejection and death, could claim that faithful discipleship should always expect to lead to prosperity.

In the Church of England

Faith in the City insisted that St Paul's statement that we are 'members one of another' was a call to work for unity in one nation, with the better off caring for the poorer – and knowing that they had much to receive from them. In the debate on *Faith in the City* in the House of Lords, Robert Runcie said, 'I believe that, if we are to have faith in the city, we must also have faith in "Comfortable Britain". I do not regard it as axiomatic that such a Britain is basically selfish, uncaring, greedy and vindictive. There is a deep fund of goodwill and altruism that can be tapped.'

There was enormous interest in the report all over the country. One of the responses of many people of all political persuasions was to say they would be prepared to pay more taxes, provided the money reached the neediest. The response to the appeal for the Church Urban Fund (CUF) came from every diocese, and established a substantial new charity. By 2001 it had raised £37 million. CUF made grants to parishes and ecumenical projects that had never dared hope they might have the money to dream of new ventures. As a result, they became more outward-looking into the community. One project in Liverpool that has thrived and become self-supporting is the Furniture Resource Centre. At the time of writing, it has a turnover of £6.5 million. It has trained, and then given regular jobs, to unemployed people, from Liverpool 8 in particular. It manufactures inexpensive furniture, obtaining contracts with Social Services in several local authorities. The pioneer of the centre, Nic Frances,[1] thought it crucial to make creative use of links with parishes that had seen themselves simply as 'givers'. He would visit these better-off parishes and raise issues about the poverty the centre was discovering in taking furniture to families who were on benefit – and what was causing the poverty. He said they needed to advertise the findings they made through CUF projects as rigorously as they did for fundraising.

At the Furniture Resource Centre, they told me of homes they entered, in which there was no cooker, no chairs and no bed. They said these cases were not out of the ordinary. These uncomfortable truths stemmed directly from the way in which the Department of Social Security's Social Fund was working out. Until two years before, money had been available for single payments – to meet special needs – mainly for furniture and the most basic domestic appliances. Now most of these grants were replaced by loans, which many poor families would not touch because of their fears of falling into debt. The Social Fund reduced the amount payable in grants nationally from £360 million to £60 million. Even including the money now made available for loans, the total offered by grants and loans together still only offered just over half of what was formerly available for single payments.

Mrs Thatcher delivered an address to the General Assembly of the Church of Scotland in 1988 – described by many as her 'sermon'. Her central claim was that the Christian message is to individual responsibility: she quoted St Paul's text, that if a man would not work, he should not eat. Each person must work and use their talent to create wealth. She praised the hymn 'I vow to thee my country' – its triumphant assertion of what she described as 'secular patriotism'. 'It goes on to speak of "another country I heard of long ago" whose King cannot be seen and whose armies cannot be counted, but "soul by soul and silently her shining bounds increase". Not group by group or party by party or even Church by Church – but soul by soul – and each one counts.' In an interview given to *Woman's Own* the previous year, she made the comment that 'There is no such thing as society. There are individual men and women and there are families.'

Kenneth Baker addressed a fringe meeting of the General Synod; he said that the churches which were finding the greatest response were those that concentrated on offering spiritual help to individuals. Even if that were true, I would still want to ask if such a headcount of numbers in the pews proved that churches were being faithful to God and his kingdom. In his book *Holiness*, Donald Nichol wrote that the market was being flooded with books on spirituality, meditation, mysticism and so forth. He said some people regard this flood as a sign that there was a turning away from material things towards spiritual realities. That was certainly one possibility; but another possibility had been suggested by a group of editors of religious journals at a recent meeting. 'They discovered that the readership of all their journals was drawn almost entirely from the upper income bracket of society; and a survey had shown their readers to have virtually no interest in articles about social justice.'[2]

Within our own diocese, there were mutterings at times that the bishop was not concerned with the suburbs, towns and villages. At a 'Bishop's hearing' before the Lambeth Conference of 1988, there was a cry from suburban parishes, 'We have needs too'. I readily acknowledged that in comfortable districts personal tragedies, family breakdown and heavy responsibilities at work brought with them a struggle to live Christ's way. Michael Henshall received some of the grumbles about the bishop's priorities – as suffragan bishops do. We agreed that he would host some meetings for me to meet 'Gatekeepers' in the Formby/Birkdale

Presenting my oil painting of the newly completed cathedral to the Lord
Mayor of Liverpool. The Archbishop of York, Stuart Blanch, looks on during
the celebration of the centenary of the city and diocese, 1980.
(Photo: *Liverpool Post* and *Liverpool Echo*)

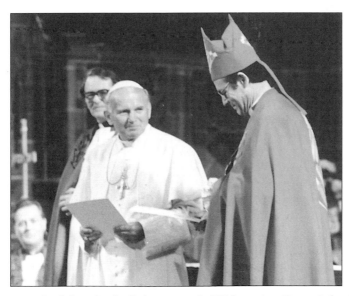

'You have a wonderful cathedral' (page 181). Welcoming Pope John Paul II to
Liverpool's Anglican cathedral, 1982. The Dean, Edward Patey, is beside him.

'If the Church leaders wanted to turn back now, we wouldn't let them' (page 176). The walk along Hope Street between the two cathedrals before we signed a Covenant for Unity, 1985. With me in the front row are: Norwyn Denny, Major Douglas Rayner, Derek Worlock, Trevor Hubbard.

With Derek Worlock and John Newton, Whit Sunday 1995, at the end of the Two Cathedrals' Ecumenical Service that had become a tradition on Merseyside.

'That's my house!' With Tony McGann, Derek Worlock and some of the Eldonians planning the Eldonian village in the old Scotland Road.

Celebrations after the cathedral service in 1993, Liverpool's first ordination of women as priests. (Photo: *Liverpool Post* and *Liverpool Echo*)

The expectations of a bishop's wife. The Frank Harris cartoon in
Grace's 'Jackdaw Kit' for wives of bishops (page 207).

The children's game at Bishop's Lodge Open Garden event.
The 'Mad Hatter' meets a friend. (Photo: Eddie Barford)

Robert Runcie launches the report *Faith in the City*, 1985. On the left is
Sir Richard O'Brien, the Chairman of the Archbishop's Commission.

'A certain joyful hope' (page 279). Derek Worlock and I meet Desmond Tutu
at Archbishop's House, Cape Town, 1989.

Grace emerges from the shacks of KTC township near Cape Town with the children who helped her find the way out.

Grace and I celebrate my recovery from a hip operation, 1994.
(Photo: Stephen Shakeshaft)

Jenny joins us for my 25th Anniversary Service as a bishop, five weeks after my hip operation. (Photo: Tom Murphy)

Grandpa and Stuart throw pebbles in the pool: one of Grace's watercolour paintings.

Leaving with balloons at the end of our farewell service in Liverpool Cathedral, 1997. (Photo: Richard Williams)

commuter belt of the diocese. These proved to be positive occasions when Christian brothers and sisters put me on the spot. And together we looked at the power that managers often had to open or shut 'gates' to employment or promotion for people from ethnic minorities or from unpopular addresses.

In Liverpool Diocese, the more affluent parishes never questioned the principle of 'quota by potential', though at times there were grumbles about its details. There was much sympathy for people who could not find a job. A key lay post in every diocese is that of chair of the Board of Finance. At the time we were working at our response to *Faith in the City*, Tom Prince became our chairman. He was Manager of Marks and Spencer in Southport. They gave him a year's paid leave before retirement, to work full-time for the diocese. That meant that, for the only time in my years, we had a full-time chairman; this came also at just the moment when an able young man, Keith Cawdron, came to be diocesan secretary. Tom Prince won the confidence of parishes by his openness and availability. One day he told me that he had grown up in a poor part of Salford. He wanted to offer for ordination, and went to see the Bishop of Manchester, Guy Warman. The bishop left him in no doubt that someone with his lack of education could not be considered for ordination. It seemed amazing to me that a young man who had been treated like that should have anything more to do with the Church. It seemed equally amazing that God had given us Tom at that particular moment as chairman. He understood Southport parishes, but also had the background that made him keen to find the resources that would enable the Church to be more open to those who had so often found it closed.

Different opinions were held within the diocesan team. Derrick Walters came to be Dean of Liverpool in 1983. He used to tell me about his father who was a South Wales trade unionist, while Derrick had become a firm supporter of Margaret Thatcher. We fell out quite seriously within the first year after he came. It wasn't about politics; he had written a piece in which he attacked 'bishops' for questioning the faith. I said that, if he meant David Jenkins, the Bishop of Durham, he should name him and make clear what point he disagreed with. The irony to me was that theologically Derrick was the nearest to a 'modernist' of anyone on our staff. Paradoxically, alongside his radical theology, he was a traditionalist about the liturgy. Both of us realised that a rift between bishop and dean would damage the Church. We worked hard to build understanding and trust, establishing regular lunch meetings every six weeks. I believe we succeeded in building firm and genuine unity. When it came to appointments of cathedral canons that were in my patronage, I discussed names from the beginning with Derrick, and made sure that he had the last word about each appointment. After all, they were going to make up his close team. In the diocese, he agreed to chair a working party that could have set fresh patterns of training, but its work was hurried. It soon became clear that he was going to give his undivided attention to the cathedral and what surrounded it. He told me the cathedral was 'a jealous mistress'. That single-mindedness limited his involvement in ecumenical partnership, which had grown strong between the cathedrals. Derek Worlock reported to me that the clergy at the Metropolitan Cathedral told him that it wasn't the same as it had been when Edward Patey was dean.

Those were what I saw as Derrick Walters's limitations. His achievements were remarkable. Very soon we saw the effects of changes he brought about: the daily celebration of choral evensong was re-established. Soon, a dead space was turned into a thriving refectory. A new visitors' centre with a bookshop was set up. The lighting – so crucial for the pink sandstone interior – was perfected, and the tower was floodlit. The number of visitors grew, and a more professional management matched their requirements. Derrick saw the organ and the choir – without a choir school, yet second to none – as the jewel in the cathedral's crown. After his death, the organist, Professor Ian Tracey, wrote, 'As a Dean, he was the answer to an organist's prayer. He was, in his own words, a Medieval Dean at heart. He saw the Cathedral very much in the medieval monastic model at the centre of the community, employer, trainer of apprentices in the various trades, builder of dwellings and workplaces and in every sense nurturing the community around it.'[3]

The private part of the housing development below the cathedral, started by Michael Heseltine's competition, had run into the sand. Derrick formed 'Project Rosemary'. He used all his contacts with the Church Commissioners, with Downing Street and the City of London, to build a Cathedral Close for the canons, and lecture rooms and students' residences for John Moores University. The legacy this development left behind will prove to be of great long-term benefit to the cathedral.

Somehow he won, at the same time, the confidence of Mrs Thatcher's Government and Liverpool City Council. At a time when confidence in the city was low, he and his team showed that they could deliver. He had a gift for persuading the most unlikely people to work together. He moved on from the buildings on the hill below the cathedral to redeveloping sixty acres around Upper Parliament Street in the heart of Liverpool 8. Joan Walters was teaching in a nursery and primary school in that district. She loved her job and had stories to tell every day of the life and needs of children and families in that hurt district. I felt sure this inside story provided an important part of Derrick's motivation. Project Rosemary delivered the new Women's Hospital, enterprise workshop units and much-needed housing association accommodation. It was a remarkable achievement. Huw Thomas in his obituary in the *Independent* wrote:

> Anyone further removed from the stage parson than Derrick Walters can scarcely be imagined. The smart grey double-breasted suit with white tie, the office with the long director's table and television screen 'flashing the FTSE 100 Index', the latest issue of *The Economist* on his desk and the air of business activity were a long way from Barchester – though Archdeacon Grantley might well have warmed to some of it!

For years he was struggling with prostate cancer, still hopeful of delivering a major millennium project for Liverpool – though unsuccessful this time. He leaned heavily on the two full-time canons, Mark Boyling and Noel Vincent, who rose to the occasion and helped maintain the cathedral's regular life. He died in 2000, a greatly valued figure in Liverpool, with lasting achievements to his name. His successor as dean, Bishop Rupert Hoare, builds on his legacy. In addition, Rupert gives a high priority to the ecumenical partnership with the Roman Catholic cathedral, and chairs the Merseyside Inter-Faith Council.

In the Anglican Communion

In many parts of the worldwide Anglican Communion, Christian witness is costly – dangerous sometimes – where there is injustice and oppression that are beyond our experience in Britain. As a diocese, we sought fresh partners in mission after completing the agreed ten-year link with the province of the Southern Cone in South America. This new link was with the Diocese of Akure in the Yoruba West of Nigeria. Grace and I made a visit in 1995, staying with our opposite numbers, Emmanuel and Alice Gbonigi. They paid us a visit in turn soon afterwards. I admired the boldness of Bishop Emmanuel in taking the risk of making sharp criticisms of the military Government that was then in power. In his address to the diocesan synod that we attended, he spoke sharply about the 'current appalling state of education in our country'. He quoted in full the Statement of the Bishops of the Church of Nigeria, that called clearly for freedom of the press to be restored, and for political detainees to be released.

Early in our three-week visit to Nigeria, we had gone to Owerri in the Ibo eastern region. I heard Bishop Benjamin Nwankiti say in his synod address there that it was not enough to keep calling for good politicians, co-operative civil service, a moral police force and an educated voting public, capable of accommodating views from a wider basis than their own simple self-interest or greed. He said, 'Good citizens of both earth and heaven do not appear from nowhere. They have to be formed, and the Church has a part to play in this formation.'

I had come to know Benjamin Nwankiti in preparations for the 1988 Lambeth Conference. Every ten years, 'Lambeth' brings together all the Anglican Bishops in the world. Benjamin had been appointed chairman – and I his vice-chairman – for one of four sections into which the work of the conference was to be divided. We were to look at mission and ministry. Ill health and death meant that I served three different chairmen before we reached the conference. There was much to receive from each of them, especially about the responsibility of the Church to stand for justice and unity in each nation. Benjamin Nwankiti withdrew because his wife fell gravely ill, dying a few months later. Eventually, James Ottley, the Bishop of Panama, proved to be a wise and firm chairman. He was later to be appointed as Anglican representative at the United Nations.

My first chairman was Festo Kivengere from Uganda, who became seriously ill, and died before the conference. Festo was a much-loved leader in the East African Revival Movement. He shared with me some of his disappointments about the Church's witness in Uganda. Eighty per cent of the population belonged to the Anglican or the Roman Catholic Church. Yet corruption in public life was widespread. Why, if the Church was so full of renewed life, was its influence so limited? One factor was the lack of partnership between Anglicans and Roman Catholics. Another was the danger that renewal movements sometimes emphasise only 'spiritual' and 'in-Church' matters concerning the individual Christian, and see social and political issues as nothing to do with the Church.

Between Anglicans and Roman Catholics

Back in Liverpool, it took my breath away when Liverpool Diocesan Synod voted formally to support *The Final Report* of the Anglican-Roman Catholic International Commission (ARCIC). There were no more than nine votes against – in the city where sectarian bitterness had reigned so long. A good number of parishes in the Protestant evangelical tradition had learned to join hands with Roman Catholics in serving the community. As Derek Worlock and I knew from our personal experience, that did not remove the theological questions on which we disagreed. They still had to be attended to. But having prayed, planned and worked together, we found that the ground had shifted when we came back to the stubborn theological differences. Now we each looked more closely at what was precious to our trusted partner – and understood more.

Handling Disagreements

The Commission's Final Report was published in 1982[4] – just before the Pope made his visit to Britain. The press, either out of ignorance or ill will – or simply to tell a complex story in headlines – reverted to the old and crudest trench-warfare language of sixteenth-century controversy. They set on one side the carefully crafted words that enabled the Commission to explore the possibility of accepting the Bishop of Rome as the 'Universal Primate' for a united church. If they had grasped what kind of primate was conceived, they would have seen it was proposing as large a change to traditionalist Roman Catholics as to Protestants. It was nearer to a 'first among equals' kind of universal primate than to the pontiff of the last thousand years' history. Instead, crude headlines created anxiety that 'the Pope was going to take over the Church of England'. Many retreated from making the effort to work at ARCIC's theology. They said it was too sophisticated. As it happened, during the week that followed the publication of *The Final Report*, I visited St Frideswyde's, Thornton, on the perimeter of Bootle. Over coffee and biscuits after the service, I asked members of the parish – who would not have seen themselves as sophisticated – what they made of ARCIC. They had no difficulties, and explained shrewdly what was at stake in the report. When I asked how they knew what it said, they told me they had discussed each of its three parts, as they had been published, at joint group meetings with members of St William of York, the neighbouring Roman Catholic parish. That joint discussion had meant that each 'side' would have made clear what was being defended at particular points.

I found it helpful to enter into their approach of trying to dig beneath the old wars of words. The second report of ARCIC – *Salvation and the Church*[5] – seemed to me to show truthfully that our churches stood on common ground for the heart of our salvation. In words that, surely, should have warmed the heart of every evangelical Christian they wrote:

> Above all it was agreed that the act of God in bringing salvation to the human race and summoning individuals into a community to serve Him is due solely to the mercy and grace of God. It is mediated and manifested through Jesus Christ in His ministry, atoning death and rising again. It was also not a matter of dispute that God's grace evokes an authentic human response of faith ... The difficulties arose in explaining how divine grace related to human response.

Much of the work that Derek Worlock and I shared was behind the scenes, in the 'engine room'. Both of us longed to see joint schools coming into being. That was frustrated for most of our years in Liverpool, because of falling rolls in the schools. As the population dropped, local authorities were closing schools rather than opening them. In Liverpool

50 per cent of all children went to Roman Catholic schools. Derek told me he had been obliged to preside over the closure of seventeen schools – many of which had not yet been paid for by the parishes. When Cardinal Heenan had been Archbishop of Liverpool, his confidence that the numbers of Roman Catholic children would not drop had led him to continue building new schools. In the event, over Derek's years, their numbers dropped by similar numbers as in the other schools.

Reflecting on that, it seems like a blind spot in Derek himself that he could not face openly the dramatic reduction in the number of priests. He discussed many difficulties with me, but never this, which was to change the shape of parishes and the pattern of a priest's life. He fostered the permanent diaconate – ordaining some seventy permanent deacons – mostly married men. But the reduction in the number of priests was dramatic. In 1975, I discovered that it took twenty-five years in the archdiocese before a newly ordained priest was appointed to his own parish. Derek's successor, Patrick Kelly, found he had to grapple with the situation when, by 2002, there were 165 parish priests to serve 226 parish churches, with 18 assistant priests. This led to change of a whole way of life. Where priests had lived with others and a housekeeper in a clergy house, now they lived alone.

Our hope for a joint school eventually came to fruition in a large new housing area, where rolls were increasing. Long negotiations led to a joint two-form entry primary school in Croxteth Park – Emmaus School – that Patrick Kelly and I visited together during my last months. It was the first newly built school for Liverpool in twenty-five years, and it meant much that the city had wanted it to be a church school. With the Government's encouragement of faith-based schools, it was heartening to learn in 2002 of the proposed City Academy in inner-city Kensington – a high school sponsored by the archdiocese and diocese jointly.

During the long wait for joint schools, the area in which progress was possible was higher education. We felt that, if teachers and others in higher education trained together, this would influence schools in the long term. There were two Roman Catholic colleges of higher education in Liverpool (Notre Dame and Christ's), and one Anglican (St Katherine's). In 1975, they were working in an informal federation. Derek and I were ex officio in the chairs of the respective colleges. For a time I resented the amount of time this committee work demanded of me. Gradually the conviction grew that here was a prize worth working for. Each of the principals had asked to see us on our arrival, to tell us of their enthusiasm to move on to closer links. There were times when we both had to hold them to their word.

One of the earliest of the many joint train journeys Derek and I made to London was in 1976 to see Gordon Oakes, Minister of State at the

Department of Education. We were literally fighting for the life of the church colleges in Liverpool. Civil servants in the Department were advising that at least two of the three should be closed. We pressed the value of the ecumenical partnership in Liverpool. Gordon Oakes was MP for Widnes, had been at Liverpool University, and saw the point. He used his authority to override his advisers. From then on, the Department funded one institute, which in turn funded two colleges. Derek and I chaired the Council of the Institute for two years at a time, with the other as vice-chairman. The politics of higher education were another world. Sometimes I would say to Jim Burke, our resourceful rector, 'Shall I write to the Minister to obtain an answer to the question we've been asking for six months?' 'No, Bishop,' he'd say. 'I'll ring my contacts in the Department, to see what they are planning.' Next, we would receive a question from the Department, very likely at the beginning of the summer vacation, demanding a detailed reply within a month.

When Jim Burke retired in 1995, he looked back on fourteen years, in which the institute had grown from 900 students to 4,500 – matching the national growth from 8 to 30 per cent of young people going into higher education. By then, we had overcome denominational fears and decided to become one college. Next we needed to agree the college's name. We argued ourselves to exhaustion. There were objections to every bright idea. The new rector we appointed was Simon Lee, aged thirty-seven, Professor of Jurisprudence at Queen's, Belfast. In the interview, he told us that he considered the institute, now becoming a college, the most significant ecumenical project in education in the country. On his first visit, following his appointment, he sounded me out about introducing the word 'hope' into the title, thinking of the use we had made of Hope Street linking the two cathedrals as a symbol of unity.

Simon Lee has brought flair, imagination and a higher profile to Liverpool Hope University College. The finances that had been carefully garnered over fourteen years were put to creative use. A major remodelling and expansion of the library brought a happy moment for us. Grace was asked to open the library, called the 'Sheppard–Worlock Library'. 'Hope on the Waterfront' was established in the Albert Dock. 'Hope in Everton' was to be a major inner-city development in Shaw Street that had once seemed such a symbol of decay and defeat in the city. It provides self-catering rooms for PGCE (Post-Graduate Certificate of Education) students, with the hope that they will do their teaching practice in the inner city and that some will then decide to stay.

Better Together

When Derek Worlock and I had been working together for ten years, we agreed that we would attempt a joint book – *Better Together*. Each would write one chapter at the beginning, describing our personal journeys before coming to Liverpool. In addition, we would include some paragraphs, printed in italics, that would allow each of us to tell a story or give a personal insight. It also enabled us to debate a disagreement. For the main body of the book, we went through a five-part process leading to an agreed text. When starting a new chapter, I would draw Derek out to talk about the themes we had already agreed, taking extensive notes. That would take at least a two-hour session. I would then write a first draft. This would go to and fro, with each of us making suggestions, criticisms and offering alternative phrases or additions. Derek, the small-print editor, generally had the last say in tidying up our grammar.

Occasionally the tasks were reversed. When we reached the final stage of our last book, *With Hope in Our Hearts*, his diary was heavily committed, so I did the detailed tidying up. We met to work through the text that had now emerged. Derek said he could accept everything, except for one matter. Wherever the word 'Gospel' had appeared, I had written it with a capital G. Derek's grammar, going back, he said, to R. A. Knox, made him argue that it should be printed with a lower case g, when the word was an adjective. I said Gospel was a great Christian word and I wanted it to begin with an upper case G. Eventually, he agreed and upper case it was. That evening, we went upstairs to his chapel and placed the text of our book on the altar – as we had done before. We offered a prayer – extempore, as we often did, Derek starting and I taking over. I prayed, 'Lord, we want this to be a Gospel book, that helps readers to believe the good news about you.' When we stood up from our prayer, Derek said, 'When you prayed that it would be a Gospel book, I couldn't stop myself wondering whether the G in Gospel was upper or lower case!' A crucial question for every author is, 'Who are you writing for?' What lay beneath my prayer that it would be 'a Gospel book' was my hope that it would speak about the love of Christ to readers who stood outside the organised life of the Church, as well as those inside. That meant trying to begin where people were, often with the messy issues of a hurt city.

In *With Hope in Our Hearts*, we included one major subject on which we disagreed, as we had in *Better Together* with the subject of the ordination of women. This time we laid out our arguments about population control. Derek had said in the past that one's attitude towards contraception was not the acid test of being a Christian. But in *With*

Hope in Our Hearts he argued that merely to limit the number of births in the Third World is to be handing greater power to the 20 per cent of the world who live in industrial society over the 80 per cent who live in non-industrial society. 'The Northern countries should try to solve the social problems created by poverty, lack of education and lack of health care, rather than try to enforce control of population and families in the South by contraception.'

I wrote that contraception should never provide a short cut to feeding the hungry world. In Argentina, I had heard fiercely propounded the argument that children were the only riches of the poor. The fears of people in the Third World that there will be no child to look after them in old age or to inherit their land are powerful motivations for having a large family.

> But there is no way in which the world will be able to feed the huge growth of population, if this continues through the improvement of health care. For me, it is an expression of our trust in the living God to believe that he provides appropriate gifts to meet new needs. In this case I believe he enables scientific technology not only to deliver better health care, but to limit the increased population which results from it.[6]

In 1983, we had both visited South America. My visit was part of a *Partners in Mission* commitment by Liverpool Diocese for ten years to the new Anglican Province of the Southern Cone. I attended the inaugural conference in Buenos Aires, and then found that my programme could be adjusted to match Derek's in visiting Lima in Peru. We went visiting together in the *Pueblos Jovenes*, the sprawling shantytowns rapidly growing around Lima. Derek particularly wanted me to travel with one Irish priest who served there. After a long conversation, I asked him what he taught his church members about family planning. His reply was, 'I don't say anything. I leave it to doctors and nurses.' But he encouraged the use of a liberation theology booklet about *Jesus and Women*. In strip cartoon form, with the Apostles appearing as South American Indians, this showed the respect our Lord showed to women in the Gospels. Some of the men had come angrily to him, demanding, 'What's got into my wife since she started coming to your church?'

The subject of abortion was an acutely sensitive one. Soon after I came to Liverpool, local leaders of the Society for the Protection of the Unborn Child (SPUC) came to see Edward Patey and me. We both felt the language they used about 'murder of an unborn child' assumed that they knew without a question that a foetus was a person from conception. We did not believe it was possible for human beings to have such certainty. No one advocates murder. But there are no agreed criteria for answering the question, 'What constitutes personhood?' Different people argue for different moments – at conception, at delivery, when the foetus achieves independent viability, a gradual development of personal status during gestation.[7]

Some years later, Allan Roberts, MP for Bootle, wrote to me that he was being put under heavy pressure by SPUC to take a 'pro-life' stand which in conscience he did not agree with. In my reply I said that there was another Christian position: I believed that abortion was always an evil, but that there were circumstances that led to greater evils. Those circumstances needed always to be spelt out and considered by more than one doctor, before concluding that abortion was the lesser of evils. Doctors in inner-city health centres had pressed me to understand what some of the greater evils were if unwanted babies were born, though that did not lead me to agree with another absolute position – 'the woman's right to choose'. In a number of discussions between Anglicans and Roman Catholics common ground was to be found. We agreed that the large number of abortions was wrong and should be reduced. We agreed that much of the public debate had failed to address the need to reduce the number of unplanned pregnancies – and so at least some of the demand for abortion. Allan Roberts said it would help him greatly if he could publish my letter. Reluctantly, for it was not a subject on which to relish becoming involved in public debate, I agreed, and he published it.

The archdiocese published a weekly newspaper, the *Catholic Pictorial*. They asked me for an interview on abortion. I told Derek who was coming to see me. He said that with this particular journalist he insisted on writing down what he wanted to say. I followed his example. As the journalist was leaving, he asked me, 'Did Archbishop Worlock know that it was me that was coming?' I said that he did. The '*Catholic Pic*' printed the interview in full on their front page. Derek was pressed to denounce me, but would not. That did not mean that Derek had 'gone soft' on abortion. He made plain to me that he held it to be wrong always. But he acknowledged that other thoughtful Christians honestly took another position, and should be respected.

Grace and I were drawn closer than ever to Derek in the long years of his illness, from the diagnosis in 1992 until his death four years later. In July 1992, John Moores University gave Grace an Honorary Fellowship. At first, she told Peter Toyne, the vice-chancellor, she did not believe the honour could be for her. He insisted that they wanted to recognise her achievements in Liverpool, through her writing and her contribution to public life, as well as her courage – now made public – in overcoming cancer and crippling fears. Derek agreed to make the speech to introduce her at the graduation ceremony – held each year in the Anglican cathedral. On Sunday he had mentioned to us symptoms that gave cause for concern about his health. That Tuesday morning, he told me he had been diagnosed with lung cancer. He asked me simply to tell Grace that he would be late, but promised that he would be there in time to introduce her. She was aware that something serious was afoot.

In fact, he made it an hour after the start of the ceremony. We saw him walking slowly down the side of the crowded cathedral with his chaplain, John Furnival. When he spoke, like the professional trooper he was, no one would have known that anything was wrong. In fact he had come straight from the hospital, where he had been told that the cancer meant the removal of a lung and then long months of chemotherapy. That gave Grace and him the common experience of being cancer patients, and brought them to a very close understanding. He was then able to talk about some dark nights of the soul in ways that the younger Derek, who needed to show that he could cope triumphantly with whatever was thrown at him, would not have done. In *With Hope in Our Hearts*,[8] he wrote: 'The greatest trial was the inability to concentrate. This deprived me of any satisfaction from prayer. Almost everyone who came to see me recited the Lord's Prayer. I remained as cold as a stone spiritually and desperately troubled by nightmares.' Grace had encouraged him to say publicly what this dark night experience was. He wrote later that people seemed surprised, even encouraged, by the fact that he found it so difficult to pray.

He faced the approach of death very openly. He determined to have a 'reconciliation week', in which he would try to speak to those with whom relationships had broken down. The first call he made was to his twin sister, Patricia. She had maintained an unswerving traditional position, and was highly critical of the changes Derek was so deeply engaged in. He found her visits oppressive. Now he was able to tell her that he loved her. One piece of information he found painful was to learn that Monsignor Jim Dunn, who had been a closely trusted colleague all through his Liverpool years, had married. During those last years, Derek talked to me quite often about the cost of celibacy, especially as he faced old age and weakness. Jim had been advised that Derek was too ill to be told. Now in 'reconciliation week' he went to see him. Clearly the news came as a shock. But Derek managed to say, 'I will defend your freedom of conscience.'

We said goodbye during the Mass we attended at his hospital bed the day before he died. At the moment of the peace, he opened his eyes, sat up and we exchanged the greeting. The following day I had to be in London. As his death approached, John Furnival rang Grace to say that Derek was slipping away. She felt a powerful wish to be near him for both our sakes. She jumped in the car and arrived at the Lourdes Hospital, intending to sit quietly in the lounge with her tapestry. John saw her arrive and invited her to sit with Derek. He died, on his birthday, early in the morning a few hours after she had left.

I was asked to speak at the vigil Mass on the night before his funeral, when the cathedral congregation was there to receive his body. I wondered whether it would be appropriate to introduce a touch of humour in what was of course a solemn occasion. But I risked it, and learned afterwards that my story was appreciated. I said:

In these last six months there has been much weakness, vulnerability: but flashes of light too. There was what he called 'reconciliation week', doing everything in his power to talk and make things right with those he had felt at odds with. There was his care for a visitor whose wife was very ill. And there were touches of the old humour: one day Grace brought him some fresh figs from the garden. She had wrapped them in fig leaves. Pointing at the leaves, he said, 'with all the treatment I've had this week, I could have done with one of those!'

19

Respecting 'the Others'

While Derek Worlock was still in vigorous health, we went on a number of journeys together. Seeing how other communities were fighting to overcome destructive divisions equipped us to see better the dangers and the possibilities facing us in Liverpool. And in some of these places of conflict our hosts encouraged us by saying that our partnership in Liverpool offered a small sign of hope. Northern Ireland was just across the sea and came top of the list. South Africa, though far away, had been the most notable example of unjust discrimination – and cricket had drawn me into its controversies. Other divisions – between faiths – were present in our own backyard in Britain. In each of these situations, a central challenge was how we treat 'the others'.

Protestants and Catholics in Northern Ireland

Our first joint visit was to the Corrymeela Community on the north Antrim coast. We met people who had suffered unspeakable violence and loss, yet were utterly committed to reconciliation. Bishop Tony Farquhar, a Roman Catholic auxiliary bishop in Belfast, told me that he had the duty of breaking the news of the murder of her son to one of this group. As he drove her across the city, he said, 'She ministered to me, rather than the other way round.'

We were given short notice when the two Archbishops of Armagh, Cardinal Thomas O'Feaigh and John Armstrong of the Church of Ireland, invited us to preach in both the Armagh cathedrals and in St Anne's Church of Ireland cathedral, Belfast, during the Week of Prayer for Christian Unity. There had been a terrible outrage when the IRA had machine-gunned a Pentecostal church at the village of Darkley the previous month and they both pressed us that our joint witness could speak positively in a dangerous situation. We preached a sermon alternately in four short parts in the Roman Catholic Cathedral in Armagh on the day we arrived. We hoped this method made it plain that we prepared in partnership. We stayed with our respective archbishops in the small town of Armagh. I was impressed by the courage of the Armstrongs. He had been appointed archbishop in his sixties from a comparatively quiet life in Dublin. They lived without staff in an exposed house. At breakfast, he told me that he had received a phone call already that morning, accusing him of being a traitor by going to the Roman Catholic Cathedral the night before.

I rang Derek to discuss how we should handle the Prayer Service that was to take place in the Church of Ireland Cathedral in Armagh that morning. They were sitting at the table after breakfast when my call came. The Cardinal's major-domo came into the room and announced, 'The Other Hill is on the phone, your Grace'! When we arrived for the Prayer Service to which clergy and ministers had been invited, we were surprised to see a BBC television van outside. We had received no notice that they would be coming. In the vestry, clergy and ministers were saying they would go home if the service was to be televised. I was grateful for responsible media that day. When we told the BBC correspondent of the fears that were being expressed, he agreed to withdraw. After the service, I asked a Presbyterian minister whether it had been costly for him to come to the service. 'Not for me,' he said, 'my congregation are very supportive.' Then he told me about a Methodist minister who was present. Whenever he went away from home, within the hour his wife would receive calls threatening to burn the house down. When we arrived that evening in the Cardinal's car at St Anne's Cathedral, Belfast, protesters thumped on the bonnet, shouting about 'Darkley'.

There were more visits and four-part sermons, and visits with John Newton, the Free Church Moderator for Merseyside. The twice-yearly 'North West Triangle' meetings of church leaders from Glasgow, Belfast and Liverpool took us to Belfast a number of times. Our first meeting there left an indelible impression on me. The Northern Ireland Housing Commission took us in a small bus along the interface between the two communities: we went in and out of the small streets along the Falls Road, the Shankill Road and the other street names that have a bitter ring through news of sectarian violence. At one point we got out of the bus to look at a small housing development of some forty 'Protestant houses' in the middle of some 700 'Catholic houses', in a largely 'Protestant' quarter. Just by the houses was a new brick wall. 'What's that for?' we asked. 'That's the Peace Line,' they said. The only way people could live with confidence was to have a wall four metres high, with a metal shield on top, to protect them from their neighbours. From then on we kept seeing the 'Peace Line'. It was one matter when it was a short-term barricade of corrugated iron and barbed wire, thrown up by the army. It seemed disturbingly long term and fatalist to see that new brick wall.

Some of the issues that arose when the North West Triangle met were common ground. Cahal Daly, then Bishop in Belfast, soon to succeed O'Feaigh at Armagh, spoke at one meeting about the large estates in West Belfast. He said, 'The involvement of the Church at the level of unemployment and other social questions is a vital witness. It is the only way which will in the end open people up again to the Gospel.'

At one of our meetings, we were given copies of *Sectarianism: A Discussion Document for Presentation to the Irish Inter-Church Meeting*. We were told that some church leaders had insisted that it could not be called more than 'A Discussion Document'. I found it a powerful statement about the way we think about 'the Others', and have returned to it repeatedly. It has much to say about how we regard, and how we treat, black people, Jews, Muslims – or Irish people – in England. It explained how sectarianism is a learnt process:

> The home, parenting, grandparenting, the street, the community, the Church, the school classroom, the peer group, the leaders, the idols, the media, macrohistory told in parables, microhistory – personal, local, recounted without fear of contradiction – and many more, feed into the life and mind of the child . . . Somewhere within that web it starts: the understanding of self as Catholic/Nationalist or Protestant/Unionist; and the understanding of the other as different, and more than that, as wrong – and worse still as unloveable, to be feared, hated, distrusted or disliked.

It is a rare occurrence for me to shed actual tears. But as I was reading the description of what it costs to break down that deeply imbedded inheritance, tears came streaming down my face. I knew that what they described was the true calling of a peacemaker:

> Are we prepared to challenge our friends, neighbours, family, when they express sectarian views in our company? To develop a relentless and courageous sensitivity to the God-created humanity of 'THE OTHER' whether he/she be Catholic or Protestant . . . has to be the work of the follower of Christ. It has to be the work of the sincere peacemaker. It starts with me. Bitter words build walls of hate. I am accountable for the bitter word said today, repeated tomorrow by my children.[1]

English people frequently speak about Northern Ireland as though all that needs doing is to bang the heads together of the two communities. In 1996 Nicholas Frayling, the Rector of Liverpool, wrote a courageous book, *Pardon and Peace*, in which he showed the part that the English have played in the tragedy of Irish divisions. He wrote: 'The conviction that Britain owes a debt of sorrow and penitence to the peoples of Ireland is the central preoccupation of this book.' He took a study leave of four months in Ireland, in which he crossed all the dividing lines in order to listen to authentic Irish voices, Protestant as much as Roman Catholic. John Newton, Derek Worlock and I wrote a Foreword. In it we said:

> He does not pretend that the way of penitence, forgiveness and reconciliation is easy. It is certain to be costly, as South Africa has found. He recognises that there are enormous fears to overcome. One of the strengths of the author's approach is that he has genuinely striven to listen to Irish people, of all shades of political and religious conviction.

Black and white in South Africa

In 1989 Derek Worlock and I were invited to go to South Africa together. Archbishop Stephen Naidoo, the Roman Catholic Archbishop of Cape Town, had met us on a visit to Liverpool. He said he wanted people in South Africa to see how such a partnership could work. Sadly, he was seriously ill while we were there. The following year, in his fifties, he died. The invitation came jointly from Stephen Naidoo and Desmond Tutu, the Anglican Archbishop of Cape Town. Grace came too. So did Derek's chaplain, John Furnival, and Julian Filachowski, the Director of CAFOD (Catholic Aid for Overseas Development). The State of Emergency was still in force. Nelson Mandela was still in prison. We did little public speaking during our eighteen-day visit, but were given unique opportunities to listen and see for ourselves.

It was a life-changing experience. We spent time, sometimes overnight, in a dozen black townships. The warmth of welcome we received from most of the black people we met amazed us. That had something to do with the way in which many church leaders had risked standing firm against the evil of apartheid. In a few situations we walked into overt anger. In Duncan Village in the Eastern Cape, we stopped to talk to a group of young men standing by a wide track with the sewage running down the side. It took a few minutes before they felt willing to speak to us.

A senior priest and his wife had us to stay in Mdantsane, a vast township near East London. It was one of the few moments when we caught the whiff of fear. One evening they told us of their daughter being tortured at the local police station. Just as they were describing a knock on the door by the police, there was a sharp rap on the front door. We froze – it could have been the police then. They had just been telling us of a raid that included searching the vicarage and the church – 'looking for a terrorist'. A week or two after our visit, we heard that their son had been killed on the border with Botswana. It sounded as though he had joined 'the armed struggle'. Another day, we sat in the Supreme Court in Cape Town, behind the families of a large group charged with treason. The realities of Section 29 were spelt out in the court: by it the Security Police could hold someone indefinitely without charge and without any visit or communication from lawyer or family. Those who were released from detention were frequently put under restriction, having to report to the police twice a day at a most inconvenient distance from their work.

When we stayed in Soweto, Grace asked the men who had been invited to join us for the evening meal if they would tell us about being driven from their homes in Sophiatown, where each of them had grown up. We had read and heard about Sophiatown from Trevor Huddleston, who had served there. He said this had been a flourishing example of a mixed-race community, which was a major reason why the Government wanted it destroyed. Over the dinner table we were told how the army surrounded the Township. Possessions were loaded on trucks, and they were taken to their new home in 'South West Town' (that became Soweto) with nothing except a key to the toilet – the only part of the home to have been built.

Trevor was remembered and honoured in South Africa. That summer, back in England, I spoke at an Independence Day rally in London at which he declaimed a fiery speech on the platform. I was introduced as 'Comrade Bishop'! At the meeting, I asked a black South African if he had seen a splendid photo in the *Independent* of Trevor with Albertina Sisulu, a distinguished figure in the struggle. He told me Albertina had said the picture of her with Trevor would do her street credibility much good!

Grace described a profound moment for her in KTC, a township of rough-and-ready shacks outside Cape Town. It was the one occasion in our time in South Africa that a television crew accompanied us. Grace had been talking with a woman inside her hut, and had asked our host to alert her when the party was moving off. She suddenly became aware that it had turned quiet outside. Looking outside, she discovered to her horror that we had all gone. Four local men stood outside. She had to face her fears and prejudices. Did she really believe that they were more likely to harm her than to help her find the way? She wrote:

Now was my chance to get rid of my prejudices for ever. Before God I cast them down on the sand at my feet, disowning them completely. I thanked the woman for talking with me, and moved over to the group of men that a moment ago had terrified me. 'Excuse me', I said, grinning, and using sign language, 'I'm lost. Could you tell me where my friends went?' They understood and grinned in return. They pointed out the direction for me to take, and I set off in trust and thankfulness. Twenty minutes later, I arrived at the edge of the Township and rejoined the party. I had not been alone, for holding my hands were children who had come out of their homes to meet me. To crown my lesson in humility, I discovered that no one in my party had missed me![2]

We were told that we had seen more of black people's life in the townships than 98 per cent of white South Africans. Grace and I spent one Sunday evening with the vestry meeting of a white parish. There was much criticism of the bishops and especially of Archbishop Tutu. We were told they did not 'preach the Gospel', or believe that the Holy Spirit could really change lives. Grace was about to publish her book *An Aspect of Fear*. She was invited to tell them a little about it. Then she asked if they had any fears. Soon, fears about their country's future poured out. The woman who had been most vociferous in criticisms told us she had never been in a black township. She said she would be afraid of herself and how she would behave. We tried to share some of the positive moments we had enjoyed in our visits to the townships – and the way in which black people we met had been so forgiving. As I have reflected on this conversation, it has seemed that the teaching that group had been given had emphasised personal faith, but could have said nothing about the greatest issue in their country.

Everywhere we found that the sporting boycott, once so vilified, was now praised as having brought the right kind of pressure for change. Captains of industry were now fighting to prevent the commercial sanctions, that in the end forced the Government to make fundamental changes. An unofficial cricket touring team, captained by Mike Gatting, was struggling through half a tour, with support dwindling away. I had written to Ali Bacher, the Chief Executive of the South African Cricket Association, asking if he would like to show me the coaching scheme he was running in the townships. Grace and I, together with Julian Filachowski, crowded into a small car with Ali Bacher and a young professional cricketer, who regularly coached in primary schools. We drove to Tembisa, a township of some 45,000 people, near Johannesburg. The most promising boys in the schools were chosen for coaching on the three permanent net wickets we saw. In turn, the best of these had been selected for the game that was taking place on a matting wicket in the middle of the ground. The most promising boys from this game were then bussed into The Wanderers ground in Johannesburg to play alongside the best from white schools.

Our reception at Tembisa was weird. It was made plain that we were expected to sit down to tea and a speech of welcome, before we could see any cricket. The speech compared The Wanderers with heaven and Ali Bacher with the Messiah! Saluting what he was trying to do, I expressed the opinion that it would take a long time to see first-class black cricketers emerge. Ali disagreed. He thought there would be some in the South African team within two or three years. In fact the first black player to play for South Africa, Makhaya Ntini, was selected for the Test team in 1997 – eight years on. I have admired Ali Bacher's commitment and persistence. In the car afterwards, Grace asked him what it was like to be called the Messiah. She went on to ask him what his motivation was for this demanding project. He thought for a while. Then he said, 'Perhaps it's because I'm a Jew.'

The greatest risk in going to South Africa seemed that I might find Desmond Tutu's feet were made of clay. I had long believed he was one of God's special people. Our visit only caused my admiration to grow. We flew into Cape Town late at night. We had understood Desmond was away, arguing the case for sanctions against South Africa in New York, or exhausted, having just arrived home. But there he was, coming to greet us with arms outstretched. We joined the clergy of the diocese for a eucharist and discussion with Desmond on this return of his from New York. He made a point of setting time aside to meet all the clergy after overseas visits during the apartheid years. He was conscious of the necessity of keeping direct communications open in a time when misinformation was deliberately spread around. Life went at a sharp pace with Desmond, and I feared that he would not make time for extended conversation with Derek. I tackled him firmly, saying that Derek Worlock was an influential figure, and it mattered that they had time together. Desmond responded with an unhurried interview – and Derek was his fan for life. He hung a photo prominently in his home of Desmond with the two of us.

Grace and I stayed at Archbishop's House in Cape Town, and felt the sparkle of worship with him in the chapel each morning. We had more time together in Durban. Desmond had invited Derek and me to address the yearly synod of the Church of the Province of Southern Africa there. In our four-part address to the synod, Derek Worlock spoke of the prophetic role of the Church: 'The remarkable feature of the church in South Africa is that its realism is lit by a certain joyful hope. That welcome note in your witness, characterised in a unique way by your Archbishop, must be right and a sign of confident hope for the future.'

At the beginning of the synod, there was a eucharist presided over by Desmond Tutu. He did something that I had seen him do, when he presided at a eucharist at the Lambeth Conference. On both occasions it brought tears to my eyes – again. He included some of the fourteen different languages that the Church of the Province uses in different settings for its worship. My ear is not attuned to African languages, and I could not follow some of the prayers and readings. When we came to the central moment in the communion service – our Lord's words of institution – he used a language I could nearly get hold of. After a moment it dawned on me that he was using Afrikaans, the language of the oppressors. That spoke volumes. He was not saying to them, 'We want to get rid of you!' He was saying 'We want you to be fully part of the Church and the nation with us!'

One day we were taken up from Durban to Pietermaritzburg. This was another moment when we felt fear. A prominent trade union leader had been murdered there that week. The Inkatha movement was strong in Natal and there were many more killings to come – with the suspicion that Government troops and police offered support to Inkatha. Near Pietermaritzburg, we visited the headquarters of Africa Enterprise, an evangelical movement. Michael Cassidy, the founder and leader, was on a mission elsewhere in Africa, but we met members of its staff. Michael Cassidy sought to bring reconciliation by talking to all parties. He believed he could do that more effectively if he did not take sides publicly. He certainly used his opportunities with the powerful to plead for peace and justice. We asked about the missions he ran in South Africa. We were told he would not line himself up with Desmond Tutu, because some of the churches that would support an Africa Enterprise mission would have withdrawn if he did. When we asked in this neutral setting about the conflict with Inkatha, one senior member of staff said he had seen Inkatha fighters emerge from buses and attack houses, and that the police had not interfered. I admired much of the work of Michael Cassidy, but did not feel in my own heart that neutrality was the right position to adopt, confronted with the plain evil of apartheid. I believed that the Christian churches needed to be seen – as Desmond Tutu was with other church leaders – marching in peaceful demonstrations with arms linked against water cannon and police dogs. 'When we stand together', Desmond said, 'we are unstoppable.'

When we arrived home, we asked if the Foreign Secretary, Geoffrey Howe, would welcome our debriefing with him on our days in South Africa. We had been given a briefing at the Foreign Office before going. It was agreed that I should be the one to play back what we had learned about Inkatha. Geoffrey Howe did not seem to welcome what I told him. I believe the Government of Margaret Thatcher bears heavy responsibility for the encouragement they gave to Inkatha, which was always a sectarian movement. They lionised Chief Buthelezi, hoping that they might find in him an alternative leadership to that of the African National Congress (ANC), which they dismissed as 'Communist'.

One British government minister had asked Robert Runcie if he could not persuade Desmond Tutu to 'make it up' with Chief Buthelezi, the leader of Inkatha, as though this was a personality problem. Bishop Michael Nuttall, our host in Durban, told me that Desmond had been going to pay a visit to the Diocese of Natal as archbishop. The archdeacon of the northern part of the diocese received a phone call threatening that Desmond would be killed if he came there. The church briefings we had received before and during our visit warned us that Inkatha was a sinister movement and that we might be used if we went to see Chief Buthelezi. The Roman Catholic Archbishop of Durban, Denis Hurley, for forty years a stalwart opponent of apartheid, showed me a loose-leaf folder containing his correspondence with Buthelezi over years. A pattern was clearly there – that was to be revealed more publicly in later years. He played along with the possibility of meetings that Hurley was suggesting, that would bring groups together for honest discussion. But when it looked as if a real meeting might happen, Buthelezi would insist that it took place in Ulundi, with him in the chair.

Derek Worlock and I were invited to speak to a fringe meeting of the Conservative Party Conference at Blackpool about our visit to South Africa. We learned that Chief Buthelezi had spoken to another fringe meeting earlier that day. As our meeting opened, a group of large young men entered and stood prominently at the back. They distributed leaflets with the heading 'ANC equals IRA'. When we asked for questions, all their hands shot up at once. We made it clear we would answer questions from all parts of the room, not just one. One Conservative MP, Peter Bottomley, was sitting on the floor. He made it clear that some Conservatives looked for justice in South Africa more keenly than supporting trade there. He insisted that we should listen to the main voices speaking for black South Africans.

The most contentious issue at that time was about commercial sanctions. Desmond Tutu showed us advice he was receiving from economists. He believed that it was in the best interests of a peaceful future for South Africa that sanctions should be adopted, even if that meant in the short term suffering for the poor. When pressed to lift my opposition to playing cricket with South Africa, I was ready to do that, if and when black South Africans told me that was their wish. It was the same with the argument about sanctions. There is little doubt that it was the threat of trade boycott that eventually brought the climbdown of the South African Government.

Other faiths

Following the Lambeth Conference of 1988, the Anglican Communion joined with the Pope and other churches in proclaiming a Decade of Evangelism. Some minority faith groups in Britain saw this as a threat. From my first day in Liverpool, there had been a warm welcome from the Jewish community. Invitations to speak came from adult groups and from King David High School. Politeness ruled the day, so that some of the more contentious topics were left on one side. I discussed sensitive inter-faith issues with the headmaster, Philip Skelker. His successor, Clive Lawton, had a sharper edge to him. The first time he came to see me, he had not sat down before he asked, 'Why is the cathedral running a Church Missions to Jews exhibition?' Before he got up to leave, he and I had agreed that we would bring together a Christian–Jewish group who would meet privately on the basis that 'we would not be polite to each other'. I valued that group greatly, understanding how Jewish friends honestly saw issues we discussed – and learning fresh depths within the Old Testament Scriptures. At each meeting one member would introduce a subject. After a year or two, we trusted each other enough to discuss 'the land of Israel'. Eventually the Jewish members were ready for the group to discuss and criticise the policies of the State of Israel, but not until we had listened to what 'the land' meant to them.

We were given a glimpse into the fear that a minority faith community can feel. Clive Lawton showed the group a video, produced by a Jewish body in order to expose what they regarded as aggressive Christian evangelism. This was portrayed as making a deliberate target of Jewish young people at moments when they were most liable to be lonely and vulnerable as new students at university. To my eyes it was slanted, but gave an astringent insight to people like me who had never known what it was to grow up in a minority community. Because of the nature of the video, Clive had shown it separately to Gentile and Jewish sixth formers. The Gentile group was appalled, upset, wondering how their Jewish friends would react: they expected them to be angry. In the event, the reaction of the Jewish group was a surprise to them. The attitude of several was characterised by fear and withdrawal: some said they would not try for a university place after all.

In 1991 – early in the Decade of Evangelism – I said as a bishop that Christians should not 'target' Jews. This was in a paper on 'Evangelism with a good heart' at the two-day ecumenical conference of clergy and ministers in Liverpool. I said:

> I believe that Jesus Christ is in an altogether unique way the Saviour of the world. I believe that His death on the cross made a sacrifice to

atone for our sins, and not for ours only, but for the sins of the whole world. The mystery of that atonement is beyond tidy theories: it is beyond time, effective for the entire human race. This is not to colonise Jewish people by claiming them to be 'latent Christians'. It does allow us to believe that there may be many people – like Abraham – living by faith who belong to other faith communities.

I said that dialogue with people of other faiths had always to be based on a deep respect for the other person's spiritual journey. That meant renouncing manipulation or exploitation of power and influence. Respect for others included being willing to share our own precious beliefs, as well as listening to what was special to them. So, in dialogue we Christians should not be coy about explaining what Christ meant to us. In our group, Clive Lawton once expounded what he understood me to believe about God's grace. I did not need to add a word, because he accurately played back what he had heard me say about my faith in the group.

I came to know Rabbi Jonathan Sacks,[3] when I was chairman of the Central Religious Advisory Committee (CRAC). He asked me if he could discuss the Reith Lectures that he had been invited to deliver on BBC Radio. We spent a morning together. I said that Jewish insights had much to say not only to the Jewish community but to all of us, and I hoped he would share them boldly. The image Rabbi Jonathan used in his Reith Lectures has repeatedly come back to mind. He said we all need to learn two languages: first a public language of common citizenship, and second the language of our own faith community. He called us to bring back into the 'moral ecology' rich biblical themes like covenant and kinship, exodus and liberation, human dignity and responsibility:

> It was a distinctive language. Quite unlike the vocabulary of consumer culture, in which we speak only of rights and entitlements, interests and choices, self-expression and success, it referred to meanings beyond . . . It was a language that linked private faith to public action . . . Faith lives not only in the privacy of soul, but in compassion and justice, the structures of our common life.[4]

Among objectives I had set myself during the two years of the Archbishop's Commission on Urban Priority Areas (ACUPA) had been to see more of the Asian presence in England. The way the visits worked out, I did not make much progress in that direction. So I asked Mano Rumalshah,[5] a member of ACUPA, if he would have me to stay in his parish in Southall for two days and give me some education. My Southall visits included a newly built Sikh temple and meeting young people who were leading an organisation for Asian youth. One evening, Mano and Sheila Rumalshah invited a wide spectrum of religious people in the district to a buffet meal to meet me. As people took their food, Mano asked me to bless the meal and the company. I said, 'We come from different faiths, respecting each other's beliefs. In dialogue I believe each of us should feel free to express our own faith fully. I hope you will understand that as a Christian I shall bless in the name of the Father, the Son and the Holy Spirit.' During the day, I had engaged in a long talk with a young Asian who said that he had no religious faith. At the end of the evening, he came over to me with tears in his eyes and said, 'There was a remarkable unity in the room when you blessed.'

The following day I met with the Southall Christian ministers' fraternal. Some voices were very critical of meeting people of other faiths in dialogue in the way that Mano did. They felt that this betrayed the uniqueness of Christ. I responded that dialogue was an approach St Paul used, and that we trod on holy ground when we listened to other people's journeys of faith. I told them about my blessing the night before and the young man's response. Mano said afterwards, 'If I was not a Christian, socially I would be in the top 10 per cent in Pakistan. Because I am a Christian, I am regarded as being at the bottom of the social pile. Of course I want people to know about Jesus Christ.'

In Liverpool, some members of the comparatively small Muslim community heard about our Christians and Jews group, and asked me if they could join. When I asked the group, members said that this would change its character and would not agree. But it was agreed that some Christians and Jews from the first group should join with Muslims in a second group – made up from the three faiths. Again trust grew gradually until we felt free to speak strongly to each other. My eyes were opened when a Muslim member, who had seemed aggressive in promoting his beliefs, said that he had been criticised severely in the mosque for meeting with us. It made me realise the cost of inter-faith dialogue for someone in his position.

Muslim immigration from the Indian subcontinent has produced the most different community in Britain – with different language, dress, religion, establishing distinct residential zones.[6] It would misunderstand the character of Muslim life to attempt to describe these communities in ethnic or national terms – as 'Pakis', for example – while ignoring religion. That does not assume that all Muslims are devout. For all that, Islam is part of their cultural and ethnic identity. At some moments, Pakistani nationalism has come to the fore; I watched Pakistan win the semi-final of the Cricket World Cup at Old Trafford, and saw the excitement and celebrations on the ground and young men driving through Manchester in high spirits, waving Pakistani flags. At other times the focus has been explicitly on Islam. For example, during the Salman Rushdie affair young people rallied round Islam as a vehicle of ethnic belonging.

The publication of *The Satanic Verses* united the Muslim community in outrage. The Council of Mosques in Bradford, with its large Muslim population, decided to burn a copy of the novel in January 1989. They wrote to the Prime Minister in November, appealing to him to ban the book, as the Indian Government had done. In Liverpool, the leaders of the much smaller Muslim community came and asked me what they should do. I expressed my distaste for films or books that portrayed Jesus in unsavoury ways; but had come to the conclusion that attacking them would only mean that more people saw or read them. That led to my belief that it was better not to give them the publicity that public protest would bring. Some years later, they reminded me of that. They told me they had taken my advice not to make public protests. Now they felt that by allowing blasphemy to go unchallenged they had failed in their devotion. They wanted Christian leaders to take up the question of the law against blasphemy, which in theory protected the Church of England, but made no mention of other faiths. Attempts to use the blasphemy laws had long been ineffective, and achieved nothing in protecting the Church of England. However, I could see how this law seemed to people of other faiths. Increasingly it seemed best to me that the law should be repealed.

The Inner Cities Religious Council (ICRC) was established in 1991, standing for government recognition of different faith communities. Robert Key, a junior minister at the Department of the Environment, wrote to the Archbishop of Canterbury, urging that the Church and the Government should find a better way of working together for the good of local communities. ICRC generally meets three times a year, chaired by a government minister, with participants from the Christian churches, including the black-led churches, Hindu, Jewish, Muslim and Sikh communities.[7] As Chairman of the Board for Social Responsibility (BSR), I agreed that one of our staff, the Revd Chris Beales, should be seconded as the first Secretary of ICRC. The Council organised regional conferences. Their first Liverpool conference made me face my own need for repentance that I had not given attention to the Muslim community. I had told myself that the lack of jobs in Merseyside meant that there was no significant fresh immigration, adding to the small, longstanding, community. That ignored the arrival of refugees, for example, from the civil war in Somalia, joining relatives who had been settled in Liverpool for years. Soon after that, I paid a visit to the mosque, and found a substantial number had come to question me about inter-faith relations and opportunities in the city.

September 11, 2001, produced new fears about terrorism based on extremist religious beliefs, with the attack on the World Trade Center in New York. In Britain, anxiety had already been created by riots in Bradford and Oldham. That led to some attacking the Government's policy of increasing the number of 'faith-based' schools. They feared these would create segregation. But housing, jobs and fear had already created segregation. In some areas there were state schools with 90 per cent Muslim children. That was the reality – together with the fact that Muslim communities had founded their own independent schools.

To say that segregation would be removed by a thoroughgoing secularism would be nonsense. In 2000, the Parekh Report, *The Future of Multi-Ethnic Britain*, said:

> There is a tendency in western democracies to believe that secular society provides the best public space for equality and tolerance . . . but secular society tends to push religion . . . to the margins of public space and into the private sphere. Islamophobia and antisemitism merge with a more widespread rejection of religion which runs through a significant part of 'tolerant' society, including the educated middle class and the progressive media.[8]

The report said that anti-racist organisations frequently appeared to be insensitive to forms of racism that targeted religious identity.

In a House of Lords' debate on education in 2002, I said that tolerance and respect for other faiths grew from confidence and security in one's own identity and faith. Bringing independent Muslim schools into the state system would mean some requirements could be made of them. A 'cluster' of schools sponsored by different faiths and the local authority could be highly creative. Moving out from the secure base of belonging to a school in which their own faith was taught, children could meet 'the others' and work out what tolerance and respect mean. Opening up the possibility of Muslim schools would send a strong message of inclusion to that community. Many of their young people felt disenfranchised and excluded from places of influence and power. Our message to those young people should be, 'We want you as full citizens.'

In Liverpool the leaders of the Muslim community had come to see me, when Liverpool Education Committee went co-educational. They asked for help from our church schools. Resulting from that approach, Archbishop Blanch Girls High School has for some years been glad to include a number of Muslim girls. Another Liverpool school with a most honourable tradition in this way is a Jewish high school – King David School. It has included perhaps 30 or 40 per cent Gentile children – with its particular appeal of specialising in music.

These years have seen immigrant communities at different stages of their developing life. Sometimes there are conflicting voices emerging – for example, 'Leave us alone. Our culture's as good as yours.' But also, 'Give us a share of the common future.' Concern for the common good meant entering into debates on a national stage.

20

Not Just in My Backyard

General Synod

Entering the public arena requires plenty of good briefing and study, and I had stuck my neck out on enough highly contentious matters. It was plainly wise to limit the number of subjects on which to speak in the General Synod. Rowan Williams wrote that modern means of communication result in 'an overload of information that needs a formidable amount of switching off'.[1] One great issue of the 1980s on which I decided to 'switch off' public involvement was that of nuclear disarmament – vital as it was to the future of the world. The Church of England published *The Church and the Bomb*, a report that received widespread attention. I was made the chairman for the televised General Synod debate.

Being made a member of the panel of chairmen amused me, because I had never contemplated raising a point of order, as some 'professional' Synod members loved to do. We drove to London for the first occasion when I was to take the chair. Grace tested me in the car on the Standing Orders that governed our procedures. I got on quite well in the chair during my three years on the panel. In the chair, there was good advice from the Synod's staff. But instinct was sometimes the best guide. The only bad mistake was on a procedural matter. That was when, against my better instinct, I listened to too much of the advice that was whispered in my ear!

I did speak on matters concerning urban mission – like racial justice, poverty, employment and resourcing the Church in UPAs. I found the Synod sympathetic when I spoke about ways of 'getting *Faith in the City* into the bloodstream of the Church', or about ecumenical partnership. When I became Chairman of the Board for Social Responsibility (BSR) there was a wider range of subjects to bring to the Synod and matters to answer at Question Time.

The divisions that ran deepest often did not reflect the old High

Church/Low Church conflicts. They were more likely to be between 'liberal' and 'traditionalist'. In the context of the Synod, those labels did not necessarily coincide with theological convictions. For example, I talked this through with Martin Hunt. He thought of himself as an evangelical and a charismatic. I had seen him vote on a series of issues in what would have been judged a 'liberal' direction. As a vicar in a large outer estate, and then of the industrial town of St Helens, he saw the need for the Church to serve people where they were, in messy, human situations.

The need to 'get *Faith in the City* into the bloodstream of the Church of England' led me to include two visits to theological colleges each year. Naturally, a high proportion of ordinands came from the 'churchgoing belt', which gave them little experience of life in UPAs. I visited most of the colleges. I would try to take them with me into that life, and to think through how we could help people who had grown up there to see that the Christian faith engaged with their lives. One visit each year for twelve years was to St John's College, Nottingham, who made me their president. Grace and I would spend twenty-four hours staying in the college. That was enriching for us. It gave time to meet staff and discuss in small groups, including an evening with couples, who were glad to think through questions with both of us about the realities of vicarage life and the public/private tensions clergy homes meet.

House of Lords

Another significant platform on which different voices can debate the common good is the House of Lords. In my maiden speech in 1981, I expressed the hope of seeing that any church presence that the nation wanted to see in Parliament would be an ecumenical one, with representatives from the other churches. Twenty years on, the shape of a reformed second chamber has still to be settled, but I hope that an ecumenical and also an inter-faith presence may be part of it.

I spoke repeatedly in the House about the effect of mass unemployment that Merseyside knew. I could contribute to the debates what I had seen and heard. Sometimes this was dismissed as 'politically slanted'. I could not avoid that. In my opinion, what looked like a slant to some in Westminster looked straight down the middle to us in Liverpool. Looking through my House of Lords speeches, I find a spread of subjects: housing; second-chance learning; cuts in public services; the coal industry; local government; nationality; immigration and asylum; football spectators; legal services; charities law; criminal justice; secure training centres; Northern Ireland; the youth service; Sunday trading; broadcasting.

I took a substantial part in debates on the last two subjects. Sunday trading brought together all the Christian churches in an effective campaign to 'Keep Sunday Special'. This was not defending strict Sabbatarian positions: it sought some sensible compromise. Mrs Thatcher's Government had brought in a bill for complete deregulation. Voices from all sides in the House of Lords spoke strongly against this. Though the Government had a huge majority, it was defeated in the House of Commons in 1986 by a cross-party vote. This made me ask whether such Christian solidarity might not win some other battles, if only we would stand together. On Sunday trading, Tesco announced in 1991 that they were going to break the law. The Government brought back a further bill. As chairman then of the BSR, I met representatives of the big stores. They spoke of a more streamlined, more modern structure to our week, rid of the clutter of regulations. They asked why there should be any interference with the freedom and the convenience of the consumer.

In the House of Lords, I said that freedom for the more powerful often removed freedoms from those in weaker bargaining positions. That included shop workers and many others who were left behind in the scramble for a streamlined world of convenience. The Shopping Hours Reform Council leaders had told me that they expected large supermarkets mostly to be in out-of-town centres. That was convenient if you had a car: many assumed that everyone in Britain now had access to a car. But the 1991 census figures for Merseyside showed a very different picture. There were wards in Liverpool where 80 per cent did not have a car. In Urban Priority Areas, and perhaps even more in rural communities, elderly people, sick people and those on the lowest incomes needed good corner shops. Those who voted for this proposal, sponsored by the big battalions, were very likely voting for further loss of such shops.

I said that the bill was of great significance to the churches. I quoted Derek Worlock's strong attack on the further secularisation of Sunday this bill would cause. I acknowledged that Christians did not have the right to lay down the law to all people about Sunday observance. However, we had the same right – no more, but no less – as other citizens to argue for what we conceived to be for the health of the whole. Communities, as well as individuals, needed a rhythm of work and rest. This creeping secularisation had its effect on the spiritual life of so many. We in the churches were often told that we had grave responsibility for strengthening moral values. Our belief was that beneath moral values, spiritual roots needed cherishing. The task of the churches would be made more difficult, if there was a further shift in the pattern of Sundays.

I had one of those moments when the apt retort came to mind just too late. Geoffrey Howe, who had been at Trinity Hall at the same time as I, had become Lord Howe of Aberavon. He said in the debate that he would keep Sunday special, but he did not need a law to compel him. That begged the question how another generation was expected to learn what he had been taught in Sunday school. The moment passed. I could have asked: 'Before the noble Lord sits down, would he tell your Lordships' House first how he himself learnt to keep Sunday special, and secondly how he hopes his grandchildren will learn to keep Sunday special?'

Just before the Broadcasting Bill came to the House of Lords, there was a telephone call from Jane Reed, who had been my editor when I wrote a column for *Woman's Own*. I had not heard from her for years. She told me she now worked for *News International*. They wondered whether I would welcome receiving a dish for Sky television, in order to watch the England cricket tour about to begin in the West Indies. For a split second I was tempted. Then I said, 'Jane, you probably don't know' (though I was sure that someone at *News International* knew) 'that I chair the Central Religious Advisory Council (CRAC) and I am expecting to be the main spokesperson for the faiths in the House of Lords' debates on the Broadcasting Bill. I think it would be rather important not to have received any present from Sky.' In the debates, promoters of Sky television argued for complete deregulation.

I became involved in some sharp exchanges in the Broadcasting Bill debates. The bill was part of Mrs Thatcher's determination to deregulate commercial life. Broadcasting was said to be hedged about with too many regulators. In 1989 I had been made Chairman of CRAC – an incongruous title if ever there was one. We were the successors to Lord Reith's 'Sunday Committee', the first advisory committee the BBC set up. Now we advised the Independent Television Commission (ITC) as well as the BBC. CRAC included representatives of the Jewish, Muslim and Hindu faiths, as well as from all the mainline churches. We challenged the proponents of the bill, when they argued that more channels and less regulation would increase quality. More channels seemed to us likely to lead to an increase in 'candyfloss' entertainment, in order to hold on to viewing audiences. When David Mellor was made the minister in charge of the bill, I went to see him. He showed patience, humour and readiness to listen to those who brought criticisms to the 'total deregulation' that some believed the Prime Minister had promised. In his hands the bill was modified considerably. (Since retirement, Grace and I try never to miss David Mellor's Sunday programme on Classic FM.)

CRAC's guidelines on religious broadcasting were that it should reflect the worship, thought and action of the principal religious traditions represented in Britain – not only Christian. In addition, it should engage with beliefs, ideas, issues and experiences in the contemporary world.

291

Some evangelical Christians, eager to gain freedom to own their own stations, in addition to the cable stations already allowed, had briefed a group of peers. They claimed that the full-blooded expression of the Gospel did not receive a fair share of religious broadcasting time.

In my speech at the second reading of the bill, I finished by saying something as a Christian to Christians:

> Much of the debate has centred round the question of broad-casting or narrow-casting. It will be possible for those who own their own cable stations to use their religious networks to encourage their friends to watch their channel. That is fine, but I should be sorry if a significant part of the Christian body turned away as a regular practice from mainline channels which are part of the united life of our nation. That would follow the philosophy that sees the Church as a fortress of light, calling individuals to separate themselves from the darkness of the world around. In contrast, I believe that the Incarnation, by which I believe God in the person of Jesus Christ entered into the thick of life, calls us in the direction of broad-casting, not narrow-casting.

In the House of Lords attacks were repeatedly made on Ernie Rea, Head of Religious Broadcasting at the BBC, and Rachel Viney, Religious Adviser to the ITC. They could not reply. I worked closely with both and saw the integrity, faith and skill they brought to maintaining quality religious broadcasting. These attacks made me indignant. I was well enough briefed to interrupt and challenge the allegations, each time they were made. I said that religious broadcasting was not perfect, but promoted an honest and sensitive attempt to share the faith on a broad platform. Staff told me that the BBC *Everyman* series had an audience of 3.5 million, and that this figure was higher than that for all the 'televangelists' in the United States put together.

Ernie Rea continued the battle within the BBC to maintain schedules. The competition for audiences and advertising revenue in the peak period between 6.30 p.m. and 10.30 p.m. has meant an ever-fiercer ratings war. ITV companies will only schedule 'programmes providing diversity' in that peak period, if they can claim to recruit a mass audience. The emphasis that wins arguments has often been on what *young* people want. That ignores the growing population of elderly people who cannot get out. A significant proportion of them would welcome diversity in programmes. However, it is a false assumption that only elderly church-goers switch on. Every survey showed that there were varying audiences, including many who did not go to church. To my regret, the erosion of religious programmes on television has continued.

Keeping staff for a religious department has also been a rearguard action. CRAC protested when the BBC announced that the Religious Department was to move out of London to Manchester. This chairman could not find it in his heart to fight too hard to argue against that move. Quality really can be produced in the North of England! The protest was that religious broadcasting was being marginalised. The reply claimed that other major departments were being moved to the regions, so that the BBC became a truly national corporation, not all centralised in the capital.

The rearguard action has been a struggle. In 2001, Ernie Rea resigned. The appointment now was to be that of a Head of Ethics and Religious Broadcasting. At first, we heard that no appointment was made, because only a small field applied. One reason why some did not apply was that the head of the relevant BBC department had said she wanted a non-believer to hold that appointment. That ignored the long and honourable record that I was defending in the House of Lords, of tolerance and determination to give space to all the main religious traditions and moral debate of human issues. The new appointment was of an agnostic, Alan Bookbinder, skilled as a producer and fair-minded. But it seemed difficult for someone who did not have a lively faith to discern the most appropriate voices in 'the principle religious traditions' – and the moments when what we had called 'a religious interpretation or dimension of life' could be shown.

Local radio has continued to play a significant part. The economic slump at the end of the 1980s brought swingeing cuts in commercial radio stations. That underlined the importance of the role of the BBC in maintaining its local radio network. The rearguard actions have been worth it. On sound radio in particular, there remains a remarkable volume of religious broadcasting, reflecting the worship, thought and action of the principle religious traditions represented in Britain.

The Board for Social Responsibility

Becoming Chairman of the BSR in 1991 meant learning to engage with a broad sweep of issues. Grappling with the Board's agenda proved stretching intellectually. It certainly helped keep me fresh during my last years as a working bishop. My colleagues in the diocese were marvellously supportive, and encouraged me to take this on. I had to introduce the BSR staff to a feature of my life that the colleagues in Liverpool already knew – that I needed a siesta to survive long working days! For these Church House days, I asked if there could be a room with two chairs for a siesta. That went for Synod days too, when it was easy to drift off during long afternoons in the overheated debating chamber. 'The BSR corridor' housed six executive staff with back-up secretaries. Each of them had a brief that made our level of staffing seem tiny. In 2001, further financial pressures brought a cut in that over-stretched staff. That meant that the Board had to make the decision to leave some important issues untouched.

I was eager that we should work in partnership with other churches wherever possible. The truth was that they often looked to us to take the lead in sustaining this mission to the nation. Modest as it was, ours was the largest church staff for social responsibility. Examples of joint work included our challenge to the introduction of the National Lottery. A Methodist staff member provided the engine room for that, but I became fully involved in public debate and in leading a delegation to the government minister. When the Board produced papers about human genetics, we looked to one of the committees within the BSR, the Science, Medicine and Technology Committee, chaired by a distinguished scientist, Professor John Polkinghorne.[2] They worked in partnership with the Church of Scotland Society, Religion and Technology Project. From the chair of Board meetings, I would press the three Board members whose expertise was in this field to argue out these complex issues of medical ethics. That needed to be in language that enabled the rest of us to understand ethical issues that were at stake. As chairman of the Board, I was asked to lead ecumenical delegations on three occasions to three different Home Secretaries about the treatment of asylum seekers. In concerns about overseas aid, we worked closely with Christian Aid. There was close partnership with the staff of the Roman Catholic Bishops' Conference for work on euthanasia.

Other major issues we engaged with included a challenge to Nestlé whose marketing methods were alleged to discourage mothers from breastfeeding; speaking to Lord Mackay, the Lord Chancellor, and his department, and supporting his proposals for divorce law reform; a submission to Lord Nolan on standards in public life; arms control; the use of force in Bosnia; drug abuse (though a gap in our staff meant we had to postpone work we wanted to do); the use of Church Commissioners' investments; legal aid; the family.

Something to Celebrate

The most controversial piece of work during my years in the chair was produced by a working party appointed by the BSR to examine the state of family life in Britain. Among its terms of reference were these questions: What is happening to families at the present time? What are the implications of current changes in family life for public policy and the Church?' Any Church body tackling the subject of family life with realism in the 1990s was bound to be divided. The majority of members of the working party, whatever their differences, wanted to start with the world as it was. Others wanted to start with God's word about marriage, and proclaim that to the world. After the working party had started its task, the General Synod asked it to include the question of cohabitation. There had been a debate in which members, like Bishop Gavin Reid, had spoken movingly of accepting members of their own family cohabiting following honest thought about it. The working party laid emphasis on 'the quality of the relationship, not its category'. On two occasions members of the working party met with the full Board. In these meetings, robust criticisms of some early drafts were offered.

The working party published its report, *Something to Celebrate*,[3] in 1995. They had received 3,000 written responses from Church groups and members to a questionnaire. This had asked about hopes and fears for families, and about how the church helps or hinders families through its practice and teaching. As in the wider Church, there were divided views in the working party and the cracks showed. They worked through much pain before the report was produced. The press made a meal of one sentence: 'The first step the Church should take is to abandon the phrase "living in sin".'[4] The background to this was the working party's reflection on a story they had been told about a couple bringing their baby for baptism; the vicar had said, 'Go away. You're living in sin.' The report commented that it might be better to invite people into a conversation, during which 'the better way' could be credibly presented. In introducing the report to the General Synod, I defended the belief that it was possible to hold a balance. Such a balance stood for our firm belief that marriage was God's best way and at the same time respected those who in conscience had decided against marriage for the moment. That was quite different from encouraging casual relationships. Accepting responsible people who cohabited included arguing with them that there was a more excellent way. I said, 'I hope we shall not back away from being the kind of church that risks debating issues in public which affect all people, believers or not. There is a price to be paid for freedom of thought and speech, a price worth paying.'

I was conscious of being the spokesperson who collected the plaudits – and the brickbats – but the quality of the BSR's work depended first and foremost on the skill and commitment of the staff. When I retired from the chair, I wrote to David Skidmore, the Board Secretary:

> I was determined to write to you on the first day of the rest of my life! These five years have been a very significant period in my own pilgrimage. I owe more than I can put into words to you for your support at so many and varied times. We've been through some fire together. I realise that has meant some personal bruising for you. Your

solidarity with your team on the corridor has been very important for them: sometimes their detailed and professional work goes with little recognition. You've insisted that we have to work within the world as it is and with the Church as it is. That takes a lot of discipline not just to free-wheel with great ideas. I guess it means that rewards we know about are long-term and subtle rather than dramatic and immediate. But they count for more than we can know in Kingdom of God reckonings.

I meant every word.

Something to Celebrate brought to the surface deep currents that had been swirling around for years. They have continued to produce fierce divisions, as the debates in Parliament over the proposed repeal of Section 28 (forbidding local authorities to 'promote homosexual behaviour') showed in 2000. Many Christians want to see the Church proclaim absolute standards. It is instructive to compare the way we approach the question of war with the approach to questions about sexual morality. In the case of war, absolute standards are expressed by pacifists, while many Christians, including me, argue that, in facing evil in the real world, a just war offers the lesser of evils at times – lesser than allowing tyrants to overrun the weak. There seems a certain inconsistency when those same people will not allow that there are questions of sexual morality when the lesser of evils becomes the best course of action.

When Pope John Paul II issued his encyclical letter *Veritatis Splendor* I was encouraged to make a statement as Chairman of the BSR: even though the search for moral absolutes was understandable, it was by no means an easy matter to establish the existence of such absolutes. The realities to which the eternal values of the Gospel must relate were constantly changing. Whether in the field of industry and economy, or medical ethics and technology, or the morality of war, Christians had to address questions which simply did not exist in a previous age. In the statement, I said:

> How then can we know 'the mind of Christ'? I believe that God's revelation of His purposes is a continuing process in which our understanding grows. Our view of authority is therefore one that encourages vigorous debate – and its consequences. It permits Christians to live together even though they reach, in good conscience, different conclusions. Perhaps we place greater emphasis on freedom of debate, rigorously tested by Scripture, Tradition and Reason, out of which firm convictions become received.

The debate about homosexual relationships has tested all the churches to the limit. In 1991, the Church of England's House of Bishops published a report, *Issues in Human Sexuality*.[5] This spoke about acceptance in a congregation of those who with conviction in their own conscience cohabited, or had 'homophile' relationships. *Issues* made a distinction for those who held public office, such as ordained men and women:

> In our considered judgement the clergy cannot claim the liberty to enter into sexually active homophile relationships. Because of the distinctive nature of their calling, status and consecration, to allow such a claim on their part would be seen as placing that way of life in all respects on a par with heterosexual marriage as a reflection of God's purposes in creation. The Church cannot accept such a parity and remain faithful to the insight which God has given it through Scripture, tradition and reasoned reflection on experience.

I had tried, without too much success, to encourage parishes to debate this report. There was reluctance on most sides. Christians were still embarrassed to speak openly about cohabiting, and especially about homosexual relationships. In 1992, my Methodist colleague John Newton was made the chairman of a working party that presented a report to the Methodist Conference[6] on sexual relationships. He and I debated the subject over a period of years, together with Canon John Elford, the Anglican Pro-Rector of Liverpool Hope College. John Elford felt that Christians within the gay and lesbian community might have seen *Issues in Human Sexuality* as reaching out to them with a readiness to listen to their understanding in an honest debate. He said it was not reasonable to expect that we were about to set aside the Church's position inside one generation.

The three of us invited a number of gay and lesbian people to meet privately with us. In one meeting, a lesbian, employed by the church in a lay ministry, reminded us that male homosexual relationships had been criminal in the eyes of the law until less than forty years previously. It would not have been possible for a male couple to go public about their relationship before then. So there was no tradition of faithful and public relationships for them to look to. That conversation made me realise how large a leap it was to expect of homosexual partners that a lifelong partnership was the ideal – and possible.

There were Christian voices within the gay movement that did not shrink from emphasising the quality of relationships, and the calling to responsible partnership. Douglas Rhymes had been one of the first in the field with his book *No New Morality*. In 1992, in his autobiography, when nearly eighty years old, he wrote that the so-called 'gay' world was often no more understanding and compassionate than the 'straight' world. Douglas Rhymes said, 'It is strangely ironic that society, Church and the gay world itself are all obsessed with the purely physical: what is done in bed becomes far more important in terms of approval or disapproval, than creative, human relationship.'[7]

Homosexuality was another of the subjects that I had made a decision not to debate publicly. In 1977 as a guest of Paul Moore, the Bishop of New York, I spent a week visiting courageous inner-city projects. In each of them Paul was spoken of as their champion – in a way that I hoped our clergy and people in UPAs might think of me. The following weeks at Louisville for the Partners in Mission Consultation with the Episcopal Church made me grasp that in that context his name stood for a different cause. Church politics buzzed with the claim that he had ordained a practising lesbian. I reflected on the way Paul's name was regarded. Rightly or wrongly, I feared my influence might be lost in fighting some tough battles in the field of urban mission if I became involved in another controversy, about which Christians became so heated.

The Wood–Sheppard Principles

One subject that remained near the top of my priorities was that of employment. Statistics kept showing that black and Asian people were less likely to find jobs – or promotion. In 1993, the Race Equality in Employment Project (REEP)[8] asked Wilfred Wood and me to give our names to ten principles for equal opportunities to put to employers. These 'Wood–Sheppard Principles' were based on the Macbride Principles for fair employment in Northern Ireland.

In following up the launch of the Principles, I was among several bishops and church leaders around the country who invited employers to meetings that considered how to put equal opportunities into effect. The most powerful advocacy came from examples of good practice that employers themselves were able to explain. In Liverpool, Littlewoods had consistently tried to keep opportunities open to black people. John Moores told me about his approach in that company. An equal opportunities policy, he said, 'has to be pushed from the top. If you leave it alone, it dies. It's about getting women and black people to the top.'

REEP continues to use the Wood–Sheppard Principles. It offers an accreditation process of monitoring, spread over eighteen months. That asks for twenty-five days' executive time. Small firms that cannot finance this may ask for a 'health check' that requires two days' executive time. The Revd Mark Nicholson is its present director, working as a member of the South London Industrial Mission (SLIM). He is also Minister of the Emmanuel Inspirational Church of God in Croydon. Customs and Excise, who had used the Principles to good effect, seconded a member of staff, David Clarke, to work for REEP.

'Unemployment and the Future of Work'

The ecumenical networks made possible a major enquiry into the great questions surrounding employment. As Chairman of the BSR, I raised the idea at our yearly meeting with opposite numbers from all the member churches of the Council of Churches for Britain and Ireland (CCBI). The Public Affairs Secretary of CCBI, the Revd Ermal Kirby, agreed to convene a 'shadow' sponsoring body of officers and represent-atives from the different churches. He invited me to chair this informal body. We were a group of individuals at that point. We had to win the support of the Boards or committees we served – like the BSR. Its Industrial and Economic Affairs Committee resolved that this subject should be their main interest for the coming years. They agreed that Ruth Badger, the staff person who served their work, should be seconded to enable the enquiry to come into being. Derek Worlock was nominated to represent the Roman Catholic Church (replaced when he became too ill by Bishop John Jukes). Another key player among the churches was the Church of Scotland. The Revd Andrew McLellan was the Secretary of the Church and Nation Committee.[9] He insisted that 'unemployment' should appear in any title for the enquiry. One afternoon, after we had worked hard for several meetings, he needed to leave early to catch a train. As he reached the door, I asked him, 'What do you think we should do?' Andrew turned, 'Go for it!' he said.

The official Church Representatives Meeting of the CCBI now appointed an 'arm's length' body, drawing its membership from the different churches. It invited me to chair this sponsoring body, with oversight of the enquiry. That would mean raising the money, agreeing terms of reference, appointing the working party and staying in touch with their work. Andrew Britton, our first choice as executive secretary, took early retirement from the National Institute of Economic and Social Research, and offered to work full time for an honorarium. He would give us three years, setting up a two-year enquiry and staying for a follow-up period. Andrew, a Reader in the Diocese of Southwark, brought his Christian faith to work in harmony with his skills as a distinguished economist. Sir Geoffrey Holland, formerly Permanent Secretary in succession at the Departments of Employment and Education, agreed to chair the working party. The authority the two of them brought undoubtedly meant that the report would be respected as a serious contribution to economic policy.

It was a huge blow for me, half way through the enquiry, when Geoffrey rang me up to tell me that, being now Vice-Chancellor of Exeter University, he had been pressed to serve on the Dearing enquiry into higher education. He felt he had to accept, and reluctantly felt he must resign from the churches' enquiry. I dropped everything else to consult with members of the sponsoring body and other allies. My anger at feeling let down produced new energy to search for a new chairman. We struck gold! Patrick Coldstream had just retired from his post as Director of the Council for Industry and Higher Education when I rang him. He agreed to take it on. Geoffrey Holland told him that he gave him a fifty-fifty chance of winning agreement for a report. Some members – who might be described as being at the more 'grass-roots end' of the working party – had feared that the eminence and knowledge of Geoffrey Holland and Andrew Britton meant that they had 'top-down' conclusions sown up already. Patrick Coldstream made a point of listening to all sides of this exceptionally diverse body. The tensions between 'grass-roots' and 'top-down' were largely resolved. Some differences remained in theological approach – never between denominational loyalties – but unanimous agreement was obtained for the report. Patrick told me that earnest prayer before and after business meetings 'really mattered, powerfully reinforcing the sense of common purpose'.

When Andrew Britton started off on the enquiry, I said to him, 'If we come back to Merseyside, and say that we are going to bring back full employment, we shall be greeted with a hollow laugh.' But the working party persuaded me that it was possible – if we had the will – to see that there was enough good work for all who wanted it. One of the important emphases in the report's slogan, 'enough good work for all who want it' was the word 'good' – good work – not 'Any old dead-end job will do'. There were specific suggestions of how more jobs could develop in the market. If some further creation of jobs in the public sector was needed, then we supported the increased tax such job creation in the public sector might require.

The report said that members had been 'shocked and saddened' by what they saw as they travelled round Britain and Ireland. In Merseyside the working party was told of 12-year-olds saying there was no point in working, because you couldn't expect to find a job. Elsewhere black youngsters said they saw no point in working at school; their elders had achieved good qualifications and had still found no decent jobs. The report had much to say about education and its importance. But it feared that this area of policy was being made to carry a frighteningly large weight of public aspiration and expectation. No improvement would make any sense, unless there were in fact jobs to be had, when the pupils left school: 'Better schooling is often prescribed as the potential cure for unemployment. In fact the converse may be nearer the truth. In areas of high unemployment there needs to be some provision of employment opportunities before we can expect any marked improvement in the achievements of school leavers.'[10]

The report provided a demonstration of what a debate such as this looks like when conducted by an explicitly Christian group. It based its position on a firmly Christian view of work. God has given all of us gifts. They are to be used, not wasted. All people are called to make their particular contribution to the life of the whole community. The working party drew on the teaching of Jesus on the kingdom of God, with its shared care and concern for all. They knew they had to move beyond the idealised call for justice and the Christian promise of future deliverance, into grappling alongside others with the detail of how justice was to be made a practical reality. They set their face against a division in society, by which one part did all the giving and the other part were only to receive.

There was potential for a damaging clash between the view of working party 'grass roots' and Church 'top brass' about the timing of publication. Our timetable had been to publish early in April 1997 after the two-year enquiry. At the beginning of the year every commentator was forecasting that the general election would take place at the beginning of May. What were we to do? The Archbishops of Canterbury and Westminster and the Free Church Moderator – John Newton – had encouraged us to launch the enquiry. We tried to keep them in step with us, hoping indeed that they might be willing to appear at the launch of the report. Dr Kathleen Richardson, who had taken John Newton's place as Free Church Moderator, was happy for us to go ahead. But, when we went to see them, both George Carey and Basil Hume felt this could be seen as the Church playing politics in the middle of an election campaign, and advised us to delay. They made it clear they accepted that it was for the sponsoring body to decide, but made the case for delaying our launch.

When we reported back, some members of the working party expressed anger. They had met with unemployed people and others very close to them during their visits around Britain and Ireland. They knew that some were excited at the thought of the churches' enquiry saying something bold in the spring. I called a meeting of the whole enquiry – sponsoring body and working party together. Careful discussion – and strong feelings – concluded with the sponsoring body voting in the presence of the working party. The vote was firmly to go ahead with publication in April. I wrote to Archbishop, Cardinal and Moderator:

There was a strong sense of there being a *kairos* [meaning a moment of opportunity] for our nation and for the Church. Members of the Working Party were aware of areas ravaged by unemployment, and unemployed people sometimes feeling that the Church is detached from their struggles. There was a strong sense that 'grass roots' people might feel deeply hurt if we were known to have postponed the Report from a time when the nation is voting about its priorities.

Each of them replied, with a warm understanding of our reasons, and their support for the enquiry.

There was keen interest in the press. Some tried to rubbish the report. The *Daily Mail*'s commentator, William Oddie, said that the bishop – that was me – was 'very ignorant of realistic economics'. In fact I did not serve on the working party that produced the report. Twelve out of sixteen of its members were lay people, with a wide range of experience. Andrew Britton in particular was a distinguished economist. *The Times* printed a major article on its leader page, saying that 'the Anglicans' had got the economics all wrong. The enquiry was in fact fully and transparently ecumenical, not Anglican, and most commentators gave full credit to that. The same day on its business page, *The Times* printed a piece from their business correspondent. In contrast to the piece on the leader page, he said, 'Most independent economic commentators are likely to find that the Churches' study is on a sound economic basis; that it has done its numbers and its work properly.'

Political leaders took the challenge of the report seriously. Gordon Brown said he would like to meet us, if Labour won the election. When he had become Chancellor of the Exchequer, he met privately with a small group of us. Both on that occasion and when we went back a year later – and in the public launch of the report in London – he made it clear that he felt as keenly about unemployment as we did. At the same time, he was defensive about our readiness to increase income tax in order to enlarge opportunities of jobs in the public sector. In the autumn, public meetings were held in the English regions, in Scotland, Wales and in the Republic of Ireland. Following on from them, a network, supported by industrial mission, was established to keep the debate alive.

Thankfully, the 1997 Labour Government restored the ideal of full employment to its objectives – abandoned as unachievable twenty years before. The New Deal became a major plank of government policy in working towards this. In 2001, I was asked by Church Action on Poverty to chair a day conference to review the churches' report on unemployment and the future of work, four years on from its publication. I asked for briefing from allies in Liverpool close to the New Deal. In Liverpool, the number of young people out of work for more than six months dropped by 68 per cent between April 1998 and October 2000. Political critics of the government programme said that those it helped to find work would have obtained jobs anyway, and that it was too expensive. But such a moment was precisely the time when it is crucial to persevere – when those furthest from the labour market had been identified.

Programmes tailored to their needs would indeed be likely to be more expensive but would be a long-term investment that would stand the nation in good stead.

Steve Little came to tell me how it was working out. Steve is a non-stipendiary minister from an inner-city parish, involved day in, day out in the voluntary sector option of the New Deal. He hoped some more flexibility could be injected; it would be possible to measure the distance some trainees had travelled in the twenty-six weeks of the programme, but still know they were not ready for employment. I asked him about the sensitive question of 'help and hassle', needed to break the 'no-job culture'. He said that most of those he knew said they were glad they were 'coerced'. One, who had completed a very successful course, told him that, if they hadn't told her she *had* to take part, she would never have done it. At that 2001 Church Action on Poverty conference, the majority of those who were providing training projects took the view that some coercion was inevitable, if the cycle was to be broken.

That same year, I risked upsetting some of my friends and allies in a debate in the House of Lords. The Government proposed to cut part of someone's benefit, if she or he failed to turn up more than once, having been sentenced to Community Service. They were right that there needed to be a stick as well as a carrot. The prize of getting people into a real job was a great one. Perhaps some of those I admired most, in their close involvement with those on benefits, might themselves have become locked into the no-work culture. Relying on benefits then seemed the only way. I would still want to argue that income support should be increased to catch up with European Union standards of benefit. But shifting the philosophy from taking benefits as a right to acknowledging that there is a citizen's contract with the State was to treat people as responsible adults.

Ed Murphy, Chief Executive of Liverpool Council for Voluntary Service, who had let me have shrewd and honest briefings in the past, wrote a letter to Steve Little, for me to see. Ed wrote that the New Deal was one of the most successful government programmes he had engaged in. In particular the voluntary sector option was now able to pay proper wages. This had transformed the way both participants and employment service staff saw the voluntary sector. 'The revival of the notion that public service is about helping people, rather than policing the benefits system, has been one of the most remarkable features of New Deal in Liverpool.' All was not sweetness and light, though. Having felt encouraged that the Diocese of Liverpool had launched its own New Deal programme, I was saddened to learn that they had pulled out of it. The reason, they said, was that over-much bureaucracy made medium-sized projects unworkable.

Another issue needed to be tackled in Whitehall. A senior civil servant who had played a leading role in the government office in Merseyside, Eric Sorensen, had now moved back to Whitehall. He told a friend that he had forgotten how deep the trenches were between government departments. When the Labour Party was still in opposition, the Urban Bishops' Panel encouraged me to ask George Carey if he would approach Tony Blair and ask if a church group might meet with shadow ministers concerned with urban policies. That led to my leading an ecumenical group of eight church leaders, who had a series of meetings with shadow ministers, led by Chris Smith. When the church group discussed our impressions of these meetings, we felt the strength of departmentalism was already having its effect. In the December before the general election, I wrote to Chris Smith, asking him if he would show the letter to Tony Blair, about the need for co-ordination of policies to meet the interlocking problems of urban deprivation. I quoted the comment Sir Stanley Holmes made to me about the Inner Areas Study when I came to Liverpool in 1975. Stanley said he had always believed the only person who could have chaired that study effectively was the Prime Minister.

Tony Blair's reply encouraged me to write again in September, following Labour coming to power. I praised the establishment of the Social Exclusion Unit, and that he, as Prime Minister, was taking hands-on interest in its work. This would make sure that government departments co-operated with the Unit. Tony Blair had sent me a copy of his speech about inner cities in June 1997 that he made at the Aylesbury Estate, now regarded as a disaster area. I wrote:

> You mention the fatalism which many people have felt about poverty and unemployment ... It matters urgently that the Welfare to Work programme delivers successfully; and what you describe in the Aylesbury Estate speech, 'Today the greatest challenge for any democratic government is to bring this new work-less class back into society and into useful work', calls for persistent policies over ten years.

Of course, it is one thing for the Government to share our passion that members of that 'work-less class' should be enabled to find themselves included and make their contribution to society – and another to deliver success.

The churches' report *Unemployment and the Future of Work* captured the moment. Many people were ready to hear an articulately presented message like this. I believe it helped the new Government to place – and keep – the Welfare to Work programme among its firm priorities. We church leaders had also pressed the crucial importance of co-ordinating policies between departments. Deep-seated social problems were never the result of one single deprivation – the jobs, the schools, the housing, the health and the transport. They result from an often confusing interlocking of all these. Achieving what was now called 'joined-up government' was a necessary base to mounting policies that would be effective in tackling urban deprivation. They are certainly needed in Liverpool.

21

Liverpool Hope

The best sabbatical

There was an obvious need to stay fresh, if I was going to stay a long time in Liverpool. Sabbaticals plainly refreshed clergy, and I knew the value for myself of the change previous sabbaticals had brought me. What were we to do this time? Perhaps we should go to India – or to an American University for a study course. Grace's spiritual director, Richard Buck, who knew us both in depth, said, 'You don't need more experiences. You've had plenty. What you need to do is to stop and think about them.' We saw, too, the value of spending time together now. We had fought to keep private space in the middle of a public life. But retirement would be very different. How would we cope with all those days together? Would we 'get under one another's feet'? Part of the value of this last sabbatical could be to prepare for living close to each other in a more confined space.

Friends lent us a cottage in the Western Highlands of Scotland. My diary dates meant that we were limited to starting on 1 February 1988. We drove up to Loch Fyne, not knowing whether the car would be able to climb through the snow to the cottage, which was the most remote in the village. We fell in love with the warm, honey-coloured hills of the Highlands' winter, almost resenting it when they turned green. Starting in February meant that we saw the whole of spring come in. After the three months of sabbatical, we had intended to make for the sun for a holiday in the last month. But how could we possibly miss seeing Argyll in May?

We spent the mornings separately in the two small ground-floor rooms. The afternoons were for exercise, walking by the loch, where we began to recognise the diving ducks and other sea birds. We met up with neighbours in the village. They gave us a warm welcome, accepting our intention to lie low while we were there. The evenings were for 'culture' – listening to music, reading poetry and plays, and listening to selected radio programmes. For several weekends we invited friends and family to come and stay.

There was time to paint. As a small boy I had concluded, without any question, that I was incapable of drawing or painting at all. Although my maternal grandfather, J. A. Shepherd, had been a distinguished artist, whose work still appeared then in *Punch* magazine, it never occurred to me that I might have inherited some skill from him. However, when Jenny was a little girl, I started to draw teddy bears for her. Grace, like the good nursery school teacher she was, spotted some possible talent, and encouraged me to attempt more. After that, each holiday would include my attempting at least one oil painting. I would be totally absorbed for three days. My style was crude, but a sense of colour started to grow.

In 1980, both city and diocese celebrated a centenary. It was agreed that, in an exchange of gifts, a painting of the completed cathedral would be acceptable to the city. The city meanwhile presented the diocese with the preliminary sketch of a painting of the Queen that hung in the Town Hall. I said to Michael Henshall, 'We shall have to find £2,000 to commission a painting.' He said, 'You can paint a bit. You should do it.' Flattered and taken aback, I saw nevertheless that there would be an advantage in a personal touch, provided the painting proved to be adequate. I agreed to make the attempt, on the understanding that Michael himself, Edward Patey, the dean, and Clifford Price, Chairman of the Diocesan Board of Finance – three people who knew their own minds – accepted the picture. It took me a week, camped out each day for our post-Easter holiday in an empty office block in Leece Street. This had once been the office of the Manpower Services Commission, from which I had seen the scaffolding taken down to reveal the newly completed west front of the cathedral. When it was ready for inspection, the three judges arrived at Bishop's Lodge, looking nervous, to view the painting. Having been left on their own, they emerged, smiling broadly, and agreed to accept my effort. Later it was an exciting moment when the Lord Mayor received it in the Town Hall.

Our Argyll sabbatical was in a painter's cottage, and the hills and water of Loch Fyne cried out for painting. Grace always had more painting skills than I, but had held back for when she had more time – and was not in competition. She now started to produce tiny but evocative watercolours. In retirement, she has joined a regular watercolour class, and, with encouragement, has expanded her paintings – and begun to sell them!

During these months, she discovered the joy of writing. Darton, Longman and Todd (DLT) had approached her to write a book. By then, she had written a diary regularly for four years, but never for publication.

She used our time in Argyll to explore this new field. During those months, I read and commented on two drafts of the first six chapters of *An Aspect of Fear*. I admired the courage and openness that made her ready to share what had often been painful experiences. She had a story to tell that has touched many readers from all sorts of backgrounds. It became a book that circulated on grapevines, as readers passed it on to family and friends. As well as those men who told her, 'I've given your book to my wife!' – men were among the many who wrote to tell her that they had recognised some of their own vulnerability in Grace's account. Twelve years later, people we meet, or who write to Grace, tell how her words brought them courage, healing and the knowledge that they were not alone.

We prepared for these months carefully, designing a more balanced, though disciplined programme of living. This included equipping ourselves with a hi-fi record player, so that we were able to fill the cottage with a wide variety of music. My taste was widened to appreciate Finzi, Bruch, Elgar, Cesar Franck, some Shostakovich, and Bach – lots of Bach. I had first heard the St Matthew Passion in the year that followed my Cambridge conversion. I went on my own to a performance in London, and was overwhelmed by the experience. Now, on our sabbatical, instead of the usual pressured clergy preparation in Holy Week, there was space to listen to the St Matthew Passion, St John Passion and the Mass in B Minor.

At the heart of the Argyll sabbatical for me was the need to be still before God, without rushing into more busyness. I determined that there need not be end products to show to anyone. There was the opportunity to keep unhurried time early every day for my attempts at spiritual exercises, mediated by the writings of Gerard Hughes.[1] In my review of the year that I shared that autumn with my colleague Michael Henshall, I wrote about the sabbatical: 'I can recollect the freshness of the presence of Christ in the months following my conversion. That awareness of His presence was quite as alive as 39 years ago; and there was a new awareness of the very close presence of my heavenly Father, together with His insistence that he is the Father of all.'

I had time to study the Bible in fresh ways, and to read more widely than for a long time. I had often found poetry distant. T. S. Eliot had been opaque. Now there was time to read and repeat aloud *Four Quartets*, until I began to penetrate Eliot's imagination. Kenneth Rose's *King George V*, Owen Chadwick's *Hensley Henson*, Alan Wilkinson's *Dissent or Conform*, and Adrian Hastings' *History of English Christianity* took me into the history of the first part of the twentieth century from different angles. Books on urban mission, that had so long been the centre of my study, were consciously left on one side. Yet, in those moments of vivid awareness of the love of God the Father, I knew he would not allow me to forget the needs of those so often left behind. He is the Father of *all*.

In the event, the sabbatical was a special gift from God. Entering into such a variety of interests took away fears that retirement might be like an empty field. It pointed me towards the rhythm of rest and creativity that is making retirement fulfilling. We both grew – in different ways. I became more comfortable with privacy and stillness; Grace was being prepared to expand her life in more public directions. In that smaller-scale living, we found a new closeness that has deepened in retirement.

Enterprise City flourishes

The refreshment from the months of withdrawal was soon tested back in Liverpool. The blessing of the sense of God the Father's presence proved as real amid the demanding pressures of a city in crisis as in the stillness of the Highlands. The crisis was still there, but gradually the confrontation of the Militant years gave way to co-operation, when Harry Rimmer became the Leader of Liverpool City Council. Liverpool owed him much. Now, partnership again became the order of the day, between the city and private and voluntary sectors – and, increasingly, between central and local government. A series of government programmes – Action for Cities, City Challenge, Single Regeneration Budget – brought investment and new buildings and projects. In addition, European money arrived, as Merseyside was granted 'Objective 1 status' – the only such area in England. The churches played a part within the voluntary sector, but there was, and still is, a question of whether the voluntary sector was given the opportunity to 'punch its weight' by comparison with the public and private sectors.

Earlier in the book I have described Liverpool's story as 'a tale of two cities'. As we moved into the 1990s, 'Enterprise City' has increasingly flourished. Office space is far cheaper than in London. There is a proven work force with the skills that offices require. Aggressive policies have brought growth to Mersey Dock and Harbour Company, which handles more goods today than at any time in the port's history. New firms have come, for example, to Wavertree Technology Park. Ford Halewood was replaced by Jaguar Halewood, and by 2002 five car-component makers had set up in Speke to supply the Jaguar car factory. Private housing developments and new hotels have burgeoned along the riverside. The city centre population that Liverpool Parish Church serves was some 3,000 in 1990. By the year 2000 it was 8,000, with the forecast that it would pass 25,000 in another decade. Visitor Survey in 2000 claimed 19 million visitors to Merseyside in the year, spending £600 million compared with £223 million in 1985. Liverpool Airport's traffic passed

2 million passengers in 2000, with further expansion expected. Merseyside Vision has large-scale developments in its sights: the Kings Waterfront Arena scheme and the Paradise Street Development Area have the highest profile. The Heritage Lottery Fund has made major grants to Liverpool. The sum of £10 million was given towards the restoration of St George's Hall – part of Liverpool's hopes to be designated European Capital of Culture in 2008. Another £27 million was given to National Museums and Galleries on Merseyside (NMGM). Part of that has upgraded the Walker Art Gallery, now to be known as the National Gallery of the North.

David Henshaw, then Chief Executive of Knowsley,[2] asked me in 1997 to come for one last visit to the borough. I asked him if he could show me results from Objective 1 status. He took me to see industrial estates, once run down, that had an efficient, prosperous look. Knowsley had made a point of processing planning requests quickly. Kirkby town centre had security cameras. There was glass in the windows of shops. He said, 'We want Kirkby to be seen as an ordinary town.' It all seemed a far cry from the Knowsley when Jim Lloyd had described the 'anarchy' of its workforce.

For a good many years, friends have been asking me whether things are better in Liverpool. There is no doubt that the answer is 'Yes'. There is a renewed confidence in Merseyside. Business sees the opportunities here, realising – as we continue to experience – that it is a good place to live. The bid for European Capital of Culture in 2008 builds on the reality that Liverpool, with its great buildings, galleries, theatres and orchestra, is a burgeoning centre for the arts.

Hurt City remains

However, it would be claiming too much to say that the whole of Merseyside has flourished along with Enterprise City. 'Hurt City' still bleeds. The refrain – and the nervous question tacked on at the end – was played to Derek Worlock and me on a visit to a large pharmaceutical firm. 'Things are better in Liverpool – aren't they?' Derek said, 'Perhaps you should ask that question across the road.' Across the road was the large outer estate of Speke. One of the directors asked what we believed the unemployment there was. Derek said, 'Perhaps 50 per cent'. 'Oh, we should put it higher than that,' came the director's reply. In the 1990s the Speke–Garston development brought new industry and commerce to the area. As in all industrial developments, the question remained, how many of these new jobs would go to people who lived 'across the road'. After all, Ford's Halewood had been just across the road for years. But its skilled workers travelled in from a wide radius.

Jobs did not necessarily go to the nearest residents, if there was a lack of skills.

In 1991, in my sermon at the institution of a new rector in Speke, I spoke of the need to build up people's self-confidence. People in Speke had many gifts, but were inclined to 'put themselves down'. After the service, a police officer, working in youth liaison in Speke, said that was true of the young people she met: 'They would have to climb several mountains of self-confidence before they could even think of going on a training course.' The rector, Michael Plunkett, told me some years later that he had not known young people so hard-faced in his UPA experience before. Those hard faces often cover up deep feelings of inadequacy or disturbance.

In February 1993, two 10-year-old boys abducted 2-year-old James Bulger from a shopping centre in Bootle, led him for two and a half miles to a railway line, where they battered him to death with bricks and an iron bar. A shudder went through us all. It shocked me to the core. The request came to broadcast *Thought for the Day* on the morning after the court's verdict. I spoke about the way in which we are encouraged to rid ourselves of inhibitions, and to harden ourselves to watch scenes of violence in films or on television. I said:

> I hope some things will always shock me and make me angry – like violence to a child . . . Sometimes people accuse us in the Church of being soft on criminals. I think that's because we insist that the Gospel is about forgiveness and new starts. People confuse forgiving with condoning . . . We need to strengthen those good inhibitions that tell us that we should never, never use violence against a child. And then, that Christian insight about the possibility of forgiveness includes even those boys. There's no condoning the sheer evil of what they've done. But they can be redeemed. We're not to consign them to the dustbin.

An old friend, Nicholas Stacey, wrote to me. At one time he had been Rector of Woolwich, and later Director of Social Services for Kent. He said how grateful he was that I had said the part about not consigning the boys to the dustbin. He told me he had several children who had committed murders when they were in care or under supervision orders. All of them had come from appallingly chaotic families. He had continued to keep in touch with one of them for fifteen years in prison; in a recent visit, the young man had, for the first time, shown respect for himself and what he could be.

After we retired, James Jones,[3] my successor, gave me a copy of Blake Morrison's book *As If*. Morrison attended the whole of the trial, and could not rid his mind of the horror that was spelt out. He persisted in his attempt to understand both what had gone on in the minds of the two boys, and the refusal of so many to contemplate forgiveness. He wrote:

> For Ralph and Denise Bulger not to forgive is human. But for a whole nation not to is inhuman. Inhuman and despairing. No forgiveness – since they've been judged to be adult abusers and murderers. No forgiveness. It chimes with the mood of the tabloids, the nation, Westminster. John Major, on juvenile crime, in the wake of the Bulger case: 'We must condemn a little more, and understand a little less'. Robert and Jon could be rehabilitated, remorseful as they are. It's inhuman not to forgive damaged children, and despairing not to try to save them. As if kids who kill come from another planet, and don't deserve the chance to be human, to atone, to repair.[4]

I continued to see divisions between the attitudes of different groups who treated each other as if they came from another planet. In 1995, a bitter and long-running dispute began in Liverpool Docks. The docks had become highly successful, turning round a larger tonnage – with no more than 400 dockers – than at any time in its history. New technology had removed the power of the workforce – 45,000 employed in the docks in 1939. Now, as church leaders, we were drawn into attempts to bring the two sides together. Derek Worlock had by now become critically ill, but his colleague, Bishop John Rawsthorne, joined me together with one or other of the Free Church leaders, in all these meetings. The closer we came to the two groups in dispute, the more we felt they inhabited different planets.

The flash point came through *Torside*, a small company run by ex-dockers who had set up the company with their severance pay. They said that the dockers had dismissed themselves by striking. The shop stewards' leaders, Jimmy Nolan and Mike Carden, and other colleagues of theirs, told us that the company was going back to casual-labour practices, with demands that some men must be willing to work impossible hours. They saw themselves as carrying a torch for dockers all over the world. They believed the National Dock Labour Scheme was just and should never have been repealed. One of the shop stewards said to us, 'My grandfather was killed on the docks. My father lost the use of his legs on the docks. I have worked all my life on the docks. These are *our* jobs.' It became increasingly clear that they did not want any kind of settlement that was likely to appear. They attempted through international action to persuade ACL, the company running the largest ships coming into the port, to boycott Liverpool.

I saw the Managing Director of Mersey Docks and Harbour Company (MDHC), Trevor Furlong, alone, and put the criticisms firmly to him. He rehearsed to me the history, as the management saw it, of resistance to changes. He believed the offer of a lump sum redundancy payment of £10,000 while maintaining pension rights had been generous. He insisted that he was himself a member of the Transport and General Workers Union, and supported unionisation. He said the company had held back on taking on new dockers, but could do so no longer. He gave me a copy of a notice circulated by some strikers, giving the names and addresses of 'scabs', and described some serious and criminal acts of intimidation.

Randell Moll, the Senior Chaplain of Mission in the Economy (formerly Liverpool Industrial Mission), managed to keep the confidence of both sides throughout the dispute. He gave us thorough briefings. He kept in touch with both Bill Morris and Jack Adams, national leaders of the Transport and General Workers Union. On Randell's advice, we took an initiative in January 1996 and again about a year later. We appealed to the dockers to accept what was the best deal likely to be offered. However, the dockers turned down the proposal at a mass meeting by a show of hands. We tried to persuade them that a secret ballot was the democratic way, and asked what they had to fear. They were adamant that it was their tradition and that they trusted each other. We heard other views – that a number of dockers and their wives wanted an agreement; they were committed to mortgages, for example, and risked losing their homes.

Two worlds with wholly different philosophies were unable to engage with each other. I had great sympathy for the dockers, and was suspicious of practices that MDHC were likely to bring in. But modern international trade had moved on. All the cards were in management's hands, and there seemed no way in which the dockers could have won a better deal. They would have been able to improve it, if they had been willing for serious negotiations. The dispute dragged on, but the dockers had no power any more, and by 1998 it had come to an end, though there remained great resentment among many of those involved.

Hillsborough

In 1989 there was a tragedy that has left deep and lasting wounds in the city. Ninety-six Liverpool fans were crushed to death at the FA Cup semi-final in Sheffield. We were spending our post-Easter break with Jenny's in-laws in the Outer Hebrides island of Barra. As we were being driven round the island, I asked if we could put the radio on to listen to the commentary on the match. We switched on at the moment when the commentators had not yet grasped what was happening. Gradually the

313

horror dawned. In the evening, Derek Worlock came on the phone to say that there would be a Requiem Mass in the Metropolitan Cathedral at 6 p.m. the next day. Liverpool had come to expect the churches to act together when there were tragedies to face. So it mattered that I should be there with the other church leaders. But there was no ship or plane to get me off the island in time.

Stephen Bellamy had just taken over as my chaplain. He persevered long after others would have given up, and eventually spoke to the coastguard at Stornoway, who said he would send a helicopter to pick me up from a field in Barra. This would take me to Prestwick, where there would be an RAF Sea King helicopter that would take me to Liverpool. It was a close-run thing to get me back in time for the Mass. Permission was given for us to land in the King's Dock, very close to the city centre. As the helicopter descended, we saw crowds surrounding the cathedral. My driver, George Walker, was waiting with my robes for a quick change in the car. A police car led us through the crowds, and I walked into the vestry at 5.59 p.m., just as the procession was about to move off.

During the following week, there were long queues stretching round Anfield football ground, as thousands waited to place flowers on the pitch – until most of it had turned into one carpet of flowers. Not one of the barriers on the Kop was visible, being covered with Liverpool scarves, poems or special mementos. Some critics thought Liverpool was going over the top. They understood little of the strong sense in the city of a family wanting to mourn together. A psychiatrist, who had treated people injured and shocked by the recent bomb blast in Enniskillen, told me, 'Liverpool will be all right.' He meant that the strong sense of belonging would serve us well in that disaster. A close friend of ours, working at Liverpool University, told us that a colleague had come in that week, and given her a big hug. He said, 'I have decided to show people how much I value them now – not wait until they're dead and tell everyone else how much they meant to me.'

Grace, who had her mother with her, had stayed in Barra, arriving home four days later. She said she felt curiously cut off from what was going on, and needed to do something to reconnect with Liverpool people. So she picked some flowers from the garden, and decided to add hers to the sea of flowers on the ground. She went to Anfield quietly and without fuss. She said that, for her, this reduced the sense of shock and helped her to move on.

Four years before, when the Heysel Stadium disaster had taken place, Liverpool Football Club closed ranks, and let us know that our offers to be present were not needed. This time, they welcomed all that we as church leaders could bring. On three occasions, while the flowers were on the pitch, they asked us to come to the ground – the last in order to conduct a short service to bring that period of mourning to a close. A year on from the Hillsborough disaster, the three church leaders were asked to lead a memorial service at Anfield. We shared the different parts of the service, as we had grown accustomed to do. It was my turn to be the preacher. I said that football terraces had always been macho places: men weren't expected to weep, or to tell each other how they were feeling. In the first fortnight after Hillsborough, many had been able to express feelings of grief or anger or guilt – perhaps feeling guilty just at having been there and survived. The memory of that fortnight of openness had stood us in good stead, for pushing down awful memories made for deeper, more lasting, wounds. Many had signed into the counselling centre. I went on:

> I wonder when it first dawned on you what day this anniversary was to fall on – Easter Day – our greatest day as Christians. God's miracle says that death is not the end: there is a greater life beyond this world. I sometimes think, when we're facing tragic death, at a funeral – or today – you look at someone like me, and say, 'Leave all the rest out. What I really want to know is this: do you really believe that it's true?' Yes, I do really believe that it's true: that God raised his Son Jesus Christ from cold death, and that those who trust in him, however simply, are raised to that greater life with him.

The BBC televised the service, with great sensitivity. When the counselling centre was mentioned, the camera focused on a counsellor listening to someone, and then on the open door to the centre that had been established. A year later, I asked its director about the response. He said that until that Easter service, they had always been able to see enquirers immediately. After the service, they had needed to make diary appointments, because so many more asked for help – a year on.

With all due respect for Everton Football Club, this experience of going through the fires with Liverpool FC and its supporters has left me an unswerving follower – albeit mostly at a distance. As with Sussex cricket, I read every reference in the papers and watch all I can on television. While Derek Worlock was still in good health, we made a point of going to Anfield together.

Co-operation and pain

Part of the strength of the Church's presence is that it still plans to be there in the next generation. By contrast, grants from Europe, central Government or charitable trusts are frequently time limited. Three-year projects cannot turn around communities of the left-behind in lasting ways. When Michael Howard was Secretary of State for the Environment,

I led an ecumenical delegation. We complained that the Government had announced the shut-down of the Urban Programme without consulting the voluntary movement and the churches, even though government ministers liked to proclaim that we were vital partners. Tom Butler, then Bishop of Leicester,[5] said, 'You need us. We are present in every estate, where other agencies have withdrawn.'

For many people in Merseyside, the ecumenical partnership at public moments and at grass-roots level brought a street credibility that allowed a fresh readiness to listen to the Christian message. The 1990s saw a world-wide call to the churches to commit ourselves to a Decade of Evangelism. We knew that some Christians feared that an attempt to proclaim the Gospel ecumenically must blunt its thrust. We were keen to show that this was not so. For example, John Newton, Derek and I delivered a three-part address at an open-air meeting in the town centre of St Helens. This was organised by St Helens Inter-Neighbourhood Evangelisation (SHINE). More than forty local churches joined SHINE, appointed a full-time secretary and sustained a programme of joint outreach throughout the Decade and beyond. We planned our addresses in consultation with each other, and believed it hung together, without any one of us pulling our punches. The three headings of our joint challenge were: to be full-time disciples of the Lord himself; to join in the fellowship of his Church; and to serve the kingdom of God in the world around us.

Derek Worlock and I were given a joint honour that we both valued very highly – to be awarded the Freedom of the City of Liverpool. Derek was a sick man by then, and found it a most emotional occasion. And so it was. He told me that retirement had been no part of the tradition in which he had grown up. He kept going in the face of increasing weakness, walking with a stick. In 1994, I had a hip replacement, and suffered a pulmonary embolism on the third day after the operation. Recuperation took time, but I managed to take part in a cathedral service of celebration of the twenty-fifth anniversary of my being consecrated as a bishop. Derek agreed to speak at the end of the service. He seemed desperately frail as he climbed up to the pulpit. And then the years fell away, as he brought hopefulness and humour to the occasion. He said that I couldn't resist upstaging him; he was walking with one stick – and I had two! Actually at that cathedral service, I managed to walk up the long aisle using my bishop's staff instead of walking sticks for the first time for five weeks. Stephen Shakeshaft had taken a photograph of the two of us, both with sticks, that was included in the National Portrait Gallery 'Photos of the Century' exhibition.

After Derek's death, there was more than a year's delay in the appointment of a successor. That hiatus allowed destructive criticisms to start rolling. The writer, Alice Thomas Ellis, was given much publicity for her traditionalist attack on Derek. She blamed him and his 'progressive' approach for the falling off in church attendance. She made no mention of the effects of secularisation on all churches in the West, which had naturally hit the Roman Catholic Church in Liverpool, as well as everywhere else. After Patrick Kelly's first few months as Derek's successor, he went on holiday to stay with cousins in the United States. He was startled to be shown in a Mid-West paper the headline, 'Archbishop faces stew' – with a story about the Liverpool aggro! He said this underlined the importance of making his commitment to ecumenical partnership clear.

Patrick has brought distinct gifts to the archdiocese and to the Merseyside churches. He is a compelling expositor of Scripture. He has priority concerns for the Roman Catholic community, facing serious reductions of clergy and uncomfortable questions of closure of some parishes. During his first weeks, he agreed to come for an evening, when he could meet Grace and me in our home, and he and I could begin to establish a working relationship. I asked if, before we talked other business, he would agree that we should each join the other at our regular morning worship once a month. Patrick agreed without hesitation, and we soon became used to his arrival, helmeted, on his bike. Keith Hobbs, now Free Church Moderator, came too, and we stayed together for a business session following our worship. I pressed Patrick to join with me in various community events, continuing to believe that it was important for us to be seen together. He agreed, but argued that the churches would be seen to be together if one of us represented the others.

The team in the Anglican diocese also changed. Michael Henshall, a year older than I am, retired in 1996, leaving me with one more year to go. The question arose whether I should appoint an older man as Bishop of Warrington – who might be expected to retire within five years or so – in order to allow my successor to have the major say in choosing his team. I was grateful to George Carey for firm advice as my archbishop. He pressed me to appoint the best person, whatever his age. John Packer came, born in Lancashire, with experience in Sheffield and as Archdeacon of West Cumbria, with towns like Workington facing heavy unemployment. He and Barbara quickly became trusted colleagues and friends.[6]

In 1991, speculation was rife about who was to succeed Robert Runcie as Archbishop of Canterbury. My name was among those being tossed around as a possible candidate for the post. Those rumours were so strong that Grace and I agreed we should be open with each other about how we might cope, if the invitation were to come our way. We were clear that part of our answer to that question would have been, 'with great difficulty!' At Liverpool I was able to make some choices of the subjects to tackle in public. The Archbishop is cornered to respond on all the most controversial issues – by media and within the church. In the General Synod, I had watched partisan members playing 'hunt the Archbishop' at Question Time. I felt it was the church at its worst. I did not covet that position, was relieved when it went to another, and felt a strong obligation to pray for him, and support him.

The media had given Robert Runcie a hard time while he was Archbishop of Canterbury, and George Carey received the same destructive treatment. In February 1993, within two years of his becoming Archbishop, the *Sunday Times* published an article by Rebecca Fowler, with headlines 'Carey the catastrophe?' It was agreed that, as one of the senior bishops, I should ask for the right to reply to the *Sunday Times* piece. Eric Shegog, well experienced as the church's communications officer, negotiated an agreement for me to write an article they would publish. The same resistance met me as when I had asked the same paper for the opportunity to reply to Brian Walden's personal attack on me. Now, I wrote a piece with the number of words for which Eric Shegog had won agreement, and then went away for a much-needed reading week. My chaplain, Tim Stratford, had to battle with the newspaper on my behalf. After long arguments, they agreed to publish a letter from me, half the length that my article had been.

I wrote that we were looking forward to a visit from the Archbishop of Canterbury to Liverpool that month. In the event, we saw a man who gave the whole of his attention to each person he met, and a pastor who was at his best when meeting people, and who understood the pressures that clergy face. I wrote that our experience was far removed from the carping tone of Rebecca Fowler's article. Her research seemed to have been highly selective: each of the attributable criticisms came from within the group which had understandably been hurt by the General Synod decision to ordain women to the priesthood. In the House of Bishops I saw a warm, team man, deeply committed to the journey towards unity, embracing all the churches which are willing to come. I went on:

> George Carey stands in an honourable tradition, human, spirited, scholarly, charitable. The Church of England does not, as the media oversimplify, consist of adversarial factions of traditionalists and liberals. Of course we have our differences, like any other family. In a world where religion can too easily become a factor in nationalist divisions, robust tolerance should rank very high among the theological virtues. It takes great moral and spiritual strength to steer a steady course in such a turbulent world. I believe George Carey is already finding that strength.

Our life in Liverpool was often turbulent. One day we were both feeling exhausted, and then realised that there was still one more commitment in the diary. It turned out to be reinvigorating. We were to visit the L'Arche community in Liverpool, which has three houses there.[7] Each house offers a home to adults with learning difficulties, supported by volunteers living alongside them. The love that flowed between each member of the community, the respect paid to each in turn over the meal, sent us home renewed in spirit. For another L'Arche occasion the three Liverpool ecumenical presidents were invited to a gathering of all the L'Arche homes in the country. The final event was in the well at the west end of our cathedral. At the end of the enactment of one of the parables of Jesus, we were all invited to dance in the 'Well'. As we danced, Grace said to me, 'I think heaven must be rather like this!' I repeated that to one of the stalwart lay helpers at the cathedral. 'Yes', he said, 'but I wouldn't want it to happen too often!' He was not so sure that such spontaneity was fitting in the cathedral.

Maintaining the Christian presence does involve pain and pressure. Paradoxically, some clergy feel that those pressures have increased as a result of one of the most positive developments in church life. Lay people have taken a greater share in ministry, and not just in response to smaller numbers of stipendiary clergy. It has been a working out of belief in the nature of the body of Christ – sometimes described as 'every-member ministry', because God has given gifts to every member of the body. Some clergy have felt that the call to the ordained ministry has been belittled by the emphasis on lay ministry. That is to misunderstand the calling to leadership. The most effective leadership is not always from the front. It is also to be the spotter of gifts and the encourager of the people of God from the middle.

I admired the way so many clergy and spouses sustained their presence in every kind of district – often at great personal cost. Financial pressures on church congregations that seemed to be all about paying the clergy their stipends and pensions made some feel beleaguered, flinching from putting the challenge for increased giving. Sometimes the feelings of being beleaguered were more literal; we were made aware of dangers at the vicarage door in 'nice' parishes as well as in UPAs, and repeated acts of vandalism against the church buildings proved wearisome and dispiriting.

Shock waves hit us all when Christopher Gray, the Vicar of St Margaret's, Anfield, was murdered outside his vicarage front door in August 1996. It seemed that another taboo – forbidding attacks on clergy – had been broken. Christopher was described by Professor Adrian Hastings as 'quite the most brilliant student I have had the pleasure of teaching'. We lost an outstanding young priest, firmly rooted in the catholic wing of our church, supporting the ordination of women, reaching across denominations and parties. He insisted on serving in a UPA parish, and was convenor of the diocesan evangelism team.

His murder highlighted questions the church had to face. The tradition that needy people – some of them, inevitably, disturbed – could come to the vicarage door was a long and honourable one. This was true especially in UPAs, where clergy were often the only professional people resident at night or over the weekend. That can make single clergy feel insecure. Where clergy are married, it is often the spouse, or children, who open the vicarage door, sharing in the risks too. We tried to make sure that clergy homes knew where skilled advice and service for needy people was available.

This was a period when, like other professionals, clergy needed to acknowledge how vulnerable they were both to physical attacks and to false accusations. Like other churches, we put in place codes of practice to safeguard protection of children, and to protect adults serving the church from false charges. I insisted that all our clergy attended one of three meetings with our Child Protection Officer, Colin Critchley, himself a professional child psychologist and non-stipendiary minister. It meant signing forms and checking with police records. It was worth it to protect children entrusted to us. One of my most bitter memories is of going to meet mothers whose children had been abused by a vicar, and, having visited him in prison, going through the solemn ceremony of deposing him, 'unfrocking' him – so that he could never minister again.

Ordination of women

That was the lowest point. One of the highest was the day in 1994 when I ordained twenty-six women to be priests. Ordaining bishops had been instructed to interview each woman before agreeing to go forward with the ordination. I was determined that this should not be seen as another hurdle women must climb over that would not have been put in front of a man. But I could see that we had reached a moment when we had put away ecclesiastical arguments, and were confirming the personal calling of God to each individual. I asked four clergy and lay colleagues to offer unhurried time to help each candidate for priesting to tease out her sense of God's calling. They then presented me with an account I could talk through with those to be ordained. Margaret Rogers interviewed six or seven of the women. With the experience of a career in higher education behind her, she told me she remembered those interviews as the most inspiring moments of her church life. I don't believe any group of priests had ever been so carefully prepared. It would be a mistake to suggest that women have brought particular gifts that men cannot possess. Gifts we may label as male or female can be part of the characteristics of either sex. I made notes of the reports that were made to me from the interviews that were testing the callings of those first twenty-six. All had previously been ordained deacon and many had served for some years as a deaconess or a parish worker before that:

> She has a ministry of encouragement, being able to persuade reluctant adult Christians that they possess gifts of which they were previously unaware.

> She has a clear vision of God's call to the Church to reach out and serve the community and the strength to hold people to the vision and challenge them where necessary.

> She has a strong empathy with people – especially with those who are bruised and marginalised – and this will enable her to be a representative as well as an enabler.

> It would have been easy in that situation to have been simply a social worker, and the church building a meeting place. Her commitment has been that she is a priestly presence in the parish, and the church building has become a powerhouse of prayer, worship and community.

> When I am uncertain what to do in any situation, she is the first person I seek out for advice, as I know she possesses the ability to listen deeply, and I value the fact that she is not afraid to say something hard if that is required.

> As a person, she has demonstrated in personality and character her ability to create, build, heal and develop relationships with people on both a social and an intellectual level.

> I sometimes say to myself that, if the Church were ever to undergo persecution, she is the kind of person I would want to have around; tough and uncompromising where truth and justice are concerned, but unashamed of her own vulnerability.

How could we have gone on wasting such God-given gifts? I have no doubt that their ordination has enriched the ministerial priesthood of our church, making it more collaborative and more aware of being servants of the whole body of Christ.

Local roots for the Church

Important as the ordination of women was to me – and the placing of them in posts that matched their gifts – at the top of my priorities I continued to keep the Church's presence in UPAs. 'Getting *Faith in the City* into the bloodstream of the Church of England' meant persistent follow-up in the diocese. I jointly chaired a follow-up committee. They quickly put me on the spot: 'You must call a meeting in each of the eight boroughs in the diocese during the next six weeks. Invite people from public, private and voluntary sectors. You must chair each meeting yourself.' At first sight that seemed like an impossible addition to the diary's demands, but I saw the point, and squeezed the dates in. There was positive response – outstandingly in St Helen's, where the leader and deputy leader of the council, and half the councillors, came. Links forged at some of these meetings led on to lasting alliances in serving the community.

Several recommendations in *Faith in the City* had been about establishing local roots for the Church in UPAs. That lay behind the argument for ordaining local non-stipendiary ministers (LNSM):[8] it said that this should be based on a 'Church Leadership Development Programme'. When Stanley Booth-Clibborn was appointed Bishop of Manchester, he and I found we had a common mind about LNSM and set up a joint Liverpool–Manchester working party to look at proposals. This built on the convictions reached with Trevor Huddleston, and described in an earlier chapter. Manchester moved ahead more quickly; we waited for our Liverpool initiative in encouraging lay ministry teams in UPAs (Group for Urban Ministry and Leadership – GUML) to provide a firm base, before introducing our own LNSM scheme. We stood by that, expecting candidates for LNSM to be part of a recognised local ministry team in other parts of the diocese or of GUML. The first men and women were ordained in the year following my retirement.

The first director of GUML was Neville Black. Over ten years, he brought long experience in inner-city parishes and passionate belief that those who had received bad experiences in school nevertheless had intelligence and gifts that could be unlocked. He had earlier led the Evangelical Urban Training Programme (EUTP – which under its more recent leader, Jenny Richardson, has taken the title UNLOCK). In Neville's ten years as director, GUML produced teams in some twenty UPA parishes. It offers a two-year training programme, using participants' experience and building up the confidence to work out Christian faith in their own urban context. It encourages people to equip themselves for service in the wider community as well as within church life. When I went to commission teams, I saw the way in which confidence had been boosted. And that confidence-building released God-given gifts that had often been trampled on at home and school.

As I arrived at St Peter's, Everton, for a commissioning service, Jane Corbett, herself involved sensitively in the West Everton Community Council as well as in the parish, waylaid me: 'You're not just going to talk about them leading the youth work and other parts of church life, are you?' 'What should I be talking about then?' I asked. 'Well', she said, 'one is involved with the Community Council, another with the Centre for Homeless people, another with the Advice Centre.' In my sermon I duly included these commitments in the wider community, as well as those that are firmly within the life of the local church there. Jane's husband, Henry Corbett, the Rector of St Peter's, had trained as a member of the GUML team, and the Reader, Mark Hedley, led the service. Mark stands as an example of how 'incomers' can play a part that does not block local leadership from emerging. As a young lawyer, he and his family moved into Everton, where they have stayed, while he has ascended the legal ladder and become a judge. In this commissioning service, he asked if he might speak personally; he said that, with the commissioning of the GUML team, he was seeing a dream fulfilled of local leadership that he had kept burning all the years he had lived there.

My enthusiasm for second-chance learning was strengthened by these church initiatives. Another honour that meant much to me was to receive an honorary degree from the Open University – an institution that has opened the door to higher education for many who might never have expected it. Further education (FE) provides the necessary bridge towards such courses or employment opportunities for many. In areas of high unemployment FE should be a major plank of government policy. In retirement I have welcomed the increased funding that the Government is giving to FE. It had long been the Cinderella in education. When I had been in Liverpool for ten years, people in the diocese asked if there was an object for which I would welcome a trust fund. The Bishop David Sheppard Anniversary Trust raised rather more than £200,000 and offers grants for second-chance learning in colleges of FE within the diocese. Meeting some at Liverpool Community College, who had received grants from us, I asked whether small sums of between £50 and £100 were really any help. They told me that they had made a significant difference to travel or finding books or equipment. And the personal interest shown to them often enabled them to find further money from other charities. The administration has been done on a voluntary basis, first by the Revd Lena Prince, followed by Lesley Conder, Rosemary Hawley and then Brenda Wolfe. They have made a point of interviewing applicants, or seeing that a colleague met them.

In 1990, I took part in a debate in the House of Lords on education and training. The debate was widely drawn, with an emphasis on equipping people to be more employable. Staff at Liverpool Community College provided stories of second-chance learning making people more employable (their Lordships like stories). I mentioned colleges of FE that I had visited in Merseyside. Employers would see there the growth of confidence, the release of intelligence and the way students were equipped with skills. One young woman had said, 'Before I started the course, I was a bored, unemployed and disillusioned single parent, with no job prospects and no ideas of how to pull myself and my son out of the rut that had developed around me.' It had been her mother, herself a student the previous year, that introduced her to the course. She learned how to study, and that she had a thirst for good books. Now she was studying for a maths course for teaching and a GCSE English language course.

I spoke of the effect on struggling schools that FE could have by giving parents new experiences like that. Liverpool Education Committee did some research in 1983 on the effect that parents' second-chance learning has on their children's schooling. I quoted some further testimonials I had received. Typical of their thrust was this: 'My attitude towards my children's education hasn't changed, but my ability to influence them has. I've always encouraged them to try really hard at school, but now the kids have seen me studying and my wife studying. Now studying is not something grown-ups impose on kids.'

Nothing presented the Church of England with a greater challenge to getting *Faith in the City* into its bloodstream than making space for black people to bring their gifts. Jim Thompson, then Bishop of Stepney, told me that he confirmed hundreds of black children, yet was seeing no black people being elected to the Bishop's Council for the area. He took an initiative to draw them in. He brought into being an informal bishop's advisory body including a number of black Christians. They made effective contributions, and grew sufficiently in confidence to stand two years later at the next Bishop's Council election – when several were elected. I felt envious when he said he confirmed hundreds of black children. That was not our experience in Liverpool, with a long-established black community in which children did not see their parents going to church any more than did their white neighbours in the inner city. But I determined to learn whatever was possible from Jim Thompson's example. Individual black Christians were present, worshipping in churches in the diocese. So I wrote to all our clergy, asking them to give an enclosed letter to any of their members 'who thought of themselves as black'. In the letter an invitation was enclosed to a meeting at Bishop's Lodge.

That meeting brought together a small group. In time, Christians from all churches came together, when we established the Churches Action for Racial Equality (CARE) project. Raising money for ecumenical action always proved difficult, but CARE project, with two full-time officers, has been the one project largely supported by the MARCEA churches in addition to finding the stipend for the ecumenical officer. Education was a main intention for CARE project – both in schools and in local churches. Black members were willing to put themselves on the line to go to 'the White Highlands' where few had known the opportunity of meeting black people. That has been a costly contribution to building bridges on which searching questions could be explored. CARE project has mounted meetings to promote the Wood–Sheppard Principles for equal opportunities in employment. It has raised issues about asylum seekers. In Liverpool, Somalis were fleeing from civil war, making for safe places with members of their families settled here. Speaking to the annual meeting of CARE in 1992 about the Asylum Bill that was then before Parliament, I said that speeded-up procedures need not mean poor arrangements for appeal. Some newspapers confused asylum with immigration, playing on their readers' fears. A small country had a right to limit the numbers that come in. It did not have a right to lay down what colour they should be. I went on: 'Asylum is a different matter: it's about people in danger. We need to spend more on seeing that appeals and legal aid are properly available with clear and fair procedures. Fortress Europe is not good on minority ethnic groups that have entered in the last hundred years, especially people with different colour skins.'

My final Church campaign as Bishop of Liverpool was to ensure that financial support was sustained for a nationwide ministry. *Faith in the City* called for potential for giving to be taken into account between *dioceses* as well as between parishes. National needs called for contributions to be made from dioceses according to their capacity to give. The Church Commissioners had often intervened with additional funds for dioceses in which historic resources were small and the number of UPAs were disproportionate. By now their finances were stretched, especially to meet the increased bill for clergy pensions.

Often church members see the need to keep their own parish afloat, and are ready to give generously to charity and to the Church overseas. Yet they may not hear the call to support the Church's presence in less affluent parts of their own country. Ten years on from *Faith in the City*, the report *Staying in the City* produced tables that compared weekly giving in UPAs and non-UPAs and between dioceses. The weekly giving in non-UPAs in my once-home Diocese of Chichester was £2.73, compared with £2.80 in UPAs in Liverpool.[9] There were many friends among bishops, clergy and lay people in the more prosperous parts of the nation who were keen to help. But sustaining a nationwide ministry in poorer parts cannot depend on private initiatives. Living as members one of another surely calls for steady commitment to a joint scheme based on thorough research into the resources each member brings to the common pool. I understand the financial pressures parishes face at the moment – especially to support clergy pensions. But I pray that this call of *Faith in the City* will be answered soon.

22

Steps Along the Shore

Late in September 1997, we said goodbye to Liverpool. Both Grace and Jenny joined me for the procession down the long nave of the cathedral at the end of the farewell service. Balloons floated down, as we moved under the tower. It had been agreed that, having greeted many represent-atives during the service, we would leave immediately. George Walker was waiting with the car at the foot of the steps. We realised quickly that friends had tied balloons to the bumper of the car, declaring, 'You're never too old to party!' We climbed into the back. I was still fully robed in my cope, and must have looked rather like a meringue. Five minutes away from the cathedral, a policeman stopped us. He ordered us to remove the balloons, as they were a potential danger and were hiding the registration number plate. George got out and removed the offending balloons. The policeman peered through the window, looking hard at me. Perhaps he wondered if we had come straight from one of the clubs in fancy dress. 'Don't do it again,' he said. 'I promise,' I said, 'I will *never* do it again!' Somehow, it seemed a true Liverpool send-off – with plenty of laughs and on the wrong side of the law.

When we told friends that we had bought a retirement house in the Wirral, across the Mersey from Liverpoool, a number commented, 'We thought you'd go back down South.' Northerners often spoke to us as though a Southerner would always prefer the South. In the end, it was clear where we felt we belonged. Many expressed pleasure that we had decided to stay in Merseyside.

The need to leave a tied house forces clergy to make a fresh decision about where to settle. We agreed to write down the features of a retirement place that each of us hoped for. Both of us included in our list having a garden and the determination not to become isolated. Grace put 'a community to belong to' at the top of her list. Next, she wanted to be able to see *water* if possible, or *hills* if there was no water, and definitely *sky*. On my list was the wish to be near enough to a big city to keep in touch with issues that had been at the centre of my life.

For four years we spent many of our days off looking at possible retirement houses. Friends and family were scattered across the country, and there was no obvious place to go. We spent a week's holiday in Brighton, wondering whether we should go back to our roots in the South. That produced a strong awareness that, after twenty-two years in Liverpool, we belonged in the North. But we knew we should move out of my successor's way. So, we ringed Manchester, thinking that we should put some distance between Liverpool and ourselves. Next, our research into the possibility of living in Leeds nearly brought us a marriage crisis. We spent a wet and foggy holiday week in November looking at houses there. Having contained her frustration for three days, Grace said, 'I'll give you one more day!' Jenny reminded us that we had never lived in Yorkshire. She asked why we did not look at West Kirby, on the Wirral, where we had quite often gone to walk round the Marina and blow the cobwebs away on a day off. 'You were always happy when you went there,' she said. West Kirby is in the Diocese of Chester, and faces away from Liverpool, even though it is only eight miles from the tunnels under the Mersey and our friends back on the other side.

The sixth West Kirby house we looked at met all the features we had written down. It's small enough to clean in a morning. It looks across the Dee Estuary where it is five miles wide to the Welsh hills, and out to the Irish Sea past Hilbre Island. We can be on the shore in two minutes. From the beginning, I loved high tide, with the sound of the sea reaching us in the garden. We also came to appreciate the times when the estuary's expanse of sand produces a huge variety of reflections of light and colour. Sunsets are sometimes as exotic as Turner's paintings, but the changing moods and light inspire me too. The garden stretches and delights us both. Although Grace is the more experienced gardener, we work together. Thanks to the generosity of Liverpool Diocese's farewell gift, we were able to create our own design. It has been rewarding to see the garden developing so quickly. As the keeper of the compost heap, it was a moment of achievement for me when it was actually steaming for the first time! Up until now, the assistance of a gardener coming two hours a week has helped us keep on top of its demands.

A supportive community

We bought the house some time before retirement, and soon found that the first hope – of a community to which we could belong – would be more than fulfilled by our neighbours. We used the house for a holiday then, and were starting breakfast when we realised that there was a message on the answerphone that we had not heard in the night. It was my Liverpool colleague, Michael Henshall, ringing to tell me the terrible news that a young vicar, Christopher Gray, had been murdered. We dropped everything, and went across the Mersey, to be there with parish, police and press, and to see Christopher's parents when they arrived that evening. When we eventually came back, near to midnight, the breakfast was still on the table, together with a note on the doormat from our neighbours on either side – who had our keys – saying how sorry they were at the news. They had seen that we had left windows wide open, and had come in to close them.

Early the following morning, I walked on the shore, as has continued to be my habit, and was given what I saw as a glimpse of glory that has stayed with me. It has put a framework round retirement. That August morning, the early morning sun, hidden by the cliffs, came from just round the corner, and lit up the many small boats moored on the estuary. My mind was on Christopher, and I thought of him lit up now by a bright light on another shore. I often remember that morning. It reminds me that, as a retired person, I am taking steps along this shore, travelling full of hope towards my own journey's end.

Neighbours – and members of the parish of St Bridget's, West Kirby – did not rush at us with demands, but allowed us to go at our own pace. There was a moment when I was anxious about their expectations: the couple from whom we bought the house very kindly threw a lunch party and invited neighbours in. One asked me, 'Do you sail?' I said I didn't sail. 'Do you play golf?' I don't play golf. 'Do you play bridge?' Thinking of acceptable West Kirby activities, I said, a little desperately, 'No. But I paint!'

Rhythm of retirement life

We agreed that the first six months of retirement should have no public commitments. As this period came towards an end, Grace said, 'This has been wonderful. Why don't we do it every year?' That made powerful sense, and I promptly agreed to keep three months each year free from any public engagements. That has given increased time for creativity, our partnership, family and neighbours. During that first six months, a major surprise added another dimension to our life. In the New Year's Honours List, I was made a Life Peer, a great honour. That introduced a London element to retirement that I had not planned, with some happy spin-offs. In addition to the life of the House of Lords, it has meant seeing more of the two grandsons who have been born in these years, and who live in London.

I took some time to reflect on what the pattern of my retirement should be. Reading the Old Testament, I came across a fresh translation of the story of Elijah – when he met with God on Mount Horeb: first came a great and strong wind . . . but the Lord was not in the wind. Then there was an earthquake, followed by fire. And the Lord was not in the earthquake or the fire. 'And after the fire a small murmuring sound . . . and a voice: "Why are you here, Elijah?" ' I wrote some headings under the title, 'Have I been hearing a small murmuring sound?' in my times of stillness and walking on the shore.

> *Build on these months, and be a retired person* – grandfather, home-making, the garden, good neighbouring, painting, singing, reading. Guard the morning pattern of stillness, my walk and physical exercises.
>
> *Establish a structure* – be part of the Christian community in the parish; accept preaching and speaking engagements beyond the parish within a ceiling of 20 in a year, expect working weeks up to 25 hours instead of 60–70 hours in 'the other life'. Keep three months each year free from public engagements.
>
> *Support Grace in her ministry.* Go with her for some of her involvements and set her free at times from chores at home.
>
> *Write a book* – in my times of stillness my mind has kept returning to writing an autobiography. We have lived through some momentous years and have a story to tell. Do some studying in the history of my own time.
>
> *Accept that there will be a London dimension.* Keep it within limits, but go for it!

I had discovered the value of having a spiritual director during the Liverpool years. Frank Wright, a canon of Manchester Cathedral, had been a sensitive and shrewd soul friend. Now he had retired further north, and we agreed that I should seek another. Canon Brian McConnell, Vicar of Altrincham, has brought vision and accountability to my retirement, when it could easily have drifted into another whirl of commitments. He regularly keeps in front of me the need for a rhythm of life in which creativity has a prime place.

Grace and I had agreed to look for some fresh activities that we could share in addition to gardening. We joined a choir together – St Peter's Singers in Heswall. Grace had kept her singing alive in Cathedral Singers during our Liverpool years, but I had not sung in a choir since schooldays, when it had been a major part of my life. Two concerts a year with sacred music from Bach to Benjamin Britton stretches, fulfils and introduces us to another circle of friends. Theatr Clwyd and The Gateway in Chester are within easy reach for plays. And we drive back to Liverpool for a dozen concerts at the Philharmonic Hall.

Retirement gives the freedom to make choices. That includes time for reading. Among the novelists whose books I have enjoyed have been Pat Barker, David Lodge, Vikram Seth, P. D. James and Joanna Trollope. I have devoured each of William Dalrymple's books – so much more than travel stories. Cricket keeps finding its place; the first book I read on retiring was Charles Williams' fine biography of Don Bradman. And then there was Dickie Bird's autobiography.

Writing my autobiography has been a three-year challenge. I believed I would write a better book if I studied some history of my own time as a background. Martin Daunton[1] kindly took me on, feeding me with a wide range of reading. The essays I wrote for him included: 'Public, private and voluntary sector answers to urban poverty'; 'What planners, politicians and economists thought a modern Britain should look like in the 1950s and 1960s'; 'Thatcherism'; and the vast subject of 'Immigration and Britain'.

Another retirement challenge was how to cope with the correspondence that would reduce greatly but still have its demands. I had dictated letters on to a tape for my secretary. Now I was on my own, though we share the contents of the mail at breakfast. I had always seen myself as incompetent when it came to machines of any kind, and had kept my distance from computers. Now, they clearly had something to offer. Grace and I put our toes in the water by sitting down at a computer in a public library for a short 'Computer Programme for the Terrified!' That encouraged me to look further, and I signed up as a student at Wirral Metropolitan College for a 'CLAIT' computer course. I climbed on the bus to Birkenhead every Saturday for thirty weeks, bought a computer and found to my surprise that I could manage – and enjoy – word processing and simple spreadsheet and emails better than I had dreamed possible.

Another bonus retirement has brought is the chance to watch more cricket than for many years. Old Trafford is an hour's drive away, where there has been a warm welcome from the Lancashire committee, who made me a vice-president of the club. I have always followed my own team, Sussex, from afar in the press. Staying with my sister on visits to Sussex has provided a base for occasional matches over the years. In 2001 I was made president of Sussex, and managed rather more days in a season when Sussex's revival burgeoned – being top of the second division and winning promotion.

That first March, we celebrated Grace's birthday with a day in London. In the morning we went to an exhibition of Bonnard's paintings. We had lunch with Jenny and Donald. Half way through the meal, they looked at each other, and said, 'Shall we tell them?' After ten years of marriage, Jenny was pregnant! We were overjoyed. In due course, Stuart and then Gilles were born, and there is the delight and the stretching of being grandparents. For me, playing on the floor, or going to the park, with these little boys is a bonus to every visit to London.

Bubbling over with that news, we went in the afternoon to the House of Lords for what Grace described in her diary as 'a redemption process'. When I had been introduced to the House as a bishop in 1980, she had felt the heavy hand of Black Rod – the senior officer responsible for the good order of the House. My mother had come for the occasion, in a wheelchair, which was placed by 'the Bar' in the debating chamber. After some time, my mother beckoned to Grace – who takes up the story:

> Unsure whether I should rise, or leave the Chamber in these circumstances, I paused before moving across to her. Bobbing down to minimise the fuss, I whispered, 'What is it Nana?' She replied in a loud whisper, 'I think we ought to go'. Before I could stand up, there was a hand on my shoulder. 'Please return to your seat, my Lady, and never do that again!' The blood drained from my face. It was Black Rod himself. I had committed the unforgivable sin of 'crossing the Bar'! I could hear the horses coming to take me to the Tower.

The same day, there were two further moments when Grace felt she had broken the rules. This experience robbed her of any sense of being at ease in the House. Now that I was to be reintroduced to the House, she was determined to discover what she was allowed to do and where she was allowed to go. There was a new Black Rod, who gave us unhurried time and a warm welcome, and gave her new confidence. In her diary, she described, 'A full and worthwhile day – potentially life-changing. Being grandparents and being a Lord and Lady all at once is a bit of a challenge, to say the least!'

Life peerage

After the announcement of the life peerage, a prompt letter arrived from Garter King of Arms, asking me not to make any plans before coming to see him. He raised the matter of my title: I had wondered whether 'Lord David Sheppard' was possible. Garter looked pained. 'But you're not the son of a duke or an earl,' he said. But he had no problems with the title I really wanted, 'Lord Sheppard of Liverpool'. He went on to ask me if I had given thought to who might be my two supporters when I was reintroduced to the House of Lords. I had wondered about asking the Bishop of Bath and Wells. His brow furrowed once more. 'But he's not the same rank as you will be.' In House of Lords terms he was a prelate and I was to be a baron. So what about asking Lord Runcie and Lord Cowdrey? After a moment's contemplation, Garter relaxed and said, 'God – and Cricket. I think that would do very well!'

As we approached retirement Grace and I both felt that we would be free from the political constraints we had felt from my calling to be a bishop. So we both joined the Labour Party. When, a few months later, I was made a life peer, it seemed natural to ask if I might sit on the Labour benches. The *Sunday Times* ran a story that this broke a tradition dating back to the Reformation, that bishops sat on the cross-benches. In fact, the history is that the bishops have sat on the separate bishops' benches – not the cross-benches – until the recent creation of life peers. I was the first bishop to receive this honour, following four archbishops, who have indeed sat on the cross-benches. Dr George Macleod of the Church of Scotland was made a life peer, as was Dr Donald Soper of the Methodist Church. George Macleod sat on the cross-benches, while Donald Soper sat on the Labour benches for many years.

As a retired person with other commitments, I do not go to the House every day. I budget for three days every other week. That makes it possible to drink in the flavour of the debates, and to make occasional interventions and speeches. I determined to confine my public interventions to a few subjects in which I had been involved – employment matters, homelessness, the youth service, asylum seekers, ecumenical partnership, Northern Ireland, faith-based schools, opportunities for young people in sport.

The reform of the House of Lords has taken up many hours of debate. I regret that the tone has sometimes become acrimonious. I have long believed that in some issues there was an appropriate party to undertake particular political changes. For example, the future of Rhodesia had to be settled by the Conservatives. The Labour Party should have dealt with trade union reform. I believed it was a betrayal of their responsibility that Labour backed away from the proposals Barbara Castle introduced under the title 'In place of strife'. In the same way, the Conservatives, in office for eighteen years with a huge majority in the House of Commons, should have been the government to tackle the reform of the House of Lords.

Because of the presence of hereditary peers, the Conservatives had a built-in majority of four to one, yet never brought in reforms that would have removed such an unjust balance of power. They could have achieved this with much less bitterness than the Labour Government faced. Some critics have been fierce in their criticisms of proposals that the reformed House would not be democratic unless it was wholly elected. I do not agree. In my view, that would make it a pale shadow of the House of Commons. Part of the strength of the House of Lords has been that it has some members who are not full-time politicians, but bring distinction and insight from particular areas of the nation's life. That can produce remarkable quality in debates. In the future, an independent panel will be able to make such appointments, alongside a proportion of elected peers. As I had said in my maiden speech back in 1980, my hopes for a reformed House include representatives of other Christian churches and of other faith communities.

There have been many attempts to attack Tony Blair for 'stuffing the House with cronies'. The facts are far different: from Labour coming to power in 1997 until the end of 2001, 245 life peers have been created. Less than half of those (114) support the Labour Party. After five years in power, Labour still commands only 28 per cent of the vote in the House of Lords (195 members out of 695). The Conservatives still have the largest number of peers (220) with cross-benchers having 181 and Liberal Democrats 65.

Still a bishop

'Once a bishop, always a bishop' matches 'once a priest, always a priest'. Finding the best rhythm as a bishop in retirement involves 'shortening my stride' – taking on fewer commitments. There has been the warmest of welcomes from the Bishop of Chester and his colleagues, joining them for ordination services and taking some confirmations. It is a rich experience for Grace and me to sit together in the congregation at St Bridget's, our parish church, as regular worshippers. I preside and preach at one early morning communion each month. My priority in public ministry now is to produce occasional papers on subjects closest to my heart, but mostly to make visits to parishes and ecumenical services in the region. So, I have gradually been discovering the churches of the Wirral – perhaps I've preached in a dozen by now.

I enjoy preaching and speaking more than ever before. Now it is possible to obey the advice we were given as students in theological college, to make a start on Sunday's sermon on Monday morning, and let it simmer and come to the boil through the week. That was not realistic for a bishop, with perhaps four or five addresses a week. It was essential then to find ways of freshening material, in order to produce from the store 'things new and old'. Now, there is much more time for solid reading. Among the theological authors, several stand out: Tom Wright, Walter Brueggemann, David Ford, Rowan Williams. When there are addresses to prepare, I can work at a draft a week ahead. The computer makes changes easy. And the time available means that Grace can read and comment on the draft. I value her eye for form and structure, and for what will engage people's attention. That sometimes means drastic rethinking, but draws out of me fresh ideas and illustrations from life.

Happily overwhelmed

There was a shock in April 2001 that threatened to destroy our hopes and plans. It was discovered that I had bowel cancer. Surgery was followed by twenty-four weeks of chemotherapy. Grace tells me that my first words when I woke up from the operation were, 'I want to get better.' A flood of calls, cards, letters, prayers and acts of love of many people made us feel happily overwhelmed. At moments when we needed help most, a friend arrived on the doorstep with a casserole or a cake. At the time of writing, a scan has given an 'all clear' message, and I feel well. I cancelled all the commitments for the months that followed the operation. The cancellations included the three-hours service on Good Friday, which was the week after coming home. But it meant I was free, just as in that sabbatical year in Argyll, for my Holy Week to be lifted up by Bach's music and the story of the Passion. As a new year dawned, friends said they hoped 2002 would be a better year. Of course I understood what they were saying – but how could another year be better?

These weeks have given me an insight into and an admiration for those in the front line of the NHS. Both my surgeon and oncologist have specialist nurses to back them up. The Macmillan nurse allotted to me in support of the surgeon, gave time to both of us – patient and carer – before I went into hospital. She gave me her phone number, and promised she would be there if I needed help or advice. The oncologist's specialist nurse sat down unhurriedly to explain just what would happen and again gave me telephone numbers and the assurance that she would be there. They were true to their word. Surgeon and oncologist's teams on the Wirral work closely together. There is a collaborative spirit about both teams, with humour and trust between them. They have been a major influence in strengthening my will to get better. When we came to Liverpool in 1975, Clatterbridge was thought of as the place you went to in order to die. Now I found that the oncology centre there was a place of hope. The support of a caring community has been a key part of healing too. It has included, too, the prayers of many church members and the laying-on of hands of our rector and the parish healing group. Just as when Grace recovered from ovarian cancer thirty-seven years ago, this whole experience has heightened my consciousness of the gift that life – and every day – is.

The experience of the NHS healing team and the commitment of so many to supporting the healing process provides a picture of what the Church both is and can be. My passion remains for the Christian Church to be there alongside those who are suffering from exclusion, especially in major cities like Liverpool and London. Just as the wider community needs to be involved both personally in caring, and corporately in supporting those in the front line of the NHS staff with sufficient resources, so it is with the Church. In the same way, reaching out to those who are excluded from the opportunities of 'Comfortable Britain' will only be effective if the whole body believes in the importance of the task, and does not leave it to a few enthusiasts. Just as the readiness of the better off to pay taxes is a vital support to the NHS, the Church's mission in Urban Priority Areas and among other groups that are excluded requires synods to vote for funding too.

Now there are steps along the shore every morning. That is part of keeping solitary time for the stillness that I value greatly. And although I miss the stimulation of belonging to a professional team that was there throughout my 'active' ministry, another sort of belonging continues. Retirement makes possible more time with Grace, with family, neighbours and friends. The chance to recollect and record some of my memories over the last three years has been its own spiritual journey – looking back with thankfulness at God's faithfulness in testing situations and at the companions he has given me on this pilgrimage. Looking forward in retirement, I see an array of choices spread before me, including the joy of watching our grandsons grow up. And in my conversations with God on those walks, I still test the hints and hunches that suggest the way my journey of faith is yet to take – a few more steps along the street called Hope.

Notes

Chapter 1: Early Stepping Stones

1 David Sheppard, *Parson's Pitch* (Hodder & Stoughton, 1964).

Chapter 2: New Directions

1 Owen Chadwick went on to be Regius Professor of Modern History, Master of Selwyn College and Vice-Chancellor of Cambridge University.
2 John Collins was to be Vicar of St Mark's, Gillingham and later of Holy Trinity, Brompton.
3 John Eddison (ed.), *Bash: A Study in Spiritual Power* (Marshalls, 1983).
4 David Watson, *You Are My God* (Hodder & Stoughton, 1983), p. 25. David Watson became a gifted evangelist. He was vicar of St Michael-le-Belfrey, York.
5 Tony Tremlett was later Bishop of Dover.
6 Cyril Bowles was later Bishop of Derby.
7 Maurice Wiles was later to be Regius Professor of Divinity at Oxford.
8 Donald Soper was Minister of the West London Mission. He regularly spoke at open-air meetings at Tower Hill. He was later made a life peer as Lord Soper.
9 Maurice Wood was later Bishop of Norwich.
10 In Gerald A. Studdert-Kennedy, *The Unutterable Beauty* (Hodder & Stoughton, 1947).

Chapter 3: East Enders

1 The National Association of Boys' Clubs is now the National Association of Clubs for Young People.
2 Grace Sheppard, *An Aspect of Fear* (Darton, Longman & Todd, 1989), p. 7.

3 David and Jean Hewitt, *George Burton: A Study in Contradictions* (Hodder & Stoughton, 1969), p. 96.

4 Alan Bullock, *The Life and Times of Ernest Bevin*, Vol. 1 (Heinemann, 1960), p. 369.

5 George Burton, *People Matter More than Things* (Hodder & Stoughton, 1965).

6 Brian Seaman went on to be Vicar of St Paul's, Elswick, Newcastle, for twenty-one years.

7 E. R. Wickham, *Church and People in an Industrial City* (Lutterworth, 1957). Wilmott and Young's *Family and Kinship in East London* was also published in 1957, the year I became warden of the Mayflower, as was Richard Hoggart's *The Uses of Literacy*. I devoured each of these.

8 Isaiah 1:16–18.

9 Roy Trevivian went to the Mayflower as chaplain, when Roger Sainsbury was the warden (1974–81).

10 Roger Sainsbury was later to be Bishop of Barking.

Chapter 4: Young People – Problems or Possibilities?

1 *The Youth Service in England and Wales* (Albemarle Report, HMSO, 1960).

2 Jim Gosling went on to be ordained. He is currently vicar of All Saints, Kenton in Devonshire. I listened to his description of growing as a youth leader on a tape recording of Sunday Group discussions. These tape recordings formed the basis of the four booklets I refer to later in this chapter.

3 The National Association of Youth Clubs is now called Youth UK.

4 Mary Morse, *The Unattached* (Pelican, 1965).

5 Jude Wild, *Street Mates* (Merseyside Youth Association, 1982), p. 31.

6 Ted Lyons went on to be ordained. He is currently vicar of Brownsover, Rugby, and Area Dean of Rugby.

7 David Sheppard, *Loving; Working; Arguing; Belonging* (Scripture Union, 1966).

Chapter 5: Evangelism – And a Cricketing Sabbatical

1 Timothy Dudley-Smith, *John Stott: The Making of a Leader* (InterVarsity Press, 1999), p. 206.

2 Peter Selby was later to be Bishop of Kingston and then Bishop of Worcester.

3 Timothy Dudley-Smith, *John Stott: Vol. 2, A Global Ministry* (InterVarsity Press, 2001), p. 27.

4 David Sheppard, *Parson's Pitch* (Hodder & Stoughton, 1964), p. 189.
5 Michael Harper was Director of the Fountain Trust, and then of SOMA (Sharing of Ministries Abroad). He later became a member of the Orthodox Church.
6 David Ford, *The Shape of Living* (Fount Paperback, 1997), p. 148.
7 *On the Other Side: Report of the Evangelical Alliance's Commission on Evangelism* (Scripture Union, 1968), p. 12.
8 John Hunter, *A Touch of Class: Issues of Urban Mission. The Story of the Evangelical Urban Training Project (Unlock)* (printed at Lancaster University, 1998), p. 26. This book is available from Unlock, 336a City Road, Sheffield S2 1GA.

Chapter 6: Justice and Peace – A New Awareness

1 Hugh Montefiore was later my colleague as Bishop of Kingston in Southwark Diocese. Subsequently he was Bishop of Birmingham.
2 Norman Anderson was Professor of Law and Islamic Studies. He was Lay Chairman of the General Synod when I became a member in 1975.
3 Alan Hill, *Peter May: A Biography* (Andre Deutsch, 1996), p. 166.
4 Quoted in Bruce Murray, 'Politics and Cricket: The D'Oliveira Affair of 1968', *Journal of Southern African Studies*, Vol. 27, No. 4 (December, 2001), quoting from NA CAB 1/1/4 (1968), Notuleboek, State Archives, Pretoria.
5 Peter Hain later became an MP and Minister of State at the Foreign and Commonwealth Office.
6 Betty Boothroyd was to become an MP, and later Speaker of the House of Commons.
7 Stephen Chalke, *At the Heart of English Cricket: The Life and Memories of Geoffrey Howard* (Fairfield Books, 2001), p. 209.
8 Stephen Verney (ed.), *People and Cities* (Fontana Books, 1969), pp. 172f.
9 Simon Phipps was later Bishop of Lincoln.

Chapter 7: Bishops and Bishoping

1 Grace Sheppard, op. cit., pp. 19f.
2 Burgess Park, a major new park in Camberwell, was named after Jessie Burgess.
3 Desmond Tutu was Archbishop of Cape Town, 1986–97.
4 John Austin later became Bishop of Aston.
5 Rodney Bomford in *Father Diamond of Deptford*, eds Rodney Bomford and Harry Potter (Ditchling Press, 1994), pp. 60ff. Canon Rodney Bomford is now Vicar of St Giles, Camberwell. David Diamond died in 1992, aged 57.

6 Donald Reeves was later Vicar of St James, Piccadilly.
7 Nicholas Frayling was then Vicar of All Saints, Tooting Bec. Later he became Rector of Liverpool. In 2002, he was appointed Dean of Chichester.
8 Quoted in Michael De-la-Noy, *Mervyn Stockwood: A Lonely Life* (Mowbray, 1996), p. 217.

Chapter 8: Glass Partition or Brick Wall?

1 David Sheppard, *Built as a City* (Hodder & Stoughton, 1973), p. 56.
2 Michael Bowen was later to be Archbishop of Southwark.
3 F. Boulard, *An Introduction to Religious Sociology* (Darton, Longman & Todd, 1960), p. 60.
4 Jim Thompson came to Southwark Diocese as Team Rector of Thamesmead. After twelve years as Bishop of Stepney, he became Bishop of Bath and Wells.
5 David Martin, *Tracts Against the Times* (Lutterworth Press, 1973), pp. 171ff.
6 Neil Wates died tragically young.
7 *Bishop Hugh – With Affection: A Retirement Tribute*, ed. Colin Buchanan (Birmingham Diocesan Board of Finance, 1987), p. 16.
8 John Gladwin was later Bishop of Guildford.
9 Later Baroness Denington.
10 Martin Daunton (ed.), *Charities, Self-Interest and Welfare in the English Past* (UCL Press, 1996), p. 9.

Chapter 9: Black and White Encounters

1 Sybil Phoenix was made a Freeman of the Borough of Lewisham.
2 David Sheppard, The Martin Luther King Memorial Lecture, 1975.
3 Wilfred Wood was the Bishop of London's Chaplain for Community Relations when I first met him. He came to Southwark Diocese as Vicar of St Laurence, Catford. He became Archdeacon of Southwark in 1982, and was made Bishop of Croydon in 1985.
4 E. R. Norman, *Church and Society in England, 1770–1970* (Oxford University Press, 1976), p. 234.
5 I quoted from this letter in The Gore Memorial Lecture, Westminster Abbey, 1981.
6 *The New Black Presence in Britain: A Christian Scrutiny* (British Council of Churches, 1976).
7 Later renamed the Committee for Minority Ethnic Anglican Concerns.

Chapter 10: Not Only . . . But Also . . .

1 Eric James, *A Life of Bishop John A. T. Robinson, Scholar, Pastor, Prophet* (Collins, 1987), p. 111.
2 *Sunday Mirror*, 7 April 1963; quoted in James, *A Life*, p. 116.
3 James, *A Life*, p. 312.
4 Ezekiel 34.
5 Robin Denniston, *Trevor Huddleston: A Life* (Macmillan, 1999), p. 135.
6 Desmond Tutu in Foreword to Eric James, *Trevor Huddleston: From a Biographer's Chair*, The Huddleston Lecture, 1999.
7 Ted Roberts was later a canon of Bradford Cathedral, and then Vicar of St James, Bermondsey, and a canon in Southwark Diocese as Adviser for Inner-City Ministry.
8 *Local Ministry in Urban and Industrial Areas* (Mowbray, 1972), the report of a working party which met under the joint chairmanship of the Bishop of Stepney and the Bishop of Woolwich.
9 David Sheppard, *Built as a City: God and the Urban World Today* (Hodder & Stoughton, 1973), pp. 406ff.
10 Leonard Hodgson, *Sex and Christian Freedom* (SCM Press, 1967), p. 29, quoted in J. V. Taylor, *The Go Between God* (SCM Press, 1972), pp. 36f.
11 Sheppard, *Built as a City*, pp. 418, 421f, 432f.

Chapter 11: Southerners Go North

1 Grace Sheppard, *An Aspect of Fear* (Darton, Longman & Todd, 1989). It was widely read, selling some 18,000 copies.
2 Alan Ripley became Vicar of St Bridget's, Wavertree, after his three years as my chaplain. He later moved to Bath and Wells Diocese, where he was Rector of South Petherton and lay training adviser.
3 Bishop Bill Flagg came to Liverpool from years as a missionary in South America. He had been Bishop of Paraguay and Northern Argentina, and then the first Anglican Bishop in Peru. When he moved on after eight years in Liverpool, he became General Secretary of the South American Missionary Society (SAMS).
4 Janet Eastwood later became Rector of Holy Trinity, Wavertree.
5 *Change or Decay: Final Report of the Liverpool Inner Areas Study* (HMSO, 1977).
6 Terry Gibson was later Archdeacon of Suffolk.
7 Samuel Brittan, *Steering the Economy* (Penguin, 1971), p. 327.
8 David Sheppard, *Bias to the Poor* (Hodder & Stoughton, 1983).
9 Christopher Smith moved on to be Team Rector of St Mary's, Walton, then a canon at Sheffield Cathedral.
10 Graeme Spiers was later Archdeacon of Liverpool.

11 Peter Spiers is Vicar of St George's, Everton.
12 Martin Hunt moved on from St Luke's, Princess Drive, to be Vicar of St Helens Parish Church. Sadly he died, still in young middle age, while visiting a coal mine there.
13 Steve Ann Henshall, *Not Always Murder at the Vicarage: A View of Clergy Marriages Today* (SPCK, 1991); *Is It a Daddy Sunday?* (Monarch, 1994).

Chapter 12: A Matter of the Affections as well as the Intellect

1 P. J. Waller, *Democracy and Sectarianism: A Political and Social History of Liverpool: 1868–1939* (Liverpool University Press, 1981), p. 238.
2 'Granny Cotton' died at 100 years of age. When I gave the blessing at her funeral service in the cathedral, I realised how she had seen the whole process of the building. Her husband Vere Cotton had been secretary to the Cathedral Building Committee, and her son Henry was later its chairman. He was also Lord Lieutenant of Merseyside.
3 The more senior Papal Nuncio, Archbishop Luigi Barbarito, had now replaced the post of Apostolic Delegate. I was told the British Government would not accept a Roman Catholic Nuncio before 1994.
4 Clifford Longley, *The Worlock Archive* (Geoffrey Chapman, 2000), pp. 138, 219.
5 David Sheppard and Derek Worlock, *Better Together* (Hodder & Stoughton, 1988), p. 4.
6 Albert Augustus David was Bishop of Liverpool, 1923–44.
7 *Tablet*, 17 February 1996.
8 Longley, *The Worlock Archive*, pp. 293ff.

Chapter 13: Staying with the Struggle

1 The Bullock Report was prepared by a Committee of Enquiry on Industrial Democracy, chaired by Alan Bullock, published in 1977.
2 Eric Heffer was MP for Liverpool, Walton, until his death.
3 David Donnison, *The Politics of Poverty* (Martin Robertson, 1982), pp. 227f.
4 Ralph Ellison, *Invisible Man* (Penguin Modern Classics, 1963). First published in the USA in 1952.
5 Bill Sefton was later made Lord Sefton of Garston. He became a good ally.
6 *The Economic Status of Coloured Families in the Port of Liverpool* (Liverpool University Press, 1940), pp. 12f.

Chapter 14: 'Costly Openness'

1 CORAT was Christian Organisations Research and Advisory Trust.
2 Galatians 3:28 (Revised English Bible).
3 David Sheppard and Derek Worlock, *With Hope in our Hearts* (Hodder & Stoughton, 1994), pp. 107f.
4 COMPASS stands for Counselling on Merseyside, Pastoral and Supporting Services.
5 *The Nature of Christian Belief: A Statement and Exposition by the House of Bishops of the General Synod of the Church of England* (Church House Publishing, 1986), p. 6.
6 James Barr, *Escaping from Fundamentalism* (SCM Press, 1984), p. 158. James Barr was Regius Professor of Hebrew at the University of Oxford.
7 John Baker was later Bishop of Salisbury and Chairman of the Church of England Doctrine Commission.
8 David Sheppard, *Bias to the Poor* (Hodder & Stoughton, 1973), pp. 175f.
9 I was quoting Alan Ecclestone, *Yes to God* (Darton, Longman & Todd, 1975), p. 17.
10 Sheppard, *Bias to the Poor*, p. 163.
11 Sheppard, *Bias to the Poor*, p. 96.
12 Sheppard, *Bias to the Poor*, pp. 71f. I was quoting Norman Snaith, *Distinctive Ideas of the Old Testament* (London, 1944), pp. 76ff.

Chapter 15: Listening to the Cries

1 Austin Smith OP, *Passion for the Inner City* (Sheed & Ward Ltd, 1982).
2 Philip Mawer was appointed Parliamentary Commissioner for Standards in 2002, after twelve years serving at Church House.
3 Lord Scarman, *The Brixton Disorders, 10–12 April 1981* (HMSO, November 1981).
4 Wally Brown was later principal of Liverpool Community College.
5 Dick Crawshaw was later Deputy Speaker of the House of Commons. He left the Labour Party and joined the SDP when that was formed. He regularly came to the diocesan 'Lay Swanwick' conference.
6 Later Sir Kenneth Oxford.
7 Margaret Simey, in *Partnership Policing in Scarman and After*, ed. John Benyon (Pergamon Press, 1984), p. 138. Margaret always insisted on being called Mrs Simey rather than Lady Simey. Her husband, a Professor at Liverpool University, had been made a Life Peer.
8 David Alton was Liberal MP for Mossley Hill, and later made a Life Peer as Lord Alton of Liverpool. He was appointed Professor of Citizenship at Liverpool John Moores University.

9 John Burrow was later Chief Constable of Essex.
10 *Loosen the Shackles*, first report of the Liverpool 8 inquiry into race relations in Liverpool (Karia Press, 1989).
11 John Miguel Bonino, *Revolutionary Theology Comes of Age* (SPCK, 1975), p. 68.
12 John Moores was later Chancellor of Liverpool John Moores University. He was known as John Moores Junior until the death of his father.
13 Michael Heseltine, *Life in the Jungle: My Autobiography* (Hodder & Stoughton, 2000), pp. 220f.
14 Richard Evans and Hilary Russell, *Stockbridge Village – Achievements and Lessons after 10 years* (European Institute for Urban Affairs, Liverpool John Moores University, 1993).
15 David Thomas later became Team Rector of Canvey Island and then Rector of Wivenhoe.
16 When the Merseyside and Region Ecumenical Assembly (MARCEA) was formed, it was agreed that we should have a lay 'Speaker'. Alfred Stocks, a Methodist, was elected the first Speaker.
17 Sir Hector Laing later became Lord Laing of Dunphail.

Chapter 16: Confrontation

1 David Sheppard, 'The Other Britain', The 1984 Richard Dimbleby Lecture (BBC, 1984).
2 Professor Michael Parkinson, *Urban Policy, 1970–95; Programmes, Priorities and Partners* (European Institute for Urban Affairs, Liverpool John Moores University, 1995).

Chapter 17: A Postcard from Spain

1 Mark Santer was later Bishop of Birmingham.
2 *Gallup Survey of Church of England Clergymen: Prepared for the Archbishop's Commission on Urban Priority Areas* (General Synod, 1986).
3 *Faith in the City: A Call for Action by Church and Nation* (Church House Publishing, 1985).
4 Pat Dearnley was succeeded as Archbishop's Officer in 1989 by the Revd Alan Davis, and by Gill Moody in 1991.
5 *Living in the City* (General Synod, 1990).
6 Adrian Hastings, *Robert Runcie* (Mowbray, 1991).

Notes

Chapter 18: Handling Disagreements

1 Nic Frances is currently Executive Director of the Brotherhood of St Laurence. This is a major church body delivering social welfare throughout Australia.
2 Donald Nichol, *Holiness* (Darton, Longman & Todd, 1981).
3 Ian Tracey in the Newsletter of the Friends of Liverpool Cathedral, Spring 2001.
4 Anglican–Roman Catholic International Commission, *The Final Report* (Catholic Truth Society/SPCK, 1982).
5 *Salvation and the Church: ARCIC II* (Catholic Truth Society and Church House Publishing, 1987).
6 Sheppard and Worlock, *With Hope in Our Hearts*, p. 84.
7 *Abortion and the Church* (Church House Publishing, 1993).
8 Sheppard and Worlock, *With Hope in Our Hearts*, p. 101.

Chapter 19: Respecting 'the Others'

1 *Sectarianism: A Discussion Document* (The Department of Social Issues of the Irish Inter-Church Meeting, 1993), p. 76.
2 Grace Sheppard, *Pits and Pedestals* (Darton, Longman & Todd, 1995), pp. 3ff.
3 Jonathan Sacks subsequently became Chief Rabbi.
4 Jonathan Sacks, *The Persistence of Faith* (Weidenfeld and Nicolson, 1991).
5 Mano Rumalshah later became Bishop of Peshawar. At the time of writing he is General Secretary of the United Society for the Propagation of the Gospel (USPG).
6 I owe much of this account to Philip Lewis, *Islamic Britain: Religion, Politics and Identity among British Muslims* (I. B. Tauris, 1994).
7 *Staying in the City: Faith in the City Ten Years On: A Report by the Bishops' Advisory Group on Urban Priority Areas* (Church House Publishing, 1995), p. 94.
8 The Runnymede Trust Commission (chaired by Bhikhu Parekh), *The Future of Multi-Ethnic Britain* (Profile Books, 2000), p. 235.

Chapter 20: Not Just in My Backyard

1 Rowan Williams, *Lent Book* (Fount, 2000), p. 19. Rowan Williams is the Archbishop of Wales.
2 The Revd Canon Professor John Polkinghorne was Professor of Mathematical Physics at the University of Cambridge and later Master of Queen's College, Cambridge.

3 *Something to Celebrate: Valuing Families in Church and Society* (Church House Publishing, 1995).
4 *Something to Celebrate*, p. 117.
5 Church of England House of Bishops, *Issues in Human Sexuality* (Church House Publishing, 1991), p. 44.
6 Report of the Methodist Conference: 'A Christian Understanding of Family Life, the Single Person and Marriage'.
7 Douglas Rhymes, *Time Past to Time Future*, quoted in Eric James, *In Season, Out of Season* (SCM Press, 1999), p. 30. Canon Douglas Rhymes was Vicar of St Giles, Camberwell, in the years when I was Bishop of Woolwich.
8 The Race Equality in Employment Project (REEP) was formed after a conference on 'The Economic Empowerment of the Black Community'. REEP published a survey of private employers – *Buried Talents* – in 1992.
9 Andrew McLellan was Moderator of the Church of Scotland in 2000.
10 *Unemployment and the Future of Work: An Enquiry for the Churches* (CCBI, 1997), pp. 145, 149.

Chapter 21: Liverpool Hope

1 For example, Gerard Hughes, *God of Surprises* (Darton, Longman & Todd, 1985).
2 David Henshaw became Chief Executive of Liverpool in 1998.
3 James Jones had been Bishop of Hull before becoming Bishop of Liverpool in 1998.
4 Blake Morrison, *As If* (Granta Books, 1997), pp. 239f.
5 Tom Butler later became Bishop of Southwark, and in 2001 Chairman of the Board for Social Responsibility.
6 John Packer became Bishop of Ripon and Leeds in 2000.
7 L'Arche is an international and ecumenical community that supports adults with learning difficulties. It was founded by Jean Vanier, a Canadian priest.
8 Local non-stipendiary ministers (LNSM) are now known as ordained local ministers (OLM).
9 *Staying in the City: Faith in the City ten years on* (Church House Publishing, 1995), pp. 132ff.

Chapter 22: Steps Along the Shore

1 Martin Daunton is Professor of Economic History at the University of Cambridge.

Index

Index